the new ULTIMATE GUIDE TO THE perfect Word

BIGGEST CRAFTER'S RESOURCE BOOK
Of Words and Journaling
More Poetry, Sayings & Quotes for
Scrapbooks, Art Journals & Crafts

Linda La Tourelle

Copyright 2015 | The Ultimate Book Company Inc.

All rights reserved. No part of this book may be reproduced or transmitted in any form by any means, electronic or mechanical, including photocopying and recording, or by any information storage and retrieval system, without the prior written permission of The Ultimate Book Company Inc.

Permission is hereby granted to the purchaser of this book to reproduce any part of this book on a limited basis for personal art and craft projects only, which are not for resale.

Commercial use of any or all of this book requires written permission and payment of any applicable licensing fees. Please direct ALL COMMERCIAL USE requests to *linda@ultimatebookcompany.com*.

The Ultimate Book Company Inc. has made every effort to verify author and source for every quote and poem used in this book, and to give proper ownership credit. However, the publisher cannot guarantee total accuracy.

In the event of a question arising from the use of a particular poem or quote, please contact the publisher to verify authorship and source. Your request for necessary corrections will be honored in future editions of this book. Any corrections will be noted on our website.

All scripture was taken from the King James Version of *The Bible*.

Contact publisher for more information:

The Ultimate Book Company Inc.
Telephone / 270 251-0022
ultimatebookcompany.com

ISBN 978-1-59978-055-9

• Proudly printed in the United States of America •

The Biggest Book of Words & Prompts for Scrapbooks, Art Journals & Crafts

Table of Contents

- Introduction
- Dedication
- Because Of Love
- Special Thanks
- Favorite Links

1 **STORYTELLING**
2 - Journaling
3 - The Purpose Of Journaling
4 - Journey To Journaling
7 **WRITER'S TOOLS**
8 - Journaling Tools
9 - A Place To Journal
10 - Journals For Everyone
11 - The Story Of Us
12 - Digital Journaling
15 **WRITING TIPS**
16 - Journaling Jumpstarts
17 - More Jumpstarts
18 - The Five W'S
19 - Doodle, Doodled & Doodling
19 - Color Your Pages With Words
21 - Word Palette / Lists Of Words
30 - My Favorite Words
31 - Overcoming Writer's Block
32 - Creative Sparks
33 - Tidbits & Tips
35 - Finish These Sentences
36 - Genealogy
37 - Historical Preservation
37 - School Days
38 - It's All About The Words
39 - Hand-Written With Love

43 **LOVE LETTERS**
44 - Love Letters In The Sand
45 - How To Write A Love Letter
45 - Gather Your Tools
46 - Get Comfortable
46 - Writing Warm-Up
46 - What Is The Purpose
47 - Written By Hand
47 - Parts Of A Letter
48 - Closing
48 - English Basics 101
49 - Intimacy Through Writing
49 - Letters For All Occasions
51 - Sentimentally Said
52 - Love Letter List
53 **GIFTS OF LOVE**
54 - The Gift Of Words
57 - Journaling For A Gift
58 - Gifts To Give
59 - Moments Worth Journaling
60 - Pearls For Daily Living
63 **SWEETEST TALE**
64 - Every Picture Tells A Story
65 - Written On Your Heart
66 - A Tapestry Of Love
67 **QUESTIONS**
68 - Questions To Answer
70 - Pregnancy & Birth
72 - Childhood
80 - Engagement & Wedding
82 - The Newlyweds
83 - Home & Family

QUOTES & QUIPS

90	ACCOMPLISH	133	▸ Birthday Friend
92	ADOPTION	134	▸ Birthday Love
94	AGE & AGING	134	▸ Birthday General
97	ALBUM TITLES	135	BOATS & SAILING
99	AMUSEMENT PARKS	135	BODY BEAUTIFUL
100	ANIMALS	135	▸ Eyes
100	ANIMAL ALPHABET	136	▸ Face
101	ANNIVERSARY	136	▸ Hands
104	APOLOGY	138	▸ Feet
104	APPLES	139	▸ Hair
105	ART & ARTISTS	139	▸ Teeth
107	ATTITUDE	141	BOOKS
107	BABY	142	BOY & GIRL SCOUTS
109	▸ Baby Baths	144	BOYS
110	▸ Baby Blanket	148	BOYFRIENDS
110	▸ Baby Firsts	149	BUGS & BEES
110	▸ Baby Food	149	BUTTERFLY
111	▸ Baby Pacifier	150	CAMPING & HIKING
111	▸ Crawling	151	CASTLES
111	▸ Growing	151	CATS & KITTENS
111	▸ Nude	152	CELESTIAL
111	▸ Sleep Time & Naps	152	▸ Earth
113	▸ Standing & Walking	154	▸ Moon
114	▸ Teething	153	▸ Planets
114	BABY ALPHABET	153	▸ Skies
114	BABY POEMS	153	▸ Stars
117	BALLET	154	▸ Sun
118	BAND	154	CHILDREN
118	BEARS	159	COLORS
119	BEAUTY	162	COMPUTER
121	BIRDS	163	COUPLES
123	BIRTH	164	COWBOYS • COWGIRLS
125	BIRTHDAY	165	CRAFTING
128	▸ Birthday Belated	166	▸ Cross Stitch
129	▸ Birthday Milestones	166	▸ Step Family
		166	▸ Knitting

167	▸ *Painting*		199	▸ *Uncle*
167	▸ *Photography*		199	▸ *Wife*
168	▸ *Quilting*		200	**FARM ANIMALS**
169	▸ *Rubberstamping*		201	▸ *Chickens*
170	▸ *Scrapbooking*		201	▸ *Cows*
170	▸ *Sewing*		201	▸ *Horses*
171	▸ *Weaving*		202	▸ *Pigs*
171	▸ *Writing*		202	**FARMING**
172	**CRYING**		203	**FASHIONISTA**
172	**DANCE**		204	**FLOWERS**
173	**DAYS OF THE WEEK**		206	**FOOD & COOKING**
174	**DOGS & PUPPIES**		206	▸ *Baking*
175	**DREAMS**		207	▸ *Barbeque - Grilling*
175	**DRESS UP**		207	▸ *Candy & Sweets*
177	**DRIVING**		208	▸ *Chocolate*
177	**DUCKS**		209	▸ *Coffee*
178	**EDUCATION**		210	▸ *Diet*
178	**ENCOURAGEMENT**		210	▸ *Fruits & Veggies*
179	**FAIRYTALES**		210	**FRECKLES**
179	**FAMILY**		211	**FREEDOM**
180	▸ *Aunt*		211	**FRIENDS**
181	▸ *Brother*		213	**GAMES**
182	▸ *Cousin*		214	**GARDENS**
182	▸ *Daughter*		217	**GIRLS**
183	▸ *Family Trees*		218	**GIVING**
183	▸ *Father*		219	**GLASSES**
185	▸ *Grandchildren*		219	**GOALS**
186	▸ *Grandparents*		220	**GRADUATION**
187	▸ *Husband*		221	**GRATITUDE**
188	▸ *In-laws*		223	**HAIR & HAIRCUTS**
189	▸ *Mother*		223	**HAPPINESS**
193	▸ *Parents*		224	**HARVEST**
195	▸ *Siblings*		225	**HEART**
196	▸ *Sister*		225	**HERITAGE**
199	▸ *Step Family*			

C | ultimatebookcompany.com

225	**HOLIDAYS**	254	**LOVE & ROMANCE**
226	▸ *Christmas*	256	**LOVE & WEDDING**
229	▸ *Cinco De Mayo*	256	▸ *Dating*
229	▸ *Earth Day*	257	▸ *Engagement*
229	▸ *Easter*	258	▸ *Pre Wedding*
230	▸ *Father's Day*	259	▸ *The Showers*
230	▸ *Fourth Of July*	260	▸ *The Wedding*
231	▸ *Halloween*	263	▸ *Wedding Reception*
232	▸ *Hanukkah*	264	**LOVE & MARRIAGE**
232	▸ *Kwanzaa*	267	**LULLABY**
232	▸ *Mother's Day*	267	**MAKE BELIEVE**
234	▸ *New Year's Day*	268	**MANNERS**
234	▸ *St. Patrick's Day*	268	**MEMORIAL**
235	▸ *Thanksgiving*	269	**MEMORIES**
236	▸ *Valentine's Day*	269	**MEN**
237	**HOME**	271	**MISCELLANEOUS**
238	**HOME – NEW**	271	**MOM & DAD-ISMS**
239	**HOME BUILDING**	272	**MONEY**
239	**HOME REPAIR**	272	**MOUNTAINS**
240	**HOUSEWORK**	273	**MOVING**
241	**HUMOR**	273	**MUSIC**
241	**ILLNESS & INJURIES**	275	**NATURE**
242	**INSPIRATION**	277	**NURSERY RHYMES**
245	**KINDNESS**	277	**OCEAN ANIMALS**
246	**KIND WORDS**	277	**PARADISE**
247	**KINGS & QUEENS**	278	**PARTIES**
248	**LAKE LIVING**	278	**PETS**
248	**LANGUAGES**	279	**PLAYING**
248	▸ *I Love You*	279	▸ *Dolls*
249	▸ *Merry Christmas*	279	▸ *Fun & Games*
249	**LIFE**	281	▸ *Kites*
250	**LOVE INSPIRING**	281	▸ *Teddy Bears*
252	**LOVE & PASSION**	282	▸ *Toys*
252	▸ *Hugs*	283	**PMS**
252	▸ *Kisses*	283	**POTTY**
253	▸ *Passion*	283	**PRAISE A CHILD**

284	**PREGNANCY & BIRTH**	315	▸	*Church Signs*
285	**PUMPKINS**	315	▸	*Faith*
286	**READING**	315	▸	*Forgiveness*
287	**REPAIRS**	316	▸	*Godparents*
287	**RETIREMENT**	316	▸	*God*
288	**ROOM SAYINGS**	316	▸	*Prayer*
288	▸ *Kitchen*	317	▸	*Scripture*
288	▸ *Bedroom*	318	**SPORTS**	
289	▸ *Family Room*	319	▸	*Archery*
289	▸ *Laundry*	319	▸	*Badminton*
289	▸ *Nursery*	319	▸	*Baseball*
289	**ROSES**	320	▸	*Basketball*
290	**SAND & SURF**	320	▸	*Body Building*
292	**SANTA**	321	▸	*Bowling*
293	**SCHOOL**	321	▸	*Boxing*
293	▸ *College*	321	▸	*Bungee Jumping*
293	▸ *Graduation*	321	▸	*Canoeing / Kayaking*
294	▸ *High School*	322	▸	*Cheerleading*
295	▸ *Prom Night*	322	▸	*Croquet*
295	▸ *School Days*	322	▸	*Cycling*
298	▸ *Teachers*	323	▸	*Disc Golf*
300	**SEASONS**	323	▸	*Diving*
301	▸ *Autumn*	323	▸	*Fencing*
302	▸ *Winter*	323	▸	*Fishing*
305	▸ *Spring*	324	▸	*Football*
307	▸ *Summer*	324	▸	*Golf*
310	**SHOPPING**	325	▸	*Gymnastics*
310	**SLUMBER PARTY**	325	▸	*Hockey*
310	**SMILES & LAUGHTER**	326	▸	*Horse Racing*
311	**SNOW**	326	▸	*Hunting*
312	**SNOWMEN**	326	▸	*Ice Skating*
313	**SOUTHERN SAYINGS**	327	▸	*Martial Arts*
313	**SPIRITUALITY**	327	▸	*Off Road*
314	▸ *Angels*	327	▸	*Racing*
314	▸ *Baptism*	328	▸	*Racquetball*
314	▸ *Children's Prayers*	328	▸	*River Rafting*

328	▸ Rock Climbing		337	THEATER
329	▸ Running		337	TIME
329	▸ Scuba Diving		339	TOWN
329	▸ Skateboarding		339	TRANSPORTATION
330	▸ Sky Diving		342	TRAVEL & PLACES
330	▸ Snowboarding		350	TREES
330	▸ Snowmobiling		350	TROUBLE & MESSES
330	▸ Snow Skiing		351	TWINS & TRIPLETS
331	▸ Soccer		351	VOLUNTEERS
331	▸ Surfing		352	WEATHER
332	▸ Swimming		354	WISDOM
332	▸ Tennis		354	WOMEN
332	▸ The Gym		355	WORK & JOBS
332	▸ Track & Field		362	YARD SALES
333	▸ Volleyball		362	ZOO • CIRCUS • FAIRS
333	▸ Walking		365	Notes & Quotes
333	▸ Water Skiing		366	People To Interview
333	▸ Working Out		i – x	Index
334	▸ Wrestling			About Us
334	▸ Yoga			Bonus Stuff
334	SUCCESS			Order Form
335	SUNDIAL MOTTOES			
225	TEA			
336	TEENS			

INTRODUCTION

Looking for the perfect words?

The New Ultimate Guide To The Perfect Word – Volume 2
The Biggest Book of Words & Prompts for Scrapbooks, Art Journals & Crafts

At last—I am so excited to share this sequel to my bestselling first volume! I wrote this all new book to help you discover the wonderful gifts that you can give to your family and friends. The priceless gifts of words that you create can be wrapped and presented anyway you choose —plain, simple, artistic, elegant—it's up to you and it's easy, too! Best of all, these gifts are free and will bring wealth beyond measure to the recipient!

The gifts are your stories, your memories from childhood to present day. You are the keeper of your memories and they are stories to be shared—valuable keepsakes that will matter now and for generations to come.

My hope is that within these pages you will find inspiration to begin to tell your stories as only you can. Your voice will speak volumes to those you love, as you impart your treasured memories through journaling.

May your journey into journaling be one of self-discovery as you learn to share your memories. May your words and your stories be your legacy of love—the greatest gift of all.

Happy journaling and many blessings...

Linda

The Biggest Book of Words & Prompts for Scrapbooks, Art Journals & Crafts

Thank You

Thena Smith
Camilla Smith
Erica Hamilton
Nicholas Gordon
Mark Seastrand
Lettering Delights
Thomas King
Lisa Fulmer

The Perfect Fonts

THANK YOU TO THESE WONDERFUL FONT MAKERS
Great fonts are available from these very creative font designers.
www.letteringdelights.com
www.inspiregraphics.com
www.nicksfonts.com

For inspiration, editing and the lovely fonts,
I thank each one of you so very much!

Favorite Links

Creative, crafty and classy are just a few of the ways to describe these amazing ladies. Their passion for crafting and scrapbooking is sure to ignite a spark in you!

Get to know them by visiting their sites and blogs. Their talent and teaching will inspire new ideas and projects. You'll truly be delighted at their sweetness, too! Be blessed!

CATHIE FILIAN | crafter, designer, television host/producer
Producer of "Craft Wars" on TLC and "Creative Juice" on DIY
hgtv.com/creative-juice • cathieandsteve.com
cathiefilian.blogspot.com

JULIE MCGUFFEE | crafter and award-winning designer
Host, "Scrapbook Memories" • "Scrapbook Soup TV"
Design • Consulting • Product Development
TV & Video Presentation Services
juliemcguffee.com • juliemcguffee.blogspot.com

TERESA COLLINS | designer who helps others live creatively
Owner "Teresa Collins Designs"
teresacollinsdesigns.com

BECKY FLECK | author, sketch designer extraordinaire
Editor of "Scrapbook and Cards Today" Magazine
scrapbookandcards.com • pagemaps.com
facebook.com/ScrapbookAndCardsToday

More about these crafty and classy ladies...
ultimatebookcompany.com

The best part of one's life consists
of friendships, old and new.
–Linda LaTourelle

You are the music,
I am the words—
Together we are writing
a symphony of...
LOVE.
–Linda LaTourelle

DEDICATION

Dearest Thomas

From early morning
through late at night—
you keep me going.
Your kindness fills my spirit
with hope and encouragement.
Your culinary skills always
offer scrumptious nourishment.
Your humor fills our home
with joyful entertainment.
Your love is the most
important endearment—
blessing our marriage
with complete fulfillment.
Thank you for your support
and faithful prayers.
With the utmost love and gratitude
I dedicate this book to you,
my husband and best friend.

Linda

The sweetest gift you'll ever know
is watching the love for your family grow.
Nothing in life will ever compare—
the blessing of family is answered prayer!
–Linda LaTourelle

The Biggest Book of Words & Prompts for Scrapbooks, Art Journals & Crafts

Dedication

Harper...
My beautiful granddaughter!
You are the sparkling jewel
that shines upon my life...
Loving you is amazing—
you are pure, sweet joy!

Hannah, Lara and Sarah...
My beautiful daughters,
loving each of you is a cherished gift...
three miracles that changed my life.
I am so thankful for our relationships
and treasure every moment we share.

Family is everything...
I am so proud of all of you
You are my greatest blessings!

I love you so very much...

Mom
& now Grandma, too!

The New Ultimate Guide to the Perfect Word – Volume 2

Special Thanks

THENA SMITH | author, poet extraordinaire
thenaspoemaday.blogspot.com

Thena has published several books and though now retired, she continues to write daily—even into the wee hours of the morning. A legend on the scrapbooking sites, Thena has lent her talents at designing and writing for various online and print publications and has given so very graciously and generously of her time to help others. Her passion for words is great, but her love for people speaks volumes. The title of her first book was born as a result of her generosity on a plethora of scrapbooking message boards and forums with everyone asking…"Where's Thena? I need a poem about…" Intuitively she would respond with words that fit the occasion. I know readers will find the poems you have so graciously shared in this book the perfect words! Thank you for being a perfect friend all these years! I am blessed and better because of your inspiration and prayers.

HERE'S A LINK TO PURCHASE THENA'S BOOKS…
blurb.com/search/site_search?search=Thena+Smith

Learn more about Thena on my website…
ultimatebookcompany.com

Because of Love

It's wonderful having a parent believe in you and encourage you to follow your God-given passions and talents. I was blessed with two parents that consistently supported my dreams, even when they might have chosen differently.

From California to Hawaii to Kentucky, they rejoiced and reassured with each endeavor I chose to pursue. For as long as I can remember, my father taught me to be independent, think for myself and seek my purpose. He always taught me —if you can conceive it, then you can achieve it, through hard work, focus and tenacity—if you believe it.

Through that teaching and my faith in knowing that the Lord provides our heart's desires, I have been blessed with the three wonderful daughters, married the love of my life and am now blessed with the most beautiful granddaughter. She is almost three weeks old and the most amazing joy. Now, in mid-life, I am enjoying writing and creating books that I hope will inspire and truly bless others.

My journey in writing this book has been somewhat bittersweet, albeit reflective, and yet is now restoring as I am pleased with the words inked upon these pages and hope that it will make my parents proud once again.

My most important passion is family. It was always pure joy to share the creative process in writing my books, with my parents. My mother was always here to edit and encourage me to stay focused—a metaphor for motherhood. She passed away in 2007 and her words of love echo softly only in my heart now. The bittersweet. Weekly long-distant phone calls with my father keep me focused and believing this book will be a success. We talk about life and love and how the only real important thing in life is family—the reflective. The road has been rough, but with my daddy there waiting for his copy, I am very excited to tell him I did it because he believed in me!

My parents have always been my best friends, supporting me in anything I wanted to do, from homeschooling to business to writing. I thank them for always being a place called home no matter how far apart we were and loving me always. Thank you Dad and Mom. I love you!

My desire is to impart the same blessings to my daughters—Hannah, Lara and Sarah and my granddaughter, Harper—may you all find the passionate calling God has for your life and may you always know the infinite depths of my love for each of you. I am your biggest fan. You can be successful at whatever you pursue—keep focus, faith and family as your foundation—they are all that really matters! I love you all—the restoring.

—Linda

Life is the most wonderful fairytale of all
–Hans Christian Andersen

Storytelling

Journaling's a treasure
worth far more than gold
There are memories to share
and stories to be told
so learn all you can
from loved ones so dear
there are jewels to gather
with each passing year
–Linda LaTourelle

JOURNALING
Cameras capture the moment—
words tell the story

Journaling: /jûr′nəh-ling/ Journaling is a written record of thoughts, experiences or events. Journaling can be a collection of simple facts or observations to be expanded upon later. Journaling can document anything and everything about life. Journals are traditionally handwritten in book or digitally composed on a computer, but may be recorded as audio or video files as well.

A camera lens brings focus to a subject, based upon the angle and light from which it is being photographed, drawing attention to the photographer's desired focal point. With subject in view, the camera captures life as seen through the eye of the lens, preserving the moment in a photographic image.

Life's moments defined within our hearts, through feelings, events and experiences, are captured in our mind's eye as memories that remain lodged within, unless shared through written or spoken word.

As the photograph is to the camera, so is journaling to the sharing of memories. Writing about memories enables others to experience life from our perspective. A picture is worth a thousand words—if you know what it's about. But without words, that photograph is meaningless to anyone that wasn't there to experience the moment.

Your life is full of stories to tell and each story can be shared through journaling. Journals can incorporate writing, artwork, photographs, memorabilia or any combination thereof. Stories bring to life memories, feelings and events—things symbolic of our daily journey. Your words are windows for others to experience your journey in a more personal way and there isn't anyone who can tell your story better than you. The journals you create will preserve memories for now and future generations.

Fill your paper with the breathings of your heart
–William Wordsworth

THE PURPOSE OF JOURNALING

The act of putting pen to paper encourages pause for thought, this in turn makes us think more deeply about life, which helps us regain our equilibrium

–Norbet Platt

Journaling can be rewarding to the writer in an abundance of ways. The list below shows how journaling can benefit your life. Perhaps you will be inspired to begin a journal or at least write on the pages of a scrapbook. You may just discover you have a passion for writing!

- ❑ An avenue to joyful thoughts
- ❑ Bless the reader and yourself
- ❑ Bring clarity to relationships
- ❑ Capture a moment or lifetime
- ❑ Empowers your self-expression
- ❑ Encourages your creativity
- ❑ Encourages self-reflection
- ❑ Explore potential ideas
- ❑ Explore your spirituality
- ❑ Focus on what really matters
- ❑ Focus on your strengths
- ❑ Foster a sense of self-worth
- ❑ Free your spirit & dream bigger
- ❑ Fresh perspectives on your past
- ❑ Greater insight into yourself
- ❑ Hear that still small voice in you
- ❑ Help to express your gratitude
- ❑ Journaling can energize you
- ❑ Opens your heart to love
- ❑ Reveal patterns in your life
- ❑ Share feelings, fears and fun
- ❑ Share your innermost thoughts
- ❑ Simple self-discovery
- ❑ Teaches writing enjoyment
- ❑ Tell a story—yours or others
- ❑ Writing is a joy you can share
- ❑ Writing can bring you balance
- ❑ Writing can relieve stress

JOURNEY TO JOURNALING

When a man is in doubt about his writing, it will often guide him if he asks himself how it will tell a hundred years hence?
—Samuel Butler

The heartbeat of your scrapbook is journaling, yet for many, writing is reminiscent of English 101—but don't worry, there's no grade! The purpose of this book is to encourage writing with tips, jumpstarts and thought-provoking questions. My hope is you will find journaling easier than you imagined and that you will quickly discover the many benefits and blessings of journaling.

Begin by simply choosing yourself a journal or a scrapbook. There are numerous styles and types of journals that you can write—one at a time or simultaneously depending on your schedule. The more creative you are, the greater the possibilities for your journaling. Journaling can be random or it can be focused. Don't worry whether you are doing it correctly; there is no right or wrong when it comes to writing. Journaling is very subjective, so write whatever feels right to you! You are the writer, the artist, the keeper of your journal and whatever feels good, feels right—just write!

Fill your journals with memories, thoughts, feelings, favorite quotes, notes, dreams, hopes, love, photographs, artwork, doodling, mementos—anything you desire. You are the author, the poet, the artist. Your journals are yours to create. You decide the type of journal you want to write—freestyle, structured, guided—start simple, let your spirit soar as your words pour onto your pages. Please note that any journal can be created as a scrapbook, as well. Select from any of the journal styles listed in the next section under "Writer's Tools."

Journals can be written in an eclectic style incorporating both your writing ability and artistic talents—filled with drawings, paintings, collages, etc. Journals or albums that tell about life in both words and pictures are my personal favorites. Capturing special moments through art, photographs and words adds dimension and gives life to the memories as you create. Down the road, as you look through your journal, you will discover an excitement as you relive those moments.

Journals can be fun, freeing, healing, inspiring, bring clarity and more. Unleash the writer, the artist, the real you within your journal or scrapbook. The cost is minimal, the rewards are plentiful and the effort can last for generations to come.

Where and when you write will flavor your writing in random ways, depending on whether you are sitting at your favorite coffee house, or on a park bench jotting your thoughts, or entrenched in your musings within the privacy of your home. More about this is in the next section, under "Writer's Tools."

Journals can be private for your eyes only or created as stories to share. Journals are a record of the your life and the lives of those whom you choose to reflect upon. As we put our stories into words, it's natural to intertwine the people who encompass our life. These types of stories can offer a deeper understanding for the reader.

Journaling helps us remember details in life that sometimes get lost as the days and years go rushing by. The things we record in our journals will one day be golden nuggets shining brightly in our recesses of our thoughts. Over the years, these nuggets build a path for us to walk down memory lane. It's great to reflect on the moments as they happen each day—as in stopping to smell the roses—AND they will be a double blessing as you or a loved one reads those stories years down the road.

Start journaling today and you'll quickly discover the infinite possibilities that lie within your soul as your words come to life upon your pages.

Oh, the things you can do, it's all up to you
create and design—it's there in your mind
just pick up your pen and simply begin
then discover how free—journaling can be
—Linda LaTourelle

The words of love
written upon your heart
are stories waiting to be told
–Linda LaTourelle

The Biggest Book of Words & Prompts for Scrapbooks, Art Journals & Crafts

Writer's Tools

A special book
a lovely pen
a quiet space
thoughts begin

Time to write
memories to share
words of love
written with care

–Linda LaTourelle

The New Ultimate Guide to the Perfect Word – Volume 2

JOURNALING TOOLS

JOURNALS | Blank books | Handmade books | Scrapbooks | Computer

PENS | Lots of pens* and pencils of different colors, thicknesses, shapes, types, metallic, watercolor, charcoal, etc. | * Pigment ink pens will last longer

"THE ULTIMATE GUIDE TO THE PERFECT WORD" | The entire series of Ultimate books are a great resource for scrapbook, journal or craft projects

THESAURUS and **DICTIONARY** | Reading them can be a great way to get creative juices flowing and expand your vocabulary at the same time

TEMPLATES | To create different size shapes or sections on pages to add variety

PAPER | Stock up on lots of sizes, colors, textures and thicknesses

CHALKS | Colorful chalks add really nice soft touches to your journaling

SCISSORS | Collect with different-shaped edges to create a variety of looks

PAPER CUTTER | Mini size tool that works for most paper cutting

FOLDERS | Great for organizing papers, articles and sorting projects

RECIPE BOX | Perfect for organizing quotes and ideas you collect

NOTEBOOKS | Great way to quickly jot ideas and thoughts as they come to you

RUBBERSTAMPS | Various designs, shapes, phrases and colorful ink pads

ADDITIONAL TOOLS | Punches | Eraser | Tape | Glue | Stapler

PHOTOGRAPHS | Photographs are a great embellishment to any journal

LAP-DESK | Enables you to write anywhere | Clipboards or folding table are alternatives

EMBELLISHMENTS | Stickers | Ribbons | Ephemera and glitter

MEMORABILIA | Terrific complements to journal about and embellish with

*The heart can see what the camera cannot
words tell others what your life is about*
–Linda LaTourelle

A PLACE TO JOURNAL

Make your journal time a cozy time, just for you. Enjoy a cup of tea or hot chocolate, with soft piano music in the background. Choose a comfy chair or sofa, with a table next to it for your tools, to relax and write.

Some writers prefer the solitude of a quiet room. Others are inspired with a view. Inside, outside, all that matters is that you are inspired to write. The seasons, the setting, the sentiments within will all help to guide your writing and set the mood that will open your mind to allow the words to flow freely. The most important thing is to be in a place and a space where you are comfortable.

Treat yourself to some nice journals or scrapbook albums and a variety of pens as you begin to embellish and write in them.

Journaling time can actually be very therapeutic and a great stress reliever. When you get ready to write, be sure to have your tools organized and close at hand.

Perhaps you want to journal simply by artistically embellishing your scrapbooks or by creating any one of the types of journals suggested in the section "Journals For Everyone" on the next page. Whatever you decide—relax, be blessed and enjoy the journey!

Don't wait for the perfect time to journal, jot down thoughts as they come to you or as events happen. You'll find these notes of great value in recalling people, places or events. Ask other family members or friends to jot down their thoughts at events and share them with you. This will be a benefit when you begin to write. Not only will you have their perspective, but they will feel like they are a part of what you are doing, especially if you are creating a family album.

If it seems like the blank page is staring you in the face, relax, breathe deep and take a break. Sip some tea or try one of the many tips offered in the section "Writer's Block" to overcome this frustrating dilemma. Just write a word or two. Most of all, keep practicing every chance you get. Like most things, the more you do it—the easier it gets. Just go for it!

Sitting alone with thoughts flowing free
precious time with just my journal and me
–Linda LaTourelle

The New Ultimate Guide to the Perfect Word – Volume 2

JOURNALS FOR EVERYONE

- ☐ Adoption
- ☐ Affirmation
- ☐ All about you
- ☐ Art journal
- ☐ Birthdays
- ☐ Blog
- ☐ Book of Lists
- ☐ Celebrations
- ☐ Child's journal
- ☐ Christmas journal
- ☐ Circle journal
- ☐ Couple's journal
- ☐ Creative writing
- ☐ Dreams
- ☐ Every Day Life
- ☐ Family Life
- ☐ Favorite quotes
- ☐ Favorite things
- ☐ Friendships
- ☐ Gardening
- ☐ Genealogy
- ☐ Grandparents
- ☐ Gratitude
- ☐ Healing
- ☐ Hobbies
- ☐ Holidays
- ☐ Homes
- ☐ Ideas
- ☐ Life events
- ☐ Love letters
- ☐ Mediations
- ☐ Memory book
- ☐ Military Life
- ☐ Milestones
- ☐ Music
- ☐ Nature
- ☐ Online journal
- ☐ Personal diary
- ☐ Poetry
- ☐ Prayers
- ☐ Pregnancy
- ☐ Projects
- ☐ Reading journal
- ☐ Recipes
- ☐ Reflection
- ☐ School years
- ☐ Scrapbooks
- ☐ Seasons
- ☐ Siblings
- ☐ Sketchbook
- ☐ Spiritual
- ☐ Sports
- ☐ Timeline
- ☐ Traditions
- ☐ Travel journal
- ☐ Vision journal
- ☐ Wedding journal

Each letter has a shape
marry these shapes into words
to share the many stories of your life
–Linda LaTourelle

THE STORY OF US
Create a simple book about your family

The following headings are a basic outline to help you begin to design a scrapbook or journal about your marriage and your family. These are just possible topics and can be personalized. The idea is to offer you a starting point to create a legacy of love for your family and generations to come.

THE TWO OF YOU | a personal description of you and your partner

THE MEETING | how, where and when you met

THE COURTSHIP | all the interesting details of your dating

THE ENGAGEMENT | tell about the proposal, parties and romance

THE WEDDING | perspectives from the bride and groom

THE HONEYMOON | describe this wonderful time together

HOME SWEET HOME | write about of your first home or apartment

LIFE AND LOVE | share the details of your newlywed life together

LEARNING | define your education, degrees and goals

WORK | describe the nature of your jobs

OUR FAITH | share how your faith binds you together with love

PLAYTIME | favorite things we share together and individually

THE BABY YEARS | from pregnancies to birth to preschool

THE GROWING YEARS | the details of raising children together

EVERYTHING ELSE | anything else that defines the story of you

The words of love written upon your heart
are stories waiting to be told
–Linda LaTourelle

DIGITAL JOURNALING
Blogs and logs

Online journaling is a very popular, easy way to journal on a daily basis. A personal blog is like an ongoing diary that can be kept private or be shared for public view.

Some of the current blogging platforms are free to use and are accessible to even the most inexperienced users. Blog hosting sites such as WordPress, Blogspot and Tumblr.com share similar, user-friendly features for composing posts with links, photos, and even video. There are a wide variety of add-on options for interactive features like RSS and email subscriptions, so your readers never miss your updates.

In addition, each offers unique features—you can link your blog to automatically feed updates to your favorite online communities and social media sites. You can even create voice posts from your cell phone.

Create a blog for any of the journal types listed in the section "Journals For Everyone." Digitizing your writing makes it easy to transfer your journal to a digital scrapbook, available online through any number of sites or as stand-alone software. My favorite software for digital scrapbooking is "My Memories Suite," available at "MyMemories.com." After reviewing several, I think this is the best and most popular software with lots of bells and whistles.

In addition to online journals / blogs, journaling can be done on your computer through a basic office program or a variety of journaling apps to journal on the run. Now there's no excuse—write from your tablet, mobile phone, computer, online, offline—it's never been easier and it can be stored in the "cloud" for fast access anywhere, anytime. What a great way to share with family, build a heritage journal or document the growth of a child, a wedding, graduation and more—perfect for grandparents, relatives or family across the miles or around the world. The possibilities to tell your story and share life with those you love are endless!

Scribbled on a page or captured on a phone
written on a computer, in a crowd or all alone.
Many stories to tell hidden in the heart—
decorate a journal and your words become art.
However you decide to write the memories
moments documented are gifts just for you and me.
–Linda LaTourelle

My Journal List

Create a list of the journal styles you would like to create

_____
_____
_____
_____
_____
_____
_____
_____
_____
_____
_____
_____
_____
_____
_____
_____
_____
_____
_____
_____

Journals can be your new best friend—
To share your thoughts and feelings,
Hopes and dreams whenever you choose

> The pen that writes your life story
> must be held in your own hand
> –*Irene C. Casserole*

Writing Tips

Writing is easy
just pickup your pen
open your mind
and words will begin

Deep in your heart
are memories galore
things you remember
are blessings for sure

–Linda LaTourelle

JOURNALING JUMPSTARTS

The years have flown too swiftly by
Sweet memories fill my mind's eye
Treasures built from day to day
Journaling helps each one to stay
–Linda LaTourelle

Just think of journaling as afternoon tea with your best friend or a walk on the beach with your significant other. Write as though you are engaged in a spirited conversation, reliving special moments or sharing sentiments from you heart. This is a time to recollect all those wonderful details. Writing is just sharing a conversation from your heart. **Whatever you can speak—you can write!**

As you begin to write, take time to explore your thoughts and when you're ready, express facts, feelings and memories by using any of the following techniques:

Report just the facts	Use your senses
Create lists	Write freestyle
Short paragraphs	Write in story-format
Add captions to photos	Speak and then write
Interview others	Write what you know

However you decide to begin writing, try to stay focused, don't worry about spelling or grammar and just write what comes to mind first. Be sure to leave room to add in more details later, as they come to mind.

Have you ever heard the saying about eating an elephant one bite at a time? Well, it's the same with journaling...it's okay to take whatever size bite you feel like at the moment. When you're at a loss for words, I've created lists of easy-to-use jumpstarts and questions. They can be used just to get you going or as stand-alone topics and techniques. These ideas are simple and will help you to build confidence in your writing. Before you know it, you'll be ready to write a book.

I have listed a few of the popular ways to warm up to journaling. Try them all or just one or two—grab your pen (or computer) and go for it.

I never completely forget myself except when I am writing and I am never more completely myself than when I am writing
–Flannery O'Connor

MORE JUMPSTARTS

WRITE A LETTER | Keep it short and sweet to someone you love. It'll make them feel good and you'll be learning how to write in a relaxed format. No pressure...just share your thoughts and feel the joy.

RAMBLE AND WRITE | Start by just writing any words that come to mind. Don't think, just write...even if you repeat yourself.

CREATE A LIST | Writing in a list format helps to streamline a jumble of ideas and helps to inspire.

WRITE A REVIEW | Write it about a person you know, a place you enjoy going, a favorite thing to do on your day off, your favorite movie or event.

WRITE YOUR LIFE STORY | But you must do it with only seven words. That's right, describe your life in seven words. They don't have to make a sentence.

READY, SET, WRITE | Set a timer for one minute. Start writing as many verbs as you can, then set it again and do it with adjectives, nouns, feeling words

10 THINGS THAT MAKE YOU SMILE | Write the top ten things made you smile today. Keeping it to today will help you focus on the joy, too.

DRAW A SHAPE AND FILL IT IN | Create a shape, fill it with words that define love to you. Get creative and really think about it.

CREATE A JOURNALING JAR | Copy some of the "Journaling prompts" in this chapter onto slip of paper, add to jar and then pick one a day and write.

USE YOUR SENSES | Sight, sound, smell, taste and touch. Using each of the five senses, write five memories from your childhood.

MORE FAVORITES | Food, friends, travels, clothes, seasons, traditions

WRITE YOUR ABC'S | Define your life one letter at a time. One word or many, using every letter in the alphabet. Get creative and artsy, too!

TELL YOUR STORY | It's the history and the heartbeat of your journaling. Just as the quote says... "How will it tell a hundred years hence?"

*Sing your song, dance your dance,
oh, the stories you will tell*
–Linda LaTourelle

THE FIVE W'S
Who, what, where, when and why?

Want the fastest way to jumpstart any journaling? Whether on a scrapbook page, in a personal diary or a themed journal—utilize this simple formula and watch the words begin to flow as pen meets paper. Keep it short or document every detail. Either way, you'll find this to be the perfect method to begin to write for most any topic.

WHO | Begin by documenting names, ages, gender, relation and any relevant facts you desire that will enable readers to identify the person or persons you are writing about. Because we all grow and change through the years, the information you share here will be of great benefit to future generations. Be sure to label any photographs or drawings.

WHAT | Describe memorable moments of the event you are writing about, sharing significant details of the occasion. Your senses will help you to record the sounds, smells, sights, tastes, and feelings of the event and your perception of all that was happening. In the stillness of your thoughts, drink in the memories and try to recreate that time through your words.

WHERE | Let your words paint a picture of the place where the memories happened and bring added perspective to the story you are telling.

WHEN | Dates and times are very important to document special occasions. It's nice to know when something occurred.

WHY | Sharing this will give depth to your journaling and reveal more about the people, the place, the event—giving meaning and reason for choosing your topic or photographs to write about.

The words that you weave will bring blessings, give meaning and tell a story that is sure to be a treasure. Remember that this something to be enjoyed, not a task to be stressed over. Relax, breath deep and relive the memories. Talk to your paper or your computer like you're telling a story or writing for your own purpose.

Journaling is as simple as talking; there's no right or wrong. It's about what you feel, what you want to share, who you want to share it with and the legacy of love you will create through your words in your journal or scrapbook.

Watch the words begin to flow as pen meets paper—
write now to relive the memories for generations to come
–Linda LaTourelle

DOODLE, DOODLED AND DOODLING
Mindless doodling inspires mindful journaling

So here's a really simple exercise to help you relax and forget that you have that bothersome writer's block—just doodle! Doodle to your heart's content—on a blank page, a scrap of paper, the back of an envelope, a napkin—anywhere that will help you realize writing is all about having fun. There's no teacher watching now, it's about whatever you feel as you get your fingers moving with pen in hand!

Doodling is a great warm-up tool to help let go of momentary thoughts that seem to be stifling creativity. Doodle big, doodle tiny, round and round, up and down, dots, squiggles, swirls, flourishes, flowers, words, letters...just wiggle your pen joyfully, playfully and smile. You get to doodle whatever you want! Enjoy the moment and let your pen dance to the music of your heart. Doodle to your heart's content and open your mind to the words that lie within. Doodling helps the left brain connect to the right brain, relaxing and opening the flow, clearing the mind allowing words to come freely and before you know it, you've written a sentence or more.

COLOR YOUR PAGES WITH WORDS
Color your pages with memories

Journaling with lively, scintillating words will bring your memories to life. Words that describe (adjectives and adverbs) are colorful adornments, lending artistic style and personality to your writing.

Think back to lessons in English 101 about adjectives and adverbs. Remember, an adjective modifies a noun (person, place or thing.) Adverbs modify adjectives, verbs and other adverbs. Adjectives and adverbs tell where, when, how, how often and to what extent. So color your pages beautiful, jazzy, joyful and more with your favorite words. Add flair, flavor, fun and feeling with the words you choose.

Words can transform a basically simple page into a treasure for the reader because they bring life to events and photographs in memorable, vivid and realistic ways. Words can set the mood or tone reflecting the writer's perspective.

A blank page can become an artistic masterpiece through the use of different papers, embellishments, colors, textures, etc. You are only limited by your imagination. Just as these elements express your creativity, writing also becomes exciting and fun through your choice of words. The feel of a page can be changed simply or dramatically with the use of a few adjectives or adverbs. Changing a color can create a boldness or softness, and so it is with the words you choose.

Get yourself a good thesaurus and you'll soon discover that there are many ways to describe something by finding different synonyms for your adjectives or adverbs. It's exciting when you realize how creative your writing can be!

Here are some examples to show how you can change the mood by substituting any of these words for "happy" and how you can describe the way someone was "walking" by using a different adverb:

HAPPY: blessed, blest, blissful, blithe, bubbly, cheerful, cheery, chipper, chirpy, content, contented, delighted, ecstatic, elated, exultant, glad, gleeful, gratified, hopped up, in high spirits, jolly, jovial, joyful, joyous, jubilant, laughing, light, lively, looking good, merry, mirthful, overjoyed, peaceful, peppy, perky, playful, pleasant, pleased, satisfied, sparkling, sunny, thrilled, tickled, tickled pink, up, upbeat

WALKING: aggressively, ambitiously, briskly, cheerfully, clumsily, delightfully, fast, firmly, gently, happily, heartily, hesitantly, hopefully, joyfully, lazily, lightly, loudly, meanly, merrily, noisily, patiently, quickly, quietly, rambunctiously, roughly, secretly, simply, slowly, steady, swiftly, wearily,

Another way to enhance your pages is by journaling in your own handwriting. Don't worry about your penmanship—it's your fingerprint and it adds a personal touch that will be cherished for generations to come. Embellish your pages with words just as you would other decorations. You can even use another family member's writing to add a special touch to a page about them—perhaps an old letter or recipe card. More information available in the section "Hand-written with Love."

Please enjoy the following section, "The Word Palette"—it's a collection of words I've gathered to help you add color and personality to your writing.

Color is the language of the poets
–Keith Crown

WORD PALETTE

An artist uses colors to paint a masterpiece, a writer uses words to tell a story. This palette of words can be used to describe feelings, people, places, events and more. These words can add color to your journaling and bring inspiration when you're at a loss for words.

ANGRY
- ☐ Affronted
- ☐ Annoyed
- ☐ Belligerent
- ☐ Bitter
- ☐ Boiling
- ☐ Enraged
- ☐ Fired-up
- ☐ Frustrated
- ☐ Fuming
- ☐ Full of fury
- ☐ Furious
- ☐ Grumpy
- ☐ Ill-tempered
- ☐ Indignant
- ☐ Inflamed
- ☐ Infuriated
- ☐ Irate
- ☐ Irritated
- ☐ Livid
- ☐ Outraged
- ☐ Provoked
- ☐ Resentful
- ☐ Stubborn
- ☐ Sulky

BEAUTIFUL
- ☐ Adorable
- ☐ Attractive
- ☐ Beguiling
- ☐ Blossoming
- ☐ Breathless
- ☐ Charming
- ☐ Classy
- ☐ Exquisite
- ☐ Gorgeous
- ☐ Hot
- ☐ Loveliest
- ☐ Lovely
- ☐ Prettiest
- ☐ Pretty
- ☐ Sexy

CREATIVE
- ☐ Adventurous
- ☐ Artistic
- ☐ Artsy
- ☐ Bold
- ☐ Brilliantly
- ☐ Dramatic
- ☐ Dynamic
- ☐ Genius
- ☐ Imaginative
- ☐ Inspiring
- ☐ Intriguing
- ☐ Organic
- ☐ Original
- ☐ Palette
- ☐ Perfection
- ☐ Sensational
- ☐ Shimmering
- ☐ Symmetry
- ☐ Talent
- ☐ Talented
- ☐ Unique
- ☐ Vibrant
- ☐ Visionary
- ☐ Zealous

DOUBTFUL
- ☐ Distrustful
- ☐ Dubious
- ☐ Hesitant
- ☐ Indecisive
- ☐ Perplexed
- ☐ Questionable
- ☐ Skeptical
- ☐ Suspicious
- ☐ Unbelieving
- ☐ Uncertain
- ☐ Wavering

EAGER
- ☐ Anxious
- ☐ Ardent
- ☐ Avid
- ☐ Desirous
- ☐ Determined
- ☐ Energetic
- ☐ Enthusiastic
- ☐ Excited
- ☐ Frisky
- ☐ Gung-ho
- ☐ High-spirited
- ☐ Hot-to-trot
- ☐ Intent
- ☐ Keen

- ☐ Perky
- ☐ Ready
- ☐ Yearning
- ☐ Zeal

FEARLESS
- ☐ Bold
- ☐ Brave
- ☐ Confident
- ☐ Courageous
- ☐ Dauntless
- ☐ Daring
- ☐ Determined
- ☐ Gallant
- ☐ Heroic
- ☐ Impulsive
- ☐ Independent
- ☐ Lion-hearted
- ☐ Self-assured

FEELINGS
- ☐ Aloof
- ☐ Ambiance
- ☐ Anxious
- ☐ Assertive
- ☐ Assured
- ☐ Atmosphere
- ☐ Aura
- ☐ Authentic
- ☐ Bashful
- ☐ Calm
- ☐ Climate
- ☐ Compassion
- ☐ Conceited
- ☐ Cozy
- ☐ Depressed
- ☐ Elated
- ☐ Emotional
- ☐ Empathetic
- ☐ Enamored

- ☐ Experience
- ☐ Flamboyant
- ☐ Fond
- ☐ Friendly
- ☐ Fulfilling
- ☐ Gentle
- ☐ Genuine
- ☐ Healing
- ☐ Heartfelt
- ☐ Honest
- ☐ Impressionable
- ☐ Jazzy
- ☐ Jubilant
- ☐ Lucky
- ☐ Manner
- ☐ Personable
- ☐ Positive
- ☐ Prayerful
- ☐ Pretentious
- ☐ Quirky
- ☐ Satisfying
- ☐ Sentimental
- ☐ Sincere
- ☐ Snarky
- ☐ Sombre
- ☐ Sweaty
- ☐ Taut
- ☐ Tense
- ☐ Thoughtful
- ☐ Tired
- ☐ Uptight
- ☐ Vibrant
- ☐ Weak
- ☐ Weary
- ☐ Worshipful

GRATITUDE
- ☐ Appreciation
- ☐ Blessed
- ☐ Grace

- ☐ Grateful
- ☐ Kindness
- ☐ Thankful
- ☐ Thankfulness

HAPPY
- ☐ Animated
- ☐ Beaming
- ☐ Blessed
- ☐ Blissful
- ☐ Bubbly
- ☐ Carefree
- ☐ Cheerful
- ☐ Cheery
- ☐ Chipper
- ☐ Chirpy
- ☐ Content
- ☐ Contented
- ☐ Dazzling
- ☐ Delighted
- ☐ Ecstatic
- ☐ Elated
- ☐ Euphoric
- ☐ Excited
- ☐ Exhilarated
- ☐ Fantastical
- ☐ Felicitous
- ☐ Festive
- ☐ Funny
- ☐ Generous
- ☐ Giddy
- ☐ Giggling
- ☐ Giggly
- ☐ Glad
- ☐ Gleeful
- ☐ Glowing
- ☐ Gregarious
- ☐ Grinning
- ☐ Happy-go-lucky
- ☐ Hilarious

- ☐ Intoxicated
- ☐ Jolly
- ☐ Jovial
- ☐ Joyful
- ☐ Joyous
- ☐ Jubilant
- ☐ Laughter
- ☐ Lighthearted
- ☐ Lively
- ☐ Looking Good
- ☐ Merry
- ☐ Optimistic
- ☐ Overjoyed
- ☐ Peaceful
- ☐ Peppy
- ☐ Playful
- ☐ Pleasant
- ☐ Pleased
- ☐ Radiant
- ☐ Relaxed
- ☐ Restful
- ☐ Satisfied
- ☐ Serene
- ☐ Silly
- ☐ Smiling
- ☐ Sparkling
- ☐ Sparkly
- ☐ Spirited
- ☐ Sunny
- ☐ Surprised
- ☐ Thrilled
- ☐ Tickled
- ☐ Tickled-pink
- ☐ Vivacious
- ☐ Upbeat

HEAR
- ☐ All Ears
- ☐ Audible
- ☐ Awareness
- ☐ Babble
- ☐ Bellow
- ☐ Buzz
- ☐ Chatter
- ☐ Chime
- ☐ Chuckle
- ☐ Comprehend
- ☐ Discern
- ☐ Eavesdrop
- ☐ Giggle
- ☐ Glean
- ☐ Hearken
- ☐ Hum
- ☐ Hush
- ☐ Learn
- ☐ Listen
- ☐ Mumble
- ☐ Overhear
- ☐ Perceive
- ☐ Pick-up
- ☐ Quiet
- ☐ Receive
- ☐ Shout
- ☐ Sigh
- ☐ Squawk
- ☐ Stammer
- ☐ Twittering
- ☐ Tuned-in
- ☐ Understand
- ☐ Warbling
- ☐ Whine
- ☐ Whisper

HURT
- ☐ Aching
- ☐ Afflicted
- ☐ Boo-boo
- ☐ Bruised
- ☐ Bump
- ☐ Crushed
- ☐ Distressed
- ☐ Heartbroken
- ☐ Injured
- ☐ Isolated
- ☐ Lonely
- ☐ Offended
- ☐ Ouch
- ☐ Pained
- ☐ Upset
- ☐ Worried

INTEREST
- ☐ Absorbed
- ☐ Concerned
- ☐ Curious
- ☐ Engrossed
- ☐ Excited
- ☐ Fascinated
- ☐ Inquiring
- ☐ Inquisitive
- ☐ Intrigued
- ☐ Obsessed
- ☐ Pre-occupied
- ☐ Stirred
- ☐ Sympathetic
- ☐ Taken
- ☐ Touched

LOOKS
- ☐ Angular
- ☐ Beautiful
- ☐ Bright
- ☐ Brilliant
- ☐ Bulky
- ☐ Clean
- ☐ Clear
- ☐ Cluttered
- ☐ Curvy
- ☐ Deep
- ☐ Different

- ☐ Drained
- ☐ Drenched
- ☐ Elegant
- ☐ Foggy
- ☐ Gigantic
- ☐ Glimmering
- ☐ Hollow
- ☐ Huge
- ☐ Humongous
- ☐ Immense
- ☐ Lacy
- ☐ Large
- ☐ Lopsided
- ☐ Luxurious
- ☐ Messy
- ☐ Metallic
- ☐ Narrow
- ☐ Oval
- ☐ Pale
- ☐ Perky
- ☐ Ruffled
- ☐ Shadow
- ☐ Shapely
- ☐ Sheer
- ☐ Shiny
- ☐ Slippery
- ☐ Small
- ☐ Speckled
- ☐ Spiky
- ☐ Spotted
- ☐ Tall
- ☐ Tidy
- ☐ Tiny
- ☐ Tilted
- ☐ Tough
- ☐ Triangular
- ☐ Translucent
- ☐ Twinkling
- ☐ Wide
- ☐ Wooly

LOVE
- ☐ Lovable
- ☐ Loving
- ☐ Devoted
- ☐ Warm
- ☐ Close
- ☐ Drawn To
- ☐ Devotion
- ☐ Sensitive
- ☐ Like
- ☐ Hold Dear
- ☐ Idolize
- ☐ Spark
- ☐ Woo

MYSTERY
- ☐ Classified
- ☐ Confidential
- ☐ Mysterious
- ☐ Private
- ☐ Sly
- ☐ Top Secret

PASSION
- ☐ Adoring
- ☐ Anger
- ☐ Burning
- ☐ Craving
- ☐ Desiring
- ☐ Devotion
- ☐ Ecstasy
- ☐ Erotic
- ☐ Fervent
- ☐ Fury
- ☐ Intense
- ☐ Jazzed
- ☐ Joyful
- ☐ Lovesick
- ☐ Lustful
- ☐ Passionate

- ☐ Sensitive
- ☐ Sensual
- ☐ Steamy
- ☐ Stormy
- ☐ Tender

PEACEFUL
- ☐ Calm
- ☐ Comfortable
- ☐ Centered
- ☐ Content
- ☐ Quiet
- ☐ Relaxed
- ☐ Serene
- ☐ Tranquil

PHYSICAL
- ☐ Able
- ☐ Active
- ☐ Alive
- ☐ Slaphappy
- ☐ Spirit
- ☐ Tone
- ☐ Touchy
- ☐ Vibes

POSITIVE
- ☐ Achieved
- ☐ Affirmative
- ☐ Approving
- ☐ Assured
- ☐ Attitude
- ☐ Certain
- ☐ Empowering
- ☐ Hopeful
- ☐ Nourishing
- ☐ Optimistic
- ☐ Powerful
- ☐ Robust
- ☐ Successful

ROMANCE
- [ ] Adoration
- [ ] Adore
- [ ] Affectionate
- [ ] Alluring
- [ ] Amorè
- [ ] Amorous
- [ ] Beloved
- [ ] Bewitching
- [ ] Blissful
- [ ] Captivating
- [ ] Courtship
- [ ] Dreamy
- [ ] Enchanting
- [ ] Fling
- [ ] Flirtatious
- [ ] Hanky-panky
- [ ] Indescribable
- [ ] Infatuated
- [ ] Intoxicating
- [ ] Irresistible
- [ ] Juliet
- [ ] Lover
- [ ] Lust
- [ ] Make love
- [ ] Mesmerizing
- [ ] Mushy
- [ ] Passion
- [ ] Poetic
- [ ] Romance
- [ ] Romantic
- [ ] Romeo
- [ ] Rose
- [ ] Seductive
- [ ] Sensuality
- [ ] Sensuous
- [ ] Sexy
- [ ] Starry-eyed
- [ ] Sultry

SAD
- [ ] Agony
- [ ] Blah
- [ ] Blue
- [ ] Cheerless
- [ ] Choked-up
- [ ] Concerned
- [ ] Crying
- [ ] Depressed
- [ ] Desolate
- [ ] Disappointed
- [ ] Discontent
- [ ] Discouraged
- [ ] Forlorn
- [ ] Gloomy
- [ ] Glum
- [ ] Heartbroken
- [ ] Heavy-hearted
- [ ] Hopeless
- [ ] Hurting
- [ ] Melancholy
- [ ] Miserable
- [ ] Moody
- [ ] Poignant
- [ ] Somber
- [ ] Sorrowful
- [ ] Sour
- [ ] Sulky
- [ ] Sullen
- [ ] Sympathetic
- [ ] Unhappy
- [ ] Sight
- [ ] Spot
- [ ] Spy
- [ ] Stare
- [ ] View
- [ ] Vision
- [ ] Watch
- [ ] Woebegone

SMELL
- [ ] Aroma
- [ ] Aromatic
- [ ] Bouquet
- [ ] Essence
- [ ] Find
- [ ] Flavor
- [ ] Fragrant
- [ ] Inhale
- [ ] Odor
- [ ] Odorous
- [ ] Perfumed
- [ ] Scented
- [ ] Sniff
- [ ] Spice
- [ ] Stink
- [ ] Whiff

TASTE
- [ ] Appetite
- [ ] Bitter
- [ ] Bittersweet
- [ ] Bland
- [ ] Buttery
- [ ] Chew
- [ ] Chomp
- [ ] Eat
- [ ] Flat
- [ ] Flavorful
- [ ] Fruity
- [ ] Hearty
- [ ] Lick
- [ ] Mellow
- [ ] Nibble
- [ ] Palate
- [ ] Pungent
- [ ] Relish
- [ ] Rich
- [ ] Ripe

- ☐ Sample
- ☐ Savor
- ☐ Savory
- ☐ Sip
- ☐ Smooth
- ☐ Sour
- ☐ Spicy
- ☐ Sweet
- ☐ Tangy
- ☐ Tantalizing
- ☐ Zest
- ☐ Zing

TIRED
- ☐ Beat
- ☐ Burnt out
- ☐ Drained
- ☐ Exhausted
- ☐ Lethargic
- ☐ Pooped
- ☐ Sleepy
- ☐ Spent
- ☐ Tired
- ☐ Weary

TOUCH
- ☐ Brush
- ☐ Bumpy
- ☐ Caress
- ☐ Clammy
- ☐ Cuddle
- ☐ Damp
- ☐ Dull
- ☐ Embrace
- ☐ Feathery
- ☐ Feel
- ☐ Fuzzy
- ☐ Gnarled
- ☐ Grip
- ☐ Grope

- ☐ Hairy
- ☐ Hard
- ☐ Hot
- ☐ Hug
- ☐ Kissing
- ☐ Knotted
- ☐ Leathery
- ☐ Limp
- ☐ Lumpy
- ☐ Oily
- ☐ Pet
- ☐ Pinch
- ☐ Poke
- ☐ Puffy
- ☐ Ribbed
- ☐ Rubbery
- ☐ Satiny
- ☐ Scratch
- ☐ Silky
- ☐ Slimy
- ☐ Smooth
- ☐ Soft
- ☐ Squeeze
- ☐ Sticky
- ☐ Velvety
- ☐ Waxy
- ☐ Wet

A FEW MORE
- ☐ Admiration
- ☐ Admire
- ☐ Affinity
- ☐ Ageless
- ☐ Agony
- ☐ Amazed
- ☐ Amazing
- ☐ Ambitious
- ☐ Amusing
- ☐ Appealing
- ☐ Appreciate

- ☐ Approving
- ☐ Astonishing
- ☐ Athletic
- ☐ Attentive
- ☐ Aura
- ☐ Awesome
- ☐ Babe
- ☐ Baby
- ☐ Behold
- ☐ Best
- ☐ Blessing
- ☐ Blue-eyed
- ☐ Bold
- ☐ Bond
- ☐ Boundless
- ☐ Bountiful
- ☐ Brainy
- ☐ Breath
- ☐ Breathe
- ☐ Brown-eyed
- ☐ Caring
- ☐ Certain
- ☐ Challenge
- ☐ Challenging
- ☐ Charmer
- ☐ Cheeky
- ☐ Cherish
- ☐ Cherishing
- ☐ Chivalrous
- ☐ Chivalry
- ☐ Classic
- ☐ Clever
- ☐ Close
- ☐ Comfort
- ☐ Comforting
- ☐ Comical
- ☐ Companion
- ☐ Completed
- ☐ Complicated
- ☐ Compliment

- ☐ Considerate
- ☐ Contemplate
- ☐ Coy
- ☐ Crazy about
- ☐ Cuddly
- ☐ Cute
- ☐ Cuteness
- ☐ Cutie
- ☐ Dainty
- ☐ Darlin'
- ☐ Darling
- ☐ Dazzle
- ☐ Dear
- ☐ Debonaire
- ☐ Decent
- ☐ Dedicated
- ☐ Deeply
- ☐ Defining
- ☐ Delectable
- ☐ Delicate
- ☐ Delicious
- ☐ Delightful
- ☐ Delirious
- ☐ Desire
- ☐ Desirable
- ☐ Desperate
- ☐ Devoted
- ☐ Discerning
- ☐ Disciplined
- ☐ Discover
- ☐ Divine
- ☐ Doll
- ☐ Doll-face
- ☐ Doting
- ☐ Dreaming
- ☐ Eloquent
- ☐ Emphatic
- ☐ Empowering
- ☐ Encouraged
- ☐ Endear

- ☐ Endearment
- ☐ Endless
- ☐ Energized
- ☐ Enigmatic
- ☐ Enjoy
- ☐ Envelope
- ☐ Eternal
- ☐ Ethereal
- ☐ Everlasting
- ☐ Exhausting
- ☐ Extraordinary
- ☐ Extraordinarily
- ☐ Extravagant
- ☐ Fabulous
- ☐ Fair
- ☐ Faith
- ☐ Faithful
- ☐ Fantastic
- ☐ Fascinate
- ☐ Fast
- ☐ Favorite
- ☐ Feast
- ☐ Find
- ☐ Fine
- ☐ Fire
- ☐ Flirt
- ☐ Flutter
- ☐ Focused
- ☐ Fond
- ☐ Fondness
- ☐ Forever
- ☐ Fortunate
- ☐ Fragrance
- ☐ Freeing
- ☐ Fresh
- ☐ Friendly
- ☐ Genius
- ☐ Gentle
- ☐ Giving
- ☐ Glad

- ☐ Glorious
- ☐ Good
- ☐ Gorgeous
- ☐ Grand
- ☐ Great
- ☐ Handsome
- ☐ Happily
- ☐ Harmonious
- ☐ Heart
- ☐ Helpful
- ☐ Hip
- ☐ Hold
- ☐ Holding
- ☐ Honesty
- ☐ Honey
- ☐ Honorable
- ☐ Hope
- ☐ Hopeful
- ☐ Huggable
- ☐ Hungry
- ☐ Idolize
- ☐ Impeccable
- ☐ Imperfect
- ☐ Important
- ☐ Incredible
- ☐ Indescribable
- ☐ Individual
- ☐ Infinite
- ☐ Innocent
- ☐ Innovative
- ☐ Inquisitive
- ☐ Insightful
- ☐ Inspired
- ☐ Integrity
- ☐ Intelligent
- ☐ Invaluable
- ☐ Invigorating
- ☐ Iridescent
- ☐ Joy
- ☐ Jubilation

The New Ultimate Guide to the Perfect Word – Volume 2

- ☐ Keen
- ☐ Kind
- ☐ Kindly
- ☐ Kindness
- ☐ Kisses
- ☐ Kissy-face
- ☐ Liberated
- ☐ Lightning
- ☐ Limitless
- ☐ Lips
- ☐ Lovable
- ☐ Love
- ☐ Love Bug
- ☐ Loved
- ☐ Lovey
- ☐ Loving
- ☐ Lovingly
- ☐ Loyal
- ☐ Lucrative
- ☐ Luscious
- ☐ Lyrical
- ☐ Madly
- ☐ Magical
- ☐ Magnificent
- ☐ Mannerly
- ☐ Marvelous
- ☐ Masterful
- ☐ Meaningful
- ☐ Melodious
- ☐ Melody
- ☐ Memories
- ☐ Memory
- ☐ Merrily
- ☐ Mine
- ☐ Miracle
- ☐ Miraculous
- ☐ Mischievous
- ☐ Modest
- ☐ Momentous
- ☐ Monumental

- ☐ Mood
- ☐ Motivated
- ☐ Motivating
- ☐ Moving
- ☐ Musical
- ☐ My Love
- ☐ Mysterious
- ☐ Need
- ☐ Nerdy
- ☐ Nice
- ☐ Notably
- ☐ Note
- ☐ Nothing
- ☐ Nourishing
- ☐ Nurturing
- ☐ Obsession
- ☐ Odor
- ☐ Old-fashioned
- ☐ Oogle
- ☐ Orgasmic
- ☐ Original
- ☐ Outgoing
- ☐ Over-achieve
- ☐ Painful
- ☐ Painless
- ☐ Palatable
- ☐ Patient
- ☐ Peace
- ☐ Perfect
- ☐ Perfume
- ☐ Perplexing
- ☐ Personal
- ☐ Personality
- ☐ Persistent
- ☐ Pleasurable
- ☐ Pleasure
- ☐ Polite
- ☐ Positive
- ☐ Potential
- ☐ Powerful

- ☐ Prayerfully
- ☐ Precious
- ☐ Pretty
- ☐ Priceless
- ☐ Prince
- ☐ Princely
- ☐ Princess
- ☐ Privileged
- ☐ Proposal
- ☐ Protective
- ☐ Purpose
- ☐ Receptive
- ☐ Reliable
- ☐ Respect
- ☐ Respectful
- ☐ Responsible
- ☐ Resourceful
- ☐ Restoration
- ☐ Revered
- ☐ Reverent
- ☐ Rhapsody
- ☐ Roving
- ☐ Satiny
- ☐ Scent
- ☐ Scrumptious
- ☐ Secret
- ☐ Sense
- ☐ Serene
- ☐ Shimmer
- ☐ Shine
- ☐ Shower
- ☐ Silky
- ☐ Sincerely
- ☐ Smart
- ☐ Smokin'
- ☐ Snuggly
- ☐ Softly
- ☐ Soulmate
- ☐ Spirited
- ☐ Spectacular

- ☐ Spontaneous
- ☐ Starlight
- ☐ Stirring
- ☐ Strength
- ☐ Strong
- ☐ Struttin'
- ☐ Suave
- ☐ Supportive
- ☐ Surprising
- ☐ Sweetly
- ☐ Sweetheart
- ☐ Sweetness
- ☐ Symphonic
- ☐ Symphony
- ☐ Taken
- ☐ Tease
- ☐ Temptation
- ☐ Tempting
- ☐ Tenacious
- ☐ Tender
- ☐ Tenderly
- ☐ Tenderness
- ☐ Thinking
- ☐ Thirsty
- ☐ Thunderous
- ☐ Timeless
- ☐ Together
- ☐ Touching
- ☐ Touchy-feely
- ☐ Traveler
- ☐ Treasured
- ☐ True love
- ☐ Truly
- ☐ Trusting
- ☐ Trustworthy
- ☐ Unconventional
- ☐ Unexplainable
- ☐ Union
- ☐ Unite
- ☐ Unity
- ☐ Unmeasurable
- ☐ Unusual
- ☐ Uplifting
- ☐ Utmost
- ☐ Valuable
- ☐ Value
- ☐ Valued
- ☐ Velvet
- ☐ Vigorous
- ☐ Voracious
- ☐ Vow
- ☐ Warmhearted
- ☐ Warmth
- ☐ Well-built
- ☐ Wild
- ☐ Wonderful
- ☐ Worship
- ☐ Yarn
- ☐ Yawning
- ☐ Yearning
- ☐ Young
- ☐ Yucky
- ☐ Zippity

COLOR

Color it bold,
color it happy,
with colorful words
like jazzy and snappy.
Your writing will dance
on the pages you'll see,
with journaling that's
so lively and free.

–Linda LaTourelle

The New Ultimate Guide to the Perfect Word – Volume 2

My Favorite Words

Colorful words make your writing come to life—
using the word palette helps to overcome writer's block

OVERCOMING WRITER'S BLOCK
The only cure for writer's block is insomnia

So you're geared up and ready to begin your journal—sitting comfy, relaxed with pen in hand (or keyboard), ready to write and then it happens—your mind is as blank as the page or monitor staring you in the face. Your enthusiasm wanes and frustration ensues, leaving you with sweaty hands, doodling with the pen or tapping your keyboard. Sound familiar? It is the bane of writers everywhere and can come at anytime —*Writer's Block*.

Don't worry—finding the perfect words for scrapbooks, journals, diaries or historical narratives for genealogy is often very trying for even the most gifted writers. Too often, the initial sentence seems to stop even before the first word is penned upon the page. As frustrating and challenging as writer's block may seem at that moment, overcoming it can be accomplished easily through timeless techniques that open the mind to pour words freely from the heart.

Whether journaling on a scrapbook page full of photographs or simply writing in any type of journal, diary or genealogy document you may find the following tips not only helpful, but great fun, too!

LIFE IS YOUR SCRAPBOOK
The moments of every day are the most inspiring

Journaling or scrapbooking is way more than documenting a special event. It's simply sharing life as it happens daily and it's easy because every day your life is filled with moments that if captured through words, photographs or video will tell the story of your life and inspire your creativity. Family, friends, work, play, home, traveling, happy, sad —so many gems to encourage the storyteller in you. What a blessing for you, your family and future generations to truly know you!

Keep it simple, keep it true,
every day is a story fresh and new!
–Linda LaTourelle

CREATIVE SPARKS

Inspire creativity using these simple tips

- ☐ Capture words, thoughts, photos and ideas using your camera, video camera or cell phone.
- ☐ Carry a notebook with you—it's great for jotting down thoughts, ideas, or observations that will give you more topics for your journal.
- ☐ Add a quote to each page of your journal that is inspirational to you or that relates to what you have already written. Write what it means to you.
- ☐ Carry a portable voice recorder or download a recording app for your mobile device. Record thoughts, children's words and even conversations with family members you don't get to see often.
- ☐ Gratitude is a great topic to journal about. A fun thing to do is count your blessings and write about them.
- ☐ Recipe Favorites: Quotes, sayings, words, etc. that inspire you.
- ☐ Collect things that inspire you—bookmarks, postcards, greeting cards, mementos, sentimental items—these are journaling sparks.
- ☐ Leave space on your pages to write as you remember more.
- ☐ Photograph every day life, as well as special events and document the details.
- ☐ Save your old love letters and reread them occasionally.
- ☐ Save emails and text messages, bookmark your favorite websites.
- ☐ Use the first page of your journal to display a beautiful poem, one you've written or a favorite written by someone else.
- ☐ Scan old photographs and memorabilia to share digitally or in print.
- ☐ There are no rules in journaling—write simple facts or embellish your pages with more personal info about you and your family.
- ☐ Create top ten lists: favorite books, authors, music, movies, hobbies, activities, foods, vacations or anything else you enjoy.
- ☐ Use extra space at the end of a journal to write a summary of the year and leave a space on the first or last page to list the contents.

TIDBITS & TIPS
Proven ideas to get you journaling more

- ☐ Find the pearls of wisdom (or joy) in each day and jot them down on little slips of paper and store them in a treasure chest, pulling one out from time to time, just to remember or share them with a family member as a special blessing.
- ☐ When it comes to journaling a pearl is a great metaphor. The pearl starts with one grain of sand, so begin with a single thought and build your writing from that thought.
- ☐ Adding just a few words will lend meaning to any page and will often inspire a bigger story.
- ☐ Simple outlines of an event make recall easier for writing later.
- ☐ Sticky notes are a useful tool to add ideas to a page until you have time to complete it.
- ☐ Pretend your page is a very close friend and just start "talking" with your pen about your day or whatever is on your heart.
- ☐ Mark off spaces on your pages to journal later, using a clear ruler or template and a soft lead pencil.
- ☐ Forget the rules—embellish, write, think outside the box, draw outside the lines—the joy of journaling is yours.
- ☐ Give yourself through words or art—it's the best gift you'll ever give.
- ☐ Learn to love lists, they are fast and easy to create on any topic.
- ☐ Forget sentences—just add single words that describe your photo or your thought.
- ☐ Checkout ads in the media to find words that zing, colors that pop and designs that draw you in.
- ☐ Pick any word—open a dictionary or thesaurus, close your eyes and point, and use the word your finger lands on to create a story.
- ☐ Be the roving reporter at your next family gathering—write a feature story, complete with headline and highlights.
- ☐ Try just adding doodles or doodling words to define or simply embellish your photograph.
- ☐ Write a love letter to your husband, child or parents, telling each of them what they truly mean to you

- ☐ For a really simple way to get yourself writing and also discover blessings, start a gratitude journal and write something every day
- ☐ Create several scrapbook page layouts with everything completed but the journaling, then choose a night to remember and free-form write / long or short paragraphs as you walk down memory lane.
- ☐ Write a book report of your life as a child or teen and give it a title, complete with references
- ☐ Make themed greeting ards for all occasions using your own words or favorite quotes and give them away for no special reason or create sets to give as a gift.
- ☐ Don't like your handwriting? Try hiding your journaling under a flap or journal onto a folded card and tuck it inside a pocket or envelope. Hidden journaling adds embellishments, too.
- ☐ If you're a blogger, print a favorite entry to add to your journal or scrapbook, or take excerpts from your blog entries.
- ☐ If you've seen a saying on a rubber stamp you really like, but can't afford to buy it, jot it down and then use your own handwriting or favorite font.
- ☐ Highlight your writing by adding color to capital letters or other embellishments
- ☐ Try adding song lyrics that match your theme, for example if you're doing a wedding album, use love songs, or for a baby album, add a lullaby.
- ☐ Print your favorite quotes, titles, journaling or just words on transparencies and layer them on your journal or album pages.
- ☐ Write about the person, your feelings, emotions behind the photo, for example, if it's about your child, journal about how fast they're growing up.
- ☐ Write your thoughts on plain paper before you add them to your scrapbook so it's easier to make changes.
- ☐ Choose a time every day to write, even if it's only for five or ten minutes and you'll soon look forward to that time and the words will flow easier.
- ☐ Create a list of goals for the next thirty days, 6 months and one year. Then as you accomplish each goal, write it in a success journal.
- ☐ Start a journal page in pencil; once you're happy with what you've written, complete it using your favorite pen. It is easier to correct your writing by using pencil first.

The Biggest Book of Words & Prompts for Scrapbooks, Art Journals & Crafts

- ☐ Start a gratitude list at the beginning of every day. When you settle in for the evening. Try to list as many things as you can that you are thankful for that day
- ☐ Pick a favorite quote every Sunday and write about what it means to you. How is it significant to your life?
- ☐ Write your own quote, just one sentence to start. Explain it's meaning.
- ☐ Write about one talent that you have and how you use it in your life
- ☐ Create a list of your ten favorite books that you have read throughout your life and why they are.
- ☐ Choose a favorite scripture and explain how it's helped you.
- ☐ Write about someone that has recently inspired you.

FINISH THESE SENTENCES...

- ☐ My idea of happiness is...
- ☐ What I appreciate most about my spouse / significant other is...
- ☐ My favorite fictional character is...
- ☐ If I could have one gift, it would be...
- ☐ I am the most productive when...
- ☐ I like the color _____ because...
- ☐ If I could travel anywhere it would be to _____ because...
- ☐ My favorite day of the year is _____ because...
- ☐ If I could change one thing about my looks, it would be...
- ☐ If I could change one thing about my life, it would be...
- ☐ The angriest letter you never sent was...
- ☐ What I like most about myself is...
- ☐ The best day of my life was....
- ☐ I hardest thing I ever did was...
- ☐ The most beautiful thing about me is...
- ☐ The most wonderful thing about my life is...
- ☐ The saddest day of my life was...
- ☐ The funniest day of my life was...
- ☐ If I could have one super-power it would be _____ because...

GENEALOGY

The descent of a family or group, traced back through history, can be interesting and informative—helping us to learn about our heritage. Use these tips to unlock your past.

- ❑ Ask family members to interview other family members, thus bringing you information from different perspectives.
- ❑ Collect photographs and mementos from various family members to scan. You'll be able to create a wider picture of your family history through mementos from others. Copy photos you can't identify and ask for family members input.
- ❑ Copy old newspaper clippings, adding details about the event from your perspective or other family members.
- ❑ Create your own fill-in-the-blank questionnaire to share with family to gather stories and genealogy. Send it via snail mail, e-mail, or social media to encourage them to be a part of creating this heritage album. When it's complete, send digital copies or printed books as gifts—what a great family project!
- ❑ Describe your spiritual markers or other milestones and write about how they have made a difference in your life.
- ❑ Describe the most influential people in your life. Dedicate a page to them and how they have influenced you.
- ❑ Describe your siblings—document their names, birthdates, where they live, special events, their relationship with you in childhood and as an adult, their interests and accomplishments.
- ❑ Draw a family tree and see how far back you can go. Then ask family members to help or visit your local genealogy library.
- ❑ Have a family reunion in your thoughts and write about the memories you have of each person that you can remember in great detail.
- ❑ Write about your parents and tell their story from your perspective. Add information about what their life was like before you were born, then how their life changed following your birth.

*If any man wishes to write a clear style,
let him first be clear in his thoughts*
–Johann Wolfgang von Goethe

HISTORICAL PRESERVATION

- ☐ Your journal is a statement about you and your thoughts, experiences and personal recollections regarding people and events in your life.
- ☐ Document the little things! Daily life is full of subjects to write about. My grandma kept a diary for years, what a wonderful blessing years later for family members to recall the memories of days long past!
- ☐ Record current events that are shaping history, by sharing your personal thoughts and opinions about them.
- ☐ Document current fads now and compare them to your childhood. Document popular fads decade-by-decade, since you were born.
- ☐ Give all your pages a date and place. A hundred years from now, someone will look at your scrapbook or journal and wonder in what century it was created.
- ☐ Be sure to identify any buildings in the backgrounds of photos, detailing locations and significance, such as family-owned, former workplace, etc.
- ☐ Be sure to record dates, times, and seasons of the year.
- ☐ Make lists of people, places and events to inspire journaling ideas.

SCHOOL DAYS

- ☐ Your school activities, organizations, clubs, degrees or goals offer a plethora of writing opportunities.
- ☐ Write about your favorite teachers, subjects, grades, friends, activities and memorable events.
- ☐ Childhood memories can be written in a single section of your journal or divided into specific topics to add more detail later.
- ☐ Document as much as you can remember from pre-school through graduation and into your college days.

Check out the "Questions" section for even more ideas

IT'S ALL ABOUT THE WORDS
Write to capture that which you will soon forget

WORDS | What's a girl to say?

All too often I hear a scrapbooker say, "journaling is the most difficult thing for me to do," in reference to adding words to layouts in their albums. Being a writer, I am amused and intrigued because for me, it is the exact opposite —I love the opportunity to write.

My passion for actual scrapbooking is great as long as it's just about collecting papers, lovely embellishments, how-to books and cool tools. However, sit me down in front of a scrapbook album to actually create a layout—and it's instant "scrapper's block"—my mind goes blank like the page staring me in the face. Thus I totally understand, though it seems it would be faster and easier to add a few words to embellish a page or define some photographs than to conquer the page layouts.

And you thought you had writer's block! I see so many amazing albums and I am so envious! You all make it look so simple and your efforts produce great artistic accomplishments and incredibly wonderful blessings for your family.

So here we are talking about how to get you journaling on your pages. The easiest way to learn is simply pick up a pen and just start writing.

Let's begin by writing baby spoon-size bites, one or two lines at a time. As you learn the art of journaling, this technique will bring instant satisfaction because you will see immediate results. Then you can expand these little morsels of inspiration into larger pieces.

Here are a few quick starts to get you going. First, add a favorite quote under a photograph or perhaps select a piece of memorabilia and write a few words about it. Next, focus on the theme of your album and create a four-line poem describing your album. Let this poem adorn the title page of your album—instant masterpiece! Lastly, put together a bulleted list of people in the photographs and next to each name write two or three words that could define each person.

Now, create a journal to record daily events. Keep entries short and include dates, for reference. This journal will be a great tool for completing layouts later. You will come to love the finishing touch that your own words add to pages and so will those who read them.

HAND-WRITTEN WITH LOVE
The ink upon the paper is colored
by the words that are hidden within your heart.

HANDWRITING | Your handwriting is uniquely you!

The other statements I hear all too often are in relation to personal handwriting—"it's too sloppy, too big, too small, my handwriting looks like a child's scribbling" and the list goes on. Some say they will just type something on their computer and print it out to embellish their work. That is okay for some things…because your words are very important for sure. What you don't realize though is just like your fingerprints, your handwriting is unique to you. And it will be a treasure for future generations to see and remember.

I feel very blessed because my mother worked with me over the years and occasionally I will find something done in her handwriting. She has been gone now for over five years and yet each time I find something she wrote, I know it's a piece of her that remains with me. I smile and at that moment relive a memory or two of our time together—a lovely pearl in my day. It doesn't matter if the words are simple or few, to me they are beautiful now —a cherished part of her that I will treasure always.

I have recipe cards, birthday and Christmas cards, and even letters from my aunts and grandmothers and old friends. Each is a piece of my heritage, insignificant to others, but to me they are a part of who I am and a heartstring to people I miss dearly.

I remember the days of writing letters and how excited we would be to receive a letter from our grandparents or other relatives. To see their handwriting and read their words was wonderful and made you feel like you could reach out an touch them.

To write a letter or note to someone is a gift of self. It is taking time to send love and that is a wonderful thing to share.

Even sending a mere handwritten note or thank you seems to be a lost art. In these days of instant gratification and high tech communication, receiving or sending a handwritten note or letter is a rarity and robs the sender and receiver of an opportunity to have a relationship through the written word.

Sadly, texting and chatting through social media seems to have replaced talking to a live person face-to-face or on the phone. The times of sitting on the porch or walking to the neighbor's for a cup of coffee and an afternoon of friendly conversation are gone for most. Technology has made us a global society which is amazing to consider, but in many ways we are a lonely society—cocooning ourselves for snippets of time, communicating very briefly and all the while really missing what was so significant in "the good old days."

Whew...nostalgia just kicked in as I thought of the precious letters and notes I have saved through the years. The connections I feel to the senders brings a smile as I reread some of them. They are symbols of the greatest gift we can ever give to anyone—our time, ourself—that is the truest expression of love, through our words.

I've said all that to encourage you to write little notes to your spouse, your children, a parent or a dear friend and realize that the words you pen may one day be priceless blessings to the recipient.

Keep a folder on your desk or a special box or drawer for these little mementos. Save them to include in an album or simply keep the collection to reread from time to time for a lift or as inspiration to create a handwritten treasure for someone else.

I found a letter
written long ago,
the sight of it and my
thoughts began to flow.
Time erases memories,
writing holds them near—
such a treasured gift
from one so very dear!
Just like a fingerprint
the slant of the pen,
handwritten words
help remember when.
Simple and so free
bless that special one;
write sweet words of love
so your legacy will live on.

–Linda LaTourelle

The Biggest Book of Words & Prompts for Scrapbooks, Art Journals & Crafts

Letters to Write

Create a list of letters you want to write

Just imagine—the words you write today are,
in essence, conversing with unseen generations
—Linda LaTourelle

> Letters are among the most significant memorial a person can leave behind them
> –*Johann Wolfgang von Goethe*

Love Letters

To write a love letter
you must begin
without knowing
what you intend to say
and end with your passion
inked upon the pages
for your beloved.
–Linda LaTourelle

LOVE LETTERS IN THE SAND

It is my pleasure to share two of my passions with you—love and writing! I hope that through these pages you will be inspired and find joy in expressing the sentiments of your heart to those you cherish most in life, in an age-old format... "The Love Letter."

Traditionally, love letters have always been written to a spouse or intended. However, love expressed in writing to those closest to us, albeit a child, parent, grandparent or even friend, is a precious gift that will last for generations to come. Love is the essence of life. This project will focus on the original purpose of love letters, but please feel free to adapt the thoughts within however you feel led, for no matter who is the recipient of your writing—it is sure to be a blessing!

Memories from the past, moments from the present and dreams for the future are the ties that bind us to our partner and our family. It has been quoted that only when we give of ourselves does true love exist. What a beautiful gift to create as you take the time to gather treasured memories into a letter for your beloved as a wonderful anthology of your feelings! May the thoughts within these pages be the tools to gently guide you to recall the quintessential ingredients of your love.

My prayer is that these words will inspire memories of the love that brought you together, encourage thoughts of the reasons you endure and give hope as you look to the future—for the best is yet to be. May this wisdom arouse the romantic within you and motivate you to keep the flame of love alive, not only through your writing, but each day you journey together through life. Love isn't love until we give it away. Share a blessing today! Create a beautiful card to hold your letter of love using your favorite scrapping supplies! This will be a treasure to behold for generations to come as your love lives on through your words! You will be amazed at the blessings that you will bestow on loved ones through the simple act of putting pen to paper—in return your cup will overflow!

As my heart poured forth upon these pages
so too did my love—in every drop of ink,
shaping each letter ever so smoothly
into words that define the essence of us
–Linda LaTourelle

HOW TO WRITE A LOVE LETTER

Love letters are the epitome of romance. Our inherent need for intimacy makes the giving and receiving of a love letter a delightful moment. Being the author of a love letter has additional rewards as you reflect upon your lover, savoring the wonderful memories of why you fell in love. It is a perfect time to write what your spoken words cannot say, with purpose and intent to excite and rekindle the intimacy you both share. Or perhaps your words can bless and encourage someone special.

Profess your deepest sentiments as you write about your beloved's endearing physical, emotional or spiritual qualities. Write openly and sincerely expressing your feelings of hope and desire, as though you were the recipient.

Heartfelt sentiments poured into a letter are most effective if they are easily read. Love letters are keepsakes and often framed, so beautiful stationery and elegant handwriting will enhance this treasure of your love.

Your soul will shine when you write this very personal letter of love and you will see that glow reflected in the eyes of the one you adore. This is a gift that will be cherished by the recipient and kept for a lifetime or longer. Memories fade with time, but your letter will be a lasting legacy of the love you share.

GATHER YOUR TOOLS

As you do, think romance and passion

PAPER | Romantic, elegant, whatever suits the occasion!
PENS | Gels, calligraphy, dip pen and ink. Spoil yourself with pens that light a spark.
EMBELLISHMENTS | Keep them simple; focus on the recipient.
STAMPS | Ask Mr. Postman, there are always beautiful stamps available.
SEALS | Add that "sealed with a kiss" look as you finish your masterpiece.
FRAGRANCE | Adds a personal touch, that can be seductive and pleasant.
DICTIONARY | For the obvious—more about this later.
NOTE PAD | To organize your thoughts before you actually write.
PHOTOGRAPH OF RECIPIENT | Keep this near you as you write.

Feel the feelings, hear your thoughts, write your heart
–Linda LaTourelle

GET COMFORTABLE

Where you write can be as important as the pen and paper you have chosen. Writing tends to flow more easily in a quiet, private, comfortable place. Creating a romantic ambiance frees the spirit and sets a warmer tone to your writing. Candlelight, aromatherapy, or incense are calming and gentle music soothes the soul enabling thoughts to flow. Having a picture of your intended recipient near you brings focus to your feelings. Sipping a favorite beverage as you begin helps to organize your thoughts. The mood you set for writing will be reflected as you write.

WRITING WARM-UP

Arm and finger exercises, neck and back stretches, sitting quietly, relaxing in prayer or meditation are all great writing warm-ups. The simple act of writing words randomly, as you think about your beloved, will loosen you up, freeing you from writer's block. Thinking about love and good things will be reflected in your writing. Remember, you're not in school, you're not being graded—you are simply speaking the love in your heart as your pen pours words upon the pages!

WHAT IS THE PURPOSE?

A simple love letter in itself is a timeless treasure that will bless beyond words (pun intended) because it comes from your heart. But it can also convey much more—an expression of love, a stage in your journey together or a special occasion. Your purpose for writing it will shape the perspective of your letter.

Focus on the recipient, begin by making notes or an outline in relation to their physical, spiritual and emotional qualities. What really stands out? The combination of these alluring qualities is the essence or soul of a person—we are body, mind and spirit.

A love letter is so meaningful. Diamonds and gold pale in comparison to the most precious of gifts—words from your heart! Everyone wants to know they are loved and when we make time to show it through something as simple as a letter, the purpose is priceless! Love letters are one-of-a-kind treasures that will bless each time they are read and reread!

WRITTEN BY HAND

The first choice in a love letter is reading your beloved's words penned in their own handwriting—it is like a fingerprint of their heart. Handwritten letters offer the most impact, because they are truly a part of the author. However, many feel their handwriting is inferior and opt to compose on their computer. Fortunately, there are many lovely fonts available that lend a handwritten feel to your letter. An additional option is to consider soliciting a professional calligrapher, in those times when you prefer a more elegant look, remember a letter penned by your own hand is a legacy only you can give.

PARTS OF A LETTER

GREETING | Do you have any endearing names with which you normally address your beloved? The greeting can be as simple as "Hello" or you may elaborate with something romantic, enchanting or fun such as "My Darling," "My Beloved," "Hey Sexy," "Dear Sweetheart" or whatever you prefer. The salutation you select can set the tone for your letter.

BODY | The body of the letter is where you will express your intentions. You may choose to ramble and be flowery in telling your feelings or you may be specific if you are writing for a particular purpose. You don't have to be Shakespeare to write the perfect love letter. All you need to know is how you feel—it's simple, write what you would speak. What makes a love letter so romantic is that it is deeply personal and it can show the recipient how well you know them. Don't write about anyone except the two of you. Be sincere and truthful; write from the heart. If you need inspiration, try checking out poetry books on love from your local library or surf the net. There are many, many styles of love letters, but the one that is the best is the one you write from your heart. To help feel at ease, pretend you are sitting right in front of your beloved. What are you feeling? What do you want to tell them? Start slowly and softly, the words always come when you search your heart—it's like whispering sweet things face-to-face, or dancing cheek-to-cheek.

CLOSING | Conclude your letter with thoughts and hopes for the future. Your closing words will be like a kiss upon their soul. Will you leave them wanting more? Will you pamper them with passion? Will you encourage and be tender with your closing? Passion, gentleness, joy? Whatever is symbolic of your love.

In closing, sum up your feelings in a few short words that will impact the reader: "Affectionately yours", "Until we meet again," "Truly and passionately yours," "Holding you in my heart," etc. Leave them wanting more!

Above all, have fun with your writing! Remember this is a gift of you, not a contest, school lesson, competition or drudgery. You are writing to the person of your dreams, perhaps your soul mate. Think about your feelings and the words will flow, full of love, full of you.

Be sure to sign your letter! When you are finished, add a light scent, neatly fold, seal and stamp the envelope. It's ready to deliver, either in person, secretly somehow or send it through the mail. The joy comes in the giving!

ENGLISH BASICS 101

VOCABULARY | Select words from the Word Palettes in the previous chapter or use a thesaurus for inspiration.

SPELLING | When writing a love letter, A+ spelling is a must—use the dictionary!

GRAMMAR | If you can't remember the rules you learned in English 101…get some help online or from a book at your local library. A romantic love letter is the opportunity to perfect your grammar skills and put your best words forward! Always strive for accuracy—a misspelled or improperly used word will distract from the elegance of your work.

> I send you a cream-white rosebud
> with a flush upon its petal tips,
> for the love that is purest and sweetest
> has a kiss of desire on the lips
> —*John Boyle O'Reilly*

INTIMACY THROUGH WRITING
A simple letter can convey love across the universe

Treasure the moments of your life together. Record them through the art of letter writing. Perhaps share a journal, writing in a more informal style, but write back and forth to each other on a regular basis. It's another way to be intimate and share things you might not share face-to-face.

My husband and I have a small personalized journal we share to write short thoughts or feelings to one another—kind of a love journal. It's a simple act that takes only a moment to accomplish, but can be a treasure forever.

Joy grows from a heart that is filled with love and passion for others. Love is to be cherished, held ever so close, nurtured, then given away. The little things you do to show your love can be a legacy for generations to come.

LETTERS FOR ALL OCCASIONS
Writing that is new and creative speaks from the heart

LOVE LETTERS IN THE SAND | Write I love you _____ with your beloved's name onto a piece of your favorite card stock using a toothpick and glue. Sprinkle fine colored sand or glitter generously over the entire piece while the glue is still wet. Wait for an hour, allowing the glue to dry, then shake off the excess sand. Once it is completely dry, frame it and wrap it as a gift.

BE A STAR | Using a mobile phone, video recorder or computer, record a short video and / or audio reading a letter you've written to that special someone. You can then upload it to an online video site for private viewing, burn it on a DVD, or send it in an email.

A LETTER A DAY | Write at least one letter a day to someone you love or appreciate. Create a list of who you will write to or let the letters flow from your heart randomly. These letters don't have to be long, just simple expressions of how you feel about the recipient. Seal with a kiss and mail.

PUZZLES OF LOVE | Write your letter and decorate it with colorful doodles or illustrations. Next, cut the entire letter into shapes to create a puzzle that will connect when pieced back together. Place cut puzzle pieces in a small box, write instructions on the box and give it with love.

A BOOK OF LOVE | Think about the top ten reasons why you love that someone special. Write a love letter about each one, then bind them together in a handmade book. Look online or visit your library for bookbinding tutorials.

A BOX OF LOVE | Remember filling a decorated box with valentines from all the kids in your class? How fun it was opening the little envelopes and reading each one! Start now, decorate a box, then for the next thirty days create one letter or valentine per day. At the end of thirty days, give your intended the box full of valentines. You don't have to wait for February, either, just pick a month and create a theme. You can design your own valentines or wait until after Christmas and pickup ready-made cards, then add your own words.

A MESSAGE IN A BOTTLE | Written with love and tied with your heartstrings, a love letter in a bottle is a unique gift to give. Find a bottle to hold your letter, close it with a cork and send it to that someone special. It's a great way to tell your family how important they are to you.

THE WEDDING LETTER | Prior to your wedding, both you and your fiancé can write a love letter detailing how you each feel about the upcoming wedding and the love you feel for each other. Place your sealed letters in a safe place and open on your 5th, 10th or 25th wedding anniversary.

SWEETHEARTS | Small hearts, big hearts, any color you want, cut them out one at a time or as a chain of love. They're perfect to sneak inside a lunch box, day planner or hide anywhere. Give your heart and make someone smile today.

JUST A SILLY LOVE SONG | Try your hand at writing a song that focuses on your love. Don't worry about perfection, just hum a little tune and add words. Record it on your phone, computer or voice mail. Singing your song to your loved one will make it even more special.

MIRROR YOUR LOVE | Grab a tube of bright lipstick and color the world of that someone special with a love note written on the bathroom mirror. It takes only a moment to reflect your feelings to the heart of the one you love. Shaving cream on shower doors works is fun, too.

THE CHRISTMAS LETTERS | Each day, for twelve days, write a letter that reflects twelve ways the recipient has blessed you and at the same time, share twelve ways you desire to bless the recipient. Then on Christmas Day give these letters as a gift of love. Try this for birthday, too.

> More than kisses, letters mingle souls
> –John Donne

The Biggest Book of Words & Prompts for Scrapbooks, Art Journals & Crafts

SEARCHING FOR LOVE | Create a crossword or word search with a secret message for the one you love—could be great way to convey a surprise.

PILLOW TALK | Using a fabric marker, doodle your words of love onto an inexpensive pillowcase. Hide it under the covers and watch the surprise on your sweetheart's face, at bedtime. For a wow effect, use a sheet instead of a pillowcase.

LANGUAGE OF LOVE | Write a letter of love, then choose your favorite language using a free online translation program and give it to your beloved. Include the translation or let them search to translate.

HIDE AND SEEK LETTERS | Hide small notes throughout your loved one's room, office or anywhere that is appropriate within your home. These little notes will add a bright spot each time one is discovered.

A PICTURE OF LOVE | Write and sign your love letter on a beautiful single sheet of paper, then add a simple embellishment or memorabilia. Next frame the finished letter. Wrap it as you choose and bless the recipient with a lasting treasure.

SENTIMENTALLY SAID

'Twas a new feeling, something more than we had dared to own before, which when we hid not; we saw in each other's eye, and wished, in every half-breathed sigh, to speak, but did not. –*Thomas Moore*

The soul that can speak through the eyes will kiss her beloved with simply a gaze. –*Linda LaTourelle*

But tell of days in goodness spent, a mind at peace with all below, a heart whose love is innocent. –*Lord Byron*

What I do and what I dream include Thee, as the wine must taste of its own grapes. -*Elizabeth Barrett Browning*

Come live with me and be my love, and we will some new pleasures prove, of golden sands, and crystal beaches, with silken lines and silver hooks. –*John Donne*

There is a place in my heart where your touch still lingers, your breath is soft in my thoughts and your words echo down deep in my soul. It's a place that belongs to only you, my love. You are a part of me always. –*Linda LaTourelle*

One word frees us of all the weight and pain in life. That word is Love. –*Sophocles*

Two lovers in the rain have no need of an umbrella
–*Japanese proverb*

Love Letter List

Create a list of love letters you want to write
and then pour your heart onto your paper

*The word that is heard perishes,
but the letter that is written remains*

–Anonymous

Gifts of Love

The greatest gift
you have to give
others is yourself.
The words within
your heart, when
shared in writing,
are priceless pearls.
Because they require
an investment
of your time—
the most precious
gift of all.

–Linda LaTourelle

THE GIFT OF WORDS

*The spaces between the lines
reveal treasures within the heart*
–Linda LaTourelle

Journals and scrapbooks are truly one of the most cherished blessings for both the designer and the reader. The time one spends pouring words and creativity upon the pages is truly an act of love that comes from deep within oneself.

Writing is a window to our soul and reveals the details of life as seen through our eyes. There is something so relaxing about sharing memories, whether it is for our own personal use to journal our thoughts, or as an heirloom to be treasured for generations to come. Time spent creating a journal or scrapbook offers a double blessing—for you and the reader.

One of the greatest gifts you can give a loved one is a journal—it is not just a book or an album, it is time you gave. That truly is a treasure unlike any other, that no money can buy.

Last Christmas, my sweet husband created the most lovely gift for me—"The Book of Us." It was an altered book, in which he shared his feelings in a very romantic way. He creatively presented his gift of love, too. He purchased several purple scarves to wrap around the book and placed it in a beautiful box hand-tied with silk ribbons. The box now holds love letters he has handwritten to me since we met. Such simple sweet blessings of love—a priceless gift!

Create a journal, scrapbook or altered book for your special someone. **The love you share will be a blessing!**

The only gift is a portion of thyself
–Ralph Waldo Emerson

Gifts Received

This seems like the appropriate place to tell you about how some very special words became treasured gifts for my husband, Thomas and I. In the fall of 2006, I had the opportunity to work with David Jarrod, a songwriter-musician from Blackpool, England and his producer, Peter Francis, who flew over to record a CD and music video project, in the studio of Thomas King.

At that time I only knew Thomas as an acquaintance, but was excited to be part of the project. A mutual friend, Tamra Fakhoorian, a songwriter-musician, worked with us on the project, along other musicians—combining music and design talents, in studio and on location, the result was a great rockumentary and CD. The CD is available on iTunes and the rockumentary and other information about David Jarrod is also available on my website listed at the bottom of this page.

David and Peter went back home to the UK and Thomas and I began dating—and a year later were planning our wedding. We had hoped that our friends would return to celebrate with us, but were unable to—but both David and Peter were there in spirit. Tamra lives close and shared a very special place during our wedding. Their gift of words was a tremendous blessing on our wedding day—David wrote and produced the following song for our wedding and Tamra also wrote and produced a special song for us. I am sharing excerpts of the lyrics for both songs, to show what truly wonderful treasures words can be when they come from the dearest of friends.

DO YOU REMEMBER

Do you remember,
the first time we touched?
Our hearts were empty,
we know this much.
But from this day,
our hearts are one,
for a love this strong.

So here we are once again,
the past's been and gone.
To the future here and now—
we have only just begun.
'Til the end of time,
we will always be,
together you and me.

–*David Jarrod* © 2008
ultimatebookcompany.com

I DO
Written and Performed by
Tamra Fakhoorian

Verse 1:
Her: The world is standing still just for us tonight.
My heart is full of joy as our fingers intertwine.
Him: There's a shower of love falling all around us.
And I only see you.
I only see you.

Chorus:
Her: Do you feel our hearts beating as one?
Him: I do.
Her: Do you hear angels singing our song?
Her: I do.
Both: Do you see our future spinning out before us?
Do you see us walking arm in arm through life?
Him: I love you for you.
Her: I'll always treasure you.
Both: How else can I bless you?
Just say "I do."

Verse 2:
Him: We've taken long paths to find each other.
It's God who led me to you.
Her: With love I thee wed with all my heart.
Her: And I'll always treasure you.
Him: I'll always be true.

The complete song can be heard on the website. It is a delight for me to share this wonderful gift with you and show you just how special your words can be to those you love. Write from your heart and the emotions will flow and you will bless someone, too.

* For commercial use—Contact Santeela Creek Publishing © 2008

JOURNALING FOR A GIFT

Too often we forget that the greatest gift we can give is ourselves. There are endless opportunities to do that. It's simple, and best of all, it's priceless. One simple, lovely idea is to make a book and fill it with your journaling, then give it as a gift.

There are books at your local library and resources online that will show you how to put together a handmade book. Personalize the cover design using a sentimental fabric or paper and embellish the pages with your creative genius—just like your scrapbook pages. What a special blessing for the recipient! Here are some ideas...

WEDDING | Fill it with scripture or lyrics from the bride and groom's favorite song, then add your blessings for a happy life.

BABY'S BIRTH | Add some quotes or parenting tips and finish it off with prayers for a joyous new life.

BIRTHDAY | Make a book of thoughtful things you will give throughout the year, like homemade muffins, a bouquet of flowers, lunch out, etc. and add a note about why that person is so special to you.

BLESSING SOMEONE | Use your journaling to honor someone who has been important in your life or who has inspired you. What a way for you to reflect, and better yet, what a blessing for that person!

GRADUATION | A good time to recall memories of the school days past. Add some quotes on success or goals and a prayer for the new journey ahead, then give them congrats like only you can.

ROMANCE | Pen the lyrics to one of your favorite love songs or better yet, write your own romantic lyrics and set them to music to create an original song for your beloved. There are many how-to websites, some with video tutorials or there are musicians and companies offering professional services to bring your words from paper to a recorded CD or even music video, if you are so inclined. I will add links to the website for DIY songwriting, as well as musicians offering their expertise as a professional service.

The ideas are endless and whatever the gift—it will be treasured always and you'll have fun creating it—Go for it!

Love is, above all, the gift of oneself
—Jean Anouilh

Gifts to Give

Give the gift of words— love straight from your heart

---

*Whatever you write, it will be a gift
and blessing because it's part of you*
–Linda LaTourelle

MOMENTS WORTH JOURNALING

There are no ordinary moments because every moment
is an extraordinary moment, an amazing gift—
if our perspective is focused on the present
–Linda LaTourelle

As you journey on through life today, take time for the little things—the details of every day—they are precious pearls. Each one is a unique moment in life. We are so conditioned to focus our journey on finding the big things in life, that we overlook the most wonderful blessings of all.

Open your senses to the simple beauty around you every day—a baby's smile, an elder's tear, the sound of the birds, the buzz of the bees, the color of the sunset, the smell of rain, your spouse's hug, the laughter of children, a flower's bloom, the whistle of wind, the touch of a hand, the taste of pure love—all these and more are gifts from above. In addition to the beauty of just being still for a time each day and observing life as it is, not past or future, but right this moment, we will discover that the daily simplicity of life offers wonderful opportunities for photography, videography and storytelling!

There are lessons to be learned, and though the paths we trod take us on our own individual journeys, the purpose is the same as it has been since time began. We are called to love one another in word, thought and deed, recognizing our natural differences. The irony is our inherent differences are stepping stones to unity. With hands to reach out, arms to offer a comforting embrace, mouths to speak words of encouragement and ears to listen with compassion, we can make a difference in our world, our community, our home, etc.

Each of us shares an intrinsic need to love and be loved, regardless of profession, financial status, talents, education, abilities, gender, health, race, religion, or any other difference. Begin today to see how changing the world can begin with one person—YOU. May we never be too busy to realize we can be a blessing to someone, anyone, right now where we are, and as a result, we too will be blessed by these pearls of life.

Within the pages of my heart
lie stories yet untold,
memories of a lifetime
are treasures to behold.
–Linda LaTourelle

PEARLS

The treasures in each day
Are like pearls upon the shore,
Gathered one-by-one—
Precious memories galore

Collect them in a glass jar,
String them upon your heart,
Moments of overflowing joy
Love's blessings to impart

–Linda LaTourelle

PEARLS FOR TODAY

Now is the time to treasure—you're making memories for life!

What lies behind us and what lies before us are tiny matters compared to what lies within us –Ralph Waldo Emerson

There are no ordinary moments because each moment is an extraordinary gift—if our perspective is focused on the present –Linda LaTourelle

The only time you're ever living is in this moment –Linda LaTourelle

Make your life a mission—not an intermission, stay focused

It doesn't matter where you have been or where you are going—now is the only moment you have to go anywhere and everywhere –Linda LaTourelle

What you are is what you have been; what you'll be is what you do now. –Buddha

Nothing is worth more than this day –Johann Wolfgang von Goethe

The living moment is everything –D.H. Lawrence

Tomorrow is a new day; you shall begin it serenely and with too high a spirit to be encumbered with your old nonsense –Ralph Waldo Emerson

Children have neither past nor future; they enjoy the present, which very few of us do –Jean de la Bruyere

You must live in the present, launch yourself on every wave, find your eternity in each moment –Henry David Thoreau

Rejoice in the things that are present; all else is beyond thee –Montaigne

The best time to plant a tree was twenty years ago—the second best time is now –Chinese proverb

I have realized that the past and future are real illusions, that they exist in the present, which is what there is and all there is –Alan Watts

Today is the first day of the rest of the best of your life –Linda LaTourelle

If not now, when?

Do it now! –Napoleon Hill

When you are looking at one another, you can't see behind –Thomas King

If you aren't in the moment, you are either looking forward to uncertainty, or back to pain and regret –Jim Carrey

Life is what happens to you when your focus is somewhere else –Linda LaTourelle

Let today be the day that you choose to become your own greatest hero –J. L. Huie

You were made with a purpose that only God knows and you must find.

There are so many wonderful things that will never get done if you do not choose to do them –Linda LaTourelle

If you do nothing unexpected, nothing unexpected happens –Fay Weldon

That whisper you keep hearing is the universe trying to get your attention –Oprah Winfrey

Every now and then, bite off more than you can chew –Kobi Yamada

What great thing would you attempt if you knew you could not fail? –Dr. Robert H. Schuller

As I ponder the memories of my life, I realize how quickly the years have come and gone. The joys and sorrows in my mind's eye are like a strand of precious pearls that, when strung together, reflect a life full of treasured blessings.

–Linda LaTourelle

Draw your chair up
close to the edge of the precipice
and I'll tell you a story
–F. Scott Fitzgerald

Sweetest Tale

Life is a scrapbook of young and old
In which our precious stories are told.
When time moves on and our memories fail
this book 'twill be sweetest tale.
We can turn the pages of times gone by
and see how the days and years did fly.
A cherished child or faithful friend
treasured every day until the end.
Blessings and miracles so rich with love,
these are our gifts from God above.

–Linda LaTourelle

EVERY PICTURE TELLS A STORY

TELLING YOUR STORY

Writing your family story can be a very rewarding accomplishment as you journey down memory lane. It will be a work-in-progress that can be created in sections as you gather photographs and memorabilia, recall events, stories and memories and piece together the history that weaves the fabric of life that is relevant to you and your family. It can be the most healing, revealing and meaningful story ever written—by you, for you and for your family.

In the following section, I have compiled lists of questions to be used as writing prompts to help you create your stories. The answers to these interesting and thought-provoking questions, in your own words or other family members, will give current and future generations the opportunity to know you and yours in a more intimate and personal way. For simplicity, the questions have been organized into sections to assist you in building a timeline of your life.

Spending quiet time in thought as you try to remember times past can be very calming, joyful and sometimes healing. Your memories are footsteps to today and a path perhaps for others to follow and learn from. Treasure the memories—elaborate on the positives, simplify the negatives and delight in each. Your experiences and your memories tell a wonderful story —the story of you and your family.

As you relax and begin to reminisce, the words will begin to flow from the memories held in your minds eye. My hope is that you will soon discover this to be a treasure in the making and a time to count the many blessings in life—as you create this legacy of love for both present and future generations.

*Our memories and stories
are the beautiful movements
in this grand symphony of life*
–Linda LaTourelle

WRITTEN ON YOUR HEART

KEEP IT SIMPLE

Let these questions about the lives of you and your family members be an introduction to a scrapbook or journal. Questions can be answered in any order that works; they will help to give you focus. You can combine the answers to create an actual story for each section of your journal or simply use them as a bulleted list.

Memories come in snippets and so as you scan the list of questions, write as thoughts come to mind. Don't wait until you have what you need for each question, just allow your mind to wander. You may not be able to answer all of the questions, but that's okay; just add what you know and interview family and friends for help, then leave the rest to the reader's imagination.

Many questions are very basic and will be easy to answer; other questions will require more time. Simply write as though you are sharing your story with a friend or family member over a cup of tea in casual conversation. If you desire words with more pizazz, please refer to the "Word Palette" located in the sections near the beginning of this book. Use a three-ring binder, a spiral-bound notebook or create a document on your computer to gather your thoughts and keep things organized while you are creating each section. Once they are complete, it will be very easy to transfer your words to your scrapbook or journal in the appropriate sections. Add photos and memorabilia to illustrate and compliment your stories. Happy journaling...may the words of your heart be a blessing to those who peruse your story!

God gave us memories so that
we might have roses in December
–James M. Barrie

A TAPESTRY OF LOVE

THE FAMILY JOURNAL PROJECT

My hope is that the story of your family will become an ongoing project for the entire family to work on collectively or individually and that you will realize the joys in writing history—your own!

Keeping a family journal isn't just about documenting facts, dates and events—it's about connecting with family members as they share a bit of themselves from day to day. Journaling in this way offers the opportunity for family to know one another better.

Because this is an ongoing project, you will need to decide on the method of journaling that works best for your family. The traditional journal can stored at home in a special spot, allowing easy access for writing or reading by other family members. Another option is to create an online journal or blog, thus giving any family member access to writing or reading at their convenience. This option really benefits family members who live farther away from each other.

One of the really great things that online family journals offers is the ability to upload photographs and even videos from anywhere in the world. What a wonderful blessing for family members who live far away to immediately see a their new grandchild, a wedding or graduation, candid shots from a family reunion or photographs from any special event or celebration! It's almost as good as being there.

To take the online journaling one step further, excerpts from the journal entries, along with online photographs, can be used to design a book which can be printed and purchased by any family member or given as a surprise gift for a particular occasion.

Whether using the questions provided in the next section or simply writing freestyle about your day, your goals and your feelings, etc, the entries in your family journal offer a unique perspective of your family and create a legacy of love that will last a lifetime or longer.

Questions

So many questions
answers unknown,
family histories
stories untold.
Life is a mystery—
no clue to the past.
Without any answers
memories won't last.
Learn all that you can
from relatives now,
capture their words
and details somehow.
Recorded or written
however you choose,
this legacy of love
is all up to you.
–Linda LaTourelle

QUESTIONS TO ANSWER

DOCUMENTING HISTORY

Scrapbooks and journals are for sharing the events of our lives with family, friends and future generations. Creating a book with lovely embellishments and amazing photographs is fun and it offers a wonderful way to document the events in your life. But photographs are limiting and only tell part of the story. It is the details, feelings, thoughts and emotions that will make your scrapbook a masterpiece of memories. It is your words that will make it a personal experience for the reader.

Telling those stories through your own voice is like wrapping a gift to share with family, friends and future generations. Words are like ribbons on a beautiful gift that weave stories together, into an interesting package the reader can't wait to open. Capturing and preserving those stories through words is easier than you think and the gift you will be giving is totally a part of you.

WRITING | Writing can be intimidating—not because it's really difficult, but because we are our own worst critic when it comes to putting words to paper. We seem to forget that we are not being judged or anything else; we are just sharing the stories of our lives through photographs and speaking from our heart. Isn't that something you do on any given day? The only difference, is this way you are communicating with your pen. All you have to do is start writing.

DIGITAL | Words can also be preserved in a very quick, visual, audible way. Easy to do and offering even more benefits than writing, recording a family documentary can be achieved through the use of a video recorder, mobile phone or voice recorder. Choose to record video and/or audio then have your transcript printed out to accompany your recording.

THE LISTS | To give you a thought-provoking and a more fun journaling process, I have compiled lists of questions that be used in a few ways.

- Straight from the list—simply use these questions as written here
- Let the questions inspire you to create your own list of questions
- Incorporate the questions into a digitally-recorded interview
- Use a combination of each of these for more personalized journaling

How you choose to answer any of the questions is a matter of personal preference—in the order listed, randomly or just using the questions for inspiration—my hope is to simplify your journaling process and turn you on to writing.

To avoid redundancy—all questions may be used to journal life stories about yourself, spouse, children or other family members. Parents and other family members can be a great help with answers, too.

If you are interviewing others to gather information, the lists of questions will be a great tool to spark conversation. Video, audio and photographs are a fantastic way to document family histories quickly, as well as capture and preserve faces and voices of family members.

The more detailed the answers, the greater the opportunity to piece together the history of your family, as evidenced through events, people, places, etc.

These questions will be a double blessing when answers can be handwritten by parents, siblings or grandparents. A computer is a fast way to document, but there is nothing as sweet as seeing the handwriting of a loved one, especially after they are gone. That memento is a treasured keepsake!

There are so many details from the moment of conception to the day a child is born and all the way through to adulthood. Whether you are journaling about yourself, as seen through the memories and mementos of your parents and family members, or writing about your own children, the goals are the same—capturing the important pieces of the journey.

Relax and allow your mind to cherish the memories and recall the moments from the beginning. Your family will love to hear your stories over and over and will want to one day share them with their own children. Photographs can tell a story, but the words written on your heart and placed upon the pages of your scrapbook or journal will be the memories treasured for generations.

PREGNANCY & BIRTH

- ☐ How did you find out about the pregnancy?
- ☐ Describe the moment you found out you were pregnant and how you felt. Where were you, who was with you, add all the details.
- ☐ How did you share the news with your significant other?
- ☐ What were the family reactions to your news? How did you share the news with any other children?
- ☐ Write about how it felt physically finding out you were pregnant.
- ☐ Describe how you felt during the pregnancy, month by month.
- ☐ Describe any pregnancy symptoms at each stage of your pregnancy.
- ☐ What were your food cravings? Did anyone indulge you?
- ☐ What was it like the first time you felt your baby move inside your tummy? Describe the physical sensations and your emotions then.
- ☐ Did you talk, read or sing to the baby in the womb? Describe in detail and perhaps detail those times with little drawings.
- ☐ Journal about each of the doctor visits from the beginning. Include the first time you heard the heartbeat, the ultrasound, etc.
- ☐ Did you know (or want to know) the gender prior to birth? Describe how you found out.
- ☐ How did you choose your baby's name? Share the meaning and origin of your chosen name. What made you choose that particular name?
- ☐ Did you take childbirth preparation classes? Were they private or with a group?
- ☐ What special ways did you pamper yourself during the pregnancy?
- ☐ Share any ways your significant other pampered you. Share his / her emotion.
- ☐ Write about any memorable moments during the pregnancy.
- ☐ If you took month-by-month pregnancy photos, create captions for each photo.
- ☐ Describe the hospital and the birthing room. Did you have home birth? Describe the setting and add photos, too.

- ☐ Share the details of your child's "birth" day. Write about the birthing experience, from the first real labor pain until the birth.
- ☐ Describe the moment you and your husband first saw your baby.
- ☐ Describe holding your baby for the first time. Write about it from your perspective and describe what it was like for other family members.
- ☐ Document baby's weight, height, hair and eye color, health and other details that you noticed from the moment of birth.
- ☐ Document the date, time and place of the birth. What was the season, what was the weather like that day?
- ☐ Include a copy of baby's hand and footprints and journal a thought around each one. Add these as a focal point on a page.
- ☐ How did you celebrate the birth of your baby?
- ☐ Describe any showers, gifts, special visitors from the "birth" day.
- ☐ Describe the baby's nursery in detail, such as the decor theme, colors, etc.
- ☐ Write about the kind of bedding, clothes, toys, etc. you chose for the nursery.
- ☐ Describe how you prepared for your baby month-by-month.
- ☐ What was your life like during the pregnancy? Describe your work, hobbies, interests, family life and situations, etc.
- ☐ Write about bringing baby home—document all the little details.
- ☐ Did you have a special outfit or blanket to bring baby home? Where and why did you get it? Describe it and include photos.
- ☐ Who drove you and baby home—were there any special visitors?
- ☐ How did you and your baby adjust to each other and being home?
- ☐ Did you choose to breast-feed or bottle-feed? Describe the experience the first time you fed your baby.
- ☐ Did your baby use a pacifier or have a special toy?
- ☐ Did you choose cloth or disposable diapers?
- ☐ Describe caring for your baby day-by-day. Was it what you imagined?
- ☐ What did you enjoy most and least about being pregnant?
- ☐ How did you pamper yourself after baby was born?

- ☐ Describe what you loved most about being a new parent.
- ☐ Write about the first month following the birth of your baby, and tell about special moments with family and friends.
- ☐ Detail the events of your first year of being a parent.
- ☐ Ask your significant other to write about any of these prompts from his / her perspective.
- ☐ Ask grandparents or siblings to share their memories, too.
- ☐ Write the little details about how your baby looked, felt or anything that will tell the story of the miracle of becoming a parent.
- ☐ There are so many details from the moment of conception or adoption, through the pregnancy to bringing baby home. Capture these in a variety of ways because life is the most wonderful miracle of all and should be celebrated.

Write your journal using any of these prompts or create your own prompts using these as inspiration. Or perhaps create lists of "firsts" and then expand upon each of those topics such as your first month of pregnancy, first heartbeat, first contraction, first day on this planet, first day home, first visitor, gifts, outing, smile, food, holiday, etc.

CHILDHOOD

Feel free to use these questions as written
or for inspiration to create your own

- ☐ List some of your favorite things, like ice cream flavor, foods, holidays, colors, type of clothes to wear, activities, etc.
- ☐ As a child, did you ever get to meet anyone famous? If so, who was it? Describe the experience and why you liked or didn't like it.
- ☐ As a child I always dreamed of traveling to… Where? Why?
- ☐ As a child, did you have a lot of friends or just a couple close friends? Write about the memories you shared with any of them.
- ☐ As a child, did you prefer being indoors or outdoors more?
- ☐ As a child, what is your happiest and most memorable holiday memory? What is your saddest holiday memory?
- ☐ At what age did you get your first car? Describe the details.

- At what age did you learn to ride a bicycle? Who taught you to ride? How long did you ride with training wheels?
- At what age did you begin dating? Describe your first date, your first kiss, your first steady, your first heartbreak, etc.
- Create a list for each month of any year in your childhood and describe your favorite things about each month.
- Create a list of childhood favorites, such as toys, games, music, foods, activities, sports, places to go, things to do, etc.
- Create a list of the places where you lived as a child, from birth until the time you moved out on your own.
- Describe a typical after-school time. Was your mom waiting for you at home, were you in an after-school program, did you go home alone, or did you stay with siblings or grandparents?
- Describe any special memories of your grandparents.
- Describe how you would spend a typical summer vacation, Christmas vacation, fall break and spring break.
- Describe any memorable adventures you had as a child.
- Describe any or all of your graduations in detail for preschool, kindergarten, middle school, high school or college.
- Describe any special achievements, awards or diplomas you received throughout your school years.
- Describe the details of your childhood bedtime rituals.
- Describe each of your parents in one or two paragraphs.
- Describe how you got to school as a child. Did you walk, ride a bike, take a school bus or go in mom or dad's taxi?
- Describe how you would spend a typical weekend as a child.
- Describe in detail your most favorite birthday party and why it was the best.
- Describe five memorable experiences you and your father shared during your childhood.
- Describe five memorable experiences you and your mother shared during your childhood.
- Describe how you learned to drive. Who taught you at what age?

- ☐ Describe any smells or sounds you experience as an adult that immediately take you back to childhood and why.
- ☐ Describe your best and worst memories of being a child.
- ☐ Describe your best and worst memories of being a teen.
- ☐ Describe the different ways you have traveled growing-up.
- ☐ Describe your feelings about the first time you drove by yourself.
- ☐ Describe three favorite family traditions during the holidays.
- ☐ Describe three favorite childhood bands or musicians. Why?
- ☐ Describe three favorite songs from your teen years. Why?
- ☐ Describe your childhood home, your bedroom, the street you lived on or the area where you lived. Use your senses to describe.
- ☐ Describe your family's special holiday traditions for Christmas, Thanksgiving, New Year's, Easter, etc. What did you like or dislike?
- ☐ Describe your favorite childhood and teenage TV shows and characters. When were they on? How long? Color or black and white?
- ☐ Describe your favorite Halloween or Harvest Day costume. Did you design it? How did you celebrate the holiday?
- ☐ Describe your favorite things to do as a child during autumn, such as cookouts, playing in the leaves, etc.
- ☐ Describe your favorite things to do during Spring, like ride bikes, collect butterflies, plant a garden, etc.
- ☐ Describe your favorite things to do during Summer, like swimming, camping, hiking, going to the park, the beach, etc.
- ☐ Describe your favorite things to do during the winter, like sledding, tobogganing, skiing, ice skating, hockey, etc.
- ☐ Describe your grandmother and your grandfather.
- ☐ Describe your most and least favorite teachers.
- ☐ Describe your perfect real or wished-for childhood vacation.
- ☐ Describe your personality, your temperament and your attitude as a child.
- ☐ Describe your siblings from your memories of growing-up.
- ☐ Describe your teenage years. Where did you like to hang out with your friends? What were your favorite activities?

The Biggest Book of Words & Prompts for Scrapbooks, Art Journals & Crafts

- ☐ Did one or both of your parents read you stories and or pray with you at bedtime? Describe those times you shared together.
- ☐ Did you believe in the Tooth Fairy, Santa Claus, leprechauns, Cupid, etc.? How old were you when you learned the truth about them? Who told you?
- ☐ Did you leave cookies and milk for Santa? What kind?
- ☐ Did you ever go to summer camp as a child? If so, write about your adventures there. What type of camp?
- ☐ Did you ever build a treehouse, a clubhouse or a fort?
- ☐ Did you ever live on a farm or have you ever visited one during your childhood? Write about those experiences of farm life.
- ☐ Did you get to spend the nights at your grandparent's? Describe how their home was different from yours.
- ☐ Did you go on family outings such as the circus, the county fair, amusement parks, etc.? Share stories about those times.
- ☐ Did you go to Vacation Bible School or church camp as a child or teen?
- ☐ Did you grow up living in a city, town or country? Write about it.
- ☐ Did you have a boyfriend or girlfriend when you were growing up? Share a story or two.
- ☐ Did you have a hero or heroes as a child? Who and why?
- ☐ Did you have a pet when you were a child? Describe the pet.
- ☐ Did you have any imaginary friends when you were a child?
- ☐ Did you have any jobs while you were growing-up? How old were you? Describe the details and your favorite job/ s.
- ☐ Did you have anything that you loved to collect as a child or teen?
- ☐ Did you have slumber parties, sleepovers, backyard campouts? Describe some of the special memories.
- ☐ Did you like school? What grade was your favorite and why?
- ☐ Did you like to draw, create things or write stories, as a child?
- ☐ Did you and your family attend church services? Describe your childhood memories of church and how it influenced your life.
- ☐ Did you participate in band, drama, choir or other academic teams in school? Describe the details.

- ☐ Did you take any lessons as a child such as piano, guitar, dance, tennis, golf, bowling, etc.?
- ☐ Did you receive your education somewhere other than a school?
- ☐ Did you watch Saturday morning cartoons? What was your favorite cartoon and cartoon character?
- ☐ Do you have a favorite author or favorite books as a child or teen? Did you read often?
- ☐ Draw a picture of your childhood home, your bedroom and the area where you lived. Describe what they were like.
- ☐ Draw a picture of what your family was like when you were a child.
- ☐ Draw a picture of yourself at each age from baby to your teen years. Try to capture how you dressed, looked, acted, etc.
- ☐ Have any events in your childhood or teen years changed you? How?
- ☐ How did you and your family celebrate major holidays such as July 4th, Halloween, Mother's Day, Father's Day, Valentines Day, Memorial Day, Thanksgiving and Christmas?
- ☐ How did you celebrate your birthday growing up? Parties, gifts, etc.
- ☐ If you could have had any gift in the world for your birthday, as a child, what would it have been?
- ☐ How did you celebrate milestone birthdays, like 16, 18 and 21?
- ☐ How did you typically spend the weekend as a teen?
- ☐ How many homes did you live in as a child? Describe each one.
- ☐ What childhood memory still makes you smile?
- ☐ If you could have changed one thing about your childhood, what would it be?
- ☐ If you had brothers or sisters, tell some stories about the things you shared and enjoyed together as kids.
- ☐ Just like the twelve days of Christmas, describe twelve favorite childhood Christmas memories.
- ☐ List three things that scared you as a child / teen.
- ☐ List ten reasons why you didn't do your homework...or did you?
- ☐ List ten things you were most thankful for as a child or teen.

- ☐ Make a list of family events you remember attending like reunions, special anniversaries, weddings, etc.
- ☐ Name of three of the most influential people and why.
- ☐ Name three goals you had as a child. Did you accomplish any of them?
- ☐ Name three strengths and three weaknesses you had as a child.
- ☐ Tell me about your best childhood friend. Why was he / she your best friend?
- ☐ Tell me about your extended family—aunts, uncles, cousins, etc..
- ☐ Tell me about your immediate family—mom, dad, siblings.
- ☐ List ten things that made you really laugh as a child.
- ☐ Write about the bravest moment in your childhood.
- ☐ List the foods you liked and disliked the most as a child or teen.
- ☐ What was the loneliest time in your childhood and why?
- ☐ Describe the most amazing moment in your childhood.
- ☐ What was under your bed as a teen? Tell all and draw a picture!
- ☐ Was school easy or difficult for you? Why?
- ☐ Was there a class / teacher that had a particular influence on your life?
- ☐ Were there any significant world events when you were a child that changed your life? Share the details of the event.
- ☐ Were there family customs you experienced in your home growing-up? Where did they originate and why? Do you still do them?
- ☐ Were you artistic as a child? Describe your favorite medium.
- ☐ Were you brought up to do chores? Describe what they were and when you did them. Did you get an allowance? How much?
- ☐ Were you involved in organizations such as scouting, 4-H Club, Campfire, youth groups or other boys and girls clubs?
- ☐ Were you involved in sports as a child? Describe the experiences.
- ☐ What activities did your family enjoy doing together?
- ☐ What did you or your siblings do at family celebrations growing up?
- ☐ What did you like most and least about yourself as a child or teen?

- ☐ What did you want to be when you grew up? Did you accomplish that desire?
- ☐ What were your grades in school? Did you study a lot or a little? Did good grades matter to you?
- ☐ What hobbies did you have as a child? Do you still enjoy them?
- ☐ What is your earliest childhood memory? Detail the memories.
- ☐ What is your most treasured memory from childhood or school?
- ☐ What kind of events did you participate in junior high and high school, like dances, pep rallies, school elections, clubs, sports, etc.
- ☐ What kind of talents did you have as a child, like art, dancing, singing, playing an instrument, sports, academic, etc.
- ☐ What made you laugh and what made you cry as a child, as an adolescent and as a teen? Share those moments.
- ☐ What season was your favorite as a child? Why?
- ☐ What is a special smell you remember from your childhood?
- ☐ What special things did you like to do with your father / mother?
- ☐ What three people did you want to meet when you were growing up?
- ☐ What five things made you feel especially loved as a child?
- ☐ What were the best and worst Christmas presents you ever got?
- ☐ What were the best and worst vacations you ever took as a child?
- ☐ What was the first Bible verse you learned as a child?
- ☐ What was the nicest thing someone did for you as a child?
- ☐ What was the nicest thing you ever did for someone else?
- ☐ What was the worst thing you ever got in trouble for as a child?
- ☐ What was your favorite activity or sport for each season?
- ☐ What were your favorite animals at the zoo as a child?
- ☐ What were your favorite things to eat for breakfast as a child?
- ☐ What was your favorite holiday to celebrate and why?
- ☐ What was your favorite month of the year? and why?
- ☐ What was your favorite summer vacation activity?

The Biggest Book of Words & Prompts for Scrapbooks, Art Journals & Crafts

- ☐ What was your favorite bedtime story and why?
- ☐ What were your most and least favorite subjects in school?
- ☐ What were your favorite games to play as a child or teen?
- ☐ What were your favorite indoor vs. outdoor activities?
- ☐ What were your favorite things to do when you visited the park?
- ☐ What were your three favorite TV shows, top ten favorite movies, top three favorite video games as a child or as a teen?
- ☐ What type of work did your father and mother do when you were growing up? Did you ever get to go to work with them?
- ☐ When you were a child did you share a room or have your own? Describe the best, funniest or toughest parts about sharing a room.
- ☐ Describe some of the characteristics of each place you have lived, like a mini travel guide of towns, cities, states and countries.
- ☐ Where have you traveled the farthest to as a child?
- ☐ Where was your favorite place to eat as a child? Describe what you liked best about the place.
- ☐ Who was your hero? What reasons made them your hero?
- ☐ Who was your "first crush?" How old were you? Describe the relationship from start to finish.
- ☐ Write a favorite poem or quote you really liked as a teen and then share why it was your favorite.
- ☐ Write a detailed short story describing your childhood—from birth until you moved out on your own.
- ☐ Write a short story describing the experience of moving out.
- ☐ Write a poem or quote that best describes your childhood.
- ☐ Write a short paragraph describing each of your siblings.
- ☐ Write a top ten list describing the funniest moments of your childhood.
- ☐ Write a short story about you and your best childhood friend. Draw pictures or add photographs. Share it with that friend.
- ☐ Write a story telling who you are. Draw a picture of you.

- ☐ Write about any family members or friends who were mentors to you growing up.
- ☐ Write about any personal or family pets from your childhood.
- ☐ Write about three things that made you feel sad as a child / teen.
- ☐ Write about three things that made you feel happy as a child / teen.
- ☐ Write about your best and worst family memories as a child.
- ☐ Write about your favorite part of growing-up.
- ☐ Write about your favorite place to hang out with friends.
- ☐ Write about your favorite school memories for elementary, junior high, high school, college, etc.
- ☐ Write about your first day of school or the first day you can remember going to school.
- ☐ Write about your funniest childhood memory.
- ☐ Write about your most embarrassing childhood memory.
- ☐ Write about what you would do during Christmas vacation.
- ☐ Write your three favorite Bible verses and what made them special.
- ☐ You were most angry as a child when…
- ☐ You were most disappointed as a teen when…
- ☐ Did you go to college? Where, when, what was it like? Document the details of your college years.

ENGAGEMENT AND WEDDING

- ☐ Where, when and how did you meet your mate?
- ☐ Was it love at first sight or did it take time?
- ☐ What first attracted to to your spouse?
- ☐ What kind of ideals and values were you searching for in a mate?
- ☐ Write about your first impressions of your mate.
- ☐ What made you know that he or she was the one you wanted to spend the rest of your life with?

- ☐ What personality traits do you admire the most about your mate? What do you like the least?
- ☐ Describe the details of your first date. Your most romantic date.
- ☐ Describe the first time you kissed. Describe when and where, the feelings, the place, the reaction for both of you.
- ☐ Describe the first time you told each other, "I love you." Where, when and how did it happen? Who said it first? Describe the moment.
- ☐ Did you and your spouse share a lot of common interests as you got to know each other?
- ☐ Choose five adjectives that describe your relationship before marriage.
- ☐ Did you have a favorite place for romantic date? Describe a typical time and a really special time.
- ☐ What song defined your relationship and your love?
- ☐ Write down your favorite poems or quotes and tell why you liked them?
- ☐ Write a detailed description of your courtship. How long did you date?
- ☐ When, where and how did you become engaged?
- ☐ Write about your pre-wedding parties, showers, etc.
- ☐ When and how did your first meet your in-laws?
- ☐ What were your fears, expectations or anticipations about getting married? Describe the feelings and emotions that you each felt.
- ☐ How old were you and your spouse when you were married?
- ☐ Describe the feelings you both had leading up to your wedding.
- ☐ Describe your feelings and emotions on your wedding day.
- ☐ Write about where you were married. How and why did you choose the place? Describe the details of the place and include drawings or photographs.
- ☐ Describe your wedding day—include as many details as you can remember with regard to the season, the weather and the setting.
- ☐ Was there a particular theme to your wedding?
- ☐ What colors did you choose for your wedding and why?
- ☐ Describe your wedding dress, bridesmaid's dresses, best man's and groomsmen's suits or tuxedos, the flowers, the music, etc.

- ☐ Describe your ceremony, your guests and the time of day. Was everyone prepared and did the wedding start on time?
- ☐ Did you write your own wedding vows? Recount them here.
- ☐ Describe your wedding ring. Any special stories about it? Describe the feeling when you first put it on.
- ☐ Were there any special songs, poems or scripture readings during your ceremony? Include the lyrics, musicians, photos, etc.
- ☐ Were there any really special, unexpected or uninvited guests?
- ☐ Where, when and how long was your reception? Why did you choose the place for your wedding and reception?
- ☐ Describe the reception. Write about the details such as your theme, colors, food, the cake, special toasts, the dancing, the music, traditions, the gifts, etc.
- ☐ Describe the funniest thing that happened on your wedding day.
- ☐ What was the happiest moment of your wedding day?
- ☐ What was your most nervous moment of your wedding day?
- ☐ Describe anything unusual that happened on your wedding day.
- ☐ Did the expectations you had about your wedding day prove to be true in reality? Were they better or worse than you dreamed?
- ☐ Did you go on a honeymoon? Describe all the wonderful details, documenting where you went and all the romantic memories.

THE NEWLYWEDS

- ☐ Describe your first year together as newlyweds and your feelings about being married.
- ☐ Describe where you lived for the very first time as a couple.
- ☐ Describe the neighborhood you lived in. Was it in the city or country?
- ☐ Write in detail about your professional careers as newlyweds. Where did you work and whom did you work with?
- ☐ Describe the way your home was furnished, including colors, styles, etc.
- ☐ Describe how you began to build a "nest" together.
- ☐ How did you handle finances and other household responsibilities?

- Who was in charge of cooking and other household chores?
- Do your remember your first fight and making-up as newlyweds?
- Did you have any family pets during your first few years before you began a family?
- Describe how you would spend a typical morning, afternoon, evening when you first married.
- How did you spend your days off? Did you have days off together?
- Write about your first vacations together, from the planning to the things you did.
- How did you celebrate your first holidays together, (birthdays, Thanksgiving, Christmas)? Did you start your own traditions or did you carry-on traditions from you families?
- What activities did you share together? What activities did you do separately?
- Describe your favorite and least favorite things about being married during that first year.
- How did you celebrate your first anniversary together? Did you eat the top of your wedding cake? Did you dress in wedding attire again?

HOME AND FAMILY

- Describe your earliest memories of your parents, siblings and grandparents. Did you live close or far away from your grandparents and other relatives?
- Create a self-portrait or character sketch for each of your immediate family members. Try first with your own family and then write about your parents and siblings. Describe them in detail so that someone who has never seen or met them will get a good idea of who they are/were. Write about them physically, emotionally, intellectually and spiritually, from your perspective.
- Choose five adjectives that describe your relationship after marriage.
- Describe family traditions for holidays, birthdays, weddings, births, graduations, celebrations, and other life events. Did your family carry on old traditions or create new ones specific to the desires of immediate family members?

- ☐ Create a family tree with your words. Begin by writing about yourself and then write about your siblings, your parents, grandparents, great-grandparents, aunts, uncles, cousins. Try to do this for each side of your family. Include details such as birth dates, where they lived, information about growing up, education, marriages, divorces, adoptions, etc.
- ☐ Describe the places where you lived growing up. Did you live in a city, town or country?
- ☐ Create drawings of the homes you lived in growing up. Include drawings of your bedroom, the yard, playhouses, etc.
- ☐ Write about the kind of work you and your spouse did growing up, before you met and then after you married.
- ☐ Did anyone in your family go to college? Describe the memories of college days for both student and family.
- ☐ Describe special or memorable vacations, events, celebrations that have held significant meaning.
- ☐ Did you follow in your parents footsteps as far as family values and goals?
- ☐ Describe three special memories of family gatherings from the time you became an adult.
- ☐ Write about any details of your parents' and grandparents' courtships and weddings. How old were they then?
- ☐ If your parents and grandparents are still living, ask them to write a paragraph or two about their life together.
- ☐ If you can, spend some time with your parents and interview them, using any of the questions in this book. Document their words in their voice. Record them and take their picture as you do the interview.
- ☐ Tell about your relationship with your in-laws. Try writing from both yours and your spouse's perspective.
- ☐ What are some family hobbies or interests that you share together?
- ☐ Write about any family members that have served in the military. List their branch, rank, responsibilities, awards, etc.
- ☐ Write about political or civic interests you and your spouse shared as a married couple.
- ☐ Write about your relationship with your parents and siblings. Share special memories that make you smile, cry, laugh, etc.

- ☐ As a parent, describe the ten best moments of your child's / children's life. Create a list, expanding your thoughts on each of those moments include details such as places, dates, etc.
- ☐ How has becoming a parent changed your relationship with your spouse and other family members?
- ☐ Is anyone in your family extremely talented artistically, musically or otherwise? Describe their talents.
- ☐ Did you have a close relationship with your grandparents? Describe your fondest memories as a child going to visit.
- ☐ Describe Christmas morning in your home and / or Christmas eve celebrations with family and friends.
- ☐ What is your favorite season and why? Detail with photographs or memorabilia.
- ☐ What is your family's favorite season? Describe what makes that season special, such as activities, foods, events and music.
- ☐ What is the your family's favorite holiday?
- ☐ Describe three family traditions during the holidays.
- ☐ What makes you laugh or cry? What is the biggest joy and the greatest sorrow in your life?
- ☐ Describe in one paragraph what you love about your spouse. Then do the same for your children, your parents and your siblings.
- ☐ Describe your family cars from the time you were married until now. Draw pictures of them. Which was your favorite?
- ☐ Describe a typical family night and three of the best ways to spend time together as a family. Write from your perspective, your spouse's perspective and your children's perspective.
- ☐ As a couple, what interests do you share? Hobbies?
- ☐ What have been the greatest accomplishments thus far for you, your spouse, your children and your family as a whole?
- ☐ What are the top ten reasons you love being married? Write from your perspective and from your spouse's.
- ☐ Describe the biggest trials or hurdles you have experienced as a married couple.
- ☐ What has been your favorite era thus far?

The New Ultimate Guide to the Perfect Word – Volume 2

- ☐ Tell about your favorite fads when you were in school and then compare them to now. How have they changed?
- ☐ What music did you enjoy as a teen or young adult, compared to now? Have your musical tastes changed or remained the same?
- ☐ Create a list of ten words that describe the strengths of your marriage and family. Then using each word, write in more detail explaining how those strengths apply to your life.
- ☐ How do you and your spouse spend quiet time together?
- ☐ How do you and your spouse spend activity time together?
- ☐ Describe common values you share as a couple with regard to raising children, money, work, extended family, traditions, etc.
- ☐ Do you share common beliefs?
- ☐ Has your spirituality changed since you were a child? How?
- ☐ What is your favorite way to spend alone time?
- ☐ What are the favorite ways you share time together, as a couple and as a family?
- ☐ Do you and your family attend church together? Where and when? Describe what part religion plays in your lives.
- ☐ Describe a typical family evening at home.
- ☐ Do you a collect things? Share the details with words and pictures.
- ☐ Write about family meal time. Describe favorite family foods, daily traditions and chores, when it comes to meal time.
- ☐ What has been your proudest moment as a parent?
- ☐ What has been your proudest moment for your children?
- ☐ What do you feel has been your greatest personal accomplishment?
- ☐ If you could live your life over, what would you do?
- ☐ Describe any life-changing events since you were married.
- ☐ Of all the things you learned growing up, either from experience or from your parents, what three lessons do you find most valuable today?
- ☐ Describe any special family heirlooms, such as a Bible, jewelry, furniture.

- ☐ Work together as a family to create a family tree using many of the online resources available for genealogy.
- ☐ Describe as much as you know about your ancestors, going back as far as you can remember. Create drawings of things you remember most about these people.
- ☐ What have been the most exciting and the most difficult times you have shared together?
- ☐ What are your plans and hopes for the future as a couple, as a family and for each of your children?
- ☐ "It was the best of times, it was the worst of times"—describe both from your's and your spouse's perspective.
- ☐ Try to include photographs or drawings to illustrate any prompts you choose to write about. Your words are most important and the picture will complete your thoughts.
- ☐ Just start writing words that describe your hopes and dreams.

The questions in each section of this book are ideas to get your thoughts flowing. They can be answered very simply or elaborated upon to really tell a story—the choice is yours.

No matter what—your words are certain to be a blessing now and for generations to come. What you write is a part of you and as such a very special gift that only you can share with those you love. It may seem like a trivial, unimportant thing to do, but the truth is, it may be the sweetest gift you ever give.

When we write from our heart, the floodgates open and the love pours forth. Enjoy every opportunity to write and tell your story through these prompts or be inspired to just write about any memory. Your family will be blessed and so will you!

P.S. Write everyday about the little things that happen, tell about the moments in-between the big events. For it is in our days and nights that life happens and though the days may be simple, they are the essence of our life and there are wonderful stories to be told and photographs that illustrate the joy in living.

Just as musical instruments
blend to compose beautiful symphonies,
the written memories of our lives
create wonderful stories to share
–Linda LaTourelle

Quotes & Quips

He wrapped himself in quotations—
as a beggar would enfold himself
in the purple of emperors

–Rudyard Kipling

ACCOMPLISH

When no one is watching
Do your very best...
It will be evidence of
Your good character!
–Linda LaTourelle

A misty morning does not mean the day will be cloudy

A handful of patience and tenacity is worth more than a bushel full of brains

Act like a king / queen—think royalty

All that we behold is full of blessings –William Wordsworth

Ambition is the road to success. Persistence is the vehicle that will get you there

A person's true worth is the good they do in this world

Assumptions can be a pathway to wisdom or the roadblock to vision –Linda LaTourelle

Be more than you think you can be, by doing more than you think you can do and you will go farther than you ever thought you could –Linda LaTourelle

Be remarkable!

Be the best you that you can be

Don't let what you cannot do interfere with what you can

Don't do anything halfway unless you are willing to be half-happy

A person's work is always a portrait of himself

Doodling inspires one to draw their dreams creatively –Linda LaTourelle

Kick off your shoes and just dance at the wonder of life

Every new day is a once-in-a-lifetime experience

Everything you have experienced in your life is for a purpose to get you to where you are now

Failure is an opportunity to turn in a new direction

For a few moments each day think of all you dare to dream. Then live those dreams into a new way of thinking. –Linda LaTourelle

God can dream a dream way bigger than you could ever imagine—designed just for you

High expectations are the secret to everything

I don't know the secret to success, but the key to failure is to try to please everyone –Bill Cosby

If you think you can, you will. If you think you can't, you won't

If at first you don't succeed, do it like your mother told you to

If you won't be yourself—who will?

Imagination is the impetus to knowledge –Linda LaTourelle

In search of my mother's garden, I found my own –Alice Walker

It's not what you look at that matters, it's what you see – Thoreau

The garden of ones mind
is planted every day—
with seeds of love and hope
or weeds that we allow to stay.
The choice is ours to make
as each day begins anew.
I pray your joys are many
and your sorrows very few.
  –Linda LaTourelle

Take the first step and have faith

Know that you can and you most certainly will *–Linda LaTourelle*

Let past experience be your compass and hope your focus

Miracles happen even when all hope is lost if you simply believe

My father gave me the greatest gift—he believed that I could do anything—and so I did

No man is free who is not master of himself *–Epictetus*

Only you can raise the bar to excel above mediocrity *–Linda LaTourelle*

Real life is creating a life of meaning by serving and fulfilling your purpose

Rivers know no hurry

Sing songs that none have sung

Sing the song in your heart

Some succeed because they are destined to, others because they are determined

You alone define your life

Start today to be what you always dreamed of being

Success is hanging on when others let go

Success is a hidden jewel and requires a map / plan to discover it

Success is not in things, it is within ourselves

The difference between ordinary and extraordinary is that measure of difference that exceeds normal expectations *–Linda LaTourelle*

The footprints on the sands of time were not made by sitting down

The happiness you feel is in direct proportion to the love you give *–Oprah Winfrey*

The right man is the one who seizes the moment

The sweet smell of success is 100% pure tenacity and hard work

There are no shortcuts to anywhere worth going

There are two choices—make progress or make excuses

There is no such thing as an unimportant day

To achieve greatness—believe in impossibilities and trust thyself

Trust yourself always

To stand strong, move forward and succeed and make certain your feet are facing the right direction *–Linda LaTourelle*

Traveling the road of perseverance requires walking forward one step at a time *–Linda LaTourelle*

Trust that no matter what happens you will be okay

Love what you do,
Do it with passion
And success shall
Reward you with
A life full of
Purpose
–Linda LaTourelle

Victory comes by persevering through adversity, with tenacity

We accomplish much when we choose to think of the infinite possibilities and try –Linda LaTourelle

What you risk reveals what you value

When one drop of water meets the ocean's shore, its power is infinite

When in doubt of what to do next, be still and the answer will come

When there is struggle, strength will come, just hold on –Linda LaTourelle

Whatever you do—do your best for God and He'll do the rest

You are braver than what you believe and stronger than you seem and smarter than you think

You don't have to see the whole staircase—just take the first step –Martin Luther King

You are the sum total of what you consume—mentally, physically and spiritually –Ted Chapman

You become what you believe

You can accomplish great things —If you think you can!

ADOPTION

ADOPTION
Across the miles
Our baby flew—
On wings of hope
Dreams came true.
With endless prayer
And faith so strong,
Our family's home
Where we belong.
So full of love
And thankful, too,
All this my child—
Because of you.
–Linda LaTourelle

A blessing to behold

A chosen family

A family just for me

A half a world away we wait

A match made in heaven

A place to belong

A real family for me

A whole new world

Across the sea, you came to me

Adopted with love

Adoption is forever

A family—because of you!

Amazing love!

And then there was you

Because we prayed…

Blessed beyond measure

Born to be our baby

> Where did you come from baby dear?
> Out of the everywhere and into here.
> –George MacDonald

Built by faith

Built by the Master's hands

Child of our heart

Children are a gift from God—
They are his reward –Psalm 127:3

Chosen and loved

Counting the days

Delight yourself in the Lord and He will give you the desires of your heart –Psalm 37:4

Delivered by hand

Destined to be ours

Dreams came true cause of you

Fairytales do come true

Family begins and ends with you

Families come from the most unexpected places

First love, first baby

First time we ever saw your face

Flyin' high to build a family

Footprints into our hearts

For this child I prayed –Samuel 1:27

From God's arms to ours

God's perfect plan—family

God's amazing grace

Hand-picked with love

Happy adoption day

Hope built our family

Hope came home today

How our journey began

I believe in miracles

I dedicate my life to you

International adoption

Into my arms—deep in my heart

It's so nice to be with you

Labor of love

Legacy of an adopted child

Love at first sight

Love built a family

Love comes in unexpected blessings

Loving hearts—chosen family

Me and my family

Meeting our child

Miracle from God

Our baby you'll be

Now faith is being sure of what we hope… –Hebrews 11:1

Oh wondrous night!

On the wings of a prayer

Our family began today

Our little miracle

Placed by God's own hands

Praise God for adoption

Precious, priceless and praise God

The best gift of our life

The moment we've waited for

To have you is to know love

W is for waiting and wishing

Waiting for a baby like you

We are family because of you

We believe in miracles

We got you, babe
Welcome home, sweet baby
When you wish upon a star
Worlds apart—love filled our heart
You and me—we were meant to be
You and me against the world
You are all we ever hoped for
You are our sunshine
You are prayer answered
You flew into our world
You were my heart's desire
You had me with just one smile
You loved me before I was born
You're all our dreams come true

AGE & AGING

I don't mind getting older
Looking forward to being retired
Just wish I could have done it
Before my warranty expired
–Thena Smith

A man is not old until his regrets are no longer dreams
After eighty—let it all hang out
Age is a journey to perfection
Blessed are the young for they shall inherit the national debt
But officer, I forgot where I was going, I had to speed
Caution—senior comin' through
Cougar meets her mate
Eat, drink and grow old merrily

MEMORY
The memory card in my brain
Has left me often pondering
I try to focus on what I must
But my mind goes a-wandering
–Linda LaTourelle

Few women will admit their age
—few men will act theirs
For exercise—visit our arthritic department
Geezer—and proud of it!
Give me my discount—I'll leave quietly!
Grace shines upon your face
Help! I'm having a senior moment!
Hi honey—I'm home & retired
Hot old woman / man
I can remember when …
I don't wanna grow up
I forget to remember
I forgot—how did I get to be so old?
I love you, you old bear
I wish I didn't know now what I didn't know then
I'm not 60, I'm 59 and a half
If I were younger, I would know more and worry less. *–Linda LaTourelle*
I grow old learning how to love
I've got an achy-breaky everything
I've got this old age thing— C.R.N. / Can't Remember Nothin'
Inside every old man is a young stud wondering what happened
It took (#) years to look this great
It's hard to be nostalgic when you can't remember anything!

USE AN ADJECTIVE TO DESCRIBE YOUR AGE!

- Flirty Thirties
- Fabulous Forties
- Fantastic Fifties
- Stupendous Sixties
- Smashing Seventies
- Exciting Eighties
- Naughty Nineties
- Happy Hundred

Be creative or funny!

It's not how old you are, but how you are old

Just me and my rocker

Leaks when laughing

Life begins at 50 / or ?

Lying about my age is easier since I forget what it is

Middle age shows in the most annoying places

Mind of a stud—body of a geezer

My mind not only wanders, sometimes it leaves completely

Needs more memory installed

O.C.D.—Old • Cute • Darlin'

Oh, to be seventy / age again!

Old age is just a state of body

Old folks boogie

Old men are the flowers of winter

Over the hill groupies

Rockin' my life away

Sowed my wild oats—shredded my wheaties—soaked in the cream

I looked in the mirror
and what did I see
all the years
smiling back at me
I'm more mature
and wiser, too—
but I'm not old,
what happened to you
–Linda LaTourelle

Support local bingo—keep seniors off the streets

The secret to longevity—keep moving

The splendor of old age is the silver in their hair

The spirit never grows old

The afternoon knows what the morning never suspected –Robert Frost

Alas! The fleeting years, how they roll on! –Horace

These are days of oldness and reminiscent of youth's boldness

This vehicle protected by an old granny / grampy driver

Three things happen as we age—first the memory goes and ... I can't remember the other two

Warning: dates in calendar are closer than they appear

When I was a boy /girl…

Wisdom comes with winters –Oscar Wilde

You're never too old to…

Youth passes as though it were a dream

I'm only as old as I want to be and that my dear, is twenty-three

YOU KNOW YOU'RE OLD WHEN...

A pharmacist is your new best friend

Getting some action means it's time to take a laxative

Memories of hot love stories ended with a kiss, a closing door and music fading

People call your vocabulary archaic

People want to give you a ride to keep you from driving

Sitting on the porch is a rocking night out

Snap, crackle and pop isn't just your cereal anymore

The hair on your chin is thicker than the hair on your head

The only exercise you get is "shake before using"

The pennies in childhood piggy bank are now collectors items

The twinkle in your eye is simply the sun reflecting off your bifocals

There's nothing left to learn the hard way

You can live without sex but not without your glasses

You can't find your car in the parking lot

You figured out the meaning of life but forgot to tell someone

You found what you were looking for but now can't remember why you needed it

You read more to remember less

You have a party and the neighbors can't hear you

You quit holding your stomach in, no matter who walks into the room

You record albums are older than your kids

You remember life before indoor plumbing

You repeat things, you repeat things and don't even know it

You sing along to the music in the grocery store

You start every other sentence with "when I was your age..."

You take your compass to walk to the store

Young men ask you for advice

Young women open doors for you

Your childhood toys can be seen in the museum

Your high school outfit is back in style

Your kids ask if you lived in "black and white olden days"

Your kids asked if you lived when dinosaurs roamed the earth

Your knee joints predict the local weather forecast

Your car is a collector's dream

Your original one-inch tattoo now stretches to a foot

You remember when it was only black and white television

You know you are getting old when you read funny lists like these and find yourself laughing.

The Biggest Book of Words & Prompts for Scrapbooks, Art Journals & Crafts

ALBUM TITLES
For Scrapbooks or Journals

A GIFT
A book of love
Written with care
Wonderful memories
I hope to share.

Stories of life,
family and friends,
details of years
that won't come again.

A gift made for you,
straight from my heart—
a priceless treasure
I hope to impart.
–Linda LaTourelle

A Bridge to the Future
A Child's Book of Family
A Family Affair
Age Journals / Milestones
A Legacy of Love
A Lifetime of Memories
A Star is Born
A Tapestry of Love
Across the Years
All About the Cat
All About You / Us, me
All-American Family
All Because Two People Fell in Love
Among My Many Journeys
An Adoption Story
Baby and Me—a Love Story
Baby's Book of Birthdays
Baby's Book of Me
Big Book of Holidays
Blessed in Our Nest
Building Our Nest / Home
Christmas Miracles
Cookbook of Love / Recipes
Daddy's / Mommy's Darlin's
Day By Day / A daily journal
Every Picture Tells a Story
Family By Choice
Family Follies
Family Scraps
Family Vacation Fun Times
From Past to Present
Generations To Love
Got Family?
Grandma's Quilts
Grandpa's Garden
Heritage and Home
Holiday Treasures
Home of the Brave
Hometown Heroes
Honor the Past, Hope for the Future
I Remember Mama / Papa
I / We Remember... / *Use As Memorial*
In Loving Memory
It's a Dog's / Cat's Life
It's All-Relative
Just Daddy / Mommy and Me
Kinfolk and Kindred Spirits
Labor Pains and Pictures
Labor, Love and Little Kisses
Legacy of a Loving Family
Lemonade Stands and Summer Fun

97 | ultimatebookcompany.com

Life According to...
Life's Little / Big Adventures
Linked by Love
Look At the Home That Love Built
Love to Last a Lifetime
Me and My Friends
Me, Myself and I
Memories Sown With Love
Milestones Remembered
My / Our Blessing Book
My Brother / My Sister
My Collections
My Life as a Child / Teen
My Life, My Love, My Family
My Mother's Quilt
My Sports Star
My Summer Vacation
Nestled and Nested
Never a Dull Moment
New Year Beginnings
Nostalgia in the Making
Oh, the Stories I Could Tell
Once Upon a Family
One Day at a Time
One Fairytale After Another
Our Anniversary Book
Our Book of Grand Adventures
Our Daily News
Our Family Pets
Our First Christmas
Our Book of Firsts
Our Love Story
Our Wedding Day
Paw Prints on My Heart
Random Ramblings

Recollections of Love
Relatively Speaking
Rich Beyond Measure
Roaring Twenties (Add year)
Rooted in Family
School Days
Scraps of History
Seasons of The Heart
Sissy / Brother 'n Me
Six Degrees of Family
Snapshots and Snippets
Spinning Tails—our Dog
Stories as Told by Mom
Story of Life
Tales and Tails—A Pet Story!
The Birthday Book
The Children's Hour (Stories)
The Family Tree (Our Roots)
The Garden Book
The History of You / Me
The Kid Behind the Photos
The Night Before Christmas
The Rest of the Story
The Story of Us
The Wonder of You
These Are The Memories of Our Life
The Vintage Years
Through the Generations
Travel Through the Pages of Time
Treasured Pages
Walk Down Memory Lane
We Remember Moments
When Life Gave Me Lemons
When Love Builds a Home
Winter Wonderland

You and Me Against the World
You Must Remember This…
Yours, Mine and Our Stories

AMUSEMENT PARKS

A day at the park
A land of imagination
A ride above the rest
A view from the top
A world of adventure
Ahoy captain!
All hands up
Bouncin' like a tigger
Brother's / sister's big adventure
Bumper car bully
Can we go again?
Carnivals, cotton candy and coasters, oh my!
Coaster fanatics
Cruisin' the carnival
Darling little Dumbo
Don't look down
Faster, faster, faster
Flying carpet ride
Get set to get wet
Getting goofy
Give it a whirl!
Got to believe in magic
Hang on for the ride!
Help me find my stomach
He's / She's got a ticket to ride
Hi ho, hi ho, here we go
Hurl-a-girl
I don't wanna grow up

I'm upside-down and inside-out
It's so much friendlier with Pooh
Jungle jammin'
Just goofin' around with Goofy
Just mad about the mouse
Kids with character
Kissin' on the carousel
Land of make-believe
Laughin' my day / life away
Let the good times roll
Let the magic begin
Let's get wet
Let's go bouncin'
Life in the fast lane
Mad as a hatter
Main Street USA
My goofy kids
On the right track
Over the top
Painted ponies
Pedal to the metal
Pilot in training
Roller coaster Romeo
Round and round, up and down
Safari adventures
Screamin' to be heard
Second star to the right
Sittin' at the top of the world
Take it to the limit
Tea party for two
The need for speed
The ultimate thrill ride
Ticket to ride
Tiltin' and whirlin'
Top speed

Tunnel of love
Twistin' and twirlin'
Up, up and flyin'
Watch me, Mom and Dad!
We can fly
We survived the roller coaster
What a bunch of characters
Where dreams really do come true
Whirlin' and twirlin'
White-knucklin' it!
Who's the fairest of them all?
Wild and wacky water ride

Out like a lion, in like a lamb
Party animal
Paws and enjoy the animals
Peanut gallery
Pets and Paws
Playing possum
Sleep and let sleep
Sly as a fox
Talk to the animals
Toad-ally awesome
Vets are a special breed
Where the wild things are

ANIMALS

All animals are equal, but some are better than others
All God's critters
Animal crackers
Animal farm
Animal lovers unite
Animal magnetism
Bad "hare" day
Beauty and the beast
Billy goat grumpy
By leaps and bounds
Creature comforts
For the love of pets
Fur-ever friends
Fuzzy wuzzy memories
I am lion hear me roar
I'm impawsable
Just me and my (pet)

Water Animals

Be kind to your web-footed friends
Come on over to my pad
Crocodile rock
Feelin' froggy
Green is my favorite color
Hop on over
Hoppy birthday to you
Kiss that frog
See you later alligator
The frog prince / princess
Toad-ally in love
Toad-ally made for each other

ANIMAL ALPHABET

Pick your child's initial.
Create a cute animal page.

- **A**pril the Antelope
- **B**ethany the Bird
- **C**ameron the Chinchilla

- **D**oodles the Duck
- **E**lijah the Elephant
- **F**aye the Flamingo
- **G**age the Giraffe
- **H**annah the Herring
- **I**an the Iguana
- **J**arrod the Jellyfish
- **K**eeli the Kitten
- **L**ara the Lioness
- **M**abel the Manatee
- **N**atalie the Needlefish
- **O**livia the Ostrich
- **P**etunia the Panda
- **Q**uintera the Queen Bee
- **R**yan the Rhinoceros
- **S**arah the Swan
- **T**homas theTiger
- **U**lysses the Urchin
- **V**ictoria the Viper
- **W**ill the Walrus
- **X**andy the Xenopus
- **Y**essie the Yak
- **Z**oe the Zebra

ANNIVERSARY

Our love has stood the test of time
Like a rock upon the shore
Fifty years so quickly have passed
And I only love you more
–*Thena Smith*

MORE

The years may come
And the years may go,
No matter what
Our love will grow—
Closer and better
Than ever before,
Season upon season,
I love you more.
–*Linda LaTourelle*

ALWAYS

May your love only grow sweeter
Through the passing years
May your life be full laughter
And only joy-filled tears.
May you always love each other
Just as much as today and more
And enjoy all the wonder
That your lives hold in store.
–*Thena Smith*

A bushel and a peck

After all these years…

A good marriage is based on a talent for friendship –*Nietzsche*

All I need is your love

A happy marriage is a long conversation that always seems too short –*Andre Maori*

Anniversary wishes and romantic kisses

Are we not like two volumes of one book? –*Valmore*

Because two people fell in love…

Because you loved me

Built to last

Celebrate our love with praise to our Lord above

A MAGIC MOMENT

A magic moment
I remember,
I raised my eyes
and you were there.
A fleeting vision,
the quintessence
Of all that's beautiful
and rare.
—Alexander Pushkin

LOVE YOU FOREVER

I will love you forever
And loving words will always say
And if I forget, please remind me
To tell you every day
—Thena Smith

First love, last love, true love

For wherever you go, I will go; and wherever you lodge, I will lodge *—Ruth 1:16*

For once in my life

Grow old with you

Happiness is my soul-mate

Here's to ____ amazing years

How lucky we are together!

I got you, babe

I love the way you love me

I promised—I do

It just gets better every year

Just the two of us

Let us be grateful to people who make us happy, they are the charming gardeners who make our souls blossom *—Proust*

Love is a circle without end, willing to give and ready to bend
—Linda LaTourelle

It had to be you

Love is above all, the gift of oneself

Love blesses the heart and confounds the mind *—Linda LaTourelle*

Love remains the same

Lucky in love

My lover my lover, my life

Oh, how we loved on the night we were wed!

Once upon an anniversary

One boy—one girl

Our love just gets better all the time

Our marriage is a duet—where you lead and I will follow

Remember the romance

Renewing our commitment

Saving forever for you

Side by side—year by year

So amazing together

So Jacob served seven years to get Rachel, but they seemed like Only a few to him because of his love for her *—Genesis*

Stuck like glue—that's me and you *—Linda LaTourelle*

Some things are meant to be, like me finding you and you marrying me *—Linda LaTourelle*

Still living happily ever after

Sweethearts for life!

Tale as old as time

Thank you for the years of love

That's how strong my love is

THE FIRST DAY
I wish I could remember
The first day,
First hour, first moment
Of your meeting me;
If bright or dim the season
It might be;
Summer or winter
For aught I can say.
So, unrecorded did it slip away,
So blind was I to see
And to for-see,
So dull to mark the
Budding of my tree
That would not blossom,
Yet, for many a May.
If only I could recollect it!
Such a day of days!
I let it come and go
As traceless as a thaw
Of bygone snow.
It seemed to mean so little,
Meant so much!
If only now I could recall
That touch,
First touch of hand in hand!
Did one but know!

–Christina Rossetti

The best of me and the best of you—that's how happily ever after comes true *–Linda LaTourelle*

The best is yet to come

The celebration continues

The color of my love

The music plays, my memories dance and the melody of us lingers on *–Linda LaTourelle*

The fairy tale continues…

25 YEARS
Twenty-five years ago
we became one
Little did we know
it would be so fun

–Linda LaTourelle

50 YEARS
Fifty years we celebrate
Sharing our life together
Family, friends and memories
Wonderful blessings we treasure

–Linda LaTourelle

The secret to a happy marriage is you loving me and me loving you

The secrets to a great marriage are playing, passion and persistent praying

The sparkle in my eyes reflects the love in your heart

The story of our love

These are the days to treasure

This I promise you forever

Through the years

Today we celebrate our love together

Together is better with you

Together—the nicest place to be

Together we have it all

Unforgettable moments together

We must be in love

We're livin' our love song

We've got a way about us

Wrapped up in your love forever

You are like honey created by the bees—you are everything that's sweet to me *-Linda LaTourelle*

With this ring I did wed!

You are the king and queen and everything in-between

10 years and just beginning

25 years—shining silver

50 years—the best years

I've been bad; can you forgive me?

Love means always saying sorry

Wish I'd learn to keep my foot out of my mouth!

Simply said—I was wrong!

To error is human; to forgive, divine   *-Alexander Pope*

Yep, it was my fault—sorry!

Yes, I'll sleep in the doghouse

You were right; I'm an idiot!

APOLOGY

Always forgive your enemies—nothing annoys them as much

Bear with each other and forgive whatever grievances you may have against one another. Forgive as the Lord forgave you. *-Colossians 3:13*

Can I buy your forgiveness—Visa or MasterCard???

Did I say—I'm sorry? I am.

Forgive me, please!

Forgive us our trespasses as we forgive them that trespass against us *-Matthew 6:12*

Forgiveness is the fragrance the violet sheds on the heel that has crushed it *-Mark Twain*

Have the last word—apologize!

I just called to say I'm sorry!

I'm so sorry for what I said. Now, what was it again?

In quarreling, the truth is always lost *-Cyrus*

APPLES

You're the apple of my eye,
Much sweeter than apple pie.
You're all my dreams come true,
There's no one quite like you.
–Linda LaTourelle

Apple blossom time

Apples of gold

Apples of love for you

Apples for the teacher

Apple-picking time

Bobbing for apples

Good apple pies are a considerable part of our domestic happiness *–Jane Austen*

He kept him as the apple of His eye *–Deuteronomy 32:10*

How do you like them apples?

It all began in a garden

Mom and apple pie

One red apple

She is the apple of my eye and the sweetness to my soul

Sweet as apple pie

The apple orchard

The shiny red apples

The apple doesn't fall far from the tree

The apple pie trees

The flowers of the apple are perhaps the most beautiful of any tree's, so copious and so delicious to both sight and scent –Henry David Thoreau

Under the apple tree—you and me

You are apple-solutely perfect

You are the apple of my eye

ART & ARTISTS

GOD'S ARTWORK
God doesn't color
within the lines
His colors aren't subdued
His artwork on earth and sky
Is the loveliest to be viewed
 –Thena Smith

MASTERPIECE
We are all artists gently guided
by our Master's hand—
painting a vision called life.
The blending of colorful emotions,
inspire us to create a magnificent
masterpiece of ourself.
 –Linda LaTourelle

A pigment of your imagination

Artfully yours

GALLERY
On the refrigerator
mommy hangs my art
when I create a picture
it brings a smile to her heart
painting, drawing or
crafting with glue
everything I make mom
I do it just for you
 –Linda LaTourelle

IT'S ART!
In pencil and crayon
In finger paint or pen
Some make me cry
And some make me grin.
What is it you ask—
That puts emotion in my heart?
It is the sweet little pieces
Of my little one's art!
 –Thena Smith

Art and soul

Art appreciation

Art is but the wine of life, deliciously fine –Linda LaTourelle

A picture is worth a thousand words

An artist at heart

An artist's apprentice

Art washes away from the soul the dust of every day life –Pablo Picasso

Art is therapy in slow motion

Artists live out loud

A work of art / heart

Be bold, color outside the lines

Broke 'n artists club

Budding artist

Caution: artist at work

TASTE OF PASTE

Oh, I love to go to school
And I love to use the paste.
I love to use it for my crafts
But I really love the taste!
I know I really shouldn't say it,
But I think that it's a waste,
To hold two pages together
With something as yummy as paste!
When the bell rings to call us for lunch,
I watch the kids that brought a bunch,
But nothing in their lunch bags taste
As good as my delicious paste!
Teacher sent a note to Mom
And in the note I read
That I could no longer bring my paste,
I must use glue instead!
I think it's really sad
And I hope it won't catch on
For what will I do, when all I have is glue
And all the yummy paste is gone??
—*Thena Smith*

Chalk it up to talent

Color me happy, color me blue, color me loved because of you

Crafty kids and a happy mom / dad

Creating a masterpiece

Dare to be extraordinary!

Every child reaches into his soul and paints his own masterpiece simply to please himself —*Linda LaTourelle*

Handprints of love

His / Her art spoke to mine

Home is where you hang your art

How fun thou art!

I draw—on paper, walls or anything

If you want to paint—just do it!

Imagine it—create it!

I made it all by myself

In art one can find them-self and lose them-self all at the same time

In every work of genius, we recognize our once rejected thoughts —*Ralph Waldo Emerson*

It's color time!

Masterpiece in the making

Mom's / Dad's treasured masterpiece

Mommy / Daddy sprinkled stars

My many colored days

My scribbles—Mom's say it's a masterpiece

One child's art is his mother's most wonderful treasure —*Linda LaTourelle*

Our moody Monet

Pavement Picasso

Painting Mom's world with the color of happiness

Painted to perfection

Pop / splat goes the easel

Scribbles and grins—that's how an artist begins

She / He discovered the artist within

Stand back and give me room

The colors of our life are many

The heart of the artist is a masterpiece —*Linda LaTourelle*

The imagination factory

The magic paintbrush / markers!

To imagine is everything

Within a child's thoughts exist a masterpiece

ATTITUDE

Anywhere is paradise; it's up to you

Attitude determines one's altitude

Attitude is everything, so have a good one

Attitude is a little thing that can make a big difference

Change your attitude—change your life

Changes in attitudes

Dare to be remarkable

Enjoy the little things in life

Excuses are reasons for failure

Happiness is an attitude

I am what I am because I choose it

If you think you can—you're right!

If you want to change your life, you must change your thoughts

In matters of style, swim with the current; in matters of principle, stand like a rock –Thomas Jefferson

It's not whether you win or lose, it's how you place the blame –Oscar Wilde

Luck is preparation meeting opportunity –Oprah Winfrey

Keep calm—think positive!

Never, never, never give up!

The heart feels things the mind does not understand

We tend to live up to our expectations of ourselves

What lies behind us and what lies before us are tiny matters, compared to what lies within us –Ralph Waldo Emerson

You color the world with love

You're my soul and my art's inspiration!

When nothing goes right—goes left

Is your attitude worth catching?

Your perception of me is not my problem

You want an attitude, I'll give you attitude with a capital "A"

BABY

AMAZING LOVE

I remember
the very instant when
I realized that in a matter
of moments, I was going to
meet my new daughter,
face to face, for the first time.
What an awe-inspiring gift
from God!
That thought
overwhelmed my soul
like nothing ever before!
And then here she was—
gracing my life,
overflowing my heart with
the most incredible love.
In that moment that my
life was forever changed,
as her first breath
took mine away—
and our life together began
as mother and child.
–Linda LaTourelle

A baby is a tiny piece of perfection

A bundle of joy

A day in the life

A honey of a baby

Addicted to baby

All in the family

The New Ultimate Guide to the Perfect Word – Volume 2

Ain't nothin' in the world like a brand new baby
Ain't she / he sweet?
All God's children
And then there was you
Baby dear, we're blessed you're here!
Baby, hold on to me
Baby love
Baby of mine
Baby! Oh, baby!
Baby's love is the best kind of love
Bald is beautiful!
Born to be loved
Bundle of love
Can't get enough of you
Center of our universe
Child of God
Cuddle bugs
Children teach us how to explore all that is around us
Cuz I'm the baby
Daddy's / Mama's little helper
Daddy's big girl / boy
Daddy's little princess / prince
Doing diaper duty
Everybody loves (name)
Fairytales do come true
For this child I prayed –1 Samuel 1:27
God's / Our little miracle
Happiness is a warm bottle
Here come the tears!
Hip, hip hooray you were born today!
Hush-a-bye baby
I'm spoiled, but not rotten!

I am baby hear me cry / laugh, grow, crawl, etc.
I am beautiful, I am wonderful, I am loved, because I am baby
I'm yours! You're mine!
I wanna be mama's / daddy's girl / boy
I want to hold your hand
Itty-bitty pretty baby
Just like a baby
Just me and my blankie
Look who's talking!
Lovable, snuggable you
Love at first sight
Love is you!
Mama's / Daddy's baby
Mirror, mirror on the wall, who's the most precious baby of all?
Mommy's / daddy's delight
My heart belongs to mommy / daddy
Nap time for (name)
One in a million
Only the best for our little darlin'
Our little Miss / Mr. Sunshine
Our little nursery rhyme
Patty cake, patty cake
Peek-a-boo! I love you!
Perfect love is a baby to love
Prince / Princess cuddle bug
Quiet! Baby's sleeping
Rock-a-bye baby
Rockin' the night away
Secret language of babies
Shake rattle and roll
Sing a song of babies

The Biggest Book of Words & Prompts for Scrapbooks, Art Journals & Crafts

Sleepy time gal / guy
So happy just to be with you!
Some kind of wonderful
Something about that face
Spoiled with love
Sweet on you!
Tales from my crib
Thank heaven for little babies
The cutest little baby face
The happiest mom / dad in the whole USA
The many faces of (name)
The next generation
The pitter-patter of little feet
There is nothing so precious as a sleeping baby
There was never a child so lovely but his mother was glad to get her baby to sleep -*Emerson*
There's only one pretty baby in the world—mine!
This thumb was made for sucking
They placed you in our arms and all our dreams came true
We believe in miracles
What a miracle!
What I love about you…
When I count my blessings, I count you as my best one
Worth the wait!
Yes, sir, that's our baby!
You are my sunshine
You are so beautiful to me!
You're just ducky and I'm so lucky!
You'll always be my baby
You've changed our lives forever

✤ *Baby Baths*

BATH TIME
Once I'm in my bubble bath
I like to stir up more.
Half the suds go in my eyes
And half go on the floor.
The fun is in the bubbles 'cause
They giggle on my skin,
And when I stick them on my face
They dangle from my chin.
And when I splash them hard enough
They pop and disappear,
And then my bath time's over 'cause
I've made the water clear.
–Nicholas Gordon © 2004

All clean now
Baby loves bath time
Bare bottoms welcome here
Bath, bed and beyond
Bathtub pals
Bear hugs and back scrubs
Bubble baby
Bubbly bubbles
Feelin' clean all over
Have beard will splash
Just ducky and me
Look at the way the bubbles pop
Pass the rubber ducky, please
Rubber ducky, you're the one
Scrub-a-dub-dub
Slippin' and slidin'
Soakin' and scrubbin'
Splish-splash, baby's first bath
Squeaky clean

Super-duper sudsy clean
Sweet cheeks
Toys in the tub, rub-a-dub-dub
Tubby time
Well, kiss my bubbles!
Wet, wild and wonderful
Where's my rubber ducky?
Wishing you a tub full of fun
You make bath time lots of fun

- ☐ Feeds Self
- ☐ Finds Belly Button
- ☐ Finds Blanket
- ☐ Finds Thumb / Toes
- ☐ Haircut
- ☐ Holds Bottle
- ☐ Holiday
- ☐ Outing
- ☐ Plays patty-cake
- ☐ Rolls over / sits-up
- ☐ Says dada / Mama
- ☐ Sleeps all night
- ☐ Smile / laugh
- ☐ Solid food
- ☐ Stands up
- ☐ Tooth
- ☐ Walking
- ☐ Waves hi and bye

♣ *Baby Blanket*

Baby loves her / his blankie
Got blankie?
I love my blankie
Just me and my blankie

- *Blanket nicknames*
    - ☐ Banky
    - ☐ Blankie
    - ☐ Fuzzy
    - ☐ Lovie
    - ☐ Manky
    - ☐ Silky
    - ☐ Snuggie
    - ☐ Woobie

♣ *Baby Firsts*

Write about each "first"

- ☐ Babysitter
- ☐ Bath
- ☐ Breast-fed
- ☐ Christening
- ☐ Christmas
- ☐ Cooing
- ☐ Crawling

♣ *Baby Food*

A hungry bear
Apple dumplin' darlin'
A tasty treat, I love to eat!
Bottle-fed
Burp baby burp
Burps are me
Feed me I'm yours
Feed me, feed me
Got milk ? / formula?
It's hard to be neat when you're learning to eat
Lip smackin' yummy
Name that food
Need milk!
PBJ—my favorite food!

Sweet potato kisses
The messiest little baby face
When do we eat?
Yummy, yummy, yummy

♣ Baby Pacifier
Paci, paci, who's got the paci?
Got binky?
I lost my binky!
I want my paci
Just me and my binkie
Oh, no, we lost the binkie!
Where did binky go?

- *Pacifiers nicknames*
  - ☐ Bibber
  - ☐ Binky
  - ☐ Num-num
  - ☐ Paci
  - ☐ Sassy
  - ☐ Sucky
  - ☐ Wubby
  - ☐ Ya-ya

♣ Crawling
Baby on the move
Baby's got her/his groove on
Bootie-scootin' boogie
I can do it
I get around
Look at her / him go!
Look out for the bump
Ready • Set • Crawl
Ready to go
Watch me crawl

♣ Growing
All things grow with love
Getting bigger all the time
Growing like a weed
Growing so big
Growing too fast
Here I grow
I'm a big kid now
Look at me grow
Ready • Set • Go
So big now
Watch me grow
You're growing so tall

♣ Nude
Bare baby bottom
Birthday suit
Brrr bottoms
Butt naked
Ditch the diaper
Free and flashy
In the buff
Nudie patootie
Sweet cheeks
The bare necessities
The littlest streaker

♣ Sleep time & Naps

Sweet dreams my baby
Sleep tight and rest
This day is done
And you are blessed!
–Linda LaTourelle

Sweet dreams my baby
Sleep tight and rest
This day is done
And you are blessed!
–Linda LaTourelle

Do you know how loved you are?
Such a precious twinkling star—
You're all our dreams come true
The best part of our life is you!
–Linda LaTourelle

Our little darling
Sleeping in her bed
Tucked-in tight
Prayers and stories read
Sleep well, my child
The whole night through
Our life is blessed
Because of you
–Linda LaTourelle

All tuckered out

Bath, bed and bedtime stories

Bedtime for babies and bears

Breakfast in bed with mommy

Caught napping

Cradle songs

Dozin' with daddy / mommy

Dream a little dream of me

Dream big, my little one

Good night sun, good night moon

I don't do mornings

If I'm not sleeping, nobody is

I love my jammies

In dreamland

Little monkey jumpin' on the bed

BEDTIME
Goodnight daylight
And having fun,
Goodnight toys,
The day is done.
Goodnight friends,
And sister and brother,
Goodnight dog
And father and mother.
Goodnight God
And everyone
Time for sleep
My bedtime's come.
–Linda LaTourelle

Tell me a story
And kiss me good-night
Pray with me daddy
And hug me real tight
- Linda LaTourelle

Sweet dreams and rest
Be yours tonight
Morning will come
And the sun will be bright
A new day of joy
With much to do
Sleep tight little one
We love you
–Linda LaTourelle

Winkin' and blinkin'
You're noddin' to sleep
Rest little one
And count the sheep
Mornin'll come soon
With fun things to do
Remember always—
How much I love you
–Linda LaTourelle

Twinkle twinkle
little star,
shining bright
wherever you are
–Linda LaTourelle

Lullaby and good night

Mama's / Papa's little snuggle bug

Night night, sleep tight

Once upon a dream

Rock-a-bye, my little baby

Sleep, baby sleep

Sleeping beauty

Slumberland express

Snoozing my life away

Starry, starry night

Such a sleepy baby

Tales from the crib

The land of nod

The wee small hours

Things that go burp in the night

Wake up little (name)

Wake-up sleepyhead

Waking up is hard to do

Who's been sleeping in my bed?

Zonked out!

✤ Standing & Walking

Baby in motion

Baby's got her groove on

Baby steps

Big steps for little feet

Both feet on the ground

MY FOOTPRINTS
Today I'll run and jump
Wade in puddles having fun,
I'll walk barefoot in the grass
And play until day is done.
One day my feet may take me
To places far and wide
Wherever life will take me
I know your love is by my side.
Perhaps I'll stroll upon the moon
Or run in some incredible race
Whatever I do, wherever I go
Will be by God's marvelous grace.
But for now I'll leave my footprints
Soft and tender upon your heart
And one day when you miss me
May my love this gift impart.
–Linda LaTourelle 2004

Chubby little toes

Come to mama / papa

Dancing feet

Footprints on my heart

Footsie wootsie, baby's tootsies

I saw her / him standing there

My brand new walking shoes

Pitter patter of little feet

Ready • Set • Stand

Ready to walk

Standin' on shaky ground

Stand up and take off

Step-by-step

Sweet little feet

Take off runnin'

Things that go bump in the day

Walking on sunshine

❖ Teething

A pool of drool
Baby's first tooth
Drooling over you
Bitin' and chewin' and hurtin'
Grinning and smilin'
Gumming it
Just gummin' it
I like to bite
It's poppin' through
Mama it hurts
My first tooth
My puffy gummy baby
Rough and red
So sore, so sad
Teething is for babies
Teething troubles
To bite or not to bite
Toddler's teething tales
Toothless wonder
Watch me drool

BABY ALPHABET

- A. Adoration
- B. Blanket
- C. Cuddly
- D. Darling
- E. Elated
- F. Father
- G. Grandparents
- H. Home
- I. In-laws
- J. Jabber
- K. Keepsakes
- L. Lovely
- M. Mother
- N. Nursery
- O. Original
- P. Prayers
- Q. Quiet
- R. Reflections
- S. School
- T. Treasures
- U. Umbilical
- V. Vacations
- W. Wishes
- X. Xtraspecial baby
- Y. Your love
- Z. Sleepy-time

BABY POEMS

LOVE YOU
Tiny fingers
And a button nose
Cheeks as pretty
As a morning rose
Wrapped in a blanket
Of pure sweet love
The most precious gift
Sent from above
–Linda LaTourelle

DAYS OF THE WEEK
Monday's child is fair of face
Tuesday's child is full of grace
Wednesday's child is full of woe
Thursday's child has far to go
Friday's child is loving and giving
Saturday's child works hard for its living
But the child born on the Sabbath
Is fair and wise and good
–Unknown

A BABY IS...
Sweetness and delight
Everything that's right
Beautiful and precious, too
The very best part of you
They fill your heart with love
And tenderness from above
–Linda LaTourelle

My life is very happy
As I tuck you in each night
Just to say a prayer for you
And hold you very tight
You are my precious child
The one that I adore
My heart is overflowing
Each day I love you more
–Linda LaTourelle

PAT-A-CAKE
Pat-a-cake,
Pat-a-cake,
Baker's man!
Bake me a cake
As fast as you can.
Pat it and sift it
And throw it up high,
Put it in the oven
For baby and I.

A GENTLE LULLABY
Sleep sweetly little baby
And in slumber may you dream
Of wonderful things yet to come
And places yet unseen
Sleep gently little angel girl
And know that you are loved,
Cradled in your own little crib
And guarded by angels from above
God bless you precious baby
Child of my heart so dear
May God bless all of your days
And keep his angels near
–Thena Smith

BABY'S LOVE
Tiny fingers
Wrapped snuggly
Around mine
Baby's love is
Simply divine
Smiles and coos
At the sound
Of my voice
Baby's love—
Oh, how I rejoice
Napping so peacefully
In slumbering rest
With baby's love—
I'm totally blessed
–Linda LaTourelle

LOOK AT ME!
Look at me—you will see
I'm having lots of fun
Life can only get better
'Cause I've just begun!
In this album are photos
Of me from the very start
Ones taken at my beginning
Nestled near mommy's heart
–Thena Smith

SUGAR GIRL
Your soft sugar kisses
And sweet baby smiles
These are the things
That make life worthwhile
–Linda LaTourelle

BABY'S FEET
A baby's feet,
Like seashells pink,
Might tempt,
Should heaven see meet,
And angel's lips to kiss,
We think,
A baby's feet.
–Algernon Charles Swinburne

Lucky is the woman who knows
the wondrous joy of a child
To love, for she has held the
Star of creation in her heart
And heart of God in her hands
–*Linda LaTourelle*

Sweetness and light
Holding you tight
That's what I love to do
–*Linda LaTourelle*

Little one
Tiny and fair
You are a blessing
And answer to prayer
–*Linda LaTourelle*

PRECIOUS YOU
A miracle pure and precious
All my dreams come true
My life was ever changed
The moment I had you
–*Linda LaTourelle*

Happiness is—
Having a baby
To hold and to love
To cherish and care for
What a gift from above!
–*Linda LaTourelle*

Joy and wonder
Someone to hug
Soft baby kisses
The one that I love!
–*Linda LaTourelle*

YOU
You're my sweetie
You're my honey
The apple of my eye
I love to hold
And sing to you—
A gentle lullaby
–*Linda LaTourelle*

My child, each and every day
Remember this to do—
Believe in love forever
And know that I love you.
–*Linda LaTourelle*

There is a little miracle
That wakes me every day
A precious tiny bundle
Whose love is here to stay
–*Linda LaTourelle*

God gave the very best
Of his goodness and grace
The moment he created
Your sweet baby face
–*Linda LaTourelle*

A tiny little
BABY
So innocent
And sweet
Will bring
Love and
Happiness
And make
Your family
Complete!
–*Thena Smith*

Mom says I'm her sugarplum
Sweet and pretty, too
She says I'm just perfect
All her dreams come true
–*Linda LaTourelle*

Children are magical
Right from the very start
One look in their eyes
They will steal your heart
–*Linda LaTourelle*

Through laughter
Smiles and tears
You'll always be
My baby dear
–*Linda LaTourelle*

AMAZING LOVE
Welcome little child
My life is ever blessed
The day you came home
I knew God sent his best
Your soft little hands
Grabbed hold of my heart
Wrapped it with love
What an amazing start!
My first look at you
And it was plainly clear
The most precious gift
Was you—my baby dear
–Linda LaTourelle

HOW DO I LOVE YOU?
How do I love you,
Let me count the ways.
I love you for this moment
And all the rest of my days.
I love you with all my heart,
And know that it is true.
There is no greater joy,
Than the love I have for you.
I love you as my baby
And every day to come.
You are the greatest blessing
So awesome and such fun.
Forever I will love you
And hold you close to me.
For you are everything
A mother could ever need.
I love you with a love so grand
And treasure every day
As you reach out your little hand
We'll make memories and play.
For in His infinite wisdom
God brought our love together
A lifetime isn't long enough
Thank goodness we have forever.
–Linda LaTourelle 2004
Inspired by Elizabeth Barrett Browning

The most beautiful view
Is the one I see
When I look at you
And you smile at me
–Linda LaTourelle

BALLET

A classic beauty

Ballerina beauty

Ballet is beautiful

Ballet is beauty in motion

Ballet keeps me on my toes

Center stage

Dancing from my soul

Dance like a prince / princess

Dancing queen

Fancy dancer

Future ballerina

Give me music and a mirror

Got shoes?

Gotta dance

Grace on her feet

Just me and my tutu

Keeping me on my toes

Look at her dance!

Music box dancer

Only when I dance

On pointe!

On the tips of my toes

Pretty ballerina

Softness and grace

Standing on the tip of my toes

Such beauty and grace—and a lovely face

The art of ballet
The dancer
The red shoes
Tippy, tippy tip-toe
Turning pointe
Tutu lovely
Tutu talented
Twirling in time
Watch her dance

BAND

A singer in a rock and roll band
Band nerd and loving it
Banner moments
Breathe in the music
Can you reed my lips?
Ebony and ivory
Forward, march!
Got band?
Got flags?
Got music?
Half-time is the best time
He's got rhythm
Heads held high
Hittin' the high notes
I love a parade
I love band / camp
It's a band thing
I've got the music in me
Keep in step
Leader of the band
Live in concert
March to the music

No strings attached
Peace • Love • Band
Proud to be a band nerd
Queen of the baton
The band plays on
The drum majorette
The family band
Watch the conductor
We've got music

BEARS

• More in "TOYS" section

Wrapped in fuzzy fur
Full of dreams and kisses
My teddy snuggles close to me
He knows my hopes and wishes
–Linda LaTourelle

A bear is always there
Bear hugs / kisses
Beary loverly
Bear-Wee-Wuvable
Beary best friend
Best friends fur life
Cross as a bear
Don't feed the bears!
Dreamin' with my teddy
Fuzzy Wuzzy was my bear
I collect teddy bears
I'm a beary special baby
I wish I were your teddy bear
Hungry as a bear
Just me and my teddy

Teddy bear, teddy bear
Hold me tight
We'll have fun
'Til the morning light
–Linda LaTourelle

No one knows me better
Than my teddy
–Linda LaTourelle

There are no hugs
Like my teddy hugs
–Linda LaTourelle

Sweetness and light
Holding you tight
That's what I love to do
–Linda LaTourelle

Ever faithful
Always there
My best friend
My teddy bear
–Linda LaTourelle

Teddy bear, teddy bear
Close to you
Smiling and happy
I love you, I do
–Linda LaTourelle

The nicest days ever can be
The days we share
My teddy and me

Just teddy and me
Let me be your teddy bear
Love bears all things
Love me—love my teddy!
Mama, papa and baby bear
My teddy hates baths—me too!
My teddy told me
Stuffed with love for you

Tattered and torn-teddy is worn
Teddy's aren't just for kids
Tender-loving bear
Teddy bears are stuffed with love
There's no bear like an old bear
There's nothing like a teddy

♣ Pooh Bear

A honey of a day
A little boy and his bear will always be playing –A. A. Milne
Did somebody say honey?
I love my hundred acres
I've got rumbly in my tummy
If you live to be one hundred, I hope to live to be one hundred minus one day
Just me and my Pooh
Lovable ole' pooh
Oh bother!
Pooh, pooh—Pooh!
Silly old bear!
The wonderful thing about...
Tigger-iffic
Sometimes, said Pooh, the smallest things take up the most room in your heart –A. A. Milne

BEAUTY

The most beautiful view
is the one I see
when I look at you
–Linda LaTourelle

Pretty little face
A smile so sweet
Every day with you
Makes life complete
— *Linda LaTourelle*

A thing of beauty is a joy forever

American beauty

Baby, you're so beautiful!

Beautiful and bossy!

Beauty and brains!

Blooming into a woman

Bodacious and beautiful

Cha-cha charming, little chick

Chantilly lace and a pretty face

Color me beautiful

Cute, cute, cute!

Don't hate me 'cause I'm beautiful

Funny face, I love you!

Glamour girls

Good morning, gorgeous

Hello good lookin'

Hello, gorgeous

Here's looking at you kid

Hey good lookin'!

Hey pretty baby!

I enjoy being a girl

I'm a heartbreaker

I'm going to be a teenage idol

Isn't she lovely?

Just call me baby

Little Miss / Mr. America

Look at that face

Lovely lady

Make over magic

Mirror, mirror, on the wall

Model in the making

Natural beauty

Oh, you beautiful doll!

Ooh la la!

Pretty as a picture

Pretty girl with the big brown eyes

Pretty little tomboy!

Pretty woman!

She must have been a beautiful baby—look at her now!

She's a heartbreaker

Simply irresistible

Smile, you are beautiful!

Sometimes all I can do is say "wow!"

The beauty of a woman only grows with each passing year

The many faces of _____

The love from a husband's heart shines on the face of his wife
—*Linda LaTourelle*

There's something about that face

True beauty comes from within

What a doll!

Which way to Hollywood?

You are so beautiful to me

You bet I'm cute!

You were never lovelier

You're beautiful and you're mine

For every beauty there is an eye somewhere to see it —*Shakespeare*

When you look
into a woman's eyes
you will see the beauty
in her heart
–Linda LaTourelle

The beauty that is in him,
is beyond comprehension
–Linda LaTourelle

Beauty is a welcome guest
–Goethe

The power of finding beauty
in the humblest things
makes life lovely
–Louisa May Alcott

To him, she seemed
simply beautiful
–Linda LaTourelle

The loveliest face I see
shines from the beauty
that lies within his soul
–Linda LaTourelle

Did my heart love till now?
forswear it, sight!
For I ne'er saw true beauty
till this night
–Shakespeare

Tell them dear, that if eyes
were made for seeing,
then beauty is its own
excuse for being
–Ralph Waldo Emerson

Perfect beauty,
as in dewdrops, lakes
and diamonds
–Henry David Thoreau

When you stop looking
for beauty, you will
discover it—within yourself
–Linda LaTourelle

When you think about
beautiful things—
always remember to think
about how beautiful you are
–Linda LaTourelle

Think of all the beauty
still left around you
And be happy
–Anne Frank

A girl should be two things:
classy and fabulous
–Coco Chanel

The beauty of a person
is not an outward adornment,
it is an inward reflection
of one's soul
–Linda LaTourelle

The most beautiful person
you should embrace
is yourself, so rejoice!
–Linda LaTourelle

BIRDS

The bird of paradise
alights only upon
the hand that
does not grasp
–John Berry

A bird's-eye view

A feather in my cap

As light as a feather

Be my twitterbug

Bird of paradise

Bless our nest

Bluebird of happiness

THE BLUEBIRD
Today at dawn
there twinkled through
The pearly mist–
a flash of blue
So dazzling bright
I thought the sky
Shone through
the rifted clouds
on high,
'Til, by and by,
a note so honey-sweet I heard,
I knew that bright flash was a bird!
—*Evaleen Stein*

Cardinal catch

Conures rock!

Cranky cockatoo

Eagle eye

Everybirdy loves some birdy

Feathers in your nest

Feed the birds

Fly like an eagle

I give a hoot!

In a bluebirds eye

Wise as an owl

May the bluebird of happiness color your day with joy

The early bird catches the worm

Kill two birds with one stone

Lovey-dovey love birds

Madder than a wet hen

Make a nest of pleasant thoughts

Naked as a jaybird

Owl be loving you always

Parakeet pleaser

Passion for parrots

Peeps galore

Perched in my soul

Polly-parrot

Polly wolly doodle all day

Proud as a peacock

Rockin' robin

Room for wrent

Song of the nightingale

Sparrow lover

This place is for the birds

Tweet, tweet

Tweeter and twitter

Voice like a nightingale

THE FIRST RED-BIRD
I heard a song at daybreak,
So honey-sweet and clear,
The essence of all joyous things
Seemed mingling in its cheer.
The red-bird rocked and shone.
The blue sky, and his feathers
Flashed o'er by golden light,
Oh, all my heart with rapture thrilled,
It was so sweet a sight!
—*Evaleen Stein*

THE EAGLE
The dome of heaven is thy house
Bird of the mighty wing,
The silver stars are as thy boughs
Around Thee circling.
Thy perch is on the eaves of heaven
Thy white throne all the skies
Thou art like lightning driven
Flashing over paradise!
—*Edwin Curran*

THE BIRD'S BATH
In our garden we have made
Such a pretty little pool,
Lined with pebbles neatly laid,
Filled with water clean and cool
When the sun shines warm and high
Robins cluster 'round its brink,
Never one comes flying by
But will flutter down to drink.
Then they splash
and splash and splash,
Spattering little showers bright
All around, 'til off they flash
Singing sweetly their delight.
–Evaleen Stein

HOPE
Hope is the thing with feathers
that perches in the soul,
And sings the tune without the words
And never stops at all
–Emily Dickinson

GRACE
Beautiful bird
Look how you fly
Gliding so gracefully
High in the sky
–Linda LaTourelle

No bird soars too high
if he soars with his own wings
–William Blake

Keep a green tree in your heart
perhaps a singing bird will come
–Chinese proverb

BIRTH

MY FAMILY
Welcome to our world
I heard my mama say
We waited oh so long
For this very special day
She looked into my eyes
Her face was all aglow
Tears ran down her cheeks
And I knew that I was home
More love than I imagined
And ever hoped to see
I am so very lucky because
I have a brand new family
–Linda LaTourelle

A baby is a gift of love

A child is born

A daddy / mommy is born

A moment to treasure

A star is born

A time to be born…

All the pain was worth the gain

All my wishes came true the moment I saw you

A whole new world

And the story begins…

Angels danced on the day you were born

Baby love is mommy's love

Baby o'mine

Blessed beginnings

Bonding for the first time

ONLY A BABY

Only a baby small,
Dropt from the skies
Only a laughing face,
Two sunny eyes;
Only two cherry lips,
One chubby nose;
Only two little hands,
Ten little toes.
Only a golden head,
Curly and soft;
Only a tongue that wags
Loudly and oft;
Only a little brain,
Empty of thought;
Only a little heart,
Troubled with naught.
Only a tender flower,
Sent us to rear;
Only a life to love
While we are here;
Only a baby small,
Never at rest;
Small, but how dear to us,
God knoweth best.

–Matthias Barr

Born free

Born to love

Bundle from heaven

Celebrating your birth

Children are a blessing

Children are a gift from God

Countdown to miracle

Cradle of dreams

Crowning glory—baby's arrival

For the first time

General hospital

Got mommy milk?

Great expectations

He's / She's a miracle

Here at last!

Here I am come and rock me

Here she / he comes!

Fearfully and wonderfully made

I made a wish and you came true

In one amazing moment, you were born and ours to love

In the beginning…

It all began with love

It's a miracle!

It's all about you, baby!

Just arrived!

Labor day

Labor of pure love

Let the joy begin

Look out world, here I come!

Look what the stork flew in!

Love and joy wrapped in a blanket of miracles

Love began at first sight

Love was born today

Make room for baby

Mine / Ours for keeps

Mirror, mirror on the ceiling, who's that baby I see screaming?

Miracles still happen

More precious than gold

My shining star was born today

New arrival

Now appearing

Now for the breast of the story

On the day you were born...

Once upon a time...

Our new arrival...

Out of my tummy, into my world

Prayers were answered today

Presenting baby (name)

Ready or not, here I come!

Small bundles, big blessings

Special delivery to us

Sweet beginnings and happy endings

Sweet blessings from above

Ten tiny fingers, ten tiny toes

The big day—you're home!

The first time ever I your face

The journey of a lifetime began the moment I heard your first cry

The miracle of life / you

The most precious gift

'Til there was you

Today love has a name

Today our love came to life

Welcome to the world, little one

What a difference you have made in my life

What a wonderful name—Baby!

When a baby is born, so is a parent

Whole lotta rockin' tonight

With your first breath, time stood still for a moment

Wrapped in my sweet mama's arms

You are everything to us

You are the sunshine of our life

Your first breath was breathtaking

Your genes are a perfect fit

You touched my life with love

BIRTHDAY

The presents are wrapped
With ribbons so bright
The cake is all decorated
For your party tonight
We're getting together
Just to celebrate you
So excited and happy
May your wishes come true
–*Linda LaTourelle*

A birthday full of dreams come true —that's what I wish for you

A cause for party and celebration

A little cake and punch made it a night to remember

A pocketful of wishes to you!

A little cake and lots of fun, we'll party 'til the day is done!

A pinch to grow an inch

Bring on the presents!

Cake Decorating 101

A woman is always younger. than a man of equal years –*Elizabeth Barrett Browning*

A world of birthday wishes to you

A year of wonder!

After all, tomorrow is another day –*Margaret Mitchell*

Aged to perfection

Ain't no cure for the common birthday—so enjoy every minute!

Always young at heart

An ageless wonder—you!

And many more!

Another year older and better too!

Another year older and better, too—oh how we love to celebrate with you!

Another year older and sweeter, too—a happy birthday from me to you!

As old as the hills! Or not!

Balloons and candles and cake, oh my!

Behold, the birthday king / queen

Birthdays are an ordinary day with added sweetness and love

Birthdays are an ordinary days to celebrate you

Birthdays are feathers in the broad wing of time –Jean Paul Richter

Birthdays are the gift of nature, but parties are the gift of friends

Birthday wishes and champagne kisses—that's what I want for you!

Birthday wishes, chocolate kisses

Born to be the icing on your cake!

Carry your childhood in your heart and always be young and happy

Celebrating the sweetness of you

Count your blessings, not the years

Counting the candles that light your happy day

Eat, drink and celebrate!

Eating my cake and wearing it too!

Enjoy every day like it's your birthday

Every birthday is a new beginning

Every day is a great day to celebrate

Forever young—forever loved

From morning 'till night, may all your wishes be bright, full of laughter and cheer with friends family near –Linda LaTourelle

Getting better all the time

Happiness on your birthday and every day throughout the year

Happy birthday to the one I love

Happy birthday to you, we love you, we do! Have great day on your birthday and many more, too!

Have a plum-good happy birthday

Having a party and you're invited!

Hey diddle-diddle, you're no longer little—Happy Birthday!

Hooray, hooray—it's a birthday day!

May you have birthday cheer and blessings throughout the year!

I'd rather have cupcakes

It's all about you—the presents and the sweet day of love!

It's for you—may wishes come true!

It's my birthday, I'm so excited!

It's not the age, it's the attitude and yours is amazing

It's the big one!

It's your birthday time again

It's your birthday—do what you want!

King / Queen of the party!

Let them eat cake!

Let's hear a cheer, Happy Birthday all year!

Life begins at (age)

Life is short, open presents first

Make a wish and blow!

Mama / Daddy sure does know how to throw a party!

Many happy returns!

May all your wishes come true!

May every candle on your cake bring a wish for every day throughout the year

May multiple blessings be sent your way as you have a happy birthday today –Thena Smith

May roses kissed in sunshine, glistening in the morning dew be only half as wonderful as the birthday planned for you –Thena Smith

May this be a very blessed birthday

May your birthday bring showers of blessings that grow the whole year through

May your cake be plenty and your wishes be more

Much love on your birthday

My favorite gift is you!

More cake, more candles, more fun, more party! More good times with you!

My greatest birthday wish was answered when I found you

No reason to pout, it's your birthday, let's shout and have a party tonight!

Oldie, but goodie!

Once upon a time there was a very special birthday...

One happy day to celebrate you and a good excuse for a party, too!

One royal birthday for a prince / princess

One year older—more beautiful, too!

Over the hill and lovin' the scenery

Pamper yourself today

Parties are a wonderful way to celebrate you!

Party down, let's paint the town!

Party fit for a princess / prince

Party time is here, let's eat some cake and cheer!

Presents and cake and friends— what fun!

Presents, cake and candles, oh my! Happy birthday, how times flies –Linda LaTourelle

Queen / King for a day!

Ready, set, blow—look at you grow!

Ready, set, blow your candles out— let's eat cake and dance

Sexy at (age)

Sharing joys along the way—our life is a blessing every day
–Linda LaTourelle

So many candles and too much cake

So much excitement, so much fun!

Someone like you makes every day seem like a birthday!

Such a wonderful birthday!

Surprise—we're having a party to celebrate your birthday!

The age of innocence

The bigger the candles, the more wishes you get

The evidence is clearly present— there's a party going on!

The guest of honor—you!

The hardest years are the ones between seven and seventy

The longer I live, the more I see that I am never wrong about anything –George Bernard Shaw

The birthday queen / king

The icing on my birthday cake—is you!

The star of the party is you!

The sweetest joy, the saddest woe is when a birthday comes and goes

The years tell us much that the days never knew –Emerson

There's no time like getting presents!

To celebrate a happy birthday together is my present for you

To the world you are you—but to me you are amazing!

Today is the day I celebrate you—my most favorite gift ever!

Today is your day—enjoy the party!

Too many candles, not enough cake!

Too much cake—so much fun!

Warm wishes, tropical kisses and a birthday in paradise with you

We're having some fun now and it's just begun!

We're just the party animals at the zoo with you—celebrate!

We're screamin' for cake!

Welcome to the birthday bash!

What a difference a year makes!

When you wish upon a candle—just close your eyes and blow!

Wish big—dream bigger!

You bring the present and I'll bring the cake and together we make a party and celebrate

You take the cake!

You're growing up too fast!

You're not getting older, you're getting better—almost perfect!

You're the icing on my cake

You're the king / queen of this party —Happy Birthday!

You're the star of the show!

Your birthday is a gift to you—and me!

Your birthday is no ordinary day, it's extraordinary because it's all about you

Your birthday is the icing on the cake of life

Youth has been a habit of hers for so long that she could not part with it –Rudyard Kipling

Youth has no age and you look beautiful today—Happy Birthday!

✤ Birthday-Belated

Oh, no! I knew I was forgetting something—your birthday!

Heard you had a great birthday—just heard a little late! Hope it was great fun—like you!

I didn't forget your birthday—I just wanted to help extend the celebration!

I didn't forget your birthday... it was a delayed reaction

It's your birthday and I cried cuz I missed it—happy day!

The Biggest Book of Words & Prompts for Scrapbooks, Art Journals & Crafts

Oops, your birthday card was lost in the mail!

Belated birthday blessings—my apologies for missing it, hope it was delightful like you!

I'm not late—I'm early in another time zone

Roses are red, birthdays are blue wish I'd been there with you

Sorry I missed your special day!

So I hope you had a terrific birthday—wish we could have been there with you to celebrate

Sorry that my wish is late, but please don't worry;
Love and prayers and wishes are not to be in a hurry!
–Thena Smith

❖ Birthday Milestones

1–ONE

ONE
One smile
One year
One candle
One cupcake
One birthday
One baby
One love
One
You!
–Linda LaTourelle

BIG SMILE
Today I'm a big kid,
With one candle on my cake.
I'll smile for all the pictures
My mommy likes to take
–Linda LaTourelle

BABY'S BIRTHDAY
Baby's turning one today
Time to celebrate
Cupcakes, ice cream
Lollipops, too!
Balloons and presents,
Let's have a big to-do.
A day to remember
And mark with a 'B'
It's baby's birthday—
Such a grand memory!
–Linda LaTourelle

ONE JOY
What joy, what fun!
Our little baby
Is turning one.
–Linda LaTourelle

One big wish!

One year old and oh so sweet!

Baby's turning one—time for some cake and lots of fun

Celebrating the first birthday

Fun to be one

Happiest one under the sun!

Happy birthday to our little one!

Having such fun now that I'm one!

Hip, hip hooray—baby's one today!

It's the big one!

It's wonderful fun, now I am one!

My first birthday party

One little candle

One love, one baby, one birthday

One year old—good as gold!

So much fun with our little one!

One-derful birthday today!

The princess / prince is one today

129 | ultimatebookcompany.com

2-TWO

TWO YOU
Let's have a party
To celebrate two!
Happy happy birthday
All our love to you!
—Linda LaTourelle

PARTY TWO
It's time to celebrate
Birthday number two
With yummy cupcakes
and ice cream for you
—Linda LaTourelle

Baby you are two and I love you

Bippity-boppity-boo, baby is two

Happy bear-thday two you!

Happy birthday to baby who's two

Happy birthday two you!

I can't believe how fast you grew, it's so amazing—now you're two!

I'm two, watch what I can do!

It's a party two-day!

One year older and adorable two!

The joy of you, now that you're two

Totally two—a party for you!

Two delightful! Two cute!

Two times the fun!

Totally two-riffic!

We can't believe you're two

Whoop-dee-do, baby is two!

Woo-hoo, now I'm two!

You are two-riffic in every way

Zippity-do—look who's two!

3-THREE

I'M THREE
My party time is here
I'm three years old today
Come celebrate with me
We'll have lots of fun you'll see
—Linda LaTourelle

HAPPY THREE
Hey! Look at me!
Today I am three
I'm as happy
As a kid can be!
—Thena Smith

Baby's happy as can be—today he / she is turning three

Birthday party number three

Hey! Hey! Three years old today!

I'm so big, can't you see? Because today I'm three!

Look and see—baby's three!

Look at me today—I'm three!

Shout it out! Baby's three!

Sweet as can be, baby is three!

Three times a lady / baby

Triple treats now that I am three!

4-FOUR

Big and bold—four years old

Finally four—time for more!

Four years old and fabulously fun

Four years, four wishes, for you

Fine, funny and four!

Hear the roar! Look who's four!

Look who's four and ours to adore

Not small anymore—today I'm four

FOUR FOR YOU
Turning four today!
My baby turns four today
How the time has flown...
Four wonderful years
What happiness I've known!
–Thena Smith

PARTY TODAY
It seems like such a dream
You're turning four today
Let's eat cake and ice cream,
Have a party and play
–Linda LaTourelle

There's a party and more for the one who is four

Three no more—today I'm four

Funny, fabulous and four!

5–FIVE

GROWING BIG
You are more grown up now
And soon you will see
How a five-year-old is given
Much more responsibility
–Thena Smith

HAPPY FIVE
Five years old
And oh so sweet.
We've lots of gifts
And a yummy treat.
So let's have fun
It's all about you
Making your wishes
And dreams come true.
–Linda LaTourelle

Ain't no jive, our kid is five!

Being five is full of fun!

Fab five!

Five is cool and so much fun, enjoy the day!

Five years old today—let's shout a big hooray!

Five times the fun—celebrating you!

Four no more!

Hi-five birthday boy / girl!

It's a high-five day for you!

Today I turned five, you see—
Look at the party made for me

6–SIX

SIX
Six years old
growing tall
time for a party
come one and all
–Linda LaTourelle

CELEBRATE SIX
It's a great day
let's celebrate quick
our sweet child
is turning six!
–Linda LaTourelle

IT'S YOUR DAY
Your birthday is a special day
And your party will be, too
You're six years old now
Time to celebrate you
–Linda LaTourelle

Happy six!

I'm six—watch my tricks!

Silly sixes
Six is great—let's celebrate!
Smart, sweet and six!
So happy you are six!
Super six
Silly, sweet and sunny—six is funny!

7-SEVEN

How special to be seven!
The world is exciting for you
With fun and games
And special friends
To go through the day with you!
–Thena Smith

Seven candles—that's lucky!
Seven's so much fun!
Seven years old—big and bold!
Simply super and seven!
Happy seventh birthday!
Super at seven!
The celebration is on for you to have a happy birthday
You rock seven!

8-EIGHT

It's a party—don't be late
Our sweet son / daughter
Is turning eight
–Linda LaTourelle

Birthday party tonight
Time to celebrate
A very cool kid
Who just turned eight
–Linda LaTourelle

Being eight is going to be great!
I'm finally eight, let's celebrate!
It's great to be eight
Let's celebrate number eight
Someone who is turning eight!
We're excited you are eight, hope your party is great!
We're having a party to celebrate

9-NINE

I'm nine and the world is all mine
It's birthday time— you're nine!
Nine is fine, so glad you're mine!
Now that you're nine, life is so fine!
One year older and oh, so fine, now that you are turning nine!
Nine times you is a whole lotta love!
Today I am nine—the party's fine!

10-TEN

A perfect ten!
Ten birthday wishes just for you, here's to making them all come true!
Today you are ten!
Ten wishes for a perfect birthday
Ten times the fun, ten times the wishes—just for you!
Ten is terrific!
Totally ten today!

13-THIRTEEN

13 and lucky!
A brand new teen at thirteen!
Celebrate being thirteen

Happy thirteen day to you!
Lucky thirteen!
No more a kid or in-between, today you are legally a teen!
Sweet teen at thirteen!
Thirteen and all grown-up
Thirteen, no longer a tween!

16–SIXTEEN

16 candles!
Sixteen betwixt and between!
Happy birthday, sweet 16
Sweet little sixteen
You are 16, going on 17!

18–EIGHTEEN

All grown up and ready to vote!
Eighteen at last!
Eighteen is a time for celebration!
Legal at last! Are you ready for a big birthday blast?
As we grow old, the beauty steals inward -Emerson
18 and still a teen, but all grown up
Where did the years go? Happy 18th!

21–TWENTY-ONE

21 and all grown-up!
I'm 21—let's celebrate!
I'm an adult! Woo-hoo!
It's the big 2-1!
Legal in every way!
You are legal now and we're so proud of you—happy 21st!

40–FORTY

39 and holding
Every birthday is a new beginning
Forty years young!
Happy 40th birthday
Life begins at 40!
Sporty at forty
Stay young—lie about your age!
The big 4-0

50–FIFTY

Fifty years is just a small start
Of the life I pray you live,
For you have so much joy
And love for others to give
—*Thena Smith*

49 and holding!
50 is golden, not olden!
A perfect ten—times five!
A reason to party—you!
Fifty, fabulous, fit and full of life
Life begins at 50
A royal birthday for the king / queen
So many candles, so much cake!
Counting the candles that light our friendship!

❖ *Birthday-Friend*

A best friend is worth a thousand birthday wishes

Birthdays come and birthdays go, but our friendship is forever

Today's a very special day
for you my friend I pray
birthday wishes all year through
and all your dreams come true.
–Linda LaTourelle

May your days be full of surprises,
And peace and joy and love
And your birthday be the best
With blessings from above!
–Linda LaTourelle

A friend like you is a wish come true

Birthday wishes for a friend

Count your age by friends not years

Dearest friend—I celebrate you!

Every birthday I love you more

Friends are the icing on the cupcakes of life

Friendship is the gift that we receive every day

Happy birthday, treasured friend

Heartfelt joy on your birthday!

It's your party, you can dance if you want to

It's all about you, my friend!

No ordinary birthday for such an extraordinary friend!

Our friendship stands the test of time, one birthday at a time

Real friends remembers your birthday, not your age

Sending warmest wishes for a magnificent day, just like you

True friendship knows no distance on a birthday

When you wish upon your candles, may all your wishes come true!

Wishing the best birthday to my best friend!

♣ Birthday Love

A cupcake, a kiss for the one I adore

Blessed on my birthday because of all the love that you give me

Completely in love, happy birthday

Every birthday I love you more

Grow old with me, the best is yet to be –Robert Browning

Happy birthday to my favorite present!

Have your cake and eat it, too!

How do I love thee? Let me count the candles

Love is the gift I give to you— Happy birthday, darling

May your cake be sweet and your party grand

The best gift on a birthday is love

Today I celebrate my love for you

Wishes and kisses—your birthday's delicious—like you!

You are all my birthday wishes

You are the best birthday present ever

You are the frosting on my cupcake

You are the icing I love to taste

You get three wishes and more!

You're my king / queen for a day —and all year through!

You are the present I wished for

Your every wish is my joyous pleasure to fulfill

✣ Birthday–General

A little cake and icing and a night to remember!

A year in the life of...

For he's a jolly good fellow

Because the birthday of my life is come—my love is come to me –Christine Rossetti

Every day is your birthday to celebrate anew, so spend each moment praising the wonder of you –Linda LaTourelle

Born to party and eat cupcakes!

Let us celebrate the occasion with wine and sweet words –Plautus

My heart is like a singing bird...

The birthday fun has just begun!

The older the fiddler, the sweeter the tune –English proverb

We are all the same age inside

We turn not older with age, but newer every day –Emily Dickinson

You are never to old to dream

You were born an original

Youth comes but once in a lifetime—celebrate each day.

Youth has no age

BOATS & SAILING

Ahoy matey
All aboard
Anchors away
Captain at the helm
Come sail away
Crazy about kayaking
Cruising for adventure
Don't rock the boat
God bless this boat and all who sail in her
If you want to swim you gotta get out of the boat
Island paradise
Just sailin'
My body is here, but my heart has gone sailing
Row, row, row your boat
Sail away
Sailing takes me away
Sailing, sailing, over the...
Shipmates
Steady as she goes
That sinking feeling
The best ships are friendships
The love boat
The old man and the sea
Whatever floats your boat
Where the ocean meets the sky, I'll be sailing back to you

BODY BEAUTIFUL

✣ Eyes

And sisters, from whose tender eyes the love in mine hath sweet replies –Phoebe Carry

Baby blues
Bright eyes
Brown-eyed girl
Can't take my eyes off of you
Dreamy-eyed
Drink to me, only with thine eyes

Your eyes are so pretty
so sparkly and bright
You captured my heart
It was love at first sight
–Linda LaTourelle

Emerald eyes

In his / her/ my daughter's eyes

In my father's / mother's eyes

In your eyes

Moms really do have eyes in the back of their heads

My eyes adore you

My mamas / daddy's eyes

Pretty little angel eyes

She's / He's the apple of my eye

Smoke gets in your eyes

Soap gets in my eyes

The eye's have it

The eyes will tell what the heart is speaking

Them-there eyes

The one with the googly eyes

Tiny tots with their eyes all aglow

The world is more beautiful when it's reflected in your eyes

Through my husband's / wife's eyes

Through the eyes of a child

Through the eyes of a grandparent

When I look into your eyes

When Irish eyes are smiling

Where'd you get those peepers?

♣ Face

BABY FACE
Sweet little baby face
True beauty at it's best
Enchanting love and grace
My life is ever blessed
–Linda LaTourelle

Dimple darlin'

Five foot two, eyes of blue

Funny face

Head, shoulders, knees and toes

Kissy-face

Love at first sight

Mama's / Daddy's little baby face

Peek-a-boo, I see you

Pretty cheeky

Puttin' on my happy face

Seeing is believing

Sweet cheeks

Sweet lips

The many faces of (name)

This is my happy face

Winkin', blinkin' and nod

Winkin' and grinnin'

♣ Hands

BABY'S HANDS
Baby's hands are tiny
Innocent from the start
Reaching deep inside
They grab onto your heart
–Linda LaTourelle

MY HANDS

My little hands play peekaboo
or wave and say how do you do
When I fall down they pick me up
or hold my little sippy cup
My little hands reach for your hug
when I am in my bed so snug
And when my hands I fold to pray
'tis thanks I give for you today.
My little hands in time will grow
but forever will my love be so
Your big hands have held me tight
and taught me how to live so right
so take this tiny print of mine
and know that your love is divine
I know you're there in all I do
Holding my hand—loving me true
–Linda LaTourelle

PERFECT HANDS

My hands are growing bigger
And can hold so much more stuff
Over all, I'd say I'm perfect
Just exactly big enough!
–Thena Smith

ETUDE REALISTE

No rosebuds yet by dawn impearled
Match, even in loveliest lands,
The sweetest flowers in all the world
Are those of a babies hand.
–Algernon Charles Swinburne

There is nothing quite so grand, as the touch of my child's hand. –Linda LaTourelle

Little hands, oh so small

Mama's / Daddy's hands love baby's hands

Mr. Thumbkin

My little hands

My sucky thumb

Patty-cake, patty-cake

Rings on her fingers

These little hands of mine

The touch of baby's hand

Thumbody's baby

Thumbody loves you / me

Touched by the hand of God

Two hands that hold your heart

Under my thumb—that's my dad

Wrapped 'round daddy's / mommy's finger

All thumbs

Clap-clap-clap

Clappin' and shoutin'

Daddy's / Mommy's hand holds baby's hand

Don't bite the hand that feeds you

Finger lickin' good

Fingerprints on my heart

Five little fingers

Give me five!

Handle with care

Hands down

Handprints on the wall

Helping hands

Hip-hip-yeah!

Holding daddy's / mommy's hand

I'm thumbody's baby now

♣ **Feet**

PITTYPAT AND TIPPYTOE
All day long they come and go—
Pittypat and Tippytoe;
Footprints up and down the hall,
Playthings scattered on the floor,
Finger-marks along the wall,
Tell-tale smudges on the door...
By these presents you shall know
Pittypat and Tippytoe.
—*Eugene Field*

Barefootin'
Barefoot in the park
Bells on her toes
Daddy long-legs
Dancin' feet
Feet, don't fail me on my first steps
Footloose and fancy-free
Happy feet
He walks on water
Hot legs
Kickin' up your heels
Head, shoulders, knees and toes
If the shoe fits
I'm still standin'
I walk the line
Little feet smell so sweet
Long and lanky
Look who's walking
My toes were made for eatin'
One step at a time
Playing footsie
Playing with my tootsies
Put your right foot in
Sneaky feet
Ten little piggies

MY FOOTPRINTS
Today I'll run and jump
Wade in puddles having fun,
I'll walk barefoot in the grass
And play until day is done.
One day my feet may take me
To places far and wide
Wherever life will take me
I know your love is by my side
Perhaps I'll stroll upon the moon
Or run in some incredible race
Whatever I do, wherever I go
Will be by God's marvelous grace
But for now I'll leave my footprints
Soft and tender upon your heart
And one day when you miss me
May my love this gift impart.
-*Linda LaTourelle* ©2004

FOOTPRINTS
My footprints are a part of me—
The foundation that they lay
Keeps me ever faithful
as I wander through each day.
—*Linda LaTourelle*

TIP TO TOE
From the top of my head
to the tips of my toes
My love for you
continually grows
—*Linda LaTourelle*

These boots are made for walkin'
Tip-toe through the tulips
The journey begins with a single step
These feet were made for walkin'
This little piggy
Tippy-toes
Too big for my shoes

Twinkle, twinkle little toes
Walking on sunshine
Watch me run

✤ Hair

WISPS
Precious and pretty
A crown of grace
Baby's soft wisps
Adorn her sweet face
–Linda LaTourelle

Baby at the barber
Baby, let your hair down
Baby's locks
Bed-head
Blondes have more fun
Brunettes rule
Buzzed and cut
Cute little carrot-top
Clipped and curled
Curly locks
Don't gimme static
Goldy-locks
Hair of gold
Hair-raising schemes
Hair we come
Lend me your comb
My first haircut
Pigtails on parade
Rag-a-moppit
Rag-a-muffin
Rockin' it red
Shearly beloved hair
Sister golden hair

Look Mom, I cut my hair
And my sister's, too.
Don't we look so beautiful?
We did it just for you.
–Linda LaTourelle

Scissors go clip, clip
Baby cries why, why
Barber says snip, snip
Momma says, oh my!
–Linda LaTourelle

What an awful day it is
I really hate to say—
My darling baby boy
Got his first haircut today!
–Thena Smith

Snip, snip, snip
Standing on end
The barber meets baby
Where's my hair
Wild and wooly
Your crowning glory

✤ Teeth

FIRST TOOTH
Such a precious little thing
That has come to light!
'tis a gem we treasure dear,
A tooth of pearly white!
–Althea Randolph

A smile like yours
A time to brush
Bite your tongue
A tooth in the hand
A wiggle and a yank—ouch!

PEARLY WHITES

Mommy calls them my pearly whites
Daddy calls them chompers
But I've brushed them every night
Since the time I was in rompers!
I stand upon my little stool
With toothbrush and toothpaste
And I brush each little tooth
Gently, but not in haste!
Mommy says if I brush my teeth
And keep them nice and clean
I will have a lovely smile
Just like a beauty queen.
Daddy agrees with mommy
That what she says is true
If you are true to your teeth
They won't be false to you!!

—Thena Smith

Bossy flossy

Brace yourself

Brushin' and flossin'

Brushing made easy

Daddy / Mommy loves the tooth fairy

Driven to extraction

Fresh and fabulous

Got toothpaste?

Grit your teeth

Gumming it

If the tooth be known

I love my teeth

I mith my tooth

Like pulling teeth

Look mom / dad, no cavities

Looth tooth

Million-dollar smile

My first looth tooth

My two front teeth

Oh, it's teething time again

One tooth, two tooth, loose tooth, bye tooth

Owie, (name) bit me!

Perfect checkup

Pearly whites

Rub my gums

Smile bright!

Sparkling white

Tales of the tooth fairy

Teething is such sweet misery

Teething drools

Teething is a numbing experience

That dentist gets on my nerves

The root of the problem

The teething story

The whole tooth and nothin' but the tooth

The tooth fairy was here

This is the way we brush our teeth

To tell the tooth

Tooth less beauty

Toothless wonder

Train tracks

Trip to the dentist

What a difference a smile makes

You make me smile

BOOKS

No man can be
Called friendless
Who has God and
The companionship
Of good books
–Elizabeth Barrett Browning

A blessed companion is a book

A book is a garden, an orchard, a storehouse, a party, a company by the way, a counselor, a multitude of counselors –Henry Ward Beeches

Books are the treasured wealth of the world and the fit inheritance of generations and nations –Thoreau

A house without books is like a room without windows –Heinrich Mann

A children's story that can only be enjoyed by children is not a good children's story in the slightest –C. S. Lewis

A room without books is like a body without a soul –Cicero

Books are lighthouses erected in the great sea of time –E. P. Whipple

Books are the bees which carry the quickening pollen from one to another mind –James Russell Lowell

Books are windows through which the soul looks out –Henry Ward Beeches

Bread of flour is good; but there is bread, sweet as honey, if we would eat it, in a good book –John Ruskin

He fed his spirit with the bread of books –Edwin Markham

Eating and reading are two pleasures that combine admirably –C.S. Lewis

Far more seemly were it for Thee to have thy study full of books, than thy purse full of money –John Byly

Good books, like good friends, are few and chosen; the more select, the more enjoyable –Louisa May Alcott

Good friends, good books—this is the ideal life –Mark Twain

I've always imagined that paradise will be a kind of library – Jorge Borges

In books lies the soul of the whole past time –Thomas Carlyle

So many books, so little time

No entertainment is so cheap as reading, nor any pleasure so lasting –Mary Worley Montagu

People say life is the thing, but I prefer reading –Logan Pearsall Smith

Reading is to the mind what exercise is to the body –Richard Stele

Reading the best books first is like eating dessert before dinner –Linda LaTourelle

Sleep less, read more

Some day you will be old enough to start reading fairytales again –C.S. Lewis

Some stories are so familiar it's like going home –Louisa May Alcott

The love of learning, the sequestered nooks, and all the sweet serenity of books –Longfellow

The world was hers for the reading –Betty Smith

That is a good book which is opened with expectation and closed with delight and profit
–Amos Bronson Alcott

The mere brute pleasure of reading —the sort of pleasure a cow must have in grazing –Lord Chesterfield

There is no friend as loyal as a book –Ernest Hemingway

To acquire the habit of reading is to construct for yourself a refuge from almost all the miseries of life –W. Somerset Maugham

To read a book for the first time is to make an acquaintance with a new friend; to read it for a second time is to meet an old one –Chinese proverb

You will never be alone with a book

To read a book is like a garden carried in the pocket –Chinese proverb

To stay calm, read a book—it is medicine to the soul

When I was ten, I read fairytales in secret and would have been ashamed if I had been found doing so. Now that I am fifty, I read them openly. When I became a man I put away childish things, including the fear of childishness and the desire to be very grown up. –C.S. Lewis

Where is human nature so weak as in the bookstore? –Henry Ward Beeches

You can never get a cup of tea large enough or a book long enough to suit me –C.S. Lewis

BOY & GIRL SCOUTS

THE PROMISE
I love to be a Girl Scout
And learn the things I do
I made a pledge of honor
And promise to be true
by serving God and others
I'll try my best each day
To represent Girl Scouting
In all I do and say
–Linda LaTourelle

A canoe for you
A'hiking we will go
A scouting experience
Adventure time
Ah, wilderness!
All around the campfire
Around the campfire
As eagles, we can fly
Badges of...
Be prepared
Bluebirds / Daisies
Boy / Girl Scout summer camp
Boy Scouting brothers
Bridging my way up
Brownie basics
Brownies, badges & belonging
Call of the wild
Camp Wanna-Have-Fun
Campfire stories
Climb any mountain
Congratulations cub
Cookies, anyone?

THE FIRST STEP
The first step toward a goal
Is the most important one,
For you must get started
Before your task is done.
The first step you take to that goal
May seem so small to you,
But it is one step closer to the task
And you must see it through.
  —*Thena Smith*

Cookies, crafts & character

Cub Scout day camp

Cub Scouting brothers

Cubbies

Eagle Scouts soar

Earning the badge

Founder's Day

Got cookies?

How a Boy / Girl Scout serves

I love cookies

I promise to do my best

Just me and my cookies

Knottin' new today!

Make new friends

Mottos, meetings & morals

Moving on up

On my honor

Outdoor adventures

Proud to be a Scout

Running with the pack

Scouting builds character

Scouting jamboree

Scouting rocks!

Serve God and my country

The oath

To God and my country

Trail blazers

Trail seekers

U is for uniform

CONGRATULATIONS GIRLS
Congratulations to each of you
Who've been so busy this year,
Moving upward together
In your scouting career.
We are all so proud of you,
And your talent we do proclaim
As we see 'cadet' after your name
  —*Thena Smith*

MORE THAN COOKIES
Scouting goes on all year long
And helps us each to grow
It's not all about the cookies—
Thought that you should know.
  —*Thena Smith*

SHE'S A BROWNIE
She is proud of her uniform
And thinks her pins are delightful
She loves having her own handbook
And finds it quite insightful.
She looks forward to the day
When a junior Girl Scout she'll be
And tries her best at her tasks
And enjoys each Brownie opportunity!
  —*Thena Smith*

BOY SCOUTS
Scouts are awesome boys
Who strive to live each day,
No matter what the situation
In the most honorable way
  —*Thena Smith*

CUB SCOUT
Congratulations Cub!
You are on your way!
We know you will be
An Eagle Scout some day!
—Thena Smith

THE BEST SEASON
Winter, summer, spring and fall,
The best season of them all,
In my opinion has to be
The season of the Girl Scout cookie
—Thena Smith

BOYS

A boy is a gift
Sent from above
Meant to cherish
And totally love
—Linda LaTourelle

TO LOVE A BOY
If he tests your patience
Beyond your last nerve
If he's noisy and wild
And throws many a curve
If he dreams of adventures,
From sun up to sun down
If he strives to do his best
Until that game he has won
If he doesn't like his bath
And won't do his math
If he tugs at your heart
And charms you with laughter
If he fills all your days
With memories long after—
It will be in these moments
With absolute joy
That you will quickly discover
He's a special little boy!
And then when he lovingly
Exclaims "you're the best!"
Your life will forever,
Be so wonderfully blessed.
—Linda LaTourelle 2004

A boy and his boots

A boy and his dad

A boy and his dog

A boy and his trucks

A boy is...

A boy leaves a mark that is forever etched upon your heart

A boy loves dirt, toys, bugs and spending time with Dad

A boy's best friend is his mother

Adventures of a boy

Ahoy matey!

All-American guy

All boy, all mine

Basketball and boys

Big boys club

Blue jean baby

Boogie-woogie bugle boy

Born to rock and roll

Boy at work

Boy genius

Boy miracle

Boy of a million faces

Boy storm coming through

Boy wizard / wonder

Boy's camp / club

Boys and their toys

Boys gone wild

A BOY IS...
Adventurous
Boisterous
Cunning
Daring
Eager
Fearless
Growing
Handsome
Inventive
Jet-propelled
Knights
Loud
Monster-loving
Negotiator
Orangutan
Presidential
Quick
Remarkable
Strong
Thinker
Unique
Victorious
Whiz-kid
Xtraspecial
Yang
Zooberific

Boys will always be an anchor in their mother's life

Boys are God's way of telling you to have fun

Boys bring moments to treasure and love without measure

If I were a rich boy...

Boys grow up to be heroes in their mother's / father's eyes

Boys just wanna be loved

Boys just wanna play rough

Boys just wanna have fun

ONE BOY
Millions of stars
But only one boy—
What a blessing,
What a joy!
–Linda LaTourelle

A BOY
Big bear hugs
Dirty-face kisses
Jumping in puddles
Dandelion wishes
Climbing a tree
Playing with toys
Such is the life
Of a happy little boy
–Linda LaTourelle

Boys love their moms / dads to the moon and back

Boys to men

Boys will be noise

Boys will steal your heart and make you love it

Boys will be boys

Boys-n-toys

Built tough to run

Computer genius / geek

Daddy's / Mama's pride and joy

Dirty blue jeans, that's my boy!

Every puppy should have a boy!

Game boy

Genuine boy

From sun-up to sun-down, a boy at play cannot be found

Boys are best—north, south, east and west

BOYFUL BLESSINGS
There is nothing like the
blessing of a bouncing baby boy
to fill your home with laughter
and your heart with love and joy
He'll hug you and he'll bug you,
and try you within—
but each precious memory
you'll treasure again and again
–Linda LaTourelle

BUDDIES
Climbing a tree,
My buddy and me—
Watching the clouds go by
Planning our day
And what to play
How the time does fly?
Let's build a fort
—no girls of course
Cause all they do is cry
–Linda LaTourelle

G.I. Joe in-training

Good night, sweet prince

Great boys think alike

Happy just to be a boy

He's all boy, through and through

He's a boy, just like his dad

He does like spiders and snails

He will move mountains one day, but for now he will just play in the dirt *–Linda LaTourelle*

He is my only sunshine

He's just a boy, but he's my boy

He's my little soldier boy

He's the kind of boy that will melt your heart

Hero in the making

Hometown hero

I'll teach you to jump on the wind's back, and away we go

I'm just a country boy

I'm youth, I'm joy, I'm a little bird that has broken out of the egg *–J.M. Barrie*

In a league of his own

It's a guy thing

In the eyes of a boy—all the world's a mountain to climb, creek to explore and trail to run
–Linda LaTourelle

It's a pirate's life for me

Just like my dad

Just like one of the big boys

Just me and my daddy / mommy

King of the hill / playground

Let's hear it for the boys

Let's make a knight to remember

Little boy, big heart

Little boys leave mud prints on your floors and love prints on your heart *–Linda LaTourelle*

Little drummer boy

Little heartbreaker

Little slugger / all star

Loud and proud—that's a boy

Mad about the boy

Male-bonding

Me and my dog and a fishing pole

Mommy's / Daddy's little / big monster / super hero

Mr. Charmer
Mr. Rough and Tumble
Mud buddy
My biker boys
My boy—the superhero of my life
My family thinks I am a superhero
Of all the animals—the boy is most unimaginable –Plato
Oh, the stories he can tell!
Oh, the things he can dream!
One boy and his dad / mom
One proud boy
One smart boy lives here with his very proud parents
Playing with toys is hard work for boys
Prince of the playground
Pure boy, through and through
Rough and rowdy
Spiderboy
Sports nut
Stories to be told
Sunshine boys
Super boy with lots of toys
Sweet boy of mine
Sweet talkin' guy
Tales of a super kid
Tall oaks from little acorns grow
That's my boy—rough and tumble!
The bigger the boys, the more they love their toys
The boy next door
The boy who could do anything
The boy who loved teddy bears
The boys of summer

The brat pack
The cleverness of a boy
The imagination of a boy
The joy of a baby boy
The laughter of a boy is his father's greatest joy
The life of a boy
The love of a boy is worth more than gold –Linda LaTourelle
The secret language of boys
The simplest of pleasures are discovered every day by a boy
The spittin' image of his daddy
The tales of a boy and his dad / pets, buddies
The wheels are turning
There he goes—my boy!
This boy's in love with you
To be a boy
Trouble is my middle name, but you can call me Prince Charming
Twinkle, twinkle little boy—you are your mama's biggest joy –Linda LaTourelle
Wanted: One boy who likes camping, fishing and hanging with Dad!
We can't all be superheroes!
What a boy wants!
When I grow up, I want to be just like my daddy
What an imagination!
Wonder boys
You are the hero of our story
You're a big kid now

BOYFRIENDS

I wanna be the reason
He stays in for the night
Waiting for my call.
He bakes a cake
For the very first time,
Just for me
He makes playlists
Full of music for two.
He hides a love note
Just to see me smile.
When I find it
I wanna be the reason
He's so in love—
With me!

—Linda LaTourelle

A real boyfriend knows your moods and loves you anyway

A real boyfriend will make you feel special no matter what

Every Day I see him and my heart twitters more and more

First love

He's definitely boyfriend material

He's my Romeo / I'm his Juliet

He's the one that I want!

He's too sexy for his jeans / boots

His smile stole my heart

His voice is music to my ears

I love him way past forever!

His love should always make you feel beautiful because you are!

I have a silly, sweet and amazing boyfriend

I love how he loves me

I wanna be your everything

I only think about him on two occasions—day and night

I would rather do nothing with him than something with anyone else

I'm 100% in like with him

I'm just wild about (name)

I've been waiting for a boy like you

If I tell you I love you, will you stay forever?

In my book of love—my prince is you

Inside-out—that's how much I want to know you right now!

It's that feeling you get when you get to see him again

Just me and my guy

King of my heart

Man-tabulous!

My boyfriend rocks!

My boyfriend—my hero!

My guy's smile would light the whole universe

Now I know what love is

Prince of passion

She knew that one look at him and she was gone

She likes him, he likes her—they just need to tell each other

The best part of my day is when I hear your voice

The more I see him, the more I love him

The perfect boyfriend is the one I love

The thoughts of the things you say keep me awake and smiling

This guy's in love with you

Wanted: boyfriend! Must love chick flicks, long slow kisses and slow dancing in the rain until dawn

Who needs a teddy to hug when you have a boyfriend like mine?

Who needs puppy love when you have the real thing?

Who wants an old boyfriend anyway?

BUGS & BEES

Along came a spider

Ants in your pants

Bee happy

Bee mine

Bee positive

Beetle brain

Bookworm boy

Bug collection / hunting

Busy as a bee

Don't bug me! I'm busy!

Good night, sleep tight, don't let the bed bugs bite

Happy bee—day!

Honey bee good!

Honeycomb bee my baby!

I bee-lieve in you! / miracles

Itsy-bitsy spider

I'm a working busy bee

Knee-high to a grasshopper

Lady bug, lady bug fly away home

Love them bugs

Mad as a hornet

My bee-utiful baby

Simply bee-utiful

Sweet as honey

The queen bee

To bee or not to bee

What's the buzz?

You bee-long to me

You're the bee's knees

BUTTERFLY

The butterfly often forgets it was once a caterpillar –Swedish proverb

Butterflies are free

From caterpillar to butterfly is a remarkable transformation we should aspire to. With hope and faith, all that we need to make us beautiful is already within us. –Linda LaTourelle

Just living is not enough, said the butterfly—one must have sunshine, freedom and a little flower - Hans Christian Andersen

Oh, what a beautiful butterfly!

Oh, how I long for the days when chasing butterflies was how I spent a sunny day

May the wings of the butterfly kiss the sun and find your shoulder to light on, to bring you luck, happiness and riches, today, tomorrow and beyond. –Irish blessing

Floating and flittering up in the sky looking so pretty, fluttering by

The butterfly counts not months but moments, and has time enough –Rabindranath Tagore

CAMPING & HIKING

A blanket of stars
A cabin in the woods
A'camping we will go
A day without camping is like—work!
A' hiking we will go
A walk in the woods
Ah, the great outdoors!
Anyone have a smoke screen?
All around the campfire
At the river's edge
Back to the basics
Beneath the moon and stars
Beware of rangers bearing gifts
Blazin' the trail
Bugs and critters and bears, oh my!
Cabins, campfires and cooking outside!
Camp more, work less
Campers have s'more fun!
Campfire cookin'—the best!
Camping in my motorhome
Camping is in-tent-sive therapy
Camping rocks!
Camping with the big boys
Camping it up
Climb every mountain
Counting the stars
Creepy crawlers
Did you hear that?
Don't feed the bears
Exploring the great outdoors
Field and stream
Getting away from it all
Gone backpacking
Good-natured
Good-bye city life...
Got marshmallows?
Got poison ivy?
Got s'mores?
Happy hikers
Happy trails to you
Here I am at Camp (name)
Hi, ho, hi ho, it's off to camp we go
Hiker's haven
Home is where the camper is
Home is where the tent's pitched
Home sweet tent
I love camping
I love camping—in my motor home
I'd rather be camping
Just another happy camper
Keep calm—go camping
Let's camp!
Mountain man / mama
Nature boy / girl
Off the beaten path
Rocky mountain high
Rough and rugged
Roughin' it!
RV camping is the life for me
S'mores and snores
Star light, star bright, don't let the bears come out tonight

Stay calm—pitch the tent

Take a hike dude!

The big hike

The call of the wild

The campers life for me

To camp or not to camp? "Where" is the question.

Trailblazers on the trail

Trailer, sweet trailer

Under the stars

Welcome to Tent City

What do we do when it gets dark?

What happens at camp stays at camp

Where are the tent poles?

Which way to the woods?

Wild in the country

You got the tent?

CASTLES

A castle fit for a prince / princess

A fine feline and her old tomcat live here

A man's home is his castle

Build you a castle

Cardboard castles

Castles in the sands

Cinderella's castle

Every king / queen needs a castle

My castle fair

My castle is where you are

Paper castles

Royal home to the knight and his lady

CATS & KITTENS

THE FAMILY CAT

I can fold up my claws
In my soft velvet paws
And purr in the sun
'Til the short day is done—
For I am the family cat.
I can doze by the hour
In the vine-covered bower,
Winking and blinking,
Through sunshine and shower
For I am the family cat.

A girl and her kitty

A great big ball of yarn and other tails of cuteness

Ain't no kitten like the one I got

Attack cat on duty

Cat-o-my heart

Cat o' nine lives

Cats for sale

Cats rule and dogs drool

Fat-bottom cat

Feline groovy

Free love—get a cat!

Furr balls and fish tanks

Go cat go!

Good cat gone bad

Happiness is being loved by a cat

Have you ever loved a kitty?

Honky-tonk kats

I am cat, hear me purr

It's a cat's world

K is for kitten

Kissin' kittens
Kittens just like to have fun
Kitty mischief
Many cats make a happy home
Meow means _____
More than a cat
Must love cats
My boss is my cat!
My cat is _____
Napping my life away
Nine lives and counting
Once upon a kitten
One cool cat lives here
Our furry friend
Paws and claws
Paws on my pillow
Pet me purr-ty please?
Purr-fectly spoiled
Purrs and pets
Puss and boots
Siamese sweetness
Spoiled and proud of it
Tale of two kittens
The cat in my hat
The cat of my dreams
The cat's pajamas
The cat who came to stay
The naughty little kitty
This is the cat's house
Three little kittens
Tommy is my cat's meow
Too purr is feline
What's new, pussycat?

What a cat wants!
When dog's away—cat's will play
Wild-cat, you make my heart purr
You're nobody 'til some kitty loves you

CELESTIAL

♣ *Earth*

All of earth is crammed with heaven
And every bush aflame with God
But only those who see
take off their shoes
—Elizabeth Barrett

The green earth sends her incense up
From many a mountain shrine;
From folded leaf and dewey cup
She pours her sacred wine.
—John Greenleaf Whittier

God gives all men all earth to love,
But, since man's heart is small,
Ordains for each one spot
shall prove beloved over all
—Rudyard Kipling

All around the world
All the colors of the earth
Celebrate Earth Day
Color my world
From the ends of the earth
Earth, a relative to all that is *–Black Elk*

Go where he will, the wise man is at home, his hearth the earth, his hall the azure dome *–Emerson*

Heaven is under our feet as well as over our heads *–Thoreau*

In a perfect world
Indescribable
It's a small world
Journey to the center of the earth
Save the planet
Sitting on top of the world
Taking the world by storm
The good earth
We are the salt of the earth

♣ Moon
Blue moon of Kentucky
By the light of the silvery moon
Fly me to the moon
Goodnight moon
How high the moon
I see the moon
In the misty moonlight
It's only a paper moon
Lasso the moon
Man in the moon
Moon glow
Moon over Miami
Moonlight madness
Moonlight serenade
My daddy hung the moon
Under a hunter's moon
You hung the moon

♣ Planets
Another galaxy
As the world turns
Beam me up
Celestial bliss
Galaxy quest

In a galaxy far away
Lost in space
Men are from Mars
Mother earth
One groovy planet
Out of this world
Planet earth
Rocket man
Save the planet
Space captain / cowboy
Speak to the earth, and it shall teach Thee *–Job 12:8*
The universe
To infinity and beyond
We are the world
What planet are you from?
Women are from Venus

♣ Skies
Blue skies
City skyline
Morning sky
Night sky
Orange sky
Where the ocean meets the sky
Red sky at night
The sky's the limit
Starry starry sky
Wild blue yonder

♣ Stars
A thousand stars
Catch a falling star
Count your lucky stars
Good morning star-shine
In the twinkling twilight

Keeper of the stars
Quiet nights of quiet stars
Reach for the stars
Shining star
Star collector
Star-crossed lovers
Star of Bethlehem
Stardust memories
Star light, star bright
Starry, starry night
Stars in their eyes
Thank your lucky stars
The stars are brightly shining
Twinkle, twinkle, little star
When you wish upon a star
Wish upon a star
Written in the stars

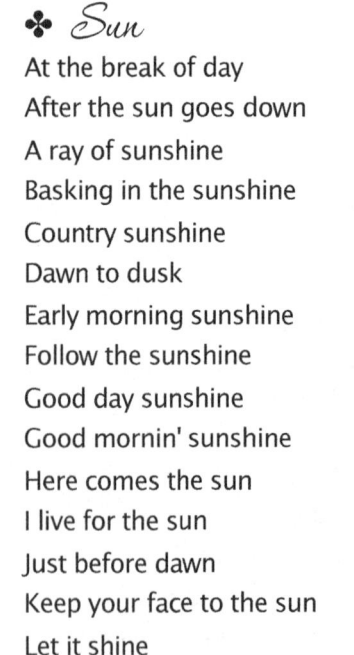

♣ *Sun*

At the break of day
After the sun goes down
A ray of sunshine
Basking in the sunshine
Country sunshine
Dawn to dusk
Early morning sunshine
Follow the sunshine
Good day sunshine
Good mornin' sunshine
Here comes the sun
I live for the sun
Just before dawn
Keep your face to the sun
Let it shine
Long about sundown

Make hay while the sun shines
Rise and shine
Shine on me
Soakin' up sunshine
Spectacular sunset
Sun light, sun bright
Sunny days are here again
Sun's comin' up
The glory of daybreak
The sun also rises
'Til the morning light
Walking on sunshine
You are my sunshine

CHILDREN

Child—a collector of strange and wonderful creatures—Guaranteed to steal your Heart with just one hug
–Linda LaTourelle

24-karat gold child

A child is sonlight from God

A chip off the old block

A day in the life of (name)

A diamond in the rough

A doll's house

A home filled with children is a home filled with love

A rich child sits often in a poor mother's lap *–Danish proverb*

Adventures of (name)

All our / my children

FOR MY CHILD I PRAY

Courage to face uncertainty,
Trust to follow your instincts
Strength to handle adversity,
Passion to keep on dreaming
Character that is kind
Commitment to work diligently
Peace that fills your mind
Integrity to live honestly
Belief in impossibilities
Tenacity to never give up
Faith to always seek truth
Know you are loved always.
—Linda LaTourelle

All about me from A to Z

All's fair in mud and war

Almost grown-up

Amazing grace

Any time is cookie time

Beloved child

Big red balloon

Blessed are the children—for theirs is a world of wonder

Blueberries for (name)

Candy today keeps grumpies away

Charmed is my middle name

Cheaper by the dozen

Child of mine

Child of one thousand faces

Child psychology for moms / dads

Childhood faces and memorable places

Childhood is a journey, not a race

Children are a heritage of the Lord

Children are our future

Children are our living jewels

Children, like flowers will bloom in life's garden when nurtured

Children fill our lives with sunshine and our hearts with love

Children learn how to live by what they see modeled at home

Children are poor men's riches

Children's wishes and bedtime kisses

Colorful characters

Comic adventures of (name)Cutie patootie and strawberry pie

Dad's / Mom's #1 fan

Daddy said it was okay!

Daddy's little buddy

Daddy / Mommy loves me best

Daddy's / Mommy's helper

Daddy's / Mommy's little prince / princess

Dancin' in the rain and jumpin' in the puddles

Dandelion wishes and marshmallow kisses

Days of our kids' lives

Did you ever have to make up your mind?

Down on the farm with Grandpa / Grandma

Family game night

Fun in grandma's attic

Fun in the mud / sun, rain, snow

Fun is contagious!

PB & J

I love peanut butter and jelly
I could eat it every day!
Mom could leave the jar out
And never put it away!
I love to spread peanut butter
Thick as can be on my bread
And then layer on the jelly
I prefer the kind that's red!
Ohhhh, yummy how delicious!
Oh, what a happy day!
For lunch I'm having my favorite—
PB&J!

–Thena Smith

Future all-star

Future ballerina, president or _____

Gettin' goofy with grandpa

Getting bigger inch by inch

God bless the child

Gold-medal Olympic kid

Got dirt? Will play!

Growing by leaps and bounds

Growing up is hard to do

Guess how much I love you

Hangin' with the big kids

Hangin' with _____

Happiness is homemade!

Happy times are here again

Hard to be neat—learning to eat

Heading for Broadway

Hooked on books

Horsin' around with Daddy / Mommy

How fun thou art!

LOVE YOU

My child, every day
Remember this to do
Believe and pray forever
Your dreams will come true

–Linda LaTourelle

I am fearfully and wonderfully made...

I can do bad all by myself

I did it myself

I don't wanna grow up

I got the preschool blues

I know what I like

I live for my children

I love my mommy / daddy

I love to laugh

I want everything and more

I want to hold your hand

I'm a big kid now

I'm the only one like me

I'm daddy's / mommy's favorite

If you give a kid some candy...

In the swing of things

Inside the mind of a child

It runs in the family

It's just my awesome imagination

It's just you and me kid!

It's the little things that matter

It's all in the genes

It's not easy being a prince / princess

Jesus loves me

Jumpin' good time

HUNGRY
Hands in the cookie jar
Fingers in the pie
Such a hungry boy
My, oh my!
–Linda LaTourelle

Just another day in Kidsville

Just another day in the sandbox

Just daddy / mommy and me

Just give me more, more, more

Just me and my child

Just my imagination

Kid's songs

Kids club—no parents allowed

Kids just wanna have fun

Kids make life a grand adventure!

King / Queen of the sandbox / playground

Kittens, kids and kites, oh my!

Legend of (name)

Let the games begin

Let the good times roll / bounce / fly

Let's go fly a kite

Lifestyles of the frazzled mom / dad

Lifestyles of the whiny and spoiled

Like father / mother, like son / daughter

Li'l gardener / farmer

Little house on the ____

Little league champ

Little people rule!!

Look who's spoiled now!

I'M GROWING
Teacher measured us today
I'm getting really tall
I think of all the feet in class
Mine are biggest of all!
My hands are growing bigger
And can hold so much stuff
Over all, I'd say I'm perfect
Just exactly big enough!
–Thena Smith

Love my little bubba

Love you forever

Lucky me

Make time for the little things

Mama's snuggle bugs

Me and my shadow

Me and my toys

Milestones and merriment

Mom / Dad always liked you best!

Mom's / Dad's little garden of love

Mommy / Daddy loves me the most

Mommy's / Daddy's little mess-maker

Mommy's little monsters

Monkey see, monkey do, monkey did!

More precious than gold

More, more, more, I want more!

Mother and child reunion

Mother knows all—Father knows best

Mud puddles & dandelions

My best friend and me

My favorite things / people

My first set of wheels

CHEERS
Bye, bye bottle
Hello cup
Watch me now
As I tip it up
–Linda LaTourelle

My heart belongs to mommy / daddy

My kid is (adjective)

My little ray of sunshine

My little red wagon

My radio flyer and me

Neighborhood kids

New kid in town / on the block

Oh, the place he / she goes!

Old dogs and children

One fish, two fish, where's the fish?

One for you, three for me!

One funny kid lives here

One great all-star

Our golden child

Our golden ray of sunshine

Our rising star

Out of the mouths of babes

Peace in the world begins with children

Please Mom / Dad, can we keep him?

Pokey little puppy

Preschool blues

Prime suspect

Prince / Princess of everything

Princess / Prince of Tantrumville

Put your hand in the hand of Dad / Mom

CHILD
A collector of wild, wooly and wonderful critters know as pets— guaranteed not to be any trouble

Raised on homegrown love

Rock star in training / practice

Roller coaster and cotton candy

Saturday in the park

See (name)! See (name) play!

See how they grow

Seems like only yesterday…

Shake your sillies out

Singing in the rain

Skip to my Lou my darlin'

Skipping rocks with Grandpa

Smart as a whip

So many toys, too many choices

Social butterflies

Some kind of wonderful

Special times with (name)

Sugar pie, sweetie cakes

Superstar of the day!

Sweet as sugar and puddin' pie

Sweet child of mine

Sweets for the sweetest child

Teach your children

Thank God for children / kids

The adventures of (name)

The age of innocence

The all-knowing child

The babysitters club
The brat pack adventurers
The children's hour
The days of kids and summer
The dish ran away with the spoon
The growing years
he handwriting's on the wall and everywhere else, too!
The imagination of a child
The kid and I
The little kid that could
The little rascals
The magic of childhood
The magic of discovery
The many faces of (name)
The measure of my love
The more the merrier
The new sneakers
The next teenage idol
The peanut butter gang
The star of the show is you!
The storybook children
The sunshine kid
The way you do the things you do
The wheels on my bike go 'round and 'round
The wild bunch
The wonder years
The world's best kid lives here
These are a few of my favorite things
This is the way we go to church
This is the way we make our beds

Thou shalt not whine!
Through my daughter's / son's, child's eyes
Through the years
Tickle me happy
Tool-time with Dad
Train up a child in the way he should go...
Two little kids went out to play
Video game maniacs
Want your children to listen— speak softly to someone else!
What a boy / girl wants
What's yours is mine, what's mine is mine!
What's a kid to do?
When I grow up I want to be...
Wiggle the whiny's away!
Wild thing, you make my joy sing!
You can't always get what you want
You color my world, the walls and my life with wonderful memories
You're one in a million!

COLORS

All the colors of the seasons
Black and white
Color me beautiful
Color me happy
Color me in love with you
Love colors everything pretty
My coat of many colors

Red roses for a blue lady
Red, white and blue
Showing his / her true colors
Techno-color
The colors of autumn / spring
The color of your love

♣ Black
Baa-baa black sheep
Black beauty
Black Friday
Little black book
Black or white
Bodacious in black
Love that licorice
Men in black
Black holes
Ebony and ivory
Little black dress

♣ Blue
Baby blue
Birth of the blues
Blue bird of happiness
Blue collar man
Blue skies
Blue suede shoes
Forever in blue jeans
Little boy blue
Love is blue
Moody and blue
My blueberry muffin
Ole' blue eyes
Once in a blue moon
True-blue friend

Violets are blue

♣ Silver
A glint of silver
Foggy and grey
He wears a pair of silver wings
Silver bells
Looking for the silver lining
Under the silvery moon
Born with a silver spoon
Sterling silver

♣ Gold
All that glitters
As good as gold!
Fields of gold
Gold rush
Golden band of love
Golden slumbers
Gold teeth
Heart of gold
More precious than gold
Worth his weight in gold

♣ Green
Big green tractor
Fried green tomaters
Go green
Green acres
Green berets
Green eggs and ham
Green peace
Green-eyed monster
Green thumbs
Jolly green grasshopper
Little green apples
Wearing of the green

♣ *Orange*

A clockwork orange
Agent orange
Orange blossom special
Orange crush

♣ *Pink*

A pink carnation and a pickup truck
Blushing pink
Color me blush
In the pink
Passionately pink
Pink Cadillac
Pink flamingo
Pink lemonade
Pretty in pink
Raspberry sherbet
Rose-colored glasses
Think pink
Tickled pink

♣ *Purple*

Deep purple
Plum purple
Purple heart
Purple mountain majesty
Purple passion
Purple people-eater
Purple rain
The color purple
When I am old I shall wear purple

♣ *Red*

Candy apple red
Cherry red
Crimson and clover
Lady in red
Little red corvette
Little Red Riding Hood
Red hats ladies
Red-hot mama
Red letter day
Red rubber ball
Red sails in the sunset
Red skies at night
Roses are red
Scarlett ribbons
Strawberry shortcake
The red balloon

♣ *Brown*

Bad, bad Leroy Brown
Brown bear
Brown-eyed girl
Brown-eyed Susan
Brown sugar
Charlie Brown
Make mine mocha
Makes my brown eyes blue
Mocha java
Mrs. Brown, you've got a...
Mud brown
Muddy river

♣ White

I'm dreamin' of a white Christmas
Pearly whites
On the wings of a snow white dove
The great white hope
Those precious pearly whites
White diamonds
White elephant
White knight
White lace and love
White noise
White on white
Winter white

♣ Yellow

Big yellow taxi
Mellow yellow
Old yeller
She wore a yellow ribbon
Sunny yellow
The yellow brick road
The yellow rose of Texas
Tie a yellow ribbon
Yellow is a happy color
Yellow polka-dot bikini
Yellow submarine

COMPUTER

A journey of a thousand sites begins with the first click
Apple is my favorite flavor
A photo is worth a thousand words and a gazillion pixels
An apple a day—keeps the viruses away
Bandwidth? How wide?
Blogger at heart
Bytes and pieces—my computer after I fix it!
Chats have nine lives
Computer programmers don't byte, they just nibble a bit
Computers saved my memory!
Crashed, corrupt and cursor—just another PC day!
Date a computer—find a wife
Dinner on the table is the sign of a broken computer
Geeky and groovy
Geek is the new pink
Get a Mac—you'll never go back!
Hard drive fixer—my hammer!
Hit any key and be refreshed
I searched online for love and found you
I got a computer—now I just need a life!
I had a life once—then I joined social networking
I live @ ...
I live—therefore I network!
I love to blog
I love my Mac
I'm just getting on for a minute
I'm just living in a virtual world
Icon do it...icon do it

The Biggest Book of Words & Prompts for Scrapbooks, Art Journals & Crafts

Jesus saves—but backup anyways
Monitors, modems, mice—oh my!
Lost in cyberspace again
Make mine Apple!
My computer is sick—it's got worms and viruses
My favorite pad—my ipad
Networking nights
Oh the life of a geek!
PC's rock! / PC's byte!
Press any key to quit!
Search and find—what?
Socially challenged
Surfin' the cyber wave
Technologically challenged
Text me
There's no place like…home.com
To err is a normal part of life—just ask my computer
To text or not to text?
When all else fails—read the manual
When all else fails—reboot
You can't teach a new mouse old clicks
You've got mail—email!

✤ *Cyber text*

:	happy
:/	sad
:/	confused
b/f	boyfriend
brb	be right back
dd	dear / darling daughter
dh	dear / darling husband
ds	dear / darling son
dw	dear / darling wife
f2f	face to face
4u	for you
g/f	girlfriend
gl	good luck
grl	girl
hb	hurry back
jmo	just my opinion
k	okay
LOL	laugh out loud
OMG	oh my gosh
peeps	people
plz	please
roflol	rolling on floor laughing out loud
thx	thanks
ttfn	ta-ta for now
ttyl	talk to you later
wfm	works for me
wywh	wish you were here
XOXO	kisses and hugs
yw	you're welcome
zzz	sleeping
2h2h	too hot to handle

COUPLES

All that I have is nothing unless you are here

By your side doing absolutely nothing is everything I want to do

I love who I've become since we became us

I love you no matter what may come our way

I made a wish for you to be mine and here we are together

I never knew for sure what I wanted until you came into my life

I only want to be with you—until forever!

Love is being with the one who completes you

Love was just a word until we met, now it's our life

More and more every day is how much I want you

My favorite letters in the alphabet are U and S because they spell you and me—together!

No one gets me the way that you do

Pinky promise—we'll love each other forever!

Side-by-side is the best place to be with you

The best of my day, the rest of my night, you are my everything!

The moment we met, I knew we were going to be together forever

The one that I adore and will love forever more—is you!

The only one for me is you!

There is no remedy for love but to love more – *Thoreau*

Thou art to me a delicious torment
—*Ralph Waldo Emerson*

Together we can do everything

It's always better when we are together

We make our own fairytales

What greater thing is there for two human souls than to feel that they are joined for life –*George Elliot*

When you need, me I'll be there

With you and me together, life makes perfect sense

You and me—that's the way it's meant to be

You are living proof that love is real

You are my home, my heart, my happiness

You are my sun, my moon and the light of my life

You are the highlight of my day, the delight of my evening and the love in my life

You are the rest of my life and the best of my love

You are my other half—my best half

You rock my world like no one else

Your hands hold my heart that beats with love for you

COWBOYS & COWGIRLS

A cowboy from the wild wild west

A girl and her boots is a lovely thing

Ain't a bull that can't be rode—ain't a rider that can't be throwed

At home on the range and rodeo

Back in the saddle again and again

Boot-scootin' boogie

Boots, chaps and cowboy hats

Cowboy-up or sit in the truck

Cowboys love guns, dogs and trucks
Cowboys / Cowgirls and cuddles
Cowgirls just wanna have fun
Even cowgirls get the blues
Future world champion bull rider
Happiness is being a cowgirl / boy
Hitch 'em up and ride 'em out
Home of an old stallion and his feisty filly
Honkey-tonk honey / hero
I've been to three county fairs and a calf ropin'
It's a cowboy thing
Just horsin' around
Keep on kicking until the clock stops ticking
Li'l buckaroo
Lovin' the cowboy life
Must love cowgirls / cowboys
Must love horses
My heroes are cowboys / cowgirls
Never kick a cow patty on a hot day
Our little cowboy / cowgirl
Pretty in pink—rockin' them spurs
Rhinestone cowboy / cowgirl
Ride 'em cowboy
Rope it, ride it, wrestle it
Ropin' my life away
The cowboy / cowgirl way
The good, the bad and the cowboy who loves her
The lady takes the cowboy
These boots are made for cowboys
Time to cowboy up and ride
Urban cowboy

CRAFTING

A creative mess
Annie get your glue gun
An original work of heart
Art from the heart
Beadin' and braidin'
Bless this mess
Crafting is the only way to relax
Crafty lady
Created to craft
Creative endeavors
Creative genius at work
Creative mess
Creative minds are rarely tidy
Eat, drink and make crafts
Girls at play
Girls just wanna have fun
Got Crafts?
Handcrafted perfection
Handmade with love
Hearts and crafts
Homemade love
I'd rather be crafting
I'm creative—you can't expect me to be neat too!
Just bead it
Keep calm—make something!
Keep calm and craft on!
Little hands make big masterpieces
Made with love
Man crafter
Meet and greet the artist
My creative clutter

My heart belongs to crafting

Neat! Did someone say neat?

No mess—no masterpiece

Old crafters never die, they just get more bazaar!

Paper trail

Peace, love, pinking shears

She's a crafty mama

Sticks like glue

The bead mistress

The magic of markers

♣ Cross Stitch

Any day spent cross-stitching is my kind of day

Bear your cross today—cross-stitch

Born to count and stitch

Colored threads and golden needles

Criss-crossed, tied with floss

Cross my stitch and hope to…

Cross-stitch addict

Cross-stitched with love

Cross-stitcher's floss with care

Crowned the counting queen

Every stitch I take, every cross I make, I'll be loving you

Handmade with love in every stitch

Hands to work, hearts to God

I will cross that stitch when I come to it

I'd rather be cross-stitchin' than cookin' in the kitchen

I'd rather be flossing and crossing with you

I'm itchin' to be stitchin'

Love is the thread that cross-stitches our lives

Making every stitch count

Quiet please, I'm counting

♣ Doodling

Brought to you by the letter "D" for doodle

Doodle me this

Doodle my life away

Doodles for dummies

Doodling inspires one to draw their dreams creatively –Linda LaTourelle

Doodle-time makes me all swirly

Doodley delightful

Doodling—not just for frustrated artists anymore

Every Day's a doodle day

I got the doodle-bug

I love to doodle

I'd rather be doodling

Let your doodle light shine

Live life by doodling on the margins with your inner spirit

Simply doodlightfully delicious

Smiles and miles of doodles

Take me away for a doodle day

♣ Knitting

Close-knit family

Counting my stitches of love

Don't needle me

Give me a skein in every color

Happy hooker

I never saw a color of yarn that I didn't like

Keep calm—keep casting on

Knit forever—clean house never

Knit one, pearl two

Knitted with love

Knitters are warm and snuggly

Knitting is cheap therapy

Knitting is my life

Made by Mom to keep me warm

One purl, two purl, give me more purls

Purls are a knitter's favorite

Purls—my passion!

Real men love knitwits

She's so knitty and witty and gay

Stay calm and knit

Things to do today—knit, purl, knit, knit and knit

Yarn snobs

❖ Painting

A day without painting is like a day without sunshine

A painting is a poem without words

All the colors of the rainbow in a painting just for you

Art is not what you see, but what you make others see –Degas

Artfully mastered by (name)

Great art picks up where nature ends –Marc Chagall

How fun thou art!

If I didn't start painting, I would have raised chickens —Grandma Moses

Let your canvas flow with the colors of your soul

Painting is silent poetry –Plutarch

Paint your world magnificent shades of you –Linda LaTourelle

Painting the pictures in your soul is poetry to my eyes

Strokes by the master

The world is but a canvas to our imaginations -Suzanne Moore

To be an artist is to believe in life –Henry Moore

❖ Photography

PHOTO DAY
It's that time of year again
To stand in line and wait
To have our picture taken—
It's something us kids hate

My hair is fixed so nicely
Clothes are fresh and clean
The kids are really goofing off
And the teacher's being mean

But I'll be good—I promise
I'll smile at the birdie and say
Cheese, please and thank you
And take a funny picture today
   –Linda LaTourelle

A flash in time

A moment in time

A not-so candid moment

A picture paints a thousand words

Budding photographer

The New Ultimate Guide to the Perfect Word – Volume 2

Candid comments

Capture the memory

Caught on film

Crop and shoot

Fabulously focused

Happily exposed

It's all about the light

Lights, camera, action

Mama's / Daddy's a big shot

Mom's / Dad's got the camera again

My self portrait

One crop at a time

Picture-perfect memories

See the light, shoot the light

Smile, you're on the camera

Snapshots and smiles

Snips and snapshots

So many pictures, so little time!

Take your best "shot"

The journey of a thousand pictures begins with the first shoot

There is nothing worse than a brilliant image of a fuzzy concept –*Ansel Adams*

This smile that broke the camera!

Through the lens with Mom— video at 11:00

Up close and personal

When my words are unclear, the camera finds my focus –*Linda LaTourelle*

There are always two people in every picture: the photographer and the viewer –*Ansel Adams*

There are no rules for good photographs, there are only good photographs –*Ansel Adams*

To photograph is to hold one's breath, when all faculties converge to capture fleeting reality –*Henri Cartier-Breton*

♣ *Quilting*

OUR FAMILY BLANKET
Grandma created a patchwork quilt
Stitched with her own sweet hands
Made from pieces of colorful fabric
Sewn together with simple strands

Each square symbolized our family
And journeys through the years
Memories of our lives together
Full of laughter, joys and tears

She loved to tell me the stories
They were her greatest treasure
Nothing else will ever compare
And cannot begin to measure

The care in grandma's stitches
Made us a blanket of love—
But her years of praying and sowing
Reaped blessings from above
 –Linda LaTourelle 2012

Another little piece of my quilt

A patchwork of love for you

A stitch in time

A true friend is like a warm quilt wrapped around your soul

Blessed are the piece-makers their stitches keep you warm

Every stitch I sew—every quilt I make—I'll be having sew much fun

Four-square and two months

From the scrap piles of life—love sewed a quilt

Happiness is a new / old quilt

I gave my family a piece of my heart

I love quilting sew much!

I'm cuttin' and piecin' and stitchin' my life away!

I sew love the piece I have when I am quilting

I sew love to quilt

Just another little piece of my art

Keep the piece—marry a quilter

Laugh a little, chat a little, stitch a little—and soon you'll have a quilt

Love the buzz at our be

Make me a blanket of love

Material girls are sew happy

My blanket of love

One hungry fabric monster lives here

Piece-ful lady is sew in love with her material man

Quilts cover generations with your love

Quilters lead a piece-ful life

Quilters make love sew fine

Quilters never cut corners

Quilting forever—housework never

Quilting is the best way to enjoy the piece and quiet

Quilted and stitched with love

Snuggling under grandma's quilt

Stung by the quilting bee

Tiny threads, scraps of fabric and love sewed this quilt

Warm and cozy—my quilt and me

With treadle to the metal, watch mama quilt!

✤ Rubberstamping

Paper, ink, stamp, emboss
It's so easy to get lost
Close the door and hide away
Let me stamp all night and day
–Linda LaTourelle

Camp stamp-a-lot!

Chocolate and stamps—sweet!

Emboss and rise

Gone stamping

Hand-stamped original

I am woman, watch me stamp

I'd rather be stamping

I could have stamped all night

I love to stamp on days that end in "Y"

MBS: must buy stamps

Made with 100% pure love

One inked and happy stamper

OSD: obsessed stamping disorder

Paper, ink, stamp!

Rubber rules and stamping's cool

Stamp by your man

Stamping leaves an impression

Stamping is the life for me

Stamp your heart out

Stamp out housework

Stamps are my addiction

Your friendship is stamped in my heart!

❖ Scrapbooking

Give me scraps, give me scraps
Let me crop all night long
Let me cut, let me stamp
Now my life is a song
Make a page, gotta scrap
It's the thing that I do
What a photo, what a book
Made with love just for you
—Linda LaTourelle 2012

Blessed are the kids—for they shall inherit the scrapbooks

Days to remember, nights to scrap

Dedicated to the one I love

Don't worry—be scrappy!

Every page I scrap is a tiny little piece of history

Fun with scissors

Gone scrap-happy

I scrapbook, therefore I am— broke

I'm scrapping my life away

Keeper of the memories

Life is a story shared between the pages of this book

Life stuck to my pages

Mama's keepsakes

Memories are like keepsakes—treasured and cherished forever

Memory is life's clock

Paper, scissors, crop

People grow on family trees

Princess / Queen crop-a-lot

Princess / Queen of scrappy land

Scrapaholic and proud of it!

Scrapbooking with the girls

Scrapbooks tell the story of life—yours, mine and ours

Scrap-happy mama

Scrapmaster extraordinaire

Scrap me to the end of love

Scraptastically creative crop

Scrappin' for Mom

So many pages, so little time

Stay calm—scrap away

Thanks for the memories

These are a few of my favorite things

These are the crops to remember

These days would be remembered and kept from generation to generation —Esther 9:28

The paper chase

This album is my legacy of love

Up close and personal

We live as long as we are remembered

Got photos? Crop, stick and scrap!

Where do I begin?

You know you're addicted to scrapbookin' when…

You never know when you might be making a memory

❖ Sewing

Sewing forever
Housework probably never
—Linda LaTourelle

A perfect fit!

Button, button—whose got the button?

170 | ultimatebookcompany.com

Friendships are sewn one stitch at a time
From my hands to your heart
Grandma made it!
Having sew much fun
Hi ho, hi ho, it's off to sew we go
Homemade love!
Home-sewn love
I am sew thankful for…
I love Miss sew and sew
Soul fed by the stitches I sew
I love sewing—and I have plenty of material witnesses to prove it
It's homemade—it doesn't get any better than this
I was cut out to be rich, but I was sewn up wrong
I'm a material girl—want to see my fabric collection?
If I stitch fast enough, does it count as an aerobic exercise?
Little Miss sew and sew
May your bobbin always be full!
My husband lets me have all the fabric I can hide!
One sewing project, like one cookie, is never enough!
Memories are sewn with love
Puttin' my treadle to the metal
Sentimental seamstress
Sew-aloha
Sew glad we're friends!
Sew in love
Sew lucky to be loved by you
Sewing mends the soul
Sew simple
Sew well, that you don't rip
So much fabric, so little time

Stay calm and sew
The love of sewing is our common thread
Stitch your stress away
You are sew special to me

❖ Weaving

A loom above
Oh, the many tangled things we weave
Over and under
Sheep thrills
Spinning wheel watch me weave
Weaving magic
Woven treasures
Looming possibilities
Take it or weave it
Woven together with love
Yarn trails
The joy of weaving

❖ Writing

All you have to do is write one true sentence— write the truest sentence you know
–Hemingway

A thousand little things every day offer opportunities to tell the details of life *–Linda LaTourelle*

Child, to say the very thing you really mean, the whole of it, nothing more or less or other than what you really mean; that's the whole art and joy of words *–C.S. Lewis*

Draw your chair up close to the edge of the precipice and I'll tell you a story –F. Scott Fitzgerald

My aim is to put down what I see and what I feel in the best and simplest way I can tell it –Hemingway

The best way to have a good idea is to have lots of ideas –Linus Pauling

We write to taste life twice, in the moment and in retrospection –Ayn Rand

Writing is creativity with a pen
Words are a lens to focus one's mind –Anais Nin

Writing is an occupation in which you have to keep proving your talent to those who have none –Jules Renard

You can make anything by writing –C.S. Lewis

CRYING

A cry for help
A cryin' shame
All teary-eyed
Behind these tears
Big girls / boys do cry
Blood, sweat and tears
Crybaby blues
Cry it out
Cry like a baby
Cry me a river
Cry on cue
Cry on my shoulder
Cryin' the blues over you
I'll cry instead
Every tear has a smile behind it
Tear after tear
Tears and joys
Tears on my pillow
You would cry too if...

DANCE

A chorus line
A pointe in time
All that jazz
All she / he wants to do is dance
Bee-bop baby
Belle of the ball
Could I have this dance?
Dance all night
Dance me to the end of love
Dance to live or live to dance
Dance through life with me—the best is yet to be
Dancin' feet
Dancin' on my daddy's toes
Dancin' with my baby
Dancing cheek to cheek
Feet don't fail me now
First recital
Getting' in the swing of things
Happy feet
I brake for dancers
I dance, therefore I am
I've got rhythm

Jitterbug girl / boy
Keep on dancin'
Let's boogie
Life is a dance
Life is simple—eat, sleep, dance!
Once a dancer, always a dancer
One good turn deserves another
Our prima ballerina
Practice makes perfect
Recital memories
Shake that bootie
Shall we dance?
Something in the way she / he moves
Step by step
Swing kids
Takes two to tango
Time to tap
Tiny dancer
Toe shoes and tutus
Two to tango
We've got rhythm
You are tutu cute!!
You make me feel like dancing
You should be dancin'

DAYS OF THE WEEK

A day in the life of...
Days of our lives
Eight days a week
Happy days are here again
Just one of those days
Lazy, hazy, crazy days of summer
My many-colored days
Oh happy day!
Our day will come
Today's the first day

♣ Sunday
Loving you Sunday morning
On any given Sunday
Palm Sunday
Sunday brunch
Sunday drives with dad
Sunday funnies
Sunday morning coming down
Sunday morning sunshine
Sunny Sunday

♣ Monday
Blue Monday
Come Monday all will be just fine
Monday Monday
Monday morning blues
Monday night quarterback
Monday's child is fair of face
Rainy Mondays
Stormy Monday

♣ Tuesday
Fat Tuesday
Groovy Tuesday
Shaky Tuesday
Totally Tuesday
Tuesday's child is full of grace

♣ Wednesday
On any Wednesday
Wacky Wednesday

Wednesday special
Wednesday's child is full of wow
Wet and wild Wednesday

♣ Thursday
Jersey Thursday
Sweet Thursday
Thirsty Thursday
Thursday's child has far to go

♣ Friday
Finally Friday
Freaky Friday
Friday night crowd
Friday night is family night
Date night Fridays
Good Friday
My man Friday

♣ Saturday
Another Saturday night
Date nights on Saturdays
Good time Saturday night
It's Saturday night—I just got paid
Isn't it Saturday yet?
Saturday in the park
Saturday matinee
Saturday morning cartoons

DOGS & PUPPIES
2 bossy dogs live here
A boy and his dog
A dog is a man's best friend
American dog

Ask me about my grand-dog
Barkin' up the wrong tree
Best of breed
Beware! One happy dog and his well-trained master live here
Big dogs don't whine
Buy one-get one flea
Dog day afternoon
Doggone cute!
Dogs just wanna have fun
Every dog has his day
Faithful friends who are dear to us always
Four-legged friend
Good ol'e dog
Happiness is a warm puppy
My dog—my best friend
Home is where my dog is
Hot diggity dog
I am puppy, hear me bark
I love my dog
I woof you!
I'm the cat's meow, even if I am a dog!
In the doghouse now
Love me, love my dog!
Lucky dog
Me and my shadow
Must love mutts / dogs
My dog's bigger than your dog
My dog can lick yours
My name is No No Bad Dog—what's yours?

The Biggest Book of Words & Prompts for Scrapbooks, Art Journals & Crafts

My Pokey Little Puppy
No cats allowed
Oh, the paws-abilities!
Old dogs and new tricks
One happy puppy
Paw prints on your heart
Pick of the litter
So many puppies
Sometimes days you're the dog, some days the hydrant
They call them puppy lovers
Trained to do his duty
Waiting for a dog like you
Walking the dog
Who's that doggie in the window?
Woof-woof means _____

DREAMS

A dream come true for me and you
Beautiful dreamer
Chasing your dreams
Dream come true
Dream lover
Dream on
Dream sweet baby dreams
Dream weaver
Dreamland express
Dreams come a size too big so that we can grow into them
Dreams of the every day homemaker
Field of dreams
Follow your dreams

In my wildest dreams
If I could reach the stars for you, I'd pull down your dreams
May all your dreams come true
Only in my dreams
Sweet dreams are made of these
To sleep, perchance to dream
You are all my dreams come true

DRESS UP

All decked out
Barely dressed
Bell-bottom blues
Best-dressed beauty
Blue jeans and pearls
Blue jean lady
Bobby socks to stockings
Clothes make the man
Designer genes
Diva in blue jeans
Fashion diva
Going in style
I have nothing to wear
I'm too sexy for my shirt
Made to model
Mirror, mirror, on the wall
Miss Fashionista
Nothing is more fun than an attic with a trunk full of clothes
Pretending is such fun
Quick-change artist
Scarlet ribbons
She rocks those jeans

So many clothes, so little time!
Struttin' her stuff
Tailor-made
The lady is dressed for the ball
The woman in red
What not to wear
When I grow-up I want to be just like my mama
Worn by time—faded with love
You're lookin' good
You've got style
You wear it well

♣ Hats

A hat for every occasion
Hang on to your hat
Hats make the man
He / She wears it well
Hiding a bad hair day
Hold on to your hat
I love hats
I'm too sexy for my hat!
Hats for every occasion
In my Easter bonnet
Love that hat-titude
Old hat, new hat
So many hats, so little time
The cowboy and his hat
You can leave your hat on

♣ Shoes

1 pair, 10 pairs, 50 pairs—who's counting?
All you really need is the right pair of shoes
Baby needs a new pair of shoes
Boots and boys
Boots, shoes, purses, oh, yes!
Even cowgirls get the boot
Give me some shoes and watch my moves
Got heels? Boots?
Have shoes? Will shop!
How much is that shoe in the window?
Just give me shoes
Keep calm and go shoe shopping
I can deal with anything as long as I have the right shoes
If the shoe fits, buy more!
It's shoe-time!
Miss goody two-shoes
No one could ever fill your shoes
Put on your dancin' shoes
Ruby red slippers
Shoe-aholic
Shoes or food—that is the question?
Struttin' those heels
The glass slipper and her prince
The red shoes
There is always room for another pair of shoes
These heels were made for dancin'
These shoes were made for running

Stepping up to fashion
What would you do for a new pair of shoes?

DRIVING

Baby you can drive my car
Back roads and boulevards
Beep beep
Behind the wheel
Bright side of the road
Caution: teen driver
Chauffeur wanted
Cruisin' on a Sunday afternoon
Cruisin' down the boulevard
Driving my life away
Enjoying the ride
Freeway of love
Get your kicks on Route 66
Greased lightnin'
Hot rod honey
In the driver's seat
Just got my license
Keep it between the lines
Keep on truckin'
King of the road
Leave the driving to us
Licensed to drive
Life in the fast lane
Life is a highway
Mr. hot rod
My car's faster than your car
My first license
No particular place to go
On the road again
Pink cadillac
Queen / King of the highway
Ready to roll
Red light—green light
Roll on down the highway
Six days on the road
Student driver
Sunday afternoon drive
The long and winding road
The wheels on my car look—oh so good, oh so good!
Two wrong turns mean we're lost
Wanna race?
Who's gonna drive me now?

DUCKS

All ducked out and no place to swim
All ducks yellow and small—how I love you one and all -Linda LaTourelle
All my ducks are in a row
Bottoms up!
Don't get your feathers ruffled
Doodle duck
Duck of the Irish
Duck soup with quackers
Feathers from my nest
I dream of ducks
I love little baby ducks
I love quackers
I'm daffy for duck soup
I'm just quackers for you
It's a ducky life

Just me and my ducky
Lucky duck is on my side
My web-footed friends
Prince / Princess duck
Quackers and milk
Quacker-jacks
Rub-a-dub duck
Rubber ducky love
Talk to the ducks
The duck stops here
The golden egg
Waddle waddle, walk, quack
Yellow and proud of it
You had me at quack, quack
You quack me up

EDUCATION

Education is the kindling of a flame, not the filling of a vessel —Socrates

The knowledge of all things is possible —Leonardo da Vinci

Education is what remains after one has forgotten everything he learned in school —Albert Einstein

Few have been taught to any purpose who have not been their own teachers —Sir Joshua Reynolds

Formal education will make you a living; self-education will make you very wealthy —Linda LaTourelle

In life, you're given a test that teaches you a lesson —Tom Bodett

It is impossible for a man to learn what he thinks he already knows —Epictetus

It is the mark of an educated mind to be able to entertain a thought without accepting it —Aristotle

Learning is a treasure that will follow its owner everywhere —Chinese proverb

Learning never exhausts the mind —Leonardo da Vincinci

Learning without thought is labor lost —Confucius

Man's mind, once stretched by a new idea, never regains its original dimensions —Oliver Wendell Holmes

Only the educated are free —Epictetus

The important thing is not to stop questioning —Einstein

The most useful piece of learning for the uses of life is to unlearn what is untrue —Antisthenes

Using the gifts and talents you are born with will lead you to learn about your purpose and make learning your passion —Linda LaTourelle

When we learn about what we love, education is easy —Linda LaTourelle

You cannot open a book without learning something —Confucius

ENCOURAGEMENT

Blessed are the hearts that can bend for they shall never be broken —Albert Camus

Don't wait, the time will never be just right —Napoleon Hill

Every blade of grass has its angel that bends over it and whispers—grow, grow —The Talmud

Every failure is a stepping-stone to your success

If plan 'A' doesn't work, choose a new letter and start again

Man is the only creature that refuses to be what he is –*Albert Camus*

Sing your song—tell your story

Sometimes the questions are complicated and the answers are simple –*Dr. Seuss*

Trust yourself, you know more than you think you do –*Dr. Spock*

When odds are one in a million—be that one

Write it on your heart that every day is the best day of the year –*Ralph Waldo Emerson*

Your past does not define who you are—it is who you are now that matters the most

FAIRYTALES

Dreams are the touchstones of our character –*Henry David Thoreau*

Thinking is the work of intellect, dreaming is pleasure –*Victor Hugo*

Give me my robe, put on my crown; I have immortal longings in me –*Shakespeare*

Fairytales do come true—it's how I met you! –*Linda LaTourelle*

Fairytales are the stories dreams are made of! –*Linda LaTourelle*

Fairytale entrance at the castle door

Fairytales—those are the stories of me and you! –*Linda LaTourelle*

Be careful what you set your heart on, for it will surely be yours –*Ralph Waldo Emerson*

Let God write the fairytale of your life and it will have a happy ending –*Linda LaTourelle*

There are no rules of architecture for a castle in the clouds –*G.K. Chesterton*

Life is full of surprises and happy-ever-after –*Linda LaTourelle*

There is nothing so sweet as finding your prince / princess

I know nothing with any certainty, but the sight of stars makes me dream –*Van Gogh*

FAMILY

A nest that's blessed

All in the family

Bless our nest

Blessed is the love of family

Families are forever

Families find meaning in the little things

Family business

Family fairytales

Family feeding frenzy

Family Feud is our favorite game

Family game night

Family man

Family portrait

Family rules

Family traditions are treasures

Focus on the family

Growing our family

Happy family gatherings

I love family

If you met my family you'd understand

In-laws and out-laws

Inspired by love

It runs in the family

It's a family affair

It's all relative

Kindred spirits

Kinfolk comforts

Life is nothing without family

Love lives here

Man, woman and child

Married with children

My family is...

My family rocks

My family, my love, my life

Need comic relief? Call family!

One big happy family

Our family heritage

Our family is complete

Relative bliss

Taste of home

The family band

The family circle

The family heirloom

The family that prays together, stays together

The gang's all here

The next generation of _____

The secret world of family

Theory of relativity

There's no place like home

Through thick and thin and back again—forever family

Together forever

We have circled and circled till we have arrived home again –*Walt Whitman*

We're a happy family

We're in this together

Yours, mine and ours

Where can one better be than in the bosom of one's family?

♣ *Aunt*

An aunt is a joy to remember your whole life through

Aunt-icipate the wonderful when Auntie comes to visit

Aunts are special friends

Aunts are sometimes like sisters, sometimes like moms, but always like friends

Aunts make life a little sweeter

A double blessing; you love like a parent and act like a friend!

Aunts like you are precious and few

I'm pretty like my aunt

In my aunt's heart grows a garden of love

Everything is nicer shared with an aunt!

Call 1-800-Auntie for spoiling

Sister, friend and mother—my aunt is like no other

Some aunts are groovy, some aunts are fun, some aunts are smart, but my aunt is everything, wonderful, all in one!

You're my aunt and my friend

✤ Brother

MY BROTHER
Someone to lean on
Someone to talk to
Someone to count on
My whole life through
—Linda LaTourelle

A brother is a friend God gave you

A brother is a special friend

A brother like no other!

A mystic bond of brotherhood makes all men one —Thomas Carlyle

Am I my brother's keeper

Being your brother is the best

Best buddies—my brother and me

Big brother / Little brother

Boogie brothers

Brothers are another word for love

Brother of mine

Brothers together—stronger than ever

Brotherly love

Brothers and sisters are as close as hands and feet —Vietnamese proverb

Brothers are a work of heart

Brothers are forever

Brothers are special—especially mine

Brothers are the best

Brothers make the best friends

Brothers share childhood memories and grown-up dreams

Celebrating brotherhood

Dear Brother

First a brother, now a friend

For the love of a brother

Forever my brother, always my friend

Growing up together

Happy or sad, big or tall, mean or nice, best of all—my brother!

Having a brother is having a best friend for life

He ain't heavy, he's my brother!

Hey big brother

I couldn't ask for a better brother

I love my brother

I'm glad God chose you to be my brother!

If I could pick the best brother—it would be you

It was nice growing up with a brother like you

Me and my big / little brother

My brother did it

My brother was once a bother— now he is my brother's a friend

My brother, my buddy / my friend

Oh, bother, oh brother!

Siblings by chance—friends by choice

Sometimes being a brother is even better than being a superhero

Soulful brothers

The best way to get a puppy is to ask for a baby brother

The brother club / brotherhood

The crest and crowning of all good, life's final star, is brotherhood –*Edwin Markham*

The highlight of my childhood was making my brother laugh so hard that food came out his nose

There's no buddy like a brother

When brothers agree, no fortress is so strong as their common life –*Antisthenes*

When I get big, I'll get even!

♣ Cousin

Born cousins—blessed as friends

Cousins have a kin-nection!

Cousins are cool

Cousin to cousin

Cute cousins

Dozens of cousins

Forever cousins

In childhood we were best of friends and cousins, too!

I love my cousins

Just me and my cousin

Kissing cousins

Lovin' cousins

My cousin—my friend

The cousin patch

♣ Daughter

And thou shalt in thy daughter see, this picture, once resembled Thee
–*Ambrose Philips*

A daughter is a gift of love

A daughter is a joy and delight who makes everything bright

A daughter is a joy forever

A daughter is a reflection of her mother's heart

Ain't she cute!

All-American daughter

All girl—that's my daughter!

All I ever wanted I found in you

Daddy's little girl

Daughter's are the flowers of life

Dear daughter…you've been a blessing from the start, with joy and love you stole my heart

Daughter of mine

Good daughters make good mothers

He that would the daughter win, must with the mother first begin –*English proverb*

I love my daughter with all that I am and want her to be happy as can be

Daughters are…

I prayed for a daughter, sweet and kind like you, I am so blessed because my prayers came true

It's a girl's thang!

Many daughters have done virtuously, but thou excellest them all —Proverbs 31:29

My blue-jean baby

A daughter is sunshine every day

My daughter, my friend, with love that never ends

My greatest treasure is my daughter

My lovely darling daughter

My pretty girl, my daughter

Old as she was, she still missed her mother sometimes

One-in-a-million daughter

She brightens my day and warms my heart, she was love and joy right from the start

One beautiful daughter

She's all girl!

She's her mother's daughter

She's my sunshine girl

To a father growing old, nothing is dearer than a daughter —Euripides

What the daughter does, the Mother did —Jewish proverb

♣ Family Trees

A legacy of love

Ancestors—the roots from whence we came

Back to our roots

Bad heir days

Dear ancestor

Every man is a quotation from all his ancestors —Ralph Waldo Emerson

Family archives

From generation to generation

Generation to generation

Kinship is all relative!

Linked by love and genes

Love endureth through all generations —Psalm 102:12

Many a family tree needs pruning

My ancestors

My family circle

Our family tree is blessed with Thee

Our legacy of love

Our roots run deep

Our roots remain as one family

Out on a limb with my family tree

Through the pages of time

The first 100 years of life are the hardest

The older love grows, the stronger it is

Watering the family tree

♣ Father

1001 reasons why I love my father...

A dad is someone who teaches you to drive the family car and your life

A dad is someone you never outgrow your need for

A day in the life of dad

A father and his car keys are soon parted

A father is someone you can lean on and learn from always

A father is someone you look up to no matter how tall you grow

A father's love warms the heart
Big bopper, my poppa
Boys will be boys until they become a daddy
Celebrating dad
Celebration of fatherhood
Color him father
Confessions of a stay-at-home dad
Conversations with my father
Dad always takes first place
Dad—another word for love
Dad-talk
Dad—a son's first hero, a daughter's first love
Dad is spelled H-E-R-O
Dads #1 fan
Dad's can fix anything—especially boo-boo's and broken hearts
Dad's day is a happy day
Dads say the funniest things
Dad's survival guide to babies
Dad's workshop
Daddy and me
Daddy's girl / boy
Daddy's little / big man
Daddy's little prince / princess
Don't wake Daddy
Dribbling with my dad
Father is a special word for love
Father knows less than Mom
Father of the year
Father still knows best
Fathers are forever
Fathers are special—especially mine!
Give Dad duct tape and he can fix anything
He's not just a dad—he's my dad!
Here's looking at you kids—Love Dad!
Hero worship—My Dad!
His father's son
I remember Daddy
I wanna be just like you, Dad!
I'm going to count to three!
In Daddy's arms
Inside the cave with Dad
It's a dad's life! / world
It's all about Daddy
It's in his hug
Just Daddy and me
Just for Pop
Just like Dad
Just me and my dad
Just one groovy dad
Keep calm and hug your dad
King of Mom's castle
Lessons from Dad
Letters to my dad
Life with Father
Like father, like son
Men behaving dad-ly
Mr. Fix-it man
MVP—Most Valuable Pop
My dad can do anything
My dad rules!
My dad—the caveman
My dad—the man, the myth and the legend
My dad's better than your dad

My daddy hung the moon
My daddy the all-star
My daddy, my hero
My father's hands
My finger may be small, but I can still wrap my daddy around it
My heart belongs to Daddy
My heart will always belong to Daddy
My hero
My pop is the greatest
My role model—my dad!
Nobody does it better than my dad!
No matter how tall I grow or old I get, my dad will always love me
No matter how tall I grow, I will always look up to my dad
No one can fill Daddy's shoes
One father is more than a hundred schoolmasters
Our dad has a heart of gold
Our dad's the greatest
Our hero, our father!
Papa loves mambo
Patio daddy-o
Portrait of my father
Proud papa
Some mornings I wake up grouchy, other mornings I let him sleep
St. Daddy's Day
Sugar daddy, sweet daddy!
Super dad
Tales from the dad-side
The best thing in my life is having a dad like you!
The coolest dad on the block

The dad's survival guide
The head of the home is the father
The joys of fatherhood begin with a child's first breath
The ideal dad belongs to me!
The love of a family begins with dad
The love of a father shines in his children's eyes
The memories of a great dad
The official sports dad
The toughest job you'll ever have and love—being a dad
The worlds greatest dad belongs to me and that make life happy as can be
Things my dad taught me...
Walking in Daddy's footsteps
We love Dad
When Daddy ain't happy—look out!
When Daddy says no, just ask Mom
When I grow up, I wanna be like Daddy
Who's your daddy?
World's best dad is mine!

❖ Grandchildren

A small grandchild is a big joy
Grandchildren—precious treasures
Grandchildren leave handprints on our hearts and our walls!
Grandchildren spoiled here!
Grandkids make life grand!
Grandkids are my reward
Grandchildren are jewels in their grandparent's treasure chest of love
Grandchildren are our compensation for growing old

So many grandkids, so little time

Grandchildren are the crowns of the aged –*Proverbs 17:16*

Grandchildren are loving doubled Generation to generation

Grandchildren are the crowns of old men

Grandkids are a grandparent's link to the future

Dearer than our children are the children of our children

Grandchildren—God's payment for gray hair and wrinkles

You think I'm spoiled? Thank Grandpa / Grandma!

Grandkids are a joy to treasure

My grandkids are the grand in my day

The grandest of all my grandkids one and all

Sunshine on any day—grandkids

Grandkids steal the key to our heart

Spoiled rotten grandchildren live here

Stay young—have grandchildren!

Grandchildren are the spark that lights a grandparent's way

Happiness is having grandchildren

Happiness is great-grandchildren

♣ *Grandparents*

"Feel free to change Grandma to Grandpa (or vice-versa) as needed "

Sitting on my grandpa's lap
Reading and singing songs,
I'm feeling so loved and happy
Think I'll stay here all day long
–Linda LaTourelle

Gold in her heart
Silver in her hair
What a special joy—
When grandma's here!
–Linda LaTourelle

A grandfather / grandmother is a father / mother with a lot of practice

A grandfather's love is like no other

A grandma is a gift of love

Grandma is a mom with extra frosting

A grandma reflects love in all she does

A grandpa is someone you never outgrow your need for!

A grandpa is a special friend

Aren't they grand? My grandparents!

Being a grandparent is almost better than being a parent

Every home needs a grandpa / grandma

Grandma fills the world with happiness Grandmas makes boo-boo's better

Grandma / Grandpa said I could

Grandma's / Grandpa's got the touch

Grandma's my name, spoilin's my fame

Grandmas are just cute little girls in big aprons

Grandmas are mommies with lots of practice

Grandmas / Grandpas are the greatest

Grandmothers are voices of the past

The Biggest Book of Words & Prompts for Scrapbooks, Art Journals & Crafts

Did you ever see a grandma
Who couldn't something say
In the ear of her little grandson
That would drive his frowns away?
—Harry I. Culler

Grandpa's / Grandma's little man / girl

Grandparents—oldies but goodies

Grandma's kitchen kids eat free

Grandparents know how to have fun

Grandparents make the world a little softer, a little kinder and a little warmer

Grandpas—little boys in a big boy body

Grandpas are short on criticism and long on love

Grannies make the world go 'round

Granny's flower garden of grandchildren

Great mothers get promoted to grandmothers

Groovy grandma / grandpa

Hangin' out at grandma's

I love my grandma's wrinkles because every one tells a story of her life

I have the perfect grandparents

I'm never in trouble when I'm with grandpa

I'm running away to Grandma's

I'm the twinkle in my grandma's / grandpa's eye

In all the world there'll never be a grandma as sweet as Thee

Grandparents know everything!

Just Grandpa / Grandma and me

Just me and my grandma

Mom won't spoil me, but Grandma will

My heart belongs to Grandma

Need a great babysitter? Call Grandma!

Over the river and down the road to Grandmother's house we go...

So many grandparents, so much love

The sweetest joy is a grandpa and his boy

There are always cookies at Grandma's / Grandpa's

There's no place like Grandma's

To Grandmother's house we go

Two proud grandparents live here

When Dad says 'no'—ask Grandpa

When I was born, so was my grandma

When I grow up I want to be just like Grandpa / Grandma

Whenever I want something I call Grandma / Grandpa

When the kids leave home they go to Grandma's

Who needs a horsey when you've got Grandpa

You put the "grand" in grandparents

♣ *Husband*

A man among men

A thousand little reasons why I love him more and more every day

Beloved husband of mine

Chivalry still reigns

From a prince to a king

Give your husband an inch and he'll rule the house and make you love it!

Happily married hubby

He's my man

Husband Training 101

Husband for sale—remote included

Husbands and wives in love

I am my beloved and he is mine

I got a cat for my husband—seemed like a fair trade

I love a man with dishpan hands

I miss my ex-husband, but my aim is getting better

Iron man in training

Man is the king of his castle until his queen comes home

Man of the year

My dearest husband

My favorite husband

My gorgeous husband

My piano man

My soul man

One wild and crazy guy

Partners for life

Perfect husbands and other fairytales

Real men ask directions!

Real men do dishes and eat quiche

Simple man, sweet husband

Tales of a terrific husband and other myths

The calmest husbands make the stormiest wives –English proverb

The almost perfect husband

The guide to training a good husband

The husband who could

The husbands guide to marriage

The ideal husband

The indulgent husband

The ladies man

The one that I love

The perfect husband

The perfect wife is one who doesn't expect a perfect husband

The proper care and feeding of husbands

What a man!

When a wife has a good husband it is easily seen in her face –Goethe

You've got male

♣ In-laws

All in the family

Doubly blessed

Family by marriage, friends by choice

Family heritage

Family is love

Getting to know you

Happiness is having your mother-in-law love you—because you love her son

I love you as my own child

In-laws and out-laws

In-laws are helpful and kind, with love in mind

Individually we are special, together we are a family

It's all relative

Kindred spirits

The Biggest Book of Words & Prompts for Scrapbooks, Art Journals & Crafts

Mother by marriage, friend by choice

Mother-in-law blues

Mother-in-laws law—remember you were once a daughter-in-law

My mother-in-law—my friend

Relative bliss is the in thing

Never rely on the glory of the morning nor the smiles of your mother-in-law *-Japanese proverb*

Next of kin

Once a bride and groom—now we are in-laws, blessed with a bigger family

Our family tree is blessed with Thee

Steppin' up to be a new family

Sweet as can be, my mother-in-law to me!

The mother-in-law dance

Through thick and thin

Treat others as you would be treated and add some extra love

We're a wacky bunch

We're all in this together

Lucky as can be, I have two families

You're like a mother to me

♣ Mother

A day in the life of Mom

A girl's best friend is her mother

A mother is the truest friend we will ever have

A mother holds her children on her lap for just a bit—but their hearts forever

I hope my child
looks back one day
and sees a mother
who was there to pray.
The years fly by
and children grow,
but to be loved
and desired
they surely will know.
-Linda LaTourelle

A mother is a special kind of friend

A mother is the blanket that warms a child when days are cold

A mother makes your heart happy

All mothers need a girl's night out

A mother takes her children everywhere she goes, if only in her heart *-Linda LaTourelle*

A mother understands a child's heart like no other

A mother's arms are made of tenderness and children sleep soundly in them *-Victor Hugo*

A mother's heart is a beautiful expression of God's everlasting love

A mother's love endures through all

A mother's love lasts forever

A mother's love never ages

A mother's arms are made of tenderness and children sleep soundly in them *-Victor Hugo*

A mother's love dries tears

A mother's love is new every day

A mother's love is the heart of the home and her family

A mother's love perceives no impossibilities

A mother's work is priceless

All mothers are working mothers

All mothers begin their lives as someone's daughter

All that I am or hope to be, I owe to my angel mother –*Abraham Lincoln*

All the words in the world can't say what a hug from Mom can

All things great and small, my mother taught me to love them all

Always kiss your children goodnight—it will bless you both with a wonderful night's sleep

An ounce of mother is worth a pound of clergy –*Spanish proverb*

As a mother, my job is to take care of the possible and trust God with the impossible –*Ruth Bell Graham*

A mother like no other

A rich child shares his poor mother's lap

As daughters, we share our mother's hearts in ways that are unique to just us

As is the mother, so is her daughter –*Ezekiel 16:44*

Ask not what your mother can do for you, ask what you can do for your mother

Because I am the mom, that's why!

Before I was a mom…

Behind every successful child is a mother's encouraging love

Being a mother has made my life complete

Blessed assurance, Mama is here. Sweet love to give for her baby dear. –*Linda LaTourelle*

Call your mother—she cares!

Domestic goddess

Don't mess with Mama!

Every mother knows when children say they are doing nothing, there's trouble ahead

Father knows best, but Mom knows better!

First my mother, forever my friend

God made you my mother and love made you my friend

Her children arise and call her blessed; her husband also, and he praises her –*Proverbs 31:28*

Home is where a mother's love surrounds her family

I always thought having you for my mother was a wonderful blessing, but those blessings are now doubled because my children have you for their grandmother

I am blessed to call you my mother

I love you Mommy because…

I love you, Mama!

I will never outgrow my love for my mother

I'm glad God chose you to be my mother!

I'm as lucky as lucky can be because the world most amazing mom belongs to me

I've become my mother more and more—and that is love reincarnated

If at first you don't succeed, do it like your mother told you

If I could choose from all the mothers in the world, Mom, I'd choose you

If love were a color, you would be the rainbow to me, Mom!

Life affords no greater responsibility, no greater privilege than the raising of the next generation –C. Everett Koop

It's good to be queen of my castle

If Mama ain't happy, nobody is!

In the sheltered simplicity of the first days after a baby is born, one sees again the magical closed circle, the miraculous sense of two people existing only for each other –Anne Morrow Lindbergh

It is the mother who can cure her child's tears –African proverb

Just me and my mom

Life began the moment I saw my mommy's face

Lifestyles of a frantic and frazzled mom

Like mother—like child

M is for Mom, Mother, Mama, Mommy and my best friend!

M is not for maid

Magical mommy moments

Mama knows everything!

Mama said there'd be days like this...

Mirror, mirror on the wall, I look like my mother after all

Mom knew that love was all that mattered in life

Mom, thanks for being you and always encouraging me to be me!

Mommies are just big little girls in aprons!

Moms are the treasures of the world!

Mothers hate four letter words like: cook, wash, iron and dust!

Mother in training!

Mother—a healer of boo-boo's, broken hearts and a friend forever

Mother—you created home for my heart forever

Mother—your love comforts always!

Mothers are roses in life's garden

Motherhood—all love begins and ends there –Robert Browning

Mothers are instinctive philosophers –Harriet Beecher Stowe

Mothers plant the seeds that grow beautiful children

Mum's a word I love!

My heart belongs to Mama

My mama said...

My mother's name is spelled L-O-V-E

My mother—I love the sound of those two words!

My mother's heart was enormous —it held enough love for her six children and all that was important to each one –Linda LaTourelle

My mother's love tucks me in and keeps me warm, if only in my heart!

My mother's prayers have always followed me

Nobody does it better than my mom

No one can hug a child like Mama!

No one is poor who had a godly mother –Abraham Lincoln

No painter's brush, nor poet's pen in justice to her fame, has ever reached half-high enough to write my mom's name

Nobody loves a child like Mama does

No matter how old a mother is, her children will always be her babies

Nothing is dearer to a mother than sharing a day with her daughter / son / children

Of course I can do anything—my mom told me I could

She always knew how to love us in just the right way

She's still doing laundry after all these years

Someone's in the kitchen with Mommy

Sooner or later we will hear our mother's words in our own voice

Super mom-tastic mother!

The art of mothering transcends generation to generation

The queen of everything—Mom

The greatest gift of all is a loving mother who gives her all

The heart of a mother is a deep abyss at the bottom of which you will always find forgiveness –Honoree de Balzac

The highest, most noble calling is that of being a mother

The love for a mother deepens with each passing year

The most important right afforded a woman is to be a mother

The most important thing a father can do for his children is to love their mother

The mother of all mothers—that's my mom!

The sounds of home make a wonderful song in a mother's heart

The wise mother is a child's greatest blessing

There is a place in childhood that I remember well, the sound of her voice and stories she loved to tell –Linda LaTourelle

There is no other, like my mother!

There is no substitute for Mother, Mom or Mama

There is only one beautiful child— and it belongs to Mama!

This is what a rocking, groovy, cool mom looks like!

Where did my mom learn all that she told me not to do?

This momster mama rocks!

Who ran to help me when I fell, and would some pretty story tell, or kiss the place to make it well? My mother –Jane and Ann Taylor

To the mother of young children there is time for everything except rest

Time is the only comforter for the loss of a mother. When God invented mothers, He gave me the best in you!

When it comes to love—mom's the word!

When thoughts of Mom are in my hearts I am never very far from home

You can fool some of the people some of the time, but you can't fool Mom anytime!

Your love helps me grow, Mommy!

Youth fades, love droops, the leaves of friendship fall; a mother's secret hope outlives them all –Oliver Wendell Holmes

❖ Parents

1000 reasons why I love being a parent

101 ways to laugh your way through parenthood

A child's greatest teacher—his parent

A happy childhood is one of the best gifts parents can give their child

All that is worth cherishing in this world is held in a parent's hands

A parents actions speak louder than any words

After leaving home, I realized my parents were so smart

An empty nest is a quiet nest

And you thought your parents were weird!

Be the kind of parent that will inspire good character, kindness, creativity in thought, word and deed –Linda LaTourelle

Be the parent you always wished you had

Be the person you would want your child to love

Be the person you want your child to be

Being a parent changes everything

Children and other hazards of parenthood

Children make us a mother or a father—love makes us a parent

Confessions of a happy parent

Don't sweat the small stuff

Dynamic duo

Everything I knew about parenting

Everything you need to know about parenting in five easy lessons

Exposing the myths of parenting

Extreme parenting

Fairly odd parents

From baby bumps to blue jeans: parenting from birth to teen

Good parent, bad parent and everything in-between

Guilt-free parenting

Happiness is being a parent

Happy parents are good parents

How fast the years fly!

I love you and you love me

I wanna be just like my momma and daddy

In search of parenthood

It is the wise parent who gives his child roots and wings

Kissing your children goodnight is a moment to treasure

Let us put our minds together and see what life we can make for our children

Lifestyles of the rich and frazzled—parents!

Life's greatest blessing and privilege, is to be a parent
–Linda LaTourelle

I'm just having a parent moment

Mamas and the Papas

Man and / or woman with child

Married with children

Meet the parents

Murphy's laws on parenthood

My parents are too hip to be square

My parents were my greatest teachers, wisest counsel and best friends

Our favorite job we ever had was being your mom and your dad

Parent's have a clear vision often seen through rose-colored glasses
–Linda LaTourelle

Parenthood: it changes lives

Parenthood—adventure of a lifetime!

Parenthood: the funny side!

Parenting is a family affair

Parenting is a labor of love that lasts a lifetime

Parenting without hassles and other wishful thoughts

Parenting: one size does not fit all; results may vary according to ingredients used

Parenting: things my mother never told me

Parents and children united in love

Parents—a mirror to a child's heart

Parents gone wild

Parents know best / know nothing

Paternity fraternity

Perfect parent's guide to surviving childhood

Parents will be parents

Perfect parenting and other myths

Planet parenthood

Pregnancy to parenthood

Surviving parenthood in ten easy lessons

Tales from a happy parent

Teach your children well that they will want to be just like you

Teach your parents well

The art of parenting

The best inheritance is time well-spent between a parent and a child

The best security blanket a child has is his parents

The best thing a parent can give to their child is happy memories

The best time to rest is after your children leave home

The blessing of a parent on a child is life-changing and eternal

The character of your child depends on you

The joys of parenthood

The light side of parenting

The most important thing a father can do for his children is to love their mother

The official guide to parenting in 100 blank pages

The parent's survival guide

The parent trap

The presence of a parent will outlast any present –Linda LaTourelle

The truth about parenthood

The ultimate guide to being a parent

The world according to parents

There is no friendship, no love, like that of a parent for the child – Henry Ward Beecher

To the world, you may just be one person, but to your child you are everything

To understand your parent's love, you must raise a child yourself

We never understand our parents love for us until we become parents

What a parent imparts to his child will echo for generations

Once you have children yourself, you begin to understand the gratitude you owe your parents

You are the bows from which your children as living arrows are sent forth –Khalil Gibran

You can't scare me...I have children!

You think you know what love is —and then you have a child and discover that it was more than you ever could have imagined –Linda LaTourelle

Yours, mine, and ours

Zen and the art of parenthood

✤ Siblings

All for one and one for all

All in the family

A sibling understands

As far as siblings—mine are the best!

Birds of a feather

Celebrating my siblings

History makers and shakers!

Oh, the secrets my siblings could tell!

Siblings are God's gift to us, as we are to them

Siblings are the friends we come home to

Siblings by chance, friends by choice

Siblings by chance, friends by love

Sibling harmony

Sisters and brothers together

Striving for birth order

There is no joy like the joy of sharing

There is no rivalry in our family—we just love to tease

To get the full value of joy you must have someone to divide it with –Mark Twain

Two of a kind

We are our sibling's keeper—the keeper of his / her's heart

We share a history

What's is yours is mine and what is mine is my own

When a child is born so is a brother or sister

When I get big, I'll get even

Where there are siblings—look out for the quibbling!

♣ Sister

A SISTER
Confidant
Counselor
Comforter
Childhood playmate
Cherished friend
–Linda LaTourelle

MY SISTER
My sister!
With that thrilling word
What thoughts unnumbered
wildly spring!
What echoes in my heart
are stirred,
While thus I touch
the trembling string!
–Margaret Davidson

A celebration of sisterhood

A ministering angel shall my sister be *–Shakespeare*

A sister is a special kind of friend

A sister is a gift of love sent to bless from heaven above

A sister is my favorite thing to be

A sister is a little bit of childhood that can never be lost

A sister knows every little thing about you and loves you anyway

A sister is a forever friend

A sister's love is for all seasons

All I ever really needed to know—my sister taught me well

All my sisters

Always my sister, forever my friend

Being sisters is pure joy

Best friends—my sissy and me

Big sis and li'l sis

Big sisters are the best friends

Big sisters are the frosting on the cupcakes of childhood!

Big / Little sisters rock

Bless you, my darling, and remember you are always in the heart –oh, tucked so close there is no chance of escape –of your sister *–Katherine Mansfield*

Brothers and sisters are as close as hands and feet *–Japanese proverb*

Childhood memories and grown-up dream

Everything is better with a sister

First my sister, forever my friend

For lots of fun—1-800-sister!

I couldn't ask for a better sister

God made us sisters—Mom made us be friends

God's design made us sisters and love made us friends forever

Happy as can be, the world's best sister is a part of me

"Help one another" is part of the religion of sisterhood *–Louisa May Alcott*

Hey soul sister...do you know I love you

I could never love anyone as much as I love my sister

A SISTER

For there is no friend like a sister
In calm or stormy weather;
To cheer one on the tedious way,
To fetch one if one goes astray,
To lift one if one totters down,
To strengthen whilst one stands.
—Christina Rossetti

I love being the little sister!

I love my sister for a million little reasons

I thank my God on every remembrance of you —Philippians 1:13

I'm glad God chose you to be my brother

I'm not afraid of the dark because my sister is always there

I'm not perfect—I'm your sister

In short, I will part with anything for you—but you I —Lady Mary Worley Montague

In the garden of life we are sisters of a different fragrance

In Thee my soul shall own combined the sister and the friend —Catherine Killigrew

In thy face, I see the map of honor, truth, and loyalty —Shakespeare

Is solace anywhere more comforting than in the arms of sisters? —Alice Walker

It is a comfort knowing your sister is there when you need her most

It's a sister thing!

Life would be empty without my sister

It's wonderful to know there is one person I can trust with all of my heart—my sister!

Just me and my sister

Keep calm—and call your sister

Little sister / Big sister

Many women do noble things, but my sister surpasses them all

Little sisters are sugar in your tea!

Memories we share, none compare

My sister is my best friend

My brother has the best sister in the world

My heart will always be close to you, my sister

My little sister wears the look our mother wore —Elizabeth Barrett Browning

My sister has the best sister ever—me

My sister is the one I turn to always

My sister shares memories that no one will ever know

My sister, my friend

My sisters don't know it, but I've envied them all my life

My sisters—wouldn't trade them for anyone else

No distance can separate the love that sisters share

No sister can compare to Thee

No sisters ever prized each other more —Tennyson

Of all the things that I've to play, I'd choose my sister any day

Only a sister can make you feel sweet and smart with just one look!

She knows if you've been bad or good—your sister! –Linda LaTourelle

Oh brother, she's my sister

She loves me just the way I am

She put her hand on her sister's and they both sat silent for a little while –Louisa May Alcott

She speaks with wisdom –Proverbs 31:26

She with her happy gaze finds all that's best –Augusta Webster

Little / Big sisters rock!

Silly, sassy, and so much fun—that's my sister!

Sisters—love 'em or leave 'em

Sister and friend—two words that mean the same

Sister by chance, friends by choice

Sister, you are amazing!

Sisterhood is a sheltering tree that will protect you and offer comfort from the storms of life –Linda LaTourelle

Sisters and chocolate make life bearable

Sisters are a part of childhood that will always remain a part of you

Sisters are forever friends

Sisters tell the best stories about you

Sisters are the best kind of friends

Sisters are the sweetest flowers in the garden of life

Sisters can be the crabgrass in the landscape of living. –Linda LaTourelle

Sisters can challenge you the most but help you to be your best

Sisters know you inside-out and love you anyway

Sisters share a special friendship that lasts a lifetime

Sisters are special—especially mine!

Sweet is the voice of a sister

The best thing about being sisters is that for a sister I have you! –Thena Smith

Sisters just wanna have fun!

The road to a sister's house is never long

The special love that sisters share is a celebration of the heart

The prettiest sister is mine

Therapy is expensive, sister's are exclusively there for you

There can be no situation in life in which the conversation of my dear sister will not administer some comfort to me –Lady Mary Worley Montague

There is no time like the old time, when you and I were young! –Oliver Wendell Holmes

Here's a special friendship that only sisters can enjoy

There's just something about having a sister like you!

There's no greater treasure than a sister

Thoughts of you always make me smile

Time spent with one's sister is refreshment to the soul

To have a sister is to see a reflection of yourself

When I get big, I'll win

To talk of childhood memories—only a sister will do

What parents don't understand—your sister always will

We wove a web in childhood, a web of sunny air –Charlotte Brontë

When I count my blessings, I count you many times

When the world doesn't understand, your sister will!

With you as my sister, the icicles tasted colder, the fireflies twinkled brighter, and the stars didn't seem so far away ~ Ludwig

You are priceless and precious

You can fool everyone except your sister

♣ Step-Family

Blending into a family

Families are born through love

Family by marriage, friends by choice

Family is love

Family is love no matter how it comes into our lives

Family of my heart

Getting to know you

I love you as my own

Individually we are special, together we are a family

Lucky as can be, I have two families

We are family

We're a wacky bunch

We're all in this together

You can go home again

♣ Uncle

A monkey's uncle

An uncle grows more treasured as time goes by!

An uncle is a gift whose worth cannot be measured except by the heart

An uncle is a joy to remember your whole life through

I not only call you uncle, I call you friend!

Say uncle

Uncle, you're forever in my heart

Undeniably naturally charismatic loving every day

Leave it to the uncles

Uncles just wanna have fun

My uncle, my buddy

When all else fails, call your uncle

Uncles like you are precious and few!

♣ Wife

A good wife and health is a man's best wealth

A natural woman

A Proverbs thirty-one wife

A wife to lean on

A woman in love

A woman's intuition is always right

Blessed and beautiful!

Blush is the color of virtue –Diogenes

Daze of our wives

Diamonds are a girl's best-friend, but so is a husband who does the dishes

Every princess needs her tiara

Everything men know about their wives—not much!

Goodnight husband, goodnight wife

Hot flashes just make me hotter

I am woman—I am exhausted

Live joyfully with the wife whom thou lovest all the days of the life... —*Ecclesiastes 9:9*

Man's blessing is an understanding wife beside him in life

My better half

My kind of wife, may lady is

My leading lady

My roller coaster wife

My so-called life as a happy wife

My wife story

My woman, my woman, my wife

Real women fix cars

Recipes from my wife

Sophisticated and sexy, too

SWAG: Southern Women Are Groovy

Tales of a military wife

That girl!

The dutiful wife

The excellent wife

The loveliest woman

The perfect wife

The secret lives of wives

The soldier's wife

The soul of a woman

The wives' club

The wives' tales

The woman's guide to men

Things learned from my husband

To be loved by a good man is the best and sweetest thing, which can happen to a woman —*Louisa May Alcott*

Whoso findeth a wife, findeth a good thing —*Proverbs 18:22*

Wild wonderful wife

Women and their friends

Women who love too much

Wonder woman

FARM ANIMALS

Animal house

Asleep in the haystack

Barnyard buddies

Counting sheep

Ewes not fat, ewes fluffy

Farming is the life for me

Flew the coop

Gentle as a lamb

Goosey, goosey gander

Grazin' in the grass

Hay good lookin'

Home, home on the farm

Horsing around at the farm

I love ewe

Like pulling hen's teeth

Mary had a little lamb

Old McDonald loves his farm

Old Mother Goose

Once upon a turkey

Pigs and sheep and cows, oh my

Stubborn as a mule

Talk to the animals
Welcome to our funny farm
Why do cows moo and pigs oink?
Wild and woolly
Wise as an owl

❖ *Chickens*

Chicken little
Chickens, cows & pigs that fly!
Dixie chickens
Don't put all your eggs in one basket
Here a chick, there a chick
Mad as a wet hen
The chicken dance
The chicken prince / princess
The little red hen

❖ *Cows*

A cow chip off the old pasture
Angus-ly devoted to you
An udder day in paradise
Can you herd my heart beat?
Cow are you?
Déjà moo—been herd before
Farmer Sonny's cows
Friends for heifer
Have an udderly delightful day
Herd the call
Holstein you close
Home, home on the pasture
Home is where the herd is
I love you dairy much
I'm head over hooves in love
In the moo-d for love
Lawn-mooer man
Manure happens
Me and my udder half
Moo kids on the block
Miss dairy princess
Moo-chas gracias
Moos flash!
Moo-sical delights
Precious moo-ments
Smoo-ches for Mom
Thinking of moo
Tomorrow is an udder day
We've moo'ved

❖ *Horses*

Back in the saddle
Blazing saddles
Giddy-up horsey
Hay is for horses
Hold your horses
Horsey, horsey, on your way
Horsin' around
Horse with no name
I love horses
Keep calm—ride a horse
Me and my pony
My little pony
Painted ponies
Pony express
Pony tales
Saddle-up
Stately steed
The mane attraction
The stable prince / princess
Wild horses

♣ Pigs

Blue ribbon pig
Cutest little piglet
Going whole-hog
Happy as a pig in the mud
Hogs and kisses
I love pigs
If pigs could fly
My favorite pig
My piggy bank
My potbellied friend
My squeaky friend
Oink! Oink!
Pig-headed
Piggy back rides
Piglets by the dozen
Pigs in love
Pigs in space
Pigs on a blanket
Pigs on the farm
Pigs on the run
Pigs to the rescue
The fattest pig
The great pig escape
The pig collector
The pig farmer
The pig kahuna
The pig prince / princess
The pig that was tickled pink
The pig who came to stay
The real dirt about pigs
Very important pig
This little piggy went to market

FARMING

AT HARVEST TIME
The harvest moon,
The flowers of June,
Bring back again
Their magic charm;
His life is spent,
In sweet content,
The man's a king,
Who owns a farm.
—Frank Willoughby

Abundant living
A day at the farm
Amber waves of grain
Barn dance tonight
Barnyard boogie
Barnyard buddies
Behind the plow
Beloved homestead
Bless this barn
Born in a barn
Born to farm
Cock-a-doodle-do
Country hoedown
Down on the farm
Eggs are chickens, too!
Farm girl / boy
Farm life journal
Farm living is the life for me
Farmer's daughter / son
Fine feathered friends
Flew the coop

From farm to table
Future farmer of America
God's little acre
Hay-cutting time
Hitch your wagon to my goat
Homegrown taters
Homegrown with love
How does your garden grow?
I'm from the country
Life on the farm
My papa drives a big red tractor
My sweet Deere—John
My tractor and me
My trip to the farm
Of farms and families
Old McDonald had a farm
One row at a time
Our farm friends
Our little house on the prairie
Papa / Mama and his / her farm
Pastures of plenty
Petunia and the potbellied piglets
Prize-winning poultry
Proud to be a farmer
Reap and ye shall sow
She thinks my tractor's sexy
Tales of the farmer's wife
Thank God I'm not a city boy / girl
The farmer's blues
The good earth
The king's farm
The rain song

FASHIONISTA

A fashion statement
A girl and her boots
All dolled-up
As long as I have the shoes to match, I can do anything
Beauty and brains, too!
Big girls need big diamonds
Chantilly lace and her pretty face
Chic and sweet
Clothes make the woman
Coat of many colors
Diva in-training
Dressed to the nines
Enamored with glamour
Forever in blue jeans
From leather to lace
Funky and fashionable
I don't do fashion
I have nothing to wear
Lady in red
Leather and denim
Lipstick and lollipops
Little black dress
Miss Purse-onality
Ms. / Mr. Fashionista
My passion's in fashion
Nothing in my closet
Pretty in pink
Pretty, pretty, hot!
Puttin' on the Ritz

Red high heels

Sassy, sexy and so sweet!

She rocks those jeans

She wears short shorts

She's a rhinestone cowgirl

She's my uptown girl

She rocks it tonight!

Shoes can be magic for a girl!

Sophisticated to the max

Star light, star bright, I wish I may, I wish I might, go shopping tonight

The queen of second-hand

These boots are made for dancin'

True beauty comes from the inside-out

Total makeover

Walking the red carpet

What not to wear

You rock those boots

You're good enough

FLOWERS

FLOWERS
Happy is the man
Whose thoughts,
Like larks,
Take liberated flight
Toward the morning skies
Who hovers over life and
Understands without effort
The language of flowers and
Voiceless things!
–Charles Baudelaire

DANDELIONS
Oh, downy
Dandelion wings,
Wild floating wings
Like silver spun,
That dance and glitter
In the sun!
You airy things,
You elfin things,
That June-time
Always brings!
Oh, are you seeds
That seek the earth,
The light of laughing
Flowers to spread?
Or flitting fairies,
That had birth
When merry words
Were said?
–Helen Gray Cone

Butterflies come to pretty flowers

Consider the lilies of the field

Flowers are the music of the ground from earth's lips spoken without sound –Edwin Curran

Flowers are the sweetest things

A PANSY
It lay upon my heart all day
With purple petals soft and bright,
I could not cast the flower away
Though it was withered ere the night
But placed it in my jewel case
To treasure more than all the rest,
For in its dust I see your face,
And in your memory am blest
–Laura Russell

ROSE

The rose is a rose,
and was always a rose,
but the theory now goes
that the apple's a rose,
and the pear is, and so's
the plum, I suppose,
the dear only knows
what will next prove a rose,
you, of course, are a rose—
but were always a rose.
—Robert Frost

APPLE BLOSSOMS

Have you plucked
the apple blossoms in the spring?
and caught their subtle odors
in the spring?
Pink buds pouting at the light,
crumpled petals baby-white,
just to touch them--a delight!
In the spring!
–William Wilsey Martin

FORGET-ME-NOT

Darling little flowers
Of a heavenly blue,
Bringing back your sweet eyes,
Tender, tried, and true.
And some tiny dewdrops
Seem to me the tears,
That you shed on parting
In the by-gone years.
Memories awaken
In this hallowed spot,
As I stoop to gather
A forget-me-not.
–Laura Russell

I will be the gladdest thing under the sun! I will touch a hundred flowers and not pick one —Edna St. Vincent Millay

Art is the unceasing effort to compete with the beauty of the flower garden's flowers and never succeeding —Marc Chagall

A violet by a mossy stone, half hidden from the eye, fair as a star, when only one is shining in the sky —Longfellow

A weed is but an unloved flower

Bread feeds the body, indeed, but flowers feed also the soul

God ever made and forgot to put a soul into —Henry Ward Beecher

Flowers follow the sun even on cloudy days

Flowers leave some of their fragrance in the hand that bestows them

I love to smell flowers in the dark...you get hold of their soul then —Lucy Maud Montgomery

If we could see the miracle of a single flower clearly, our whole life would change —Buddha

Let the beauty we love be what we do —Rumi

More than anything, I must have flowers always, always

Wild about wildflowers

Our finest flowers are often weeds transplanted —Elbert Hubbard

Wildflowers are like friends—they always come back

Where flowers bloom so does hope —Lady Bird Johnson

One must have sunshine, freedom and a pretty flower

ORIGIN OF VIOLETS
I know, blue modest violets,
Gleaming with dew at morn
I know the place you come from
And the way that you are born!
When God cut holes in heaven,
The holes the stars look through,
He let the scraps fall down to earth,
The little scraps are you
—*Unknown*

GATHER THE WILDFLOWERS
Gather the wildflowers
For rich and for poor,
Lowliest cottage
Or stateliest hall,
Childhood and old age
Their bright smiles allure,
Free as the sunbeams,
They blossom for all.
—*Martha Lavinia Hoffman*

LAVENDER
Sweet lavender!
I love thy flower
Of meek
And modest blue,
Which meets the morn
And evening hour,
The storm, the sunshine,
And the shower,
And changeth
Not its hue.
—*Agnes Strickland*

THE LOTUS
In the deep
Sequestered stream
The lotus grows,
blooming fresh and fair
In the morning sun.
—*Li Bai*

FOOD & COOKING

♣ Baking

A pinch of this, a dash of that

A tasty tradition

At home on the range

Baked with love

Baker / chef in training

Baking is my life

Blue ribbon baker

Boiling Water 101

Chief cook and dishwasher

Cinnamon and spice—so yummy and nice

Cooking in the raw

Dough, re, me loves to cook!

Eat, drink and be merry

Everyone loves to be kneaded

Flour power and sweet cream

From the kitchen of...

Green eggs and ham

Guess who's coming to dinner

Happiness is licking the spoon

Hey good lookin', what's cookin'?

Home-baked love

I could have baked all night

I'd rather be cooking

I kiss better than I cook

If you knew sushi, like I make sushi

I knead you more every day

Life is uncertain—eat dessert first

Live • Laugh • Bake
Lovin' from the oven
Mama Mia, that's a spicy meatball
Mama's kitchen
Happy are the memories of mom's apple pie
Prince / Princesses don't cook
Shall we gather in the kitchen?
Someone's in the kitchen with mama
Something's fishy around here
Still hot—even when I'm cookin'
Sugar pie, honey bunch
That little old baker mom
That's a one spicy mama!
The messy gourmet
There's no place like Mama's kitchen
The spice of life
The sweet fruits of summer
Welcome to my kitchen

♣ Barbeque-Grilling

A man and his grill
BBQ Cook-off Champion
BBQ Hall of Fame
Beverly grillbillies
Big Daddy's bbq
Man meets grill
Commander-In-Chef
Danger: men cooking
Finger-lickin' good
Firehouse special
Girls / men who grill
Grillin' queen / king
Grill master—he's the man
Grill sergeant
Hot Mama's BBQ
Legendary pit master
Licensed to grill
Look out! Dad's cooking!
Mr. / Ms. Sizzle
Much ado about BBQ
Real men don't use recipes
Real men wear aprons
Sauced and spicy
Smokin' hot
Some like it hot
The grill of his dreams
The legendary grill master
Up in smoke
Vintage chef
Where there's a grill, there's a way
Where's the beef?

♣ Candy & Sweets

All you need is love and a dozen cupcakes
A slice of the sweet life
Anytime is cookie time
A thing of beauty is Mom's coconut cake
Baby cakes
C is for cookie
Cake artist at work
Candy, cookies and cakes, oh my!
Candy kisses and marshmallow wishes
Coffee gets me out of bed, cupcakes are the reward

Cookie monsters live here

Cookies anyone?

Crazy for cupcakes

Crumbs and cravings

Cupcake queen

Got cookies?

Got cupcakes?

Have your cake and eat it too

How sweet it is to have your cake and eat it, too!

I do desserts

If you give a kid a cookie,,,

I'll have my cake and eat it, too

I love you more than cupcakes

Keep calm—bake cookies

Life's short—eat dessert first

Lollipop girls / boys

Love at first bite

Make cookies—not war

Me want cookie!

My sweet tooth

One cupcake is worth a thousand smiles

Peace • Love • Cupcakes

Sharing a cupcake is sharing your heart

Sugar and spice for your delight

Sugar shack

Sugar, sugar

Sweet beginnings

Sweetie pie

Sweets are us

Sweet shoppe and sundaes

Sweets for the sweet

The candy lady / man

The trail of the cookie thief

This is the sweet life

Who took the cookie from the cookie jar?

You are the icing on my cupcake

You are the sweet in my dreams

You take the cake

♣ *Chocolate*

A day without love is like a day without chocolate

All I want is peace, love and chocolate every hour

Anytime is chocolate time

Chocoholics anonymous dropout

Chocolate! Need I say more?

Crafting and chocolate—the perfect way to spend a day

Do not disturb: chocolate tasting in progress

Fifty shades of chocolate

Hand over the chocolate and no one gets hurt

Happy is the wife whose husband brings her chocolate!

He's like chocolate—sweet and creamy inside, sensual and dreamy outside *–Linda LaTourelle*

I am woman hear me roar—I need chocolate, give me more!

I am a woman of many dark moods—chocolate

I'd rather have chocolate than diamonds or gold

Handle life with prayer and chocolate

Just me and my chocolate

If at first you don't succeed, try chocolate!

If there is no chocolate in heaven, I'm not going!

I love a man with chocolate on his breath

I never met a chocolate I didn't love

Life's too short, eat chocolate

Life without chocolate is—sigh

Love is all you need—along with a whole lotta chocolate

Make mine triple chocolate!

Man doesn't live for chocolate, but to a woman it is the sweetness of life

Melt her heart with chocolate

Momma said there'd be days like this—no more chocolate

My favorite color—chocolate

My secret rendezvous with chocolate

Nobody knows the truffles I've seen

One taste of his chocolate drenched kisses and my heart was irrevocably taken

PMS and chocolate go together like birds of a feather

Quitting chocolate is for sissies

Starvation diet—no chocolate!

Headache cure: take two chocolates, a long hot bath

The best cure for anything is love covered in chocolate

The best things in life are chocolate

The key to my heart is chocolate

Too much chocolate is—simply wonderful!

Warning—serious chocoholic lurking!

When all else fails—try chocolate

When I get old and lonely I shall write love stories and eat chocolate

Will work for chocolate!

❖ *Coffee*

Anytime is coffee time

Coffee and Thee are perfect for me

Coffee or you? Wait 'til I wake up

Don't criticize my coffee, you may be old and weak one day

Eat, sleep and drink coffee

Give me coffee—no one gets hurt

Happiness is coffee and you

Happiness is a great book and an even better cup of coffee

He is the sugar and I am the cream—together we make a rich, hot, steamy cup of love

I don't do mornings until I've had my coffee

I'd stop drinking coffee, but I'm no quitter

I love you a latte

Instant human—fill with coffee

Keep calm—make it decaf

Life is too short for cheap coffee

Make mine mocha and give me a latte

No questions until I've had my ~~second~~ third cup of coffee!

Must love coffee

My morning cup of ambition

Sleep is a poor substitute for coffee

Two cups and my engine is revved and ready!

Wake up and smell the coffee

What I love about coffee, I love about you—waking up slowly with you warms me inside-out—your aroma invites kisses that taste delicious

With coffee, anything is possible

You are the cream in my coffee

♣ *Diet*

Chocolate is an important part of a balanced diet

Dieting is not a piece of cake

Eat dessert first and you won't be hungry for anything else

I've been on a diet for two weeks and so far all I've lost is fourteen days

Mind over platter

My goal in life is to weigh what my drivers license says I do

Never, never, never quit

One large coffee—hold the morning

Take twice as long and eat half as much

Think thin—eat trim—you win!

Tomorrow's another diet

♣ *Fruits & Veggies*

A is for apple

American as apple pie

Apple dumplin' darlin'

Apple, peaches, pumpkin pie

Back to the same old "rind"

Berry beautiful

Carrot cake counts as a serving of vegetables

Cool as a cucumber

Fruit of the vine

Little apple dumpling

If life is a bowl of cherries, why do I get so many pits!

I like to eat apples and bananas

Like peaches and cream

Mom's apple pie

She's the apple of my eye

Shiny apples, yummy pie—make me happy all the time

Strawberry girl

Top banana

Tutti-frutti what a cutie

Veggie gourmet

FRECKLES

A smattering of freckles

Counting freckles one-by-one

Freckles are for kissing

Freckles are fairy kisses

Sun-kissed with love dots

Teeny-tiny baby speckles

Tiny freckles make you look fine

FREEDOM

At least once a day, allow yourself the freedom to think and dream for yourself –*Einstein*

Peace is the climate of freedom

We cannot defend freedom abroad by deserting it at home –*Edward R. Murrow*

A wise and frugal government, which shall leave men free to regulate their own pursuits of industry and improvement, and shall not take from the mouth of labor and bread it has earned—this is the sum of good government –*Thomas Jefferson*

Celebrate freedom

Freedom forever

Freedom isn't free

Freedom lies in being bold –*Robert Frost*

Journey to freedom

Let freedom ring

Stand for freedom lest ye fall for anything less

FRIENDS

A circle of friends are a like a carousel that brings you joy

A friend is a present you give to yourself –*Robert Louis Stephenson*

A friend is a treasure and a comfort

A friend is someone who reaches for your hand and grabs hold of your heart

A friend is a gift to treasure always

A friend is someone you can do nothing with and really enjoy it

A friend is what the heart needs all the time –*Henry Van Dyke*

A friend is a special hug from God

A friend may well be reckoned the masterpiece of nature –*Emerson*

A helping hand shows a loving heart

A single rose can be my garden—a single friend, my world –*Leo Buscaglia*

A smile is the shortest distance between friends

A true friend is one soul in two bodies –*Aristotle*

All that we love deeply becomes a part of us –*Helen Keller*

Chance made us neighbors, hearts made us friends

Even though we live so far apart, you're always here in my heart

Everything can be a grand adventure when you have a friend to share it –*Linda LaTourelle*

Few delights can equal the mere presence of one whom we trust utterly –*George MacDonald*

Friends love at all times

Friendship is the sweetest bloom

Friendship lives forever in the heart

Friends are kind to each other's hopes and cherish each other's dreams –*Henry David Thoreau*

Friends are music for the heart

Friends are the best collectibles!

Friends are the sweetness of life

Friends brings sunshine into our life

Friends know the art of giving from the heart because they paint with love

Friends rekindle the flame of love when the winds of life blow heavy upon us –Linda LaTourelle

Friends always in sunshine or rain

Friends—through good times, through bad times!

"Friendship is a very comforting thing to have." said Christopher Robin –A. A. Milne

Friendship is always a sweet responsibility, never an opportunity –Khalil Gibran

Friendship is love without wings –Lord Byron

Giggles, secrets and sometimes tears

Good friends make good times great

Gorgeous, goofy, gabby girls

Hanging together again and again

I awoke this morning with devout thanksgiving for my friends, the old and the new –Ralph Waldo Emerson

I count myself in nothing else so happy as in a soul remembering my good friends –Shakespeare

If you see someone without a smile share yours

In a garden of friendship, is where love blooms so beautiful

Insomuch as any one pushes you nearer to God, she is your friend –French proverb

It is in the shelter of each other that the people live –Irish proverb

Friends add beauty to each day

Let us be grateful to people who make us happy; they are the charming gardeners who make our souls blossom –Marcel Proust

Neighborhood pals

Of all the treasures on this earth, true friends are way beyond measure

One joy scatters a hundred griefs –Chinese proverb

Planting seeds of friendship

"Stay" is a charming word in a friend's vocabulary –Louisa May Alcott

The happiest memories are of making new friends, while still enjoying the old –Linda LaTourelle

The journey to a friend's house is never long

The tree of friendship grows and is rooted in love

With a little help from my friends

There is no possession more valuable than that of a good and faithful friend –Socrates

Through love, through friendship, a heart lives more than one life –Anais Nin

What wonderful blessings we will find in one another, if we will but look! –Linda LaTourelle

When friendships are real, they are not glass threads or frost work, but the solidest things we know –Emerson

Whenever I think of you, I smile inside

You give me reasons to smile

✣ Best-Friends

A best friend is the greatest of all blessings

Best friends are our chosen family

Best friends help us write the story of our lives

Best friends' love is beyond measure

Best friends 'til the end!

First friends—now best friends

Happiness is a friend like you

Happy is the heart that holds a friend close

How blessed we are to be friends!

I felt it shelter to speak to you –*Emily Dickinson*

Just me and my bestie

Life-long friends

Old friends—best friends

Special friends bring special memories

The best of times with the best of friends

There is something very wonderful when our soul connects with another in friendship –*Linda LaTourelle*

Two are better than one...for if they fall, one will lift up the other –*Ecclesiastes 4:9*

Were we not friends from childhood? Have I not loved Thee long? –*Emily Brontë*

You'll always be my best friend because you know too much!

✣ Girlfriends

The best kind of friend is a girlfriend

Between girlfriends—friends need no words

Me and my girlfriends

Girlfriends lift you up when the world lets you down

Girlfriends see the best in us

Girlfriends are God's way of taking care of us

There's no friend like a girlfriend!

"We'll be friends forever, won't we, Pooh?" asked Piglet. "Even longer," Pooh answered. –*A.A. Milne*

Girlfriends forever

Girlfriends love to have fun

Happiness is a girl's night out

GAMES

✣ Bingo

☐ Bingo—it's my number!
☐ Bingo queen
☐ Eat • Sleep • Play Bingo
☐ Got Bingo?
☐ Grandma's my name—Bingo is my game
☐ Happiness is winning!
☐ I just need one more number
☐ It's Bingo somewhere!
☐ Is there any other game?
☐ Monday night Bingo
☐ My heart belongs to Bingo
☐ That's a Bingo!

♣ Board games

- ☐ All's fair in love and Monopoly
- ☐ Back to the start
- ☐ Calling your bluff
- ☐ Cheaters never win
- ☐ Collect $200
- ☐ Deal the cards
- ☐ Final answer?
- ☐ For the win!
- ☐ Game night
- ☐ Got game?
- ☐ Hands down
- ☐ In the game of life
- ☐ Make my play
- ☐ Play fair
- ☐ Poker face
- ☐ Puzzled?
- ☐ Read 'em and weep
- ☐ Roll them dice
- ☐ Spin the wheel
- ☐ You cheated!
- ☐ You lose / You win
- ☐ Your move

♣ Chess

- ☐ Be the queen
- ☐ Checkmate
- ☐ Chess master
- ☐ I love chess
- ☐ King of the board
- ☐ Lucky play

♣ Word games

- ☐ Anagram lover
- ☐ Crossword's my game
- ☐ Got dictionary?
- ☐ How do you spell...?
- ☐ Seven-letter word
- ☐ This boggles my mind
- ☐ Triple word score
- ☐ Your word against mine

GARDENS

I planted a little garden
To work in every day—
For many happy moments
And a quiet place to pray
—Linda LaTourelle

A beautiful garden is your reward for doing God's yard work

A beautiful rose lives here with a thorny old soul!

A garden in spring is a lovely thing

A gardener tills it like it is

A garden at sunrise is a lovely way to start the day

A garden is a thing of beauty and a passion forever

A'gardening we will grow

A beautiful garden is a joy forever

As is the gardener, so is the garden

Ah, sunflowers! Who countest the steps of the sun   *–William Blake*

All the flowers of tomorrow are in the seeds of today

As for me and my garden we love to sit and listen to the birds singing and the wind blow

MY WORK TODAY
I meant to do
my work today,
But a brown bird sang
in the apple tree,
And a butterfly flitted
across the field,
And all the leaves
were calling me.
And the wind went sighing
over the land,
Tossing the grasses
to and fro,
And a rainbow
held out its shining hand,
So what could I do
but laugh and go?
–*Richard le Gallienne*

Better homes and beautiful gardens

Beware, our garden dragons like to snap

Bless the birds and bless the bees and please bless my garden with no more weeds –*Linda LaTourelle*

Blooming creations

Butterflies and bird songs make a happy garden

Dandelions and morning dew, quiet time spent with you –*Linda LaTourelle*

Gardening is not for pansies!

Even the tiniest garden can yield the biggest dreams –*Linda LaTourelle*

From tiny seeds come beautiful blessings

Garden of weedin' and love

Garden recipe: equal parts love and water and sunshine

How I love to sit in my garden,
To think and dream and rest.
Life is at peace in my garden,
It's there I feel so blessed.
–*Linda LaTourelle*

Gardening tills my soul

Gnome sweet gnome

Grab a hoe, weed every row and watch your garden grow

Hoe-made happiness in my garden

I fought the weeds and the weeds won

I go to the garden to pray

I like my garden when it rains

I love that place between the garden and the wall when it's just the two of us

I love the sweet perfume of lilacs scenting the morning breeze

I went to a garden party...

I'm not getting old, just need repotting

If I had a single flower for every time I think about you, I could walk in my garden forever

If we see the miracle of a single flower clearly, our whole life would change –*Buddha*

If you would have a mind at peace, a heart that cannot harden, go find a door that opens wide upon a lovely garden –*French proverb*

How does your garden grow?

In the garden, time stands still and all is right with the world

It takes thyme to become an old sage

It's off to plant we go, hi hoe, hi hoe!

Life in a garden is down and dirty

May all your weeds be wildflowers

My secret garden

May you have butterfly mornings filled with dandelion wishes, all on a sunny day!

More than anything, I must have flowers always, always –Monet

Nothing is more completely the child of art than a garden –Sir Walter Scott

Oh, lovely garden, thou art my sunshine on even the cloudiest of days! –Linda LaTourelle

One is closer to God in a garden than anywhere else on earth

Perfumes are the feelings of flowers –Heinrich Heine

Recipe for a lovely garden: equal parts of water and sunshine with a double serving of love

Love began in a garden

Just me and my garden

Scatter seeds of joy and watch love bloom

Send in the clouds, pour on the rain, the garden is thirsty and needs watering again –Linda LaTourelle

Sow kindness, gather love

Squirrels and moles and bugs, oh my!

The fruits that paradise hath known are still in earthly gardens hung –Oliver Wendell Holmes

The heavens declare the glory of God; the skies proclaim the work of His hands –Psalm 19:1

The hours I spend with you I look upon as sort of a perfumed garden, a dim twilight, and a fountain signing to it –George Moore

The earth is good to me

The poetry of the earth is alive in the garden   –Linda LaTourelle

The red bird sang in the apple tree as I worked in my garden, happy as could be

The sun shines, birds sing—garden angels the flowers bring

There are flowers everywhere, for those who bother to look –Matisse

There is peace in the garden and His beauty along the path

This place is for the me and the birds

Though an old man I am but a young gardener –Thomas Jefferson

To weed or not to weed is every gardner's lament!

Welcome to my garden, would you like to sit awhile with me?

What delicious solitude between my garden and me! –Linda LaTourelle

When you have only two pennies left in the world, buy a loaf of bread with one, and a lily with the other –Chinese proverb

When you kneel in your garden, take time to pray

Where may one indulge in day-dreams, if not in a garden! Where the lilies grow, that's where you'll find me

Winter, summer, spring and fall— in my garden I love them all

The Biggest Book of Words & Prompts for Scrapbooks, Art Journals & Crafts

Won't you come into my garden? I would like my roses to meet you

Who loves a garden still his Eden keeps —*Amos Bronson Alcott*

Wild roses are fairest, and nature a better gardener than art —*Louisa May Alcott*

GIRLS

100% original
All girl
All she needs is love
American girl
An old-fashioned girl
Authentic girl
Bayou girl
Beary cute princess
Bee-utiful dreamer
Big girls love diamonds
Birthday girl
Brown-eyed girl
Calendar girl
Chicks 'R' Us
City girl / country girl
Classic and chic
Classic lady
Cool chic
Daddy's little girl
Dance, little girl
Diamond girl
Diva in-training
Down-home girl
Dreamy-eyed girl
Girl of my dreams
Girls in charge
Girls just gotta have fun!
Girly girls
Glamour gals
Good morning little schoolgirl
Grace was in her steps
Groovy girls
Happiest girl in the whole USA
Has anybody seen my gal?
Hello little girl
Her royal highness
I saw her standing there
I'm a big girl now
I'm a girl, hear me roar!
I'm not spoiled—I just know what I want
If my tiara fits...
Isn't she great
It's a girl thing!
It's not easy being a princess
Just one of the girls
Kiss the girl
Legends of the mall
Like mother, like daughter
Little girls are made of...
Little lady
Little Miss sunshine
Little princess
Lovely little lady
Mamma's girl
Material girl
Miss Independent
Modern woman
More sugar than spice

217 | ultimatebookcompany.com

Most beautiful girl
My baby girl
My favorite brunette
My motorcycle mama
My pretty baby
Never underestimate the power of a girl
No ordinary girl
One girl is worth more usually than twenty boys –J.M. Barrie
One polished little lady
Our little princess
Rhinestone cowgirl
Rock 'n' roll girl
Ruffles and lace
She enjoys being a girl
She loves you
She's a stubborn one
She's just a girl, but she's my girl
She's my Cinderella girl
She's simply irresistible
Silly girl
Smart and sassy
Smiles are the soul's kisses
Southern girl
Sugar girl
Sunshine girl
Sweet and sassy
Sweet baby girl
That girl!
That's the way a girl does it
The girl most likely to _____
The littlest flower girl
The most beautiful girl in the world!
The princess of quite-a-lot

The queen of hearts
This girl's in love with you
The sunshine girls
Valley girls
V.I.P. Very Important Princess
What are little girls made of?
What's a girl to do?
Where the girls are
Who's that girl?
You are my sunshine
You grow girl

GIVING

A bit of fragrance always clings to the hand that gives you roses
–Chinese proverb

Giving your love is the best thing you can give –Linda LaTourelle

Find a garden to sow into today for a harvest tomorrow

Give and it shall be given back to you

The giving tree bears much fruit

God can't give us peace and happiness apart from himself because there is no such thing
–C. S. Lewis

He who brings a gift will find his heart will open

It is more blessed to give than to receive –Proverbs 11:25

I know God won't give me anything I can't handle. I just wish he didn't trust me so much
–Mother Teresa

The more one sows, the greater his harvest in due season

Sometimes the smallest thing you give to someone can ultimately be the biggest blessing –Linda LaTourelle

In helping others, we help ourselves

To give little is to receive much

To whom much is given is much required –Luke 12:48

Whatever you receive—give back –Linda LaTourelle

When it comes to giving, some people stop at nothing, while others nothing can stop –Linda LaTourelle

GLASSES

100% cool-looking

Eye have a vision

Groovy glasses

I can see clearly now

I see fine

It's in the shades

Looking at the world in a new way

Love them glasses

Rose-colored glasses

Seeing is believing

She's / he's looking good!

Simply irresistible!

Sunshine shades

Spectacular specs

GOALS

A goal is a wish your heart makes and works hard to get it

An aim in life is the only fortune worth finding –Robert Louis Stephenson

A goal is a map full of obstacles, road-blocks and directions that when followed intently and tenaciously, will lead you to your desired place –Linda LaTourelle

All that you need to accomplish your goal are right there in your imagination –Linda LaTourelle

Achieving your goals will be accomplished by perseverance and hearing the truth within you, not opinions that come from others –Linda LaTourelle

Be yourself—it's the greatest opportunity for achieving your goals –Linda LaTourelle

Go forward—it's the only direction that works. –Linda LaTourelle

Life is but a matter of choices— what are yours? –Linda LaTourelle

Motivation is what gets you started. Habit is what keeps you going –Jim Ryun

Stay where you are and you will never be where you want to go – Linda LaTourelle

The important thing is not to stop questioning –Einstein

The life of heaven must be begun here on earth –L. M. Montgomery

The smallest goal can lead to the biggest dream –Linda LaTourelle

To get where you're going, you must follow your dream –Linda LaTourelle

To the person who does not know where he wants to go, there is no favorable wind –Seneca

When you know what you want to do, make a plan and follow it one step at a time and each day you will be a little closer to fulfilling that plan —Linda LaTourelle

Who says you can't hold the world in your hands? The opportunity exists every day to try —Linda LaTourelle

You are never too old to set another goal or to dream a new dream —C. S. Lewis

GRADUATION

Diploma in hand
Lessons all learned
Time to get working
There's money to earn
—Linda LaTourelle

Best wishes on a bright future

Big cheers for a winning year!

Cheers to the graduate!

Time to toss the hat!

You made it!

Great minds have purposes —Washington Irving

I'm so proud of your achievement

The future belongs to those who believe in the beauty of their dreams —Eleanor Roosevelt

Life is my college. May I graduate well, and earn some honors. —Louisa May Alcott

Go confidently in your goals

Oh, the possibilities! Go for them!

Where your talents and the needs of the world cross lies your calling —Will Durant

Hope is a waking dream. Your hopes and dreams are now coming true.

Looks like you made it!

Hats off to you

Present graduate—success!

Success is measured by the mark you leave for others

With flying colors you soared!

Let the pomp and circumstance begin

Beautiful tomorrows begin today

All you need to know you learned a long time ago

Today is the beginning of the real deal—working for a living!

GRATITUDE

A thankful heart is the greatest virtue —Cicero

A thankful heart is not only the greatest virtue, but the parent of all other virtues —Cicero

I awoke this morning with devout thanksgiving for my friends, the old and the new —Emerson

Everything in your life is deserving of your gratitude daily

For all things I give praise

Gratitude is key to living a simple life

Give thanks for little and you will discover much

GRATITUDE

For flowers that bloom
About our feet
For tender grass,
So fresh, so sweet
For song of bird,
And hum of bee
For all things fair
We hear or see,
Father in heaven
We thank Thee!

–Ralph Waldo Emerson

THANKS

For each new morning
With its light,
For rest and shelter
Of the night,
For health and food,
For love and friends,
For everything
Thy goodness sends.

–Ralph Waldo Emerson

Find the good and praise it

Gratitude is the sign of noble souls –Aesop

Gratitude turns what we have into more than we could imagine

He is a wise man who does not grieve for the things, which he has not, but rejoices for those which he has –Epictetus

Count your blessings, name them one by one, you'll be surprised what God has done

Gratitude is the heart's memory –French proverb

He who knows that enough is enough will always have enough –Lao Tzu

If the only words you speak today are thank you, that is enough

Gratitude is seeing the joy and blessings in every moment

Gratitude is the fairest blossom which springs from the soul –Henry Ward Beecher

Gratitude is not only the greatest of virtues, but the parent of all the others –Cicero

In everything by prayer and supplication, with thanksgiving, let your requests be made known to God –Philippians 4:6

Of all the blessings I ever knew, the greatest one was when I met you

When I started counting my blessings, my whole life turned around –Willie Nelson

You cannot do a kindness too soon because you never know how soon it will be too late –Ralph Waldo Emerson

Blessings flow towards gratitude –Lao Tzu

Nothing is more honorable than a grateful heart –Seneca

Let us be grateful to people who make us happy; they are the charming gardeners who make our souls blossom –Marcel Proust

One can never pay in gratitude; one can only pay in kind somewhere else in life –Anne Morrow Lindbergh

The best way to pay for a lovely moment is to enjoy it –Richard Bach

The invariable mark of wisdom is to see the miraculous in the common —*Emerson*

The river of blessings flows to the ocean of gratitude and back again

There is a humble, quiet joy that brings calmness to a life lived in gratitude —*Linda LaTourelle*

Wake at dawn with a winged heart and give thanks for another day of loving —*Kahlil Gibran*

When eating bamboo sprouts, remember the man who planted them —*Chinese proverb*

When you are grateful fear disappears and abundance appears —*Anthony Robbins*

When you change the way you look at things, the things you look at change —*Wayne Dyer*

You"ll never be happy with more 'til you're grateful for you have

HAIR & HAIRCUTS

Almost cut my hair
Baby, let your hair down
Bald is beautiful
Baldy but goody
Bee-bop a doo-wop
Big hair day
Blonde bombshell
Do-it-yourself haircut
Dreadlock holiday
Extreme makeover
Flowers in your hair
Future barber
Gentlemen prefer blondes
Get a haircut
Glamorama gal
Godly locks and the three hairs
Greasy kids stuff
Hairlairious
Hair today, gone tomorrow
Hair's best friend
Hairspray & hot rollers
Hair we are
He's so vain
I have a brand new hairdo
I'm having a bad hair day!
I've got sleepy hair
Just got my ears lowered
Let your hair hang down
Letting our hair down
Lifestyles of the hunky and hairless
Locks of love
Long-haired lady
Love that hair
Matted and messy
Only my stylist knows for sure
Ponytails and popsicles
Scarlet ribbons in her hair
Silver ribbons
Spiked up and spiffed out
Strawberry curls forever
The long and short of it
What a do!

HAPPINESS

Sunsets and moonbeams
And long talks
Sharing dreams
Twirling and laughing
And dancing on sand
Being together
Just holding your hand
These are a few of
My favorite things—
Life with you
The love that it brings
Is joyful and pleasing
And all that I need
I am thankful
I am blessed
I am loved
–Linda LaTourelle

100% pure smile

A giggle a day keeps grumpies away

A merry heart is healing to the soul

A smile as sweet as spring

A smile begets a smile

A wink and a smile

Belly-laughing is such fun

Be the smile that brightens someone's day

Dimples galore

Do good and you will feel good

Don't worry, be happy

Grins and giggles

Fill each hour with joyful thoughts and you will be happy

Happiness depends on ourselves
–Aristotle

I see your tickle spot!

Happiness grows by sharing

Happiness is a habit

Happiness is hearing your inner voice joyfully singing

Happiness is living in the present

Happiness is sharing your blessings with others

Happiness is the sunshine of the soul

Happiness is yelling "Bingo!"

Happiness is…

Happiness lives right there inside you—just feel it

Happy dance

Happy days are here again

Happy everything

Happy times—you and me!

I hope I always give you reasons to smile

I like boys who make me smile

I love to laugh

If you're happy and you know it, then your face will surely show it

I'm happy as I can be!

Joy comes in the morning

Laugh louder—smile bigger

Laugh, love and smile

Laughing all the way

Living happily ever after is a daily choice

Let the sunshine in

Make each day your masterpiece
–John Wooden

Mona Lisa smile

Ode to joy
Put on a happy face
Shut-up and smile
Silly and happy—that's how you make me feel
Smile more—worry less
Smile when you feel like crying
Smile—it makes you beautiful
Smiles bring sunshine
So much silliness
Some smiling good times
Stay calm and laugh / smile
Sweet, sweet smile
The key to happiness is you
The language of a smile is universal
The only joy in the world is to begin –Cesare Pavese
The way to be happy is to strive daily to make others happy
The world looks brighter from behind a smile
There is no key to happiness, the door is always open for you
To be happy at home is the ultimate result of all ambition –Samuel Johnson
True happiness is giving it away
Where's your tickle spot?
When you're smiling, the whole world smiles with you
Who could resist that smile?
You are someone's reason to smile
You are the reason I smile
You make me smile
You will be as happy as you make up your mind to be
You will never be happier than you expect –Bette Davis
You would smile too, if it happened to you
Your smile brightens my day
Your smile is the prettiest

HARVEST

A bountiful harvest
A harvest of memories
Always remember how good the God of Harvest is daily
Barns full of treasure—a farmer's work measured
Bringing in the sheaves
Fields of gold
Happy harvest
Harvesters of love
Harvest moon
Harvest seeds of love and life in your garden
Preserving our harvest
Reaping the harvest
The sweetest harvest is raising a family
Sharing the harvest
Shine on harvest moon
Sowing seeds of gratitude in the soil of prayers will bring a harvest aplenty to bless the soul –Linda LaTourelle
The thankful receiver bears a plentiful harvest –William Blake
Under the harvest moon with you

HEART

A good heart is better than all the heads in the world –*Edward Bulwer–Lytton*

A thankful heart is a happy heart

Being the spark to light a heart is to be the love for everyone –*Linda LaTourelle*

The love on my heart is written exclusively for you

Flowers and hearts and love, oh my!

Give thanks with a grateful heart

Home is where your heart is

It is only with the heart that one can see rightly; what is essential to the eye –*Antoine de Saint-Exupéry*

It is wisdom to believe the heart –*George Santayana*

King / Queen of my heart

Let me call you sweetheart

I love to call you tweet heart

Love is a work of heart

Gentlest heart, the kindest spirit —hold close those you love –*Linda LaTourelle*

The heart is a free and fetter's thing—a wave of the ocean, a bird on a wing –*Julia Pardoe*

No sky is heavy if the heart be light –*Winston Churchill*

My heart belongs to you!

Be sure, where I may roam, my heart is with your heart at home –*Emily Brontë*

HERITAGE

A little bit of history

Blast from our past

If memories would last forever

Oldies but goodies

Just another groovy generation

Yesterday, yesteryear

Those were the days

Sweet remembrances

From then to now

Stories from the olden days

A moment in time

Look how far we've come

It was the best of times...

HOLIDAYS

A holiday to remember

A year full of holidays

Holiday goodies

Holiday guests

Holiday happenings

Holiday hugs and mistletoe kisses

Holiday hustle and bustle

Holiday images

Holiday memories shared with friends are a gift of love

Holiday on ice

Holiday spirit

Holiday traditions

Holiday treats

Home for the holidays

Hooray for the holidays

It's all relative
It's good to be home
Jolly holidays
Kindred spirits
Magical holidays
My holiday best
Same time next year
The holiday kitchen
Together at last
We gather together
Winter holidays

❖ *Christmas*

For unto us a child is born,
unto us a son is given...
His name will be called
wonderful counselor;
mighty God,
everlasting Father;
Prince of Peace
–Isaiah 9:1

'Tis the season
1st Christmas for us
A caroling we go
A Christmas to remember
A claus for celebration
A holly jolly Christmas
A merry little Christmas
All I want for Christmas is my two front teeth...
All is calm, all is bright
All the trimmings
All through the house
All wrapped up for Christmas!

In the hearts of all children,
Christmas is about family,
Traditions and love
–Linda LaTourelle

Are you naughty or nice?
Away in a manger
Babes in Toyland
Baby's 1st Christmas
Bah humbug!
Be jolly, by gosh, by golly!
Believe in miracles
Believe in the magic of Christmas
Christ is the heart of Christmas
Christmas blessings
Christmas comes but once a year
Christmas glows with love
Christmas memories live forever
Christmas morning magic
Christmas tree shopping
Christmas wishes
Christmas wishes—love, peace, joy
Christmas with all the trimmings
Claus & company
Claus & Elves Inc
Cool yule
Countdown to Christmas
Country Christmas
Cozy Christmas
Crazy about Christmas
Deck the halls

Don't open until Christmas

Down the chimney he came...

Do you hear what I hear?

Everyone's a kid at Christmas

Faith, hope & love

Family and friends are the true gifts of Christmas

Feliz Navidad

For unto us a child is born –Isaiah 9:6

Gingerbread boys / girls

Girls and boys love Toyland

Glad tidings we bring!

Good friends share love and memories at Christmas

Got Jesus?

Got presents?

Happy birthday, Jesus!

Happy holly-daze

Have you been naughty or nice?

Have yourself a merry little Christmas

He's making a list and checking it...

Here we go a'caroling

Holly jolly Christmas

Home for the holidays

Home is the heart of Christmas

Homespun Christmas

Ho • Ho • Ho

Hunting for the perfect tree

I'll be home for Christmas

In search of the perfect tree

I will honor Christmas in my heart, and try to keep it all the year –Charles Dickens

I love Thee, Lord Jesus

It came upon a midnight clear

It's beginning to look a lot like Christmas

Jesus—the reason for the season

Jingle bells—Jingle all the way

Jolly old Saint Nicholas

Joy to the world

Just what I've always wanted

Keep the spirit of Christmas throughout the year

Keep the wonder of Christmas in your heart

Let's meet under the mistletoe

Lighting of the tree

Little drummer boy

Little town of Bethlehem

Making spirits bright

May your Christmas cheer last throughout the year

May your days be merry and bright

Meet me under the mistletoe

Memories of the holidays

Meowy Christmas

Merry and bright

Merry Christmas baby

Merry Christmas to all and to all a good night!

Merry kiss moose

Milk and cookies and more!

No place like home for the holidays

Not a creature was stirring, not even a mouse...

Now dash away, dash away, dash away all

O' Christmas tree

O' little town of Bethlehem

Oh, Holy Night!

On Dasher, on Dancer...

Ornament extravaganza

Our first Christmas together

Our little stocking stuffer

Parade of the wooden soldiers

Peace on earth good will to men

Please come home for Christmas

Presents and carols and lights—oh my!

Remember Jesus is the reason for the season

Ring the bells! It's Christmas!

Rockin' round the Christmas tree

Sights and sounds of Christmas

Silent night, holy night

Spreading Christmas cheer

Storybook Christmas

Surrounded with love

The best gift of all

The first noel

The greatest story ever told

The most wonderful time of the year

The ornaments of our home are the family and friends that gather together

The spirit of Christmas is the laughter of children

The stockings were hung

The twelve days of Christmas

The wind blew cold, the stars shone, the snow lay white on field and wood, and the Christmas moon was glittering in the sky —*Louisa May Alcott*

There's magic in believing

There's no place like mom's kitchen for the holidays

'Tis the season

To grandma's / grandpa's house we go

Tree lighting tradition

Trimming the tree

Twas the night before Christmas

Twinkle sparkle Christmas Star

Up on the rooftop...

Visions of sugar plums

We wish you a merry Christmas

We're dreaming of a white Christmas

We're having a twinkly, jingly, ringy-ding-dingly Christmas

While visions of sugar plums danced in their heads

What's under the tree for me?

White Christmas

Who's that up on the roof?

Will work for milk and cookies

Wrapped with care

You'd better not pout!

You're all I want for Christmas

You are my Christmas song

Cinco de Mayo

Celebrate Cinco de Mayo
Fiesta and siesta today!
Happy Cinco de Mayo
Time to celebrate

Earth Day

Be kind to the planet
Bless the earth
Circle of life
Less is more
Live a life of repurpose
Live well now for the future
Old mother nature
Pollution solution
Save the planet
Solutions, not pollution
This land is our land

Easter

My favorite snacks
Are fun to eat
They make no noise
Not even a peep
—Thena Smith

A basket full of goodies
A hunting we will go
A visit with the rabbit
A tisket-a-tasket, I found my Easter basket
Basketful of goodies
Basketful of love
Baskets and bunnies

Little peep critters
Of yellow, pink or blue
Are fun to see
And taste yummy too!
—Thena Smith

Baskets of fun
Bunnies and baskets
Bunny crossing
Bunny treats
Celebrating one Lord
Christ is risen today
Coloring Easter eggs
Counting the jelly beans
Cute and fuzzy as a bunny
Easter baskets full of love
Easter blessings
Easter parade
Easter Sunday best
Easter is a day for bunnies
Easter's on its way
Egg-hunting extravaganza
Egg-painting zone
Hallelujah, He is risen
He is risen
Here comes Peter Cottontail
Hip hop hooray, Easter's today!
Hippity hoppity, Easter's on its way
Hoppy Easter
I love chocolate on my eggs
I love jelly beans
In my Easter bonnet
It's, Easter for peep's sake
Jesus Christ is risen today
One cute Easter chick
Painting Easter eggs

Rejoice! He is risen!
Some bunny loves you
Spring flings and Easter things
The ears are the best part
The Easter bunny came!
The Glory of Easter
The greatest story ever told
The hunt is on

♣ Father's Day
Original verses by Linda LaTourelle

Blessed indeed am I to call you my father! Happy Dad's Day!

Dad you taught me to love by loving me! Here's to you on Father's Day!

Dad, I'll never outgrow my love for you!

Dear ol' dad—I celebrate you!

Father knows best—father is best!

I am the luckiest girl / boy in the world because I have the sweetest dad in the world

If I was to choose a dad...you'd be the only one! Happy Father's Day!

Happy Daddy Day!

Love comes in many ways—but the best is with a dad like you!

Mom chose the best when she chose you to be our dad! Happy Father's Day!

My dad, the superstar! Hope you have a bright and shining Father's Day!

My heart belongs to you, Daddy—I love you!

Happy Father of the Year!

No matter how tall I grow—I will always strive to measure up to you, Dad! Happy Father's Day!

The greatest gift I ever had, it came from God, I call him Dad

There's no dad like my dad! and I'm glad!

To the dad with a heart of gold —my dad!

When I grow up I want to be just like you dad! Happy Father's Day!

To our pop—he's the greatest!

You are the leader of our home and the keeper of my heart

Love, your daughter / son!

You'll always be my Daddy!

♣ Fourth of July

A star-spangled day
All-American / boy, girl, family
America remembers
America the beautiful
American pride
American spirit
And the rocket's red glare
As American as apple pie
Born in the USA
Born on the fourth of July
Celebrating the 4th
Diamonds in the sky
Fireworks are fantastic
Forever in peace may it wave
From the heart of America
God bless America

God bless the USA
Happy birthday, America
Happy 4th of July
Have a star-spangled day
Hip hip hooray for the USA
Home of the brave
Hurray for the red, white and blue
I love a parade
I love the USA
I'm a yankee doodle dandy
In God we trust
Independence Day
I pledge allegiance to our flag
Land of the free
Land that I love
Let freedom ring
Life, liberty and the pursuit of happiness
Li'l firecracker
Made in America
My American hero
Old Glory
One nation, under God
Patriot games
Proud to be an American
Rally 'round the flag boys
Remember our heroes
Stars and stripes forever
Sweet land of liberty
That noise you hear is the sound of freedom
The greatest American hero
The red, white and blue

This is America
This land is my land
Three cheers for the red, white and blue
United we stand
With liberty and justice for all
You're a grand old flag

♣ Halloween

A Halloween spooktacular
A howlin' good time
A spooky Halloween
Are you a scaredy-cat?
Be afraid, be very afraid
Be the ghostess with the mostess
Beware! Beauty and the beast live here
A monstrously good kid
Carvin' out some good times
Caution! Low-flying bats
Caution! Monster crossing!
Costumes on parade
Count down to candy
Creatures of the night
Don't be a scaredy-cat
Dressed to thrill!
If the broom fits, fly it!
Jack-o-lanterns light the night
Mom's / Dad's little monsters
Monster mash
Monsters on parade
My other car is a broom
No tricks, just treats
Oh, what a tangled web

Our little pirate is a treasure
Please park brooms at the door
Ready, set, glow
Sweets for the sweet
That's the spirit
Trick or treat, have a sweet
Who is that masked boo?

♣ Hanukkah

Colorful candles burning bright
Dreidel, dreidel
Eight nights of lights
Festival of Lights
Health and happiness
Holy, Holy, Holy
Holy lights
Joy and light
Latkes, latkes, good to eat
Let it glow, let it glow, let it glow
Light one if you've got one
Light up my life
Lighting the Menorah
May love and light fill your home and heart at Hanukkah
Menorah magic
One candle more
Rejoice in the festival
Shalom
Spin, spin, spin
The lights of Hanukkah
The Star of David
These lights are holy
We kindle these lights

♣ Kwanzaa

A celebration of family, community and the common good

A thousand fibers connect us with our fellow man –Herman Melville

Care for each other and our community

Celebrate the good life

Happy Kwanzaa

Hope is the pillar of the world

Kwanzaa is the day to celebrate

No man is free who is not a master of himself –Epictetus

To stumble is not to fall, but to go forward faster –African proverb

♣ Mother's Day

Original verses by Linda LaTourelle
© 2012 / unless otherwise noted

Thanks for the love you give,
For everything you do.
Your sacrifice and caring,
There's no mom like you.
I love you. Happy Mom's Day!
There is a flower of human kind,
A flower sent from above;
'Tis pure untarnished motherhood;
It's fragrance mother love.
  –Harry L. Culler

All that I am or ever hope to be is because you believed in me—I love you, Mom!

Mama, you always knew best, thank goodness! With love…

Dear Mother,
If every thought of mine for you
Could turn into a violet blue,
Then on a flowery path you'd stray,
For violet-thoughts
Would pave your way,
Dear mother!
–Aletha Randolph

I'm so glad that God chose you to be my mother!

My mother's heart is a beautiful expression of God's everlasting love for me

Happy Mother's Day to the best mom in the world—from the one who knows for sure, love your daughter

In all the world, I got the best—you! Happy Mother's Day! If I was to choose from all the mothers in the world, there would be no choice, it would always be you. Happy Mother's Day, Mom!

It is so wonderful to have a holiday to celebrate you! Happy Mother's Day!

My mom is the best mom!

Mom, no matter how old I get, I will never outgrow my love for you. Happy Mama's Day!

The love I have for you deepens year after year. You are so very special so precious and so dear. Happy Mother's Day!

Today is Mother's Day, so let's go out and play, it's time to celebrate, so get ready for our date

ONLY ONE MOTHER
Hundreds of dewdrops
To greet the dawn,
Hundreds of bees
In the purple clover,
Hundreds of butterflies
On the lawn,
But only one mother
The wide world over.
–George Cooper

Mom—thanks for loving me always and teaching me to love

Mom, you are first-class and teach me how to live every day—Happy Mother's Day!

Mom, you are the one who loves us no matter what; you care and worry endlessly. On this special day we want to say thank you for everything you do. Happy happy Mother's Day!

There will never be another, so special and so sweet, except my loving mother, who makes my life complete. Happy Mother's Day!

Nobody does it better when it comes to loving a family than our mom. Happy Mother's Day!

Of all the gifts that life has to offer, a loving mother is the greatest of them all

Mother's Day is the perfect time to tell you just how beautiful you are

One-in-a-million Mom—you!

This heart, my own dear mother, bends, with love's true instinct, back to Thee! –Thomas Moore

There is no velvet so soft as a mother's lap, no rose as lovely as her smile, no path so flowery as that imprinted with her footsteps —*Archibald Thompson*

When God created mothers, He gave me the very best! Happy Mom's Day!

You're always there to understand, to love and see me through

♣ New Year's Day

Ring out the old, ring in the new,
Ring, happy bells, across the snow:
The year is going, let him go;
Ring out the false, ring in the true.
—*Alfred, Lord Tennyson*

After midnight and beyond

A new year with old friends

A new year, a new beginning

A night to remember

A time to celebrate

A toast to the new year

An end of an era!

Auld lang syne

Blast into a new future

Brand new year

Cheers to the new year

Confetti rain

Goodbye 20__, hello 20__

Hats, confetti, noisemakers... must be a new year!

Here's to the new year

In the midnight hour

In with a bang

It was a very good year

Kisses at midnight

Midnight kiss

New Year's resolutions

Oh, what a night!

Painting the town tonight

Poppin' the cork

Ringing in the new year

Ring out the old—ring in the new

'Round midnight

Ten, nine, eight…

The confetti falls

The morning after

Watching the ball drop

Welcome to 20__

What are you doing New Year's Eve?

♣ St. Patrick's Day

A kiss for luck

A little bit of blarney

Best o'luck

Blarney blast

Blarney spoken here

Christmas in Killarney

Erin go bragh—Ireland forever

Feelin' Irish

For love of Ireland

Green eggs and ham

Happy St. Paddy's Day

Happy St. Patrick's Day

I'm feeling lucky
I'm looking over a four-leaf clover
I'm the lucky one
Irish blessings
Irish lassie
It's a pot of gold
Kiss me, I'm Irish!
Kiss the blarney stone
Leprechaun kisses
Li'l leprechaun
Looking for leprechauns
Lucky in love
Luck of the Irish
Luck of the leprechauns
Luck o' the Irish today!
Lucky charmers
Lucky four-leaf clover
Lucky me / you
Lucky to have each other
Mom's pot o' gold
My end of the rainbow
My favorite leprechaun
My four-leaf clover
My lucky charm
My pot of gold at the end of the rainbow
My pretty Irish girl
My wild Irish rose
Oh, blarney!
Our little leprechaun
Surround yourself in green
The end of the rainbow
The wearin' of the green
Today everyone is Irish
Top o' the mornin' to ya
Top of the morning
V.I.P.—Very Irish Person
When Irish eyes are smiling
You are magically adorable
You're my lucky charm

✤ Thanksgiving

A bunch of turkeys
A day of thanks
An attitude of gratitude
A time to give thanks
America the bountiful
Be thankful always
Be ye thankful for bountiful blessings
Bless this food
Bushel of blessings
Carving memories
Cornucopia of blessings
Count your blessings
Eat drink and be merry
Family, turkey and football, oh my!
Family, faith and food
Feasting with the pilgrims
Feast your eyes on this
Friends, family, food and football!
Give us this day our daily bread
Giving thanks for the simple things in life
Gobble 'til you wobble
Gobble! Gobble!
God is good, God is great
Happy turkey day

Horn of plenty
In everything give thanks
It's turkey day!
Let us be thankful unto the Lord
Let's get stuffed
Let's talk turkey
Lord's blessing and bounty
May the bounty of the season fill your heart and home with blessings and joy each day
Nap time for dad / mom
O, the Lord's been good to me
Our table runneth over!
Pass the turkey / dressing
Pilgrims and Indians remembered
Praise God from whom all blessings flow
So much to be thankful for
Stuffed with stuffing!
Thank you God, for everything
Thankful for family and...
Thankful hearts, helpful hands
Thanks for the giving
Thanksgiving bounty
Thanksgiving Day parade
Thanksgiving traditions
There shall be showers of blessings
Turkey and dressing
Turkey and family trimmings
We are thankful for...
We gather together to ask the Lord's blessings...
We give thanks for...
We thank God
What a bunch of turkeys!
What a feast!
What we are thankful for...

♣ Valentine's Day

1st valentine
A day for love
Be my love
Be my sweetie
Be my valentine
Call me Cupid
Candy kisses
Caught by Cupid's arrow
Cupid's cuties
Forget love—let's fall in chocolate
From my heart to yours
Gifts of love
Gifts of wine and roses
Give Cupid a chance
Happy love day!
Happy Valentine's Day
Hearts and kisses
How do I love Thee, let me count the ways...
How sweet it is to be loved by you
Hugs and kisses
I love you!
I want you for my valentine
I'm sweet on you
My funny valentine
My heart belongs to you!
My sweetheart
Nothing is sweeter than you

Red hot, get me!
Sweeter than candy
Sweets for the sweet
The perfect valentine
There's always time for chocolates and flowers
V is for Valentine
Will you be mine?
Won't you be my Valentine?
You make my heart sing
XOXOXOXOX

HOME

Give me a house
To call my own,
Family and friends
To call it a home.
The year's at spring
And day's at morn;
God's in his heaven,
All's right with the world.
–Robert Browning

A place to call home
All the comforts of home
Around the house
Awe, the nursery
Back home in (town)
Backyard fun
Backyards and BBQ's
Be it ever so humble
Beach house
Bring it on home to me

This house is our home
It's where love lives,
Our family grows
and God gives
blessings galore

Cabin in the mountains
Casa sweet casa
City house / Country house
City sidewalks
Dome sweet dome
Dreams of the every day homemaker
Feels like home to me
For there we loved and where we loved is home *–Oliver Wendell Holmes*
From our balcony
Happiness lives in this house
Happy little home
Hello walls
Hi-rise living
Home away from home
Home-fires burning
Home, sweet home
Home that our feet may leave, but not our hearts *–Oliver Wendell Holmes*
Hometown advantage
Honey, I'm home
House beautiful
In the neighborhood
Is it raining at your house?
Knock and the door shall open
Lady of the house
Lawn and order

Leave the porch light on
Let's play house
Life in small-town America
Little old log cabin
Love built our house
Love makes a home
Love shack
Love thy neighbor
Mi casa es su casa
My home
My old Kentucky home
On a country road
On the lanai
On the porch swing
One room, but it's our room
Our hacienda / ranch
Our inheritance
Our little hide-away
Our little old tax shelter
Our mansion
Our nest is blessed
Our refuge
Our sugar shack
Queen / King of my double-wide
Shelter from the wind
Stairway of love
Take me home to my country roads
The family abode
The glass house
The great room
The home-place
The love nest
The master suite
The royal palace

There's no place like home
This old sidewalk
Two cars in the yard
Two-story house
Upscale neighborhood
Upstairs downstairs
Wall-to-wall love
Where the sidewalk ends
White picket fence

HOME - NEW

A home of our own
A place to call home
A spouse and a house
Bless our new home
Cottage for sale
Finally ours!
First homes are special
Home with a loan
Independence day!
It's a buyer's market / sellers
Moving day
New home smell
Open house
Our dream house
Our house is a very fine house
Our new pad
Our old homestead
Remembering our heritage
Signed, sealed and moved!
Sold! Celebrate!
We are homeowners
Why I loved my house

HOME BUILDING

Adventures of building a new home
Barn raising and blessings
Blueprints and footprints
Bob the builder
Bringing down the house together
Building your dream house
Building fences
Building memories
Building our home one prayer at a time
Built with love and sweat
Constructed with love
Dream-home builder
Extreme home makeover
Fiddler on the roof
Home and garden
Home improvement
Home remodel in ten easy lessons
House Building 101
House raising experience
How we built our house
How to build a garage
Keep calm—call the contractor
Life as a house
One piece at a time
Some assembly required
This home designed by (name)
The house that (name) built
The house my spouse built
This old / new house
Under construction
We've got the plans
When all else fails, read the plans
Your home is your castle

HOME REPAIR

A constructive opportunity
Dare to repair
Do it yourself
Our money pit
Do-it-yourself
DIY—save money
He's a real tool man
Honey-do list
How I spent my summer vacation
The hapless handyman
This old dump
Mr. / Mrs. Fix-it
BYOT—bring your own tools
Fresh paint—don't touch!
Weekend remodelers
Don't fence me in
Duct tape expert
Tool time
My husband's / wife's a power man / woman
My hammer can fix anything
If I had a hammer...
Man of many vises
My husband—the hammer head
Renovation vacation
The nuts and bolts of things

Where's my crowbar?

Power tool collector

Rent-a-hubby

Handy-dandy fix-it man

Happy home repair

Have hammer, will travel

Measure once, cut twice

HOUSEWORK

A man with an apron and mop is so sexy and sweet to love

All work and no pay makes a underpaid homemaker

Aphrodisiac: Watching my husband do housework in the buff every day

Bless this mess!

Clean house is a sign of the boss coming for dinner!

Cleaning and scrubbing can wait

Cleaning-impaired today

Cleanliness is next to impossible

Cure for messy house: hire a maid

Dishwashing is an equal-opportunity

Enter at your own risk

Help wanted: please apply in kitchen

House quarantined due to illness —sick of cleaning

Housework is a family affair

Housework? Why bother!

How come Daddy doesn't have to clean his room?

I cleaned the house yesterday, too bad you slept through it

I do not do housework on days that end in "Y"

I don't do windows, floors, laundry or anything else that relates to housework

I'd rather be… cleaning? Not!

I don't like 4 letter words: cook, dust, wash or iron

I'm not super-wife—deal with it!

I'm sorry you seem to have mistaken me for someone who does floors and windows

I'm too pretty / handsome to do housework

If a woman's work is never done, then why begin?

Keep calm—avoid cleaning

M is for marvelous Mother, not maid!

Make yourself at home—the vacuum is in the hall closet and cleaning supplies are under the sink

Messy houses are happy houses

My schedule is too busy, no time for housework

Never let them see you sweep

National proclamation: housework is cancelled until further notice

Not tonight dear, I have housework

Notice: due to illness, this kitchen is closed—I'm sick of cooking!

Our butler and maid resigned

Our laundry room has the latest dirt!

Please excuse the mess—we want you to feel at home

Real men do housework with a smile

Room service closed yesterday

Sex begins in the kitchen

The great American cleaning machine—Mom

The perfect man does the cleaning, cooking and laundry and then takes you shopping

W stands for wonderful wife—not washing windows or waxing floors

When you need some time alone, just start washing the dishes!

Whenever I feel like cleaning, I lie down until the feeling goes away

You have two choices: do the housework or ignore it

You make housework look so easy

HUMOR

Blah, blah, blah!

Did I say I was here to impress you?

Everyone has an opinion, some are just stupid

Got a clue? I didn't think so

He has a photographic memory, just no memory card

He's / She's such a lousy cook, he / she can't even boil toast

How wonderful it is to do nothing, and then rest afterward

I haven't had my coffee yet—you might want to go back to bed

I'm never late—things don't start until I get there

I've been doing nothing for years, why should I change now?

Don't worry, be silly

Keep calm and laugh

If I wanted your opinion, I'd tell you to send me a letter

Life is good now that I don't care what you think anymore

My attitude problem suits me just fine, so what is your problem?

No snowflake in an avalanche ever feels responsible –*George Burns*

Sarcasm? What does that mean?

So did we forget to eat our bowl of morning sunshine?

Talk nerdy and tweet to me!

The lab called, your brain is ready

The way to a woman's heart is through the door of the mall

Young, old—they're just words!

Too bad that all the people who know how to run the country are busy driving taxicabs and cutting hair –*George Burns*

Warning—I argue politics and religion

You want my attitude? Which one? Bad or worse?

ILLNESS & INJURIES

A cry for help

A kiss will make it better

A pound of cure

A stitch in time

A time to heal

As tears go by

Big boys do cry

Blood, sweat and tears

Boo-boo time

Break it to me gently

Bumps and bruises

Crocodile tears
Cry like a baby
Doctor, doctor give me the news
Doctor's orders
Feelin' stronger every day
Give me a break
Healing hands of time
How to cure the common cold
Humor heals
I haven't got time for the pain
Just what the doctor ordered
Kiss the hurt away
Mom / Dad, I don't feel so good
Mommy / Daddy kiss it and make it better
Mom never told me there'd be days like this!
My boo-boo's better now
My first scar
On the mend
Owie-wowie ouch!
Rest, keep warm and drink liquids
Saturday night fever
Sign my cast
Speckles and spots
Stitch by stitch
The agony of de-feet
The bruise brothers
The cure is worse than the cause
The healing touch
The leg-bone's connected to the knee-bone
Them's the breaks
This too shall pass

Time heals all wounds
What's up doc?
Wipe out!

INSPIRATION

You are who you are
Whatever you're doing—
If it's working thus far
Just keep on groovin'!
–Linda LaTourelle

A cup of tea, ten minutes of quiet and your world is at peace

Always remember that you weren't created to be like anyone else

Anything can seem impossible until you have done it

Aspire to be classy, courageous, clever, kind and compassionate

Always believe that something wonderful is going to happen and it will!

At any given moment, you have the power to start again

Be happy, one smile at a time

Be yourself—everyone else is taken

Choose to surround yourself with those you want to be like and you will become like the people you are around

Don't wait for happily ever after… it's here right now

Don't forget to always stay true to who you are

Choose what inspires you and seek it

Don't let anyone dull your sparkle

PEACE

Still waters are quiet,
My soul is replete.
Next to a river
I hear His voice speak.
How pleasant and calm
And refreshing to be
Nearer my God
Much closer to Thee.

Nowhere on earth
Brings such a peace.
The water it soothes
Bringing forth a release
From troubles and toils
Of day to day living.
Oh, His grace is so good
Ever loving and giving.

–Linda LaTourelle ©2012

Eat the elephant one bite at a time

Don't let yesterday take too much time from today

Do what you feel to be right, because you'll be criticized anyway *–Eleanor Roosevelt*

Enjoy the simple things each day

If we change the things we do, we will change, too

In the darkest of times, love can always be found, turn to the light

It's all up to you, whatever you do

It's always fun when we do the impossible

It's the little victories that move us towards the bigger victories

His grace is sufficient—just believe!

It's up to you to find the beauty in the ugliest of days

IT'S UP TO YOU

Though trials may come
And surely they will
Remember my friend
They're just small hills.
Be strong, work long,
Try harder each day
Each step of the journey—
Believe and pray.
And soon you will see
Dreams do come true;
Whatever your goals—
They're all up to you.

–Linda LaTourelle ©2012

Escape from boredom—dream big!

Keep happy thoughts and you'll have a happy life

Let your past make you better today than you ever imagined

Life is a bundle of wonderful little joys and blessings every day

Life may not always be easy, but it can surely be worth it

Look for the meaning in the little things of every day

Make a difference in someone's life and you'll make a difference in yours

Mediocrity knows nothing higher than itself, but talent immediately recognizes genius *–Sir Arthur Conan Doyle*

Need something? Get on your knees and pray—stand to your feet and work

Hope and faith bring success

Never give up something that you can't go a day without thinking about

No matter how hard the past—you can always begin again

No one can make you feel inferior without your consent —*Eleanor Roosevelt*

One bad day does not a bad life make

Rejoice in hope, be patient in tribulation, be constant in prayer

Remember it's not what you have in your life that counts, it's who you have in your life

Remember to tell yourself it is okay to do things your way

Repeat after me—I know I can, I know I can, I know I can

Savor giggly moments—they're grand

Seek all that is good in today and you discover blessings galore

So storms are here—just ride the waves and float

Sometimes when we make the wrong choice, it can bring us to the right place

Perhaps things will fall apart so that better things can come together

The greatest accomplishment in life is to become the person God created you to be

That little light of yours—let it shine

What others think of you matters not

The journey to finding yourself is a wonderful one—if you let it be

Everything will be okay

The key that unlocks the door to anything in my life, albeit success, joy or peace—is me!

The little things in my life, piled one upon another, have built a stairway that climbs to the heavens

The plans He has for me are way bigger than any I could have imagined for myself

Think sparkly and you will always shine like brand new tiara

To look back while running forward —we are sure to fall and miss the road that lies in front of us

Today is another tiara day—it's full of bling and sparkles, look for them

Warning: the reflection in this mirror is beautiful because what you see is real

The reflection in the mirror is exactly as beautiful as you believe

You are individual instrument playing in the symphony of life

What we choose each day—we can change, if we will only take a chance

What you do speaks so loud that I cannot hear what you say —*Emerson*

When I am old I shall eat chocolate, dance in the rain, hold hands with you and count each day as pure joy

You can make everything beautiful

When we put God first, our perspective becomes clearer

Watch out—that boy / girl may one day change the world!

When you decide where you want to go—move totally towards that direction and don't look back

When you feel like quitting remember what it was that made you begin in the first place

When you stop chasing the wrong things, the right ones will start finding you

Where you invest your love, you will invest your life

Who you are is exactly who you choose to be each day

With his love and extraordinary grace—I can do anything

Work hard each day, remember to play, make time to pray, and you will be okay –Linda LaTourelle

You are amazing and don't you ever forget that!

You are braver than you think

You are perfect exactly as you are

You are free to choose its true, but the consequence of your choice is not for you to choose

You are the one and only, true and original you—so don't try to be a poor imitation of someone else

You are whoever you believe yourself to be and can do whatever you permit yourself to do

You can change yourself by extending love and kindness daily

You can make your life have a brand new beginning—right now!

You know what you need to do, just move out of your own way and go for it

So you don't know how to swim— dog-paddle and keep moving forward

KINDNESS

Compassion is the basis for all morality

God won't ask how many friends you had, but if you were a friend

Be the change you want to see

Blessed is the servant who loves his brother as much when he is sick and useless as when he is well and can be of service to him. And blessed is he who loves his brother as well when he is afar off as when he is by his side, and who would say nothing behind his back he might not, in love, say before his face. –St. Francis of Assisi

I expect to pass through
this world but once.
Any good, therefore, that I can do
or any kindness I can show
to any fellow creature,
let me do it now.
Let me not defer or neglect it
for I shall not pass this way again.
–Stephen Grellet

If there is to be any sweetness— let it begin with me –Linda LaTourelle

Don't wait for people to be friendly, show them how to be

Being kind is better than being right

Be kind, you are a walking blessing

Even if I knew that tomorrow the world would go to pieces, I would still plant my apple tree –Martin Luther

Love is patient and kind...
–1 Corinthians 13:4

Kindness and love are never wasted

Kindness is the golden chain by which society is bound together –Goethe

Simple things like "thank you" sometimes are the biggest blessing in someone's day

Prayer of
ST. FRANCIS OF ASSISI
Lord, make me
An instrument of your peace;
Where there is hatred,
Let me sow love;
Where there is injury, pardon;
where there is doubt, faith;
Where there is despair, hope;
Where there is darkness, light;
Where there is sadness, joy.
O divine master,
Grant that I may not so much seek
To be consoled as to console;
To be understood as to understand;
To be loved as to love.
For it is in giving that we receive;
It is in pardoning
That we are pardoned;
And it is in dying that we
Are born to eternal life.

To be beautiful, be kind

Leave a little kindness wherever go

Better to be kind than right

It is higher and nobler to be kind

Kindness is a gift you give away and it will always come back to you

Your kindness is pure joy to me

Kind words can be short and easy to speak, but their echoes are truly endless —*Mother Teresa*

Never look down on anybody unless you're helping them up —*Jesse Jackson*

Never miss an opportunity to make someone happy

Be the living expression of God's kindness —*Mother Teresa*

The echoes of kindness are endless

Gentlest heart, the kindest spirit—hold close those you love —*Linda LaTourelle*

Be always kind and be always blessed

Let no one ever come to you without leaving better and happier

Reflect upon your blessings and your joy will overflow —*Linda LaTourelle*

The essence of love is kindness

The only people with whom you should try to get even are those who have helped you

The truest greatness lies in being kind —*Ella Wheeler Wilcox*

To give what you have is less important than to share who you are —*Linda LaTourelle*

When words are both true and kind, they can change the world —*Buddha*

You cannot do a kindness too soon, for you never know how soon it will be too late —*Emerson*

KIND WORDS
♣ *For Children*

All you need is love and a warm puppy

If I could choose from all the world—my only choice would always be you

I love you more than all the world

I love you more than all the trees in the whole wide world

My heart is overflowing with you!

I love you more than all the candy in the candy store

I love you more than all the rainbows

Smile because you're beautiful

I know exactly how to make you smile—see, it worked!

Kind words, like fresh-baked sugar cookies, taste delicious and we always want more

The best thing about today is you

You make me smile

You are my sunshine and my laughter in every day

✤ *For A Spouse*

All I need is your love and a box of chocolates

All you need is love and two cupcakes

One kiss for me and one love for you

I love to remember the day we met

I love that moment when I look up to find you smiling at me

Every day is a groovy day with you

It's past your bedtime—do you want me to rock you to sleep

Everywhere I go, there you are—wrapped round my heart

I'm wearing the smile you gave me—thank you!

The best part of my day is seeing you smiling at me

The best part of me is you

We will always be best of friends

You are my fairytale come true

You put the happy in my day!

You're my sunshine day!

KINGS & QUEENS

A knight to remember

A royal party

Content's a kingdom and I wear that crown –*Thomas Heywood*

Crown for the king

'Cuz I'm the princess, that's why!

Dancing queen

If I were king

I want it all and I want it delivered

King / Queen for a day

King of rock

King of the hill

King of the road

Kings and queens

King of kings

Like a queen / king

Mississippi queen

My knight in shining armor

Princess / Prince love a lot

Prince / Princess on parade

Queen crop-a-lot

Queen love-a-lot

Queen of everything

Queen of hearts

Queen of the kitchen

Snow queen

Supreme queen

The boy who would be king

Treat me like a king and I'll serve you like a queen

We three kings /queens

LAKE LIVING

A day at the lake is worth ten in town
Ah, this is the life!
Delight in the simple things
Down by the bay, let's go and play
Eat, sleep and fish all day
Flip flops and summer sun, being at the lake is so much fun
Give me a home by the edge of the shore and I'll be at home forever more
Go jump in the lake
Happily ever after at the lake
I'd rather be lost at the lake than found at home
In the swim of things
It all began at the lake
Lake house—the perfect place to hide with the one you love
Lake life doesn't get any better than this
Lake livin' is the life for me!
Lake resort—come early, fish late
Lake rules…no shoes, no clothes, no work, such fun
Lakeside adventures
Leave your shoes at the door and worry no more!
Life is better at the lake
Life slows down at the lake
Need a brake? Go to the lake!
One day at the lake…is worth a month in the city
Once upon a vacation
Our cabin, our home, our retirement
Rise and shine—to walk the dog
Still waters run deep
Swim all day, fish all night
These are the days of sweet relaxation
Wearin' out my ski's at the lake
What happens at the lake—stays at the lake

LANGUAGES
"I Love You"

Albanian—Të Dua
Chinese (mandarin)—Wǒ Aì Nǐ
English—I Love You
Eskimo—Nagligivaget
Filipino—Mahal kita
Finnish—Mina rakastan sinua
French—Je T'aime
German—Ich liebe dich
Greek—S'agapó
Hawaiian—Aloha Au La 'Oe
Hungarian—Szeretiek
Irish—Gráím thú
Italian—Ti amo
Japanese—Suki desu
Polish—Kocham cię
Russian—Ja Tebá lúblú
Spanish—Te Amo
Swedish—Jag Älskar Dig

"Merry Christmas"

Afrikaans—Geseënde Kersfees
Czech—Veselé Vánoce
Danish—Glædelig jul
Dutch—Vrolijk kerstfeest
Filipino—Maligayang Pasko
French—Joyeux Noël
German—Froeh Weihnachten
Hawaiian—Mele Kalikimaka
Irish—Nollaig Shona
Italian—Buon Natale
Japanese—Kurisumasu Omedeto
Navajo—Merry Keshmish
Norwegian—God jul
Portuguese—Feliz Natal
Spanish—Feliz Navidad
Vietnamese—giáng sinh vui vẻ
Welsh—llawen nadolig
Yugoslavian—Cestitamo Bozic

LIFE

A moment's pause to watch the glory of a sunrise or a sunset is soul satisfying, while a bird's song will set the steps to music all day long –Laura Ingalls Wilder

Be the author of your life story

Carpe diem! / seize the day

Count your blessings every day

Dear life, I love you

Enjoy life doing what others say cannot be done

Explore • Dream • Discover

For the soul of every living thing is in the hand of God, and the breath of all mankind –Job 12:10

For once in my life...

Goodness is the only investment that never fails –Thoreau

I may not be where I should be at this point in life, but at least I'm not where I once was

I wanna love my life away with you

It's the moments, not milestones, that matter most

Just to be is a blessing. Just to live is holy. –Abraham Heschel

Keep calm—enjoy life!

Life begins the moment you start living it

Life is a garden that grows with the light of love

Life is about love and love is life

Life is a party—so eat cupcakes

Life is a song, so sing along

Life is about living with purpose—find yours

Life is beautiful—so think pretty thoughts!

Life is either a daring adventure on nothing at all –Helen Keller

Life is full of shadows, follow the sunshine

Life is a gift, enjoy the wrapping and all that is inside

Life is grand!

Life is precious!

Life is trying things to see if they work –Ray Bradbury

Life is whatever we make it

Life's a journey, not a destination

Life's not fair? So get over it!

Life's too short to drink cheap wine

Life's too short, eat more chocolate

Live authentically by being who you were created to be

Live truth and you will shine

Living a little, laughing a little

Love life! Love yourself!

Love of my life

Make the rest of your life be the best of your life

One of life's greatest gifts is the opportunity to give

Pretend to be normal, pretend to be weird, but don't ever pretend to be anyone but the person you were created to be

Remind yourself that life isn't about being perfect—it's about being real

Savor life's simple pleasures

The art of life is to know how to enjoy little and endure much

The best is yet to come

The less of routine, the more of life –Amos Bronson Alcott

The sweet, simple things of life are the ones that matter most

The way to be happy is to make others happy

To live a positive life one must lose the negative mindset

To realize how wealthy you are, count the things you have that money can't buy

Wake up every morning and say today is going to be a wonderful day, and it will be. It's true!

We're here to put a dent in the universe –Steve Jobs

Whatever you do in life, do it the best you can!

When life gives you garbage, repurpose it

Where others see but the dawn coming over the hill, I see the soul of God shouting for joy –William Blake

LOVE INSPIRING

Inspirational love quotes by Linda LaTourelle

Are you the one that will make my heart undone?

By chance we found each other, by choice we love each other and by grace we are one together

Every little thing you do shows me how many blessings I can count each night

He made me wonderful—because he loved me

Hello, I love you!

His words breathed life into her soul, his kisses brought passion to her life and so they loved

Holding your hand is on my top ten list of "happy things to do"

I like mornings better when they begin with coffee and you

I love to take naps, as long as you are my blanket

I love you more than broccoli

I used to dream about times like this—reality is so much better, now that you're in my reality

If you marry—let it be to one that will bring you hope, happiness and honor all the days of your life

If you will love me when I am at my worst, think of how amazing it will be when I am at my best!

In life, the only thing I want more of is you

Kissing your lips is one of my three favorite things to do every day

Look for the beauty—it's right there within yourself

Love believes all things…

Love me when I least deserve it, because that's when I really need it

Mama always said everything will be okay—Mama was always right

Mama told me there were men like you—I just had to find you to believe her

Marriage is an opportunity to be doubly-blessed

Old or young, together we dance this dance of love

Once you can embrace that you are the only you—an original—you will be amazing!

One little step in the right direction led me to you

One of my favorite ways to spend the day is daydreaming with you

P.S. You are loved!

Sailing on rough seas help one to be a far better navigator

They believed that they could—and so they did!

Simply put—you are the completeness of me

Sometimes I just have to pinch myself as I look at you and then I am awakened to the realization that you are not just a dream, but my one true love

The best thing to do every day—celebrate being together

The best things in life are not things—they are you and me together

The brightness in his / her eyes reflects the smile in his / her heart

The hours I spend with you are the hours I treasure the most

The number one thing that gives me joy each day—you!

The words that you tell me echo to my soul that I am loved

You were the words written on my heart that only He would know. Through all the galaxies, planets, continents and perhaps a million light years our journey brought us together, oh what amazing grace!

Together there is always hope

When I prayed for love and found it—I was awestruck at how much God knew every desire of my heart

With you I am at home, beside you I am at peace

You are my summer sun and my winter blanket. You are the color of autumn and sweet aroma spring. Together we celebrate the seasons of our life and the joy of each new sunrise gives birth to another day of loving each other.

You are the chocolate on my lips and the music in my heart

You know what? I love you!

Your love is like honey, warm from the summer sun, melting into my soul

Your smile is my sun on the cloudiest of days

LOVE & PASSION

♣ Hugs

1000 hugs and kisses

A kiss without a hug is like a flower without the fragrance

Hold me, thrill me, love me

Huggable, lovable you!

Hugs are the best gift to give every day

Hugs, kisses and stars wishes

I love you a bushel and a peck and a hug around the neck

I'm so huggable!

Mom / Dad hugs are the best hugs

My favorite place is inside your hug

We are two hearts wrapped in love and a hug

We carry our mother's / father's hug in our heart forever

When I fell into your hug—love captured my heart

You be the kiss and I'll be the hug—wrapped-up together, what sweet love! *–Linda LaTourelle*

♣ Kisses

A kiss and a promise

And then he kissed me

A thousand kisses deep

Candy kisses

Caught smoochin'

Every little kiss

Greet ye one another with a kiss of charity... *–1 Peter 5:14*

I kiss better than I cook

Hogs and kisses

How delicious is the winning of a kiss at love's beginning *–T. Campbell*

How many toads do I have to kiss?

Is not your kiss the very autograph of our love?

Just one kiss

Kisses are messengers of love

Kiss me once, kiss me twice

Kiss the cook / girl / boy

Kisses sweeter than wine

Let us kiss each others eyes and laugh our love away *–Yeats*

Lovers can live on kisses and cool water

Love was in his kiss

My favorite place–inside your hug

Never a lip is curved with pain, that can't be kissed into smiles again –Bret Harte

Never been kissed

Now that's a kiss!

Prelude to a kiss

Pucker up and kiss me

Sealed with a kiss

Smooches and snuggles

Smoochie fest

Take me by the earlaps and match my little lips to your little lips –Platus

So kissable

Sweet smooches

The kiss of a lifetime

Two lips together

World's best kisser

Your kiss, I can't resist

Your kiss is best things in life list

♣ Passion

Amorous adventures

An affair to remember

Burning love

Do you think I'm sexy?

Fantasy for you

Feel like makin' love

Have you really loved a woman?

He felt now that he was not simply close to her, but that he did not know where he ended and she began –Leo Tolstoy

I like my body with your body

I'm here, what's your next wish?

I'm in the mood for love

In the wee small hours of the morning

Isn't it romantic?

It's in his / her kiss

Just pucker up and blow

Lost in love's dance

Love slave

Love's delight

Love's ecstasy

Love's melody

Lovealicious

Lovers' waltz

Lovin' the night away

Lying in your loving arms again

Makin' whoopee

My lover and me

Naughty and nice

One more kiss

One night together

Ooo-la-la

Our love nest

Our romantic hideaway

Paint your love all over my world

Prince / Princess of passion

Ready for romance

Rock me all night long

Rock me baby

Romance 101

Romance on the high seas

Romancing the night away

Romantic interlude

Sensual and seductive

Sexy and so sensual

Slip into something comfortable—my love!

Romantic rendezvous

Take my breath away

The look of love

Thou art to me a delicious torment –*Emerson*

Whisper sweet nothings

LOVE & ROMANCE

The following verses are written by Linda LaTourelle, unless otherwise noted

100% in love with you

All I want to do is grow old with you

All rights reserved—for you

Awwuh... I love you so much!

Do I ever cross your mind?

By chance we found each other, by choice we love each other and by grace we became one together

Elation is when my head turns to find you staring at me

Every little thing you do shows me how many blessings I can count each night

Baby, our first kiss—is the beginning of forever for us

Everywhere I go, there you are—wrapped 'round my heart, keeping me warm

Let every day be a slow-dance day

THE DANCE

He's rebel and romance
And wild and loving
Sexy and sweet
He stole my heart.
Strong and stubborn,
His love's got the best of me.
Holding him close
I'm breathlessly free.
There's a feeling
So powerful as we
Dance through our life
Touching each other
I'm blessed as his wife.
We fuss and we fight
And love with a thunder
Nothing comes close
To the magic and wonder
Of loving a man
That God made for me
His perfect fit is
Everything I need.

–Linda LaTourelle
Dedicated to my husband, Thomas!

Give your love to the one who takes your breath away

He drives me crazy with that smile that makes me love to kiss him

His love always makes me feel pretty

His prayer told him that I was the one he'd waited for

Home is the person that you want to be with every moment

Everything reminds me of you

I am totally not a morning person, but for you I'll make an exception

I could sit all day and do nothing with you

I hope I always give you a reason to smile

I imagined life with you and it's all coming true

I only think about you on two occasions—day and night

I just want to be your princess

I love to lay with my head on your chest, listening to your heart beating, knowing it's full of love for me

I smile when I see your name on my caller ID

I started missing you tonight as soon as we said good-bye

I wanna be your everything

I want to always be your favorite hello and hardest goodbye

I want to be the one you can't live without

I want to be your favorite good morning hug and goodnight kiss

I will look at no one else—I'm waiting for the one that will dance me to the end of love

I wrote your name over and over to see how we would look together

If I could choose anyone—it would always be you

If I stole your heart would you come find me and take it back?

If love was a storybook, ours would be love at first sight— through the happy ending

If you want me to fall for you, please hold me close

I wish you love—for us

If you would marry a man / woman —let him / her be one that will bring you hope, happiness and honor all the days of your life

In my book of love—you are my dedication

I just wanna be with you!

In my book of love, you are my once upon a time and my happy ever-after

In my fairytale—my prince / princess is you!

Inside-out, that's how much I love you

Kiss me 'til you feel the love, hold me 'til you know how much

Little girls always want to be a princess

Laugh with the one you love

Love deeply, feel passionately, grow together

Love reminds you that nothing else really matters

Mama told me there were men like you—I just had to grow up to believe her

Mornings are always better with you, coffee and sugar

In my favorite book, the story begins as we fall in love, and through each chapter the crescendo builds to a happy ending –*Linda LaTourelle*

My favorite reflection is you looking back at me

My favorite thing is when he / she holds my hand because he / she wants to

My heart is happy because you are in it

> You know that place between sleep and awake, the place where you can still remember dreaming? That's where I'll always love you That's where I'll be waiting
> — J.M. Barrie

AA.My home is anywhere you are

Never forget the butterflies you felt at the moment you first kissed

Once in your life there will be someone you'll never forget and you'll always remember the exact moment it all began

So I'm old-fashioned—just love me

Stay beautiful—you are, you know

S.W.A.G.—Simply • Wonderful • Amazingly • Gorgeous

The best way to stay close to someone you love is simply be their best friend

Small things become great, when done with love

Our love is infinite

Remember when we'd kiss goodnight at the door and I would pray you home, counting the minutes until we saw each other again?

When we are old, we shall eat chocolate, dance in the rain, hold hands and count each day as pure joy—just being together

The man who loves a woman will always make her feel beautiful, even on her worst of days

The sound of his voice is music to my ears—our own love song

The sparkle he puts in her eyes outshines the twinkles from the stars

The thoughts of the things you say keep me awake and smiling

What I want more of is you!

With his love I can do everything with extraordinary grace

Written with love—all the letters are in my heart

You and me—so groovy together

You and me—true friends through all eternity

You are the best part of my everything

You are the voice in my heart

You asked me why I love you—I said for the million little reasons that are you

Our first kiss was the beginning of forever

Your love is the closest thing to my heart

You're amazing just the way you are

Your smile turns my world upside down

LOVE & WEDDING

♣ *Dating*

A night on the town

A teen in love

Addicted to love

Ain't love grand?

Baby's in love

Bit by the love bug

Blind date
Boy meets girl
By the light of the silvery moon
Can't get you out of my mind
Can't fight this feeling
Can't take my eyes off of you
Chain of love
Come up and see me sometime
Crazy little thing called love
Dream lover
Every day I fall more in love with you
Fairytale love affair
Falling in love
Fanning the flames
Feeling groovy
Flirtatious and bodacious
Funny face, I love you
He / She loves me—he / she loves me not...
Hello, I love you
High-school sweethearts
Holding hands together
How delicious is the winning of a kiss at love's beginning
How right it is to love you
How sweet to be loved by you
I loved you from the moment we met
I only have eyes for you
I probably love you about a million times more than you could imagine
I wanna be loved by you
It's a date!
Just you, just me—just right!
Looking for Mr. / Miss Right

Love at first sight
Love is being silly together
Lucky in love
Made for each other
More and more every day
Opposites attract
Perfect harmony
She likes him, he likes her—they just need to tell each other
So this is love
Some enchanted evening
The bachelor
The dating game
The dos and don'ts of dating
The flame
The laws of attraction
The start of something big
The very first moment I beheld him, my heart was irrevocably gone *–Jane Austen*
'Til there was you
Today I met the boy / girl I'm going to marry
What a wonderful evening!
Wild thing, I think I love you!
With you is where I like to be
You had me at...hey there, darlin'
You're the one
You've captured my heart

✤ *Engagement*

A divine romance
A kiss to build a dream on
A love story
A ringing endorsement

An engaging evening
And the story begins
And the two shall become one
And they called it "puppy love"
Be my love
Born to love you
Can't help falling in love with you
Can't live without you
Courtship behavior
Days of wine and roses
Diamonds are a girl's best friend
Engaged at last!
Fooled around and fell in love
Grow old with me, the best is yet to be
He popped the question!
He proposed! I accepted!
How deep is your love?
I found my Prince Charming
I love you—those three words are you, inside of me—hopelessly devoted to you
I loved you from the first moment I saw you
I've been waiting for a boy / girl like you
Match made in heaven
Matchmaker matchmaker make me a match
May I have this dance for the rest of my life?
On bended knee
Read all about us
Rules of engagement

The love of my life
The most romantic proposal
The proposal
There is no remedy for love but to love more –Thoreau
The search is over
There is no instinct like that of the heart –Lord Byron
They gave each other a smile with a future in it –Ring Lardner
The story of us
This magic moment
My second love is better than my first –Vernon Hamby, * Dedicated to his one true love—Jamie Hamby
To get the full value of joy, you must have someone to divide it with –Mark Twain
We're engaged!
What are you doing for the rest of your life?
When a man loves a woman
When I fall in love, it will be forever
When I look into your eyes
Will you marry me?
You're the love I prayed for
Your words are poetry to my heart!

♣ *Pre-Wedding*

A license to wed
A walk down Lovers' Lane
Ain't no cure for love
Aisle be there
Aisle style
All things grow with love

Bachelor / bachelorette party
Be our guest
Bride-to-be
Can'T take my eyes off of you
Can't help falling in love with you
Dedicated to the one I love
Fairytales do come true
Get me to the church on time!
Getting hitched
Getting ready from head to toe
Goin' for the gold / silver
Goin' to the chapel and we're gonna get married
Going bridal
Good-bye single life
Head over heels in love
He says, she says—they do
How do I love thee, let me count the ways
I love him / her and that is the beginning of everything
I'm not rushing into being in love. I'm finding fourth grade hard enough —Lara LaTourelle, age 9
In love with my best friend
Just me and my girls
Love story—me and you
Made for each other
My fairytale told me that I'm going to marry you one day
My mother's hope chest
On the road to I do
One fine day
One who walks a road with love
will never walk the road alone
Otherwise engaged
Our dream come true
Our journey to the chapel
Our love story begins
Perfect together
Playing for keeps
Pre-wedding jitters
Saving all my love for you
Take my breath away
The boy / girl I'm going to marry
The countdown
The decorating crew
The love of my life
The man of my dreams
The shoe fit
The wedding planner
This guy's girl's in love with you
True romance
Tunnel of love
We're getting married in the morning
We're tying the knot
You are cordially invited

♣ *The Showers*

A sweet new beginning
Bridal shower surprise
Every bride has her day
It started with a kiss
Showers of blessings for the bride and groom
Love is blooming
My you be showered with joy

She's getting married, so let's have a party

Showers of blessings

Showered with love

Surprise bridal shower

There will be showers of gifts

Your presence is requested

♣ The Wedding

PLEASURES
Come live with me
And be my love,
And we will some
New pleasures prove
Of golden sands
And crystal brooks,
With silken lines
And silver hooks.
—John Donne

A million little reasons why I love you...

A moment like this

And I love her

And then he kissed me...

At last!

A wedding to remember

All because two people fell in love

All because we fell in love

And they lived happily ever after

And she shall wear pearls

Baby, I do

Baby, I'm yours

Because you love me

Be still and know my love

LOVE
He is the half part
Of a blessed man
Left to be finished
By such as she:
And she a fair
Divided excellence
Whose fulness of
Perfection lies in him
—William Shakespeare

Blushing bride

Bouquet of roses

Bride and groom

Bridezilla Wear-fare

Can you feel the love?

Chantilly lace, what a pretty face

Chapel of love

Cheek to cheek

Child bride

Cinderella's wedding

Circle of love is neverending

Daddy's / Mama's little girl / boy

Dearly beloved

Do everything with love

Everlasting love

Fairytale wedding

Father / Mother of the bride—full of pride

Father / Mother of the groom

For better or worse

Forever and always

Forever yours

From this moment on

The Biggest Book of Words & Prompts for Scrapbooks, Art Journals & Crafts

ALL I HAVE TO BRING TODAY
It's all I have to bring today,
This, and my heart beside,
This, and my heart, and all the fields,
And all the meadows wide.
Be sure you count, should I forget,
Someone the sum could tell,,
This, and my heart, and all the bees
Which in the clover dwell.

–*Emily Dickinson*

Groomed to perfection

Happy is the bride

Hawaiian wedding song

Here comes the bride

His and hers

I am my beloved's and my beloved is mine

I do, I do!—We did!

I do—love you!

I found the one whom my soul loves. I held him, and would not let him go. –*Song of Solomon 3:4*

I have finally found my place in this world—next to you!

I love Thee with the breath, smiles, tears, of all my life!

I love you always and forever

I love you not only for what you are, but for what I am when I am with you –*Elizabeth Barrett Browning*

I love you 'til the day after forever

I melt with you

I pledge my love to you

I smile because we fell in love

I Thee wed

I wanna love you forever

I'll love you for always

In front of God and these witnesses

In holy matrimony

In sickness and in health

In the chapel, in the moonlight

Introducing Mr. and Mrs. (name)

It's a wonderful life

It's official!

It's our wedding and we'll dance if we want to

June bride / choose month

Just like Romeo and Juliet

Just married

Just the two of us

Just to feel my love

Keep calm and marry your beloved

Keep calm and say I do

Keeper of my heart

Kiss the bride

Let love be your guide

Let's elope!

Little band of gold / silver

Lovely bride

Lucky in love

Made for each other

Magnificent bride

Man of the hour

Marriage is being doubly-blessed

Married…at last

Meet the newlyweds

Men in black
Modern bride
Modern romance
Mother / Father of the bride / groom
Much ado about something
My best friend
My bride and joy
My bridesmaids
My eyes adore you
My heart belongs to you
My husband / wife—pure love!
My mate for forever
Now join hands, and with your hands, your hearts –*Shakespeare*
Now we are married
Oh, happy day!
Once upon a love story
Once upon a time
Our little flower girl
Our special day
Our two hearts make one!
Our vows
Our wedding day
Pearls of love
Petals of love
Portrait of a bride and groom
Prelude to a kiss
Pretty in white
Pretty maids all in a row
Property of the groom / bride
Put your hand in mine
Royal wedding

Runaway bride
Sealed with a kiss
Something old, something new, something borrowed, something blue
So happy together
Stand by your man
Suit yourself
The bells on our wedding day
The big day
The day that two became one
The flame
The glory of love
The in-laws
The kiss
The members of the wedding
The money shot
The pledge and the promise
The perfect dress
The princess bride
The union of two people
The way you look tonight
The wedding march
The wedding singer
The wedding song
They live happily ever after
This diamond ring
This I promise you
This ring has no beginning, no end
Till there was you
To have and to hold
Today, I marry my best friend

Today, tomorrow and always
Tonight I celebrate my love
Two hearts—two lives—one love
Two little words—spell love
Two shall become one
Tying the knot
Veiled intentions
Vows tenderly spoken
We are one in love
We gather together to ask the Lord's blessings
We've only just begun
Wedded bliss
Wedding bell blues
Wedding crashers
Will you marry me?
With this ring, I Thee wed
Words of love
You are so beautiful
You have not chosen one another, but I have chosen you for one another –C. S. Lewis
You look wonderful tonight
You were always the only one

♣ Wedding Reception

A cruise to remember
A great time was had by all!
A night to remember
A thing of beauty is a joy forever
A toast to the bride and groom
Away we go!
Best man's / Maid of Honor's speech
Best wishes for the happy couple
Bless the bride and groom
Blissfully wedded
Bubbles and rice, wishes so nice
Cake in the face
Champagne wishes and romantic kisses
Cut the cake
Cheek to cheek
Daddy's little girl is all grown up
Dance me to the end of love
Dancing with my daddy
Did my heart love 'til now? Forswear it sight, for I ne'er saw true beauty 'til this night –Shakespeare
Eat, drink and blessed to be married to my best friend
From here to eternity
Get the party started
Happily ever after
Happiness is being married to your best friend
Hello Mr. (name) / Hello Mrs. (name)
Here's lookin' at you, kid
Honeymoon in Hawaii
Honeymoon in Vegas
I could have danced all night
I hear a melody of love
It takes two to tango
It's honeymoon time!
It's in their kiss
It's our song
Together is a wonderful place to be
Together we have it all
Tonight we celebrate our love

Two hearts—one cake

Welcome to the family

You are my once upon a time, all my dreams come true, you're the one I can't live without, my happily ever-after, too!

You make me feel like dancing

You are my daydreams, my sweet dreams and everything in-between

You taught me the meaning of love

You, the night, the music and me together—that's amoré!

LOVE & MARRIAGE

You are the moonbeam
on the winter sky
You are the light that makes
my heart sigh
You are my reason why
–Linda LaTourelle

A groovy kind of love

Abstract love

Ain't nothing sweeter than love

All about love

April love

Autumn of our love

Baby, you got what it takes

Back in baby's arms

Beautiful in my eyes

Because I see, therefore I love Thee
–Emily Dickinson

Because of you...

Book of love

Can't stop loving you

Can't buy me love

Doubt thou the stars are fire, doubt that the sun doth move; doubt truth to be a liar, but never doubt I love *–Shakespeare*

Echoes of our love

Follow your heart

For the first time

For the love of you

For where your treasure is, there will your heart be also

Have I told you lately that I love you?

Here I am, come and take me

Hold you in my arms forever

Homemade love

Hot stuff

I am my beloved, and my beloved is me *–Song of Solomon 6:3*

I can't stop loving you

I got you, babe!

I hold you in my heart

I know what love is because of you

I love being loved by you!

I love her and that's the beginning of everything *–F. Scott Fitzgerald*

I love you this much!

I love you to the moon and beyond

I love you truly, madly, deeply

I would fall in love with her again

I'll love you for all of time

I know what love is because of you

Love is an irresistible desire to be irresistibly desired

If you live to be a hundred, I want to live to be hundred minus one day, so I never have to live without you –*Winnie the Pooh*

It must be love

It's only love

It's simple...I love you with all my heart!

It's only puppy love

Jungle love

Just to be near you

Keeper of my love

Let me call you sweetheart

Let there be love

Life is sweeter because of you

Life is the flower—love is the honey

Love conquers all

Love is a gift we can give every day

Love is all there is

Love is me, love is you—dancing cheek to cheek

Love is patient; love is kind; love never ends

Love is pulling together

Love spoken here

Love is the enchanted dawn of every heart –*De La Martine*

Love is the key that opens the heart

Love is the morning sun sparkling in her / his eyes

Love is the gift of oneself

Love is the only gold –*Alfred Lord Tennyson*

Love is you—love is me

Love itself

Love letters in the sand

Love lives here

Love makes life richer

Love me tender

Love never fails

Love of my life

Love takes two—me and you!

Love unchained

Love will find a way

Love will keep us together

Love, love, love

Love, sweet love

Loving you is loving life

Loving you is the best way to spend a lifetime!

Loving you Sunday morning

Loving you—lovin' me

Lucky in love

Me and my baby

Melancholy baby

Mood indigo

More and more every day

Music of the heart

My babe

My baby and me

My beloved

My heart is yours

My little sugar pie

My love is like a circle with no end

My one and only

My own best friend

My sweetest days are spent with you

Nothing is sweeter than you

Now and forever

Now I know what love is

Of all God's gifts to me, you're my favorite

Of all the music that reached farthest into heaven, it is the beating of a loving heart –Henry Ward Beeches

Only with you

Only from the heart can you touch the sky –Rumi

Only love can be divided endlessly and still not diminish –Anne Morrow Lindbergh

Our love is beautiful

Painted love

Perhaps love...

Say that you love me

Seasons of the heart

Secret love

Serendipity

Singin' love's tune

So much in love

So they lov'd as love in twain— had the essence but in one; two distinct, divisions none –William Shakespeare

Star-crossed lovers

So, fall asleep love, loved by me, for I know love; I am loved by Thee –Robert Browning

So this is love

Sugar babe

Sugar, sugar

Sweet, sweet love

Sweet nothings

Sweet on you!

That's amoré! Sweet amoré!

The best thing to hold onto in this world is each other

The gift of love

The greatest of these is love

The missing piece of my puzzle

The moment eternal—just that and no more—when ecstasy's utmost we clutch at the core. While cheeks burn, arms open, eyes shut, and lips meet –Robert Browning

The power of love

The story of us

The sweetest joy, the wildest woe— our love story is ever so

The sweetest things that your lips shall touch are mine

The way that you love me

There is no end. There is no beginning. There is only the infinite passion of love that consumes us. –Linda LaTourelle

There"s no remedy for love but to love more

There's nowhere that I'd rather be, than simply alone with Thee

These things remind me of you

This thing called love

Together is a wonderful place to be

Too marvelous for words

We are shaped and fashioned by what we love –Goethe

We wrote the true romance

What's the earth with all its art, verse and music worth— compared with love, found, gained, and kept? –Robert Browning

We can do no great things, only small things with great love –Mother Theresa

Where there is great love, there are always miracles

Whatever our souls are made of, his and mine are the same
–*Emily Brontë*

Wild nights wild nights were I with Thee. Wild nights would be our luxury. –*Emily Dickinson*

You and me against the world

You are my sunshine

You are the best of my life

You are like a flower that blossoms in spring and the one for whom my heart joyously sings

You are the love of my life and keeper of my soul

You feel wonderful tonight

You make my heart sing

You mean the world to me

You're the cream in my coffee

You're my cup of tea

You're my sweetheart

You're nothing short of my everything

You're too good to be true

Your love keeps lifting me higher

You're the poem written upon my heart

LULLABY

All the pretty little horses

Golden slumbers

Go to sleep, my little baby

Hush, my baby, don't you cry

Lay Thee down now and rest, May thy slumber be blessed

Lullaby and good night, thy mother's delight...

Sweet baby of mine,
Sleep gently and rest.
Forever my love—
You will always be blessed.
My darling I love you,
My baby so fair.
You're a gift that is
So precious and rare.
I cherish and adore you
With all of my heart.
You were
My special child
Right from the start.
–*Linda LaTourelle*

All through the night

Hush, my little bird

Little baby sweetly sleep

Lula, lula, lullaby

Mozart's lullaby

My little morning star

My precious little one

Rock-a-bye, baby

Sleep baby sleep

Sleep, my little one

Someone to watch over me

Sweet hour of sleep

When you wish upon a star...

You are my sunshine...

MAKE BELIEVE

Dream a little dream

To invent, you need a good imagination and a pile of junk
–*Thomas Edison*

Dream my beautiful child of the endless possibilities that are before you. Play and pretend –Linda LaTourelle

If you can't believe, just make believe—that's magic!

Imagination—it's a grand thing to have!

Imagination is more important than words –Albert Einstein

Imagination is the highest kite that one can fly –Lauren Bacall

It's only make-believe

Many live in the ivory tower called reality; they never venture on the open sea of thought –François Gautier

Oh, what an imagination!

Once upon a time in the land of make-believe…

Welcome to the land of pretending, a place where joy is never-ending

You cannot depend on your eyes when your imagination is out of focus –Mark Twain

The great pretender

Your imagination, my dear fellow, is worth more than you imagine –Louis Aragon

MANNERS

Always be polite

Be kind, be polite

Being polite is always nice

Forgive me please

Good manners make for great kids

Good manners show respect for everyone, especially yourself

I'm sorry

Manners are free to give and a treasure to receive

Manners make the man

Manners really matter

May I please?

Pardon me / Excuse me

"Please" and "thank you" are the magic words

"Please" and "thank you" mean a lot

Polite children delight grown-ups

Polite people are right people

Remember the golden rule…

Respect your elders

Thank you very much

Treat others like you want to be treated

Yes ma'am, no sir

Your manners are a mirror that reflects the real you

MEMORIAL

A moment in time

An everlasting love

An honor to know such a hero

And God shall wipe away all tears

Angels watching over you

Earth has no sorrow that Heaven cannot heal

Eternal life

Faded memories

For old times sake
Forever in my heart
Forget me not
Gone but not forgotten
In the palm of His hand
I thank God for every remembrance of you
I will always love you
In loving memory
In our arms for a short time, in our hearts forever
In remembrance
In the house of the Lord forever
It was an honor to be part of your life
Love without end
Loving memories comfort the pain in our hearts
The memory remains
To honor and remember
Watching us from heaven
We'll one day reunite

MEMORIES

A bucket of memories
A happy ending
A time to remember
A walk down memory lane
A walk to remember
Always and forever
I love remembering
Lookin' back at yesterday
Make a nest of happy memories
Marvelous, magnificent memories
Memories are made of this

MEMORIES
A book of love
Written with care
Wonderful memories
I hope to share

Stories of life,
Family and friends,
Details of years
That won't come again

A gift made for you,
Straight from my heart—
A priceless treasure
I hope to impart

–Linda LaTourelle

Memories of days gone by
Moments in time
Moments to remember
Our very special memories
Seems like only yesterday
Sentimental journey
These are the days of us
These memories of you
Things I remember most
Those were the days
Treasured memories
Unforgettable moments
We made memories
Yesterday's memories

MEN

A boy who loves a girl
A good man is hard to find
Ah men!
Babe magnet

The New Ultimate Guide to the Perfect Word – Volume 2

Babes in boyland
Beau-dacious
Boy meets girl
Crush-worthy
Five-card stud
Give a man an inch and he will be ruler of your heart
He's a man among men
He's so fine—he's my man
He's da man
Honey dude
Hubba-hubba hubby
If at first you don't succeed, try it your wife's way
In the company of men
It's a guy thing
It's good to be a man
Juliet and her man
Just me and my man
Ladies' man
Lover man / boy
Macho, macho man
Mad about the boy
Male call
Man for all seasons
Man of honor
Man of many vices
Man of my dreams
Man of steel
Man of the hour
Man-tastic
Man oh, man
Manly presence
Me and my man

Men—we're just better
Mr. Right / Mr. Wrong
Mr. Style
My man
One wild and crazy guy
Plays with cars
Quite the stud
Real men don't eat quiche
Rocket man
Sportin' and suave
Suave and debonair
Sugar daddy
Super stud
Tales from the man cave
The gentleman's club
The lady's man
The male animal
The male species
The man I love
The object of my affection
The quiet man
The right stuff
The rubber-band man
The strongest man in the world
The Y chromosome
This guy's in love with you
This is a man's world
Tie-coon
To know him is to love him
Too sexy for his jeans
What a man needs!
What a man wants!
When a man loves a woman
World's best husband / boyfriend

You've got male
World's best lover
You take my breath away

MISCELLANEOUS

Almost famous
Bits and pieces
Can you believe this?
Character is who you are when no one is watching
Don't rush me—I'm waiting until the last minute
Don't try this at home
Dwell in possibility thinking
Ever stop to think and forget to start again?
High hopes
Hip to be square
I did it my way
I'm gonna let it shine
Isn't that special?
It's not the end of the world—just the intermission
Just bee-boppin' around
Made to order
Many are called, few are chosen
No rest for the weary
Razzle-dazzle
Scatter joy—reap happiness
See what I can do!
Simply magical
The best things in life are not free, but priceless
The more things change, the more they stay the same
There's one in every crowd
There's always tomorrow!
This and that
Variety is the spice of life!
What's happening?
Whazzup!

MOM & DAD-ISMS

A little soap and water never hurt
Are you deaf?
Are you heating the outdoors?
Back in my day…
Bored? If you're bored, I'll give you something to do
"Can't" never did anything
Candy is not for breakfast
Do as I say, not as I do
Do I look like your maid?
Do you think I'm running a taxi service?
Don't make me stop this car!
Go to your room!
Eat your vegetables, they'll make you strong
Go ask your father / mother
Go play, it's a beautiful day outside!
I don't have to give you a reason
"I don't know" is not an answer
I know what's best for you
I'm going to give you until the count of three and then…
I'm your mom / dad, that's why!
If I want your opinion, I'll ask for it

If I've told you once, I've told you a thousand times...
If you're too sick to go to school, you're too sick to play
Isn't it past your bedtime?
Mom's have eyes in the back of their head
Money doesn't grow on trees
Mother / Father knows best
No jumping on the bed
Now you listen to me, buster!
You're going to put your eye out
So you think it's funny?
Some day you will thank me for this
Stop picking your nose!
Wait until your father gets home
Wash your hands and use soap
Were you born in a barn?
What do I look like, a bank?
What do you think this is—a restaurant?
When I was a kid...
When I was your age...
Who said life was fair?
You call that a haircut?
You have an answer for everything, don't you?
You think I'm made of money!
You'll always be my baby
You'll eat it and you'll like it!
You'll live by my rules
Your face is going to freeze like that
You're the oldest, you should know better

MONEY

A penny saved is a penny earned
Baby, you're a rich man
Broke, bothered and bewildered
Cheaper by the dozen
Common cents
Follow the money
For richer or poorer
I wish the buck stopped here; I sure could use a few
It's a free country as long as you can afford to live in it
Money can't buy me love
Money talks! Mine says bye
One for the money
Pennies from heaven
Rags to riches
The best things in life are free
The million dollar question...
The road to riches
Time is money
We're in the money
Work hard for my money
Zip, zilch, nada

MOUNTAINS

Ain't no mountain high enough
Big Rock Candy Mountain
Blue Ridge mountain memories
Coming round the mountain
Faith moves mountains

Fire on the mountain
Go tell it on the mountain
God of the mountains
Heading for the hills
I can move mountains
In the canyon
In the valley
Love can move mountains
Mountain climber
Mountain memories
My Ozark mountain home
On Blueberry Hill
On top of Old Smokey
Over the hill and far away
Purple mountain majesties
Rocky Mountain high
Scaling new heights
The peak of perfection

MOVING

A real home
All packed up and ready to go
A moving experience
A moving moment
Across the miles
Boxes, boxes, boxes
Boxed, taped, crated and pooped
First apartment
Here come the movers
Home owners—the bank and us
House for rent
It's a lovely day in the neighborhood
Landlord blues
Let's get packing
Let's get the show on the road
Moving day is here
Moving on
On the far side of town
On the move again
Our house is a very fine house
Packed-up and ready to roll
Room for rent
Smart move
Thinking outside the boxes
Trailer for sale or rent
We came to stay
Ye old homestead

MUSIC

A chorus line
A symphony of love
All jazzed up
All that jazz
Are we not formed, as notes of music are, for one another, though dissimilar? *–Percy Bysshe Shelley*
Bee-bop baby
Boogie woogie baby
Clef-hangers
God gave us music that we might pray without words
Fried chicken and a country song
Half-time belongs to the band
He who sings scares away his woes *–Miguel de Cervantes*

Hard-rock lover
Heart of rock and roll
Hey Mister DJ...
High voltage rock
How can I keep from singing
I haven't understood a bar of music in my life, but I have felt it
  –Igor Stravinsky
I hear a symphony
I play the notes as they are written, but it is God who makes the music
  –Johann Sebastian Bach
I love country music
If music be the food of love—play on! *–William Shakespeare*
If the king loves music, it is well with the land *–Mencius*
If the music's too loud, you're old
In music the passions enjoy themselves *–Nietzsche*
In music, there is harmony—in harmony, there is peace
In my heart, there rings a melody
Jazz clubs and other stories
Jitterbug swing
Jukebox Saturday night
Just an old-fashioned love song
Just keep on singing
Let's go, rockabilly
Life is a song to sing
Life is the song, love is the music
Make a joyful noise unto the Lord
Make mine Mozart
Make your own kind of music
Mama sang me a song
Mr. Piano man

Music can name the unnamable and communicate the unknown
  –Leonard Bernstein
Music expresses that which cannot be said and on which it is impossible to be silent *–Victor Hugo*
Music is a higher revelation than all wisdom & philosophy *–Beethoven*
Music is love in search of a word
  –Sidney Lanier
Music is the language of the spirit
Music is the one incorporeal entrance into the higher world of knowledge which comprehends mankind but which mankind cannot comprehend *–Beethoven*
Music is the poetry in motion
Music is the sound of the soul
Music is the universal language of mankind *–Longfellow*
Music is the wine that fills the cup of silence *–Robert Fripp*
Music of the heart / night
Music teachers are in perfect harmony with their students
Music teachers open the ears to hear with the soul
Music to cry by
Music—the universal language
Musicians duet better!
My love song to you
My melody of love
My music notes
Name that tune
Note-able
Pickin' and grinnin'

Rock around the clock

Rock-a-bye your baby with a Dixie melody...

Roll over Beethoven

Shake that tambourine

Sing to the Lord a new song; sing to the Lord all the earth *-Psalm 96:1*

Sing, sing a song

Singin' in the rain

Singin' the blues

Sounds of music

Strike a chord

Sultans of swing

The beat of my own drum

The fiddler and the lady

The jazz singer

The music is not in the notes, but in the silence between *-Mozart*

The music man

The pauses between the notes is where the art resides *-Arturo Schnabel*

The song of love

The sound of music

The treble maker

There is nothing in the world so much like prayer as music is *-William P Merrill*

They're playing our song

We should consider every day lost on which we have not danced at least once *-Nietzsche*

What passion cannot music raise and quell! *-John Dryden*

Where the deepest word ends, there music begins with its super-sensuous and all-confounding intimations *-Herman Melville*

Where words fail, music speaks
-Hans Christian Andersen

Where words leave off, music begins *-Heinrich Heine*

Without music life would be nothing *-Linda LaTourelle*

You are the music in my life, the song in my heart *-Linda LaTourelle*

You make my life a song *-Linda LaTourelle*

Your love is the music of my heart

NATURE

TO NATURE

Nature, I would be thy child,
sit and worship at thy feet;
read the truth upon thy face,
wait upon thine accent sweet.
I would put my hand in thine,
bow my head upon thy knee,
live upon thy love alone,
fearless, trusting all to Thee.

-Mary Morgan

Adopt the pace of nature: her secret is patience *-Ralph Waldo Emerson*

Amber waves of grain

Let us permit nature to have her way: she understands her business better than we do *-Montaigne*

At the gates of the forest, the surprised man of the world is forced to leave his city estimates of great and small, wise and foolish *-Emerson*

Nature sings the sweetest song

Back to nature

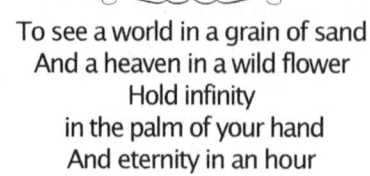

To see a world in a grain of sand
And a heaven in a wild flower
Hold infinity
in the palm of your hand
And eternity in an hour
—*William Blake*

Breath of fresh air

Designed by Mother Nature

Everybody needs beauty as well as bread, places to play in and pray in, where nature may heal and give strength to body and soul alike —*John Muir*

To sit in the shade on a fine day and look upon the verdant green hills is the most perfect refreshment —*Jane Austen*

God's country

Look deep, deep into nature, and then you will understand everything better —*Albert Einstein*

In all things of nature there is something of the marvelous —*Aristotle*

Nature always acts in the simplest of ways

Nature does not hurry, yet everything is accomplished —*Lao Tzu*

Nature is beauty at rest

Nature is the art of God —*Emerson*

Nature lover

Nature uses as little as possible of anything —*Johannes Kepler*

One touch of nature makes the whole world kin —*Shakespeare*

Only God can make a tree

Pure, natural and unspoiled

BEAUTY
The Creator's love is painted
On the hills and in the trees.
His beauty it surrounds us
In the flowers and the seas.
The wonders of His making
Gleam brightly in the sun,
Beckoning us to treasure
From morn' 'til day is done.
—*Linda LaTourelle*

Splendor in the grass

The beauty of nature

The good earth

The landscape belongs to the person who looks at it —*Ralph Waldo Emerson*

The promised land

This land is your land...

The sun does not shine for a few trees and flowers, but for the wide world's joy —*Henry Ward Beeches*

Uncharted territory

Until man duplicates a blade of grass, nature can laugh at his so-called scientific knowledge —*Thomas Edison*

Rustic countryside

Scenic wonders

Where the wild things are...

We do not inherit the earth from our ancestors, we borrow it from our children —*Navajo proverb*

Whoever loves and understands a garden will find contentment within —*Chinese proverb*

What a wonderful world!

Wild roses are fairest, and nature a better gardener than art –*Louisa May Alcott*

WOOD NOTES

Pondering shadows, colors, clouds
Grass-buds, and caterpillar shrouds
Boughs on which the wild bees settle,
Tints that spot the violet's petal
–*Ralph Waldo Emerson*

Flowers are nature's poems,
In blue and red and gold;
Every change from bud to bloom,
Sweet fantasies unfold
–*Ralph Waldo Emerson*

NURSERY RHYMES

Diddle, diddle, dumpling
Eeny, meeny, miny, moe
Five little speckled frogs
Hey diddle diddle
If wishes were horses
If you're happy and you know it
It's raining, it's pouring
Ladybug Ladybug
Little Boy Blue
Little Polly Parrot
Mary had a little lamb
Mary, Mary quite contrary
My fair lady
Old McDonald had a farm
Old Mother Goose
One, two—buckle my shoe
Pat-a-cake, pat-a-cake
Rock-a-bye baby
Row row row your boat
The cat and the fiddle
The cow jumped over the moon
The farmer in the dell
The muffin man

OCEAN ANIMALS

A crabby adventure
A whale of a good time
Don't be so crabby
Fish goes to school
Fish out of water
Fish tales
Happy as a clam
He's the oyster—I'm the pearl
Mobster lobsters
Peanut butter and jellyfish
Slippery as an eel
Star of the sea
Swims like a fish
Under the sea

PARADISE

Almost paradise
Color of paradise
Honeymoon in paradise
Just another day in paradise
Kisses from paradise
Lost in paradise
My garden of paradise
Paradise is where love dwells
Paradise is for lovers
Paradise found / lost
Surfer's paradise

PARTIES

A dream come true!
A night to remember
A time to celebrate
Celebrate good times
Cordially invited
Dancin' the night away!
Get the party started
Grandma's party
House party
I'm so excited
It's my party
It's time to party!
Let the festivities begin!
Let's go to the hop
Life of the party
Masquerade charade
Midnight at the oasis
Oh, what a night!
Once upon a party!
Paint the town
Parents away—children will play
Party like a rockstar
Party of the century
Party till the cows come home
Saturday night fever
Sleepover and pizza party
Some enchanted evening
The morning after
We're havin' some fun now

PETS

See also: Animals, Cats, Dogs

A boy / girl and his pet
Adventures of the pet-sitter
A passion for pets
A perfect pet for mom / dad
A pet and his / her master
A pet named _____
A tail of two pets
Adopted pets are the best pets
All about pets
Animal crackers in my soup
Breed all about it
Cheaper by the dozen
Furry friends family
Have you hugged your pet today?
I love my vet
I love runts
If I could talk to my animals
King / Queen of my lap
Marking the spot
Millions of pets
My beloved pet
Mystery at the kennel
Oh the pets you can get when you go to the vet!
My favorite pet story
Old pet—new pet
Our family supports adoption
Pet shop around the corner

Pet shop lullaby
Pets are us
Pets for sale / free
Pets make a house a home
Pets on parade
Pick a pet, any pet
Please mom, can we keep him?
Princess Petunia and her pets
Support your local shelter
Tails from the pet shop
The best pet ever
The critter diaries
The happiest pet
The house of a hundred pets
The pet of many colors
These are a few of my favorite pets
This home is property of the pets
To all the pets I've loved before
We love to breed
Which pet can I get?

PLAYING

♣ Dolls

A doll's alphabet
A doll's house
A doll named _____
A girl / boy and her / his doll
Baby's baby doll
Doll collector at heart
Dolly and me
Guys and dolls
Just me and my dolly
Mommy's / Daddy's little doll
My best friends are dolls
My paper doll
Never too old to play with dolls
One can never have too many dolls
Rag doll
She's only a paper doll
The best-loved doll
What a doll!
What's a doll to do?

♣ Fun & Games

A hard day's play
A real swinger
All's fair in love and play
Barefoot in the park
Blind man's bluff
Cat's cradle
Checkmate
Comic adventures
Connect the dots
Crack the whip
Dad's / Mom's just wanna have fun
Do not pass go
Dodge ball
Domino—watch 'em go!
Double letter score
Duck, duck, goose
Fairytales do come true
Families that play together, stay together
Farmer in the dell

Flashlight tag
Follow the leader
Following the leader
Freeze tag
Fun and games
Fun-sational
Game of life
Games kids play
Get a clue
Getting' goofy
Gin rummy
Go directly to jail
Go fish!
Go speed racer!!
Happy-go-lucky
Heads-up, seven-up
Hide and seek
Hokey pokey
Hop on pop—let's play!
Hopscotch
Horse play
Hot and cold
Hot lava
Hot potato
I love to play
I'd rather be playing
I've been dealt a good hand
If you're happy and you know it...
Imagination is grand
In the swing of things
Jump rope contests
Jumpin' for joy
Jumping rope
Just a swingin'

Just make believe
Just my luck!
Keep away
Kick the can
Kickball
Kid games and nursery rhymes
Kid stuff
Kids at play
King me
Laughing all the way
Leap frog
Let the fun begin
Let the games begin
Let the good times roll / bounce / fly
Let's go fly a kite
London Bridges
Marco Polo
Mom's day at the park
Mommy / Daddy and me play date
Mother may I?
Musical chairs
Name that tune
Oh, what an imagination!
Pin the tail on the donkey
Play as you go plan
Play date with mom / dad
Play today, sleep tomorrow
Playing around the playground
Playing dirty in the mud
Playing with my toys
Playmate, playmate, come out and play with me and we'll have fun you'll see...
Playing checkers with _____

Playtime is my favorite time
Pretending is fun
Red light—green light
Red rover, red rover
Relay races
Rock, paper, scissors
Rummy!
Scavenger hunt
Scrabble time!
Shoots and ladders
Simon says
Skipping stones
Skipping stones in the creek
Sleep means no play
Sorry!
Staring contests
Stickball
Swing kids
Swing time!
Swingin' around
Tag, you're it!
Take the time to play
The games kids play
The more the merrier
Tic-tac-toe
Treasure-hunting
Tug of war
Two little kids went out to play
We'll have fun, fun, fun
Wheelbarrow races
Who's got the rook?
You sank my battleship

♣ Kites

A boy / girl and a kite
A great day for kite-flying
Aim high
Blowing in the wind
Brace yourself
Come fly a kite
Everyone knows it's windy
Five little kites
Flying high
Go fly a kite
Gone with the wind
Happy winds-day!
Have kite—will fly!
Higher and higher
It's a blustery day
Let's go fly a kite
The kite-eating tree
The wind beneath my wings
Up, up and away
Windy day

♣ Teddy Bears

A beary special baby
A boy / girl and his / her teddy
A tale of two bears
As cuddly as a teddy bear
Beary cute and cuddly
Beary sweet
BFF / Bear Friends Forever
Cinnamon bear
Everything in life I will share—
except for my teddy bear

Furry best friends
Fuzzy wuzzy is my bear
Going on a bear hunt
Hope you are bear-ing up well
I'm in bear-adise with my teddy
I love bears
I love you beary, beary much
If you love me—you've gotta love my teddy
Just another day in bear-adise!
Life would be unbearable without my teddy
Little hearts never fear when teddy bear is near
Love bears all things and bears love me
Never too old to play with teddy bears
A teddy bear defeats the grumbles
Teddy and me
Just me and my teddy bear
Teddy bear! Teddy bear!
Teddy bears are always there
Teddy bears' picnic
Teddy was his name-o
The beary best of friends
The story of our baby bear
There's nothing like a warm and fuzzy teddy bear
This home loves bears
Unbearably beautiful
Where, oh where is my teddy bear?
You are my teddy bear
You make me so beary happy

♣ Toys

A boy, a dad and a go-cart
A doll's house
A visit to the toy shop
All my stuffed animals
Babes in Toyland
Broomstick buckaroo
Building blocks of love
Hula hoop
I love the toy store
I love to color
Jack-in-the-box
Jungle gym
Like a kid in a toy shop
Me and my boomerang
Me and my toys
My favorite things
My little red wagon
My toys are not your toys!
My toys! My toys!
My toy story
Old toy trains
Puzzle place
Red rubber ball
Rockets, planes and flying machines
So many toys, too many choices
The marvelous toy
Toys are my passion
Toys in Toyland
Wind me up and watch me go

PMS

Pardon my screaming
Pardon my sobbing
Pass my sweatpants
People make me sick
Perfect man syndrome
Perpetual munching spree
Perplexed man syndrome
Pimples may surface
Playful mood syndrome
Perfectly myself syndrome
Poor me syndrome
Provide me sweets
Puffy mid-section
Punish my spouse
Pure male stupidity
Pushing my sincerity
Push me stupid
Warning: do not disturb me
Warning: estrogen level high

POTTY

All grown up
All pooped out
Bye-bye diapers, hello undies
Diaper free—hooray for me
Grin and flush
Happy to be potty-free
He's / She's a big kid now
I got my big girl / boy panties
I love to potty
I made poopy
I'm a big kid now
It's my potty and I'll pee if I want to
Look what I can do!
No more doo-doo in my pants
No training needed
Potty animals / monster
Potty like a big boy
Potty pooper
Princess / Prince of the potty
The Prince's / Princess' throne
Whole lot of pottyin' going on

PRAISE A CHILD

Awesome job
Brave kid
Did I say you're fun?
Excellent effort
Go for it!
I love your laugh
I'm proud of you
Job well done
Looking great
Nice work
Super show
Terrific talent
There's no one else but you!
Totally correct
What a winner!
Wow! Way to go!
You are so smart

You did it!
You made it
You make me so proud!
You rock!
You rocked it!
You're remarkable!

PREGNANCY • BIRTH

9 months and counting
A child is born
A girl? A boy? Just love and joy!
A new baby to love
A bundle of joy—a girl or a boy!
A part of me!
A star is born
A time to be born
A whole new world
A womb with a view
Ah, sweet mystery of life!
Almost here
And the gender is…
And then there was you
And then there were ____
Appearing soon
As I looked at your tiny, beautiful, sweet face for the first time, I knew I had found my calling—to be your mommy / daddy and love you forever
Babies are a gift from God
Baby oh, Baby
Barefoot and pregnant
Been waiting for a girl / boy like you
Before you were conceived…

Bigger and bigger, day by day
Born innocent
Celebrating new life
Conceived in love
Counting the months
False alarm
Gift of our love
Got chocolate? / pickles
Great expectations
I loved you the first moment I felt you move inside me
In due time
In the beginning
It's a miracle?
It's in his/her kick!
Just the two of us
Kick up your feet—let's womba!
Labor day
Labor of love
Lady in waiting
Life before pregnancy was…
Life has begun
Look at that belly grow
Look what you did to me
Make room for baby
Mama, mama can't you hear my heartbeat?
Million dollar baby
Miracle baby
Miracles do happen
Mom / Dad in waiting
Mommy / Daddy to be
Month by month, day by day
My life began the moment I

opened my eyes and saw my mother's loving face smiling at me –Linda LaTourelle

New family under construction

I hear you mommy / daddy

Nine months and counting

Now look what you've done!

Oh how I smiled on the night you were born

Once upon a time...

Our gift from the Lord

Past-due

Peek-a-boo

Pink or blue—we love you!

Pregnant at last

Pregnant pause

Ready for baby

Romper womb

Room to grow

Sent from above

She's having my baby

She's somebody's baby

Small things come in big tummies

Sneak-peek at baby

Somebody to love

Stretched to the limits

Suddenly you were here and all my prayers were answered

Sweet beginnings

Sweet blessings from above

Ten tiny fingers and toes

Thanks be to God for His indescribable gift! –1 Corinthians 9:15

The day you were born, I was too, as your mother

The miracle of life / love

The most precious gift

The waiting game

There is no friendship, no love, like that of a mother for her child –Henry Ward Beeches

Today, love has a name...

Tummy-carried with love

Two pink lines and one big smile

We're pregnant!

Weighting for baby

What a belly!

What a difference you've made in my life

What a miracle!

When I heard your first cry, my life was forever changed. I knew at that moment you and I were connected forever with a love made in heaven just for the two of us. –Linda LaTourelle

Womb enough for two

Womb to move

Womb with a view

You grow girl!

You're a part of me

You're late, you're late for your very important due date!

Your story begins...

PUMPKINS

A pumpkin for baby

Baby's first pumpkin

Costumes and pumpkins and candy, oh my!

Cutest little pumpkin in the patch

Happiness is a jack-o-lantern
Hayrides and pumpkins
How to carve a pumpkin
I'm a pleasing pumpkin
In search of the perfect pumpkin
It's pumpkin time
Lookin' for the great pumpkin
Daddy's / Mommy's pumpkins
Our li'l pumpkin
Peter, peter, pumpkin eater
Pickin' pumpkins with mama / papa
Pumpkin Carving 101
Pumpkin hall of fame
Pumpkin pie, oh my!
Ready, set, glow
The frost is on the pumpkin
The great pumpkin
The great pumpkin caper
The great pumpkin venture
The perfect pumpkin
The pick of the patch
The pumpkin and the pie
The pumpkin parade
The pumpkin pie party

READING

A book is the most effective weapon against intolerance and ignorance –LBJ

To produce a mighty book, you must choose a mighty theme –Herman Melville

Man is known by the books he reads

Adventure is just a page away

All booked up

As a boy I was saved from a life of ignorance by my library

Book lovers never go to bed alone

Bookworm baby

Bored? Read a book!

A child learns to read on the lap of his / her parent

It's all happening at the library

I am part of all I have read

I can read now

If you do not have the time to read, you do not have the time to lead

I live / love to read

My favorite stories

No entertainment is as cheap as reading, nor any pleasure so lasting –Lady Montague

Once upon a story...

Once upon a time...

Once you learn to read, you will be forever free –Frederick Douglass

Read every day and you'll keep the cobwebs away

Reading rocks!

Reading is to the mind, what exercise is to the body –Richard Stele

So many books, so little time

Some books are to be tasted, some are to be swallowed and some few are to be chewed and digested –Francis Bacon

There is an art of reading...

The more that you read the more that you'll know and the more that you know, oh, the places you'll go! –Dr. Seuss

The storyteller

There is more treasure in books than all the loot on Treasure Island –*Walt Disney*

Today a reader—tomorrow a leader –*Margaret Fuller*

To learn to read is to light a fire; every syllable that is spelled out is a spark –*Victor Hugo*

What is reading but silent conversation? –*Walter Savage Landor*

REPAIRS

A big hammer fixes everything
A work in progress
Bang, bang, zzzz, $$$
Bulldozer boyz / girlz
Call me tool-man / woman
Caution: men / women at work
Duct tape professional
From start to finish
Home improvement
I came, I tooled, I built
I can fix anything...almost!
If I had a hammer...
Just call me super stud!
Man / Woman of many vises
Measure once—cut how many?
Mr. / Mrs. Fix-it
Room for improvement
Some assembly required
The honey-do crew
The wrecking crew
Tool time man / woman

Tough as nails
Under construction
On the eve of destruction
Who needs more power?

RETIREMENT

A blast from the past

Absolute freedom from working or not!

A retired husband is a wife's best friend (and vice-versa)

Age is an issue of mind over matter. If you don't mind, it doesn't matter. –*Mark Twain*

Being old takes up a lot of time!
Bring on the grandkids
Everything old is new again
Finally, some vacation time
Genuine geezer and proud of it
Golden oldies
Golden years or olden years?
Happy to be healthy
It's a vacation every day!
I worked hard to retire
If you can't be glamorous, settle for cute!
In the autumn of my years
It's a constant coffee break
It's not age, it's attitude
I've earned every wrinkle
Little ol' lady / man from...
Life begins at retirement
Memories of the times we left behind

My retired husband / wife has now given me a full-time job

Not quite vintage!

Now I can have coffee anytime

Ode to retirement

Old age hath yet his honor and his toil *—Alfred Lord Tennyson*

Retired and ready to rock and roll

Retired and happy

Retired—now I can really work!

Retirement is a full-time job

Retirement is not for the lazy

Retirement, when every day is Sunday afternoon!

Retirement: when weight goes up and energy goes down

Retirement: world's longest lunch hour

Since retirement my wife / husband has become my shadow

Spending my kid's inheritance

The golden years

The autumn of life

The winter of our discontent

Time marches on to its own beat

Turn back the hands of time

Twice as much time—half as much money

Two rounds of golf a day...sweet retirement!

We are young at heart!

Wrinkled was not one of the things I wanted to be when I grew up!

ROOM SAYINGS

♣ *Kitchen*

Eat well • Laugh often • Love much

Friends and family gather together

The kitchen is the heart of the home

Eat, drink and be merry

Never trust a skinny cook

Bon appetite!

Delicious moments with my family

Home is where mom's / dad's cookies are

Spice it up!

Bless all who gather here

Sit long, talk much

Café familia

Mom's / Dad's kitchen is seasoned with love

♣ *Bedroom*

Always kiss goodnight

How sweet it is to be loved by you

Holding you is holding everything

I found the one whom my heart loves

I love you to forever and back

Together is a wonderful place to be

Live • Love • Laugh

Look what happened when we fell in love

A touch is worth a thousand words

The Biggest Book of Words & Prompts for Scrapbooks, Art Journals & Crafts

The best things in life—me & you
Two souls with but a single thought
Cozy together
This is where the magic begins
I am my beloved's and she / he is mine

♣ *Family Room*

Faith • Family • Friends
So happy together
There's no place like home
Let the good times roll
Family is everything
Love came home and a family was born
Home is where love resides
Love grows in little / big houses
Home is the best place to be
A place for family and friends
The fruits of our family are sweet
Home—where our story is written
A circle of love

♣ *Laundry*

Clean and fresh
It'll all come out in the wash
Laundry help—inquire within
Self-serve laundry
A load a day keeps the smell away
Sock-it-to-me
Looking for a mate
One load at a time

♣ *Nursery*

The cow jumped over the moon
Sweet dreams and goodnight
Every good and perfect gift is love sent from above
A star danced and you were born
Lullaby my little one
One sweet child lives here
This room belongs to a princess / prince
I'll love you forever, my baby you are
Once upon a time...
I see the moon, the moon sees you
Your first breath took mine away
Twinkle, twinkle, precious star
A love like no other
A wee bit of love
All of God's grace

ROSES

A bit of fragrance always clings to the hand that gives roses
A rose lives here with an old thorn!
A single rose can be my garden... A single friend, my world –*Leo Buscaglia*
Gather ye rosebuds while ye may
God gave us memories that we may have roses in the winter of our lives –*Linda LaTourelle*
I love to go to my garden alone, while the dew is still on the roses
Rambling rose
Sweet as a rose

The roses wind with laziness and such a gentle ease

There is simply the rose; it is perfect in every moment of its existence –Ralph Waldo Emerson

Roses are red, violets are blue, flowers are sweet, but not as sweet as you!

I never promised you a rose garden –Lynn Anderson

May your day be filled with sunflowers & roses

May roses kissed in sunshine, glistening in the morning's dew, be only half as wonderful as the day in store for you –Thena Smith

Take time to smell the roses

When we want to have more roses, we must plant more roses –George Eliott

SAND & SURF

BESIDE THE SEA
Come walk with me
along the shore
Where we can talk
of love and more.
We'll dance together
on the sand,
Cheek to cheek,
hand in hand.
Searching for pearls
and ocean's treasures,
Timeless moments
none can measure
What a perfect beginning
for you and me
Laughing and loving
beside the sea!
–Linda LaTourelle

All along the seashore
A bright sunshiny day
A quick dip
A walk on the beach
Aqua kid
At one with the sea
Buried treasure
At the end of the pier
At the lake
At the water's edge
Attack of the crab monsters
A whale of a time
Back in the swim of things
Bahama Mama
Bathing beauties
Basking in the sunshine
Beach babe
Beach boys / girls
Beach bum
Beachcombing is my passion
Beachy-keen
Beating the heat at the beach
Beauty and the beach
Beyond the sea
Building sand castles
By the sea
By the shore
Catchin' the big wave
Coast of Carolina
Coney Island baby
Cool clear water
Coral reef
Cowgirl in the sand
Dancing on the beach

Days of sand and shovels
Discover the wonder of waves
Distant shores
Down by the ocean / sea
Down by the seashore
Enchanted sea
Fantasy island
Footprints in the sand
Good things come to those who wade
Harbor lights
Hit the beach running
I'd rather be at the beach
I love the sand between my toes
I love to write your name in the sand
Island getaway
Island girl / boy
It came from beneath the sea
Just chillin' at the beach
Keepin' my head above water
Let's go surfin' now
Life's a beach
Lifeguard in training!
Li'l sandman
Living water
Love letters in the sand
You and me, down by the sea
Meet me by the seaside
Michael, row the boat ashore
My first bikini
Ocean adventures
Ocean of love
Ocean-front property
Of sun, sea and sand
Official beach bum
On the beach
On the waterfront
Our treasure island
Pacific Coast Highway
Pearly shells
Playing in the sand
Pool time
Poolside adventures
Ride the wave
River rats
Rollin' on the river
Row, row, row your boat
Sail away
Sand between my toes
Sand castles
Sand in your shoes
Sand-sational
Sea breeze
Sea cruise
Sea for yourself
Sea shells and sunshine
Sea you in September
Sea, sand and surf
Seashells by the seashore
Seaside getaway
Seaside treasures
Shall we gather at the river?
Ship on stormy seas
Sittin' on the dock of the bay
Skinny-dipping
Snorkeling is such fun
Somewhere beyond the sea
Still waters run deep

Stranger on the shore
Strollin' on the beach
Summer skies and golden sunsets
Surf city
Surf, sand, fun
Surf's up
Surfer boy / girl
Surfin' safari
Surfin' USA
Taking the plunge
Testing the waters
The bluest water I ever saw
The boys / girls at the beach
The ever-constant sea
The little mermaid
The love boat
The old man and the sea
The river is wide
The sand, the sea—you and me
The surf and the sand—ain't life grand?
The river of life
Through the sand
Thunder Island
Treasures from the sea
Under the boardwalk
Walkin' on sunshine
Wave reviews
We forgot the sunscreen
We love the beach
We'll sing in the sunshine
We're having a heat wave
We're shorely having fun

Wet and wild
Wet n' wild
Whale of a time
Where the ocean meets the sky
White sands beach
You, me, and the sea

SANTA

A visit with Santa
At the top of Santa's list
Baking cookies for Santa
Cookies for Santa
Dear Santa, I want it all!
Dear Santa, I was very, very good
Desperately seeking Santa
Feeding the reindeer
Here comes Santa Claus
I believe in Santa
I love Santa
I saw mommy kissing Santa Claus
Just for Santa
Look what Santa brought me!
Mrs. / Mr. Claus
Must be Santa
North Pole—help wanted
Over the top
Rockin' the red!
S is for Santa Claus
Santa and the Mrs.
Santa baby
Santa Claus is coming to town
Santa, please stop here!

Santa stops here

Santa stuffs stockings; the rest of us stuff our faces!

Santa was here

Santa's little helper

Santa's elf

Santa's pit stop

Santa's workshop

Secret Santa surprise

This house believes in Santa

Waitin' for Santa

We believe in Santa!

Will work for cookies

Who needs Santa when you have grandma / grandpa!

Yes, (name), there is a Santa Claus

SCHOOL

♣ College

All classes lead to graduation

Believe in yourself

Big man on campus

College-bound

College is where you go to find yourself or get lost

College or bust

Dorm furnishings by mom

Dorm living is the life for me

Dorm sweet dorm

Fantastic freshman

Frantic finals

Dean's List and proud

I love college

Jewel of a junior

Keep Calm and Study

Keep Calm and Just Graduate

Majors and minors and me

Mid-term memories

My professor talks while I'm trying to sleep

Off to college

Oh the places you'll go

Old, broke and still paying my student loans

Party tonight, my dorm

Ready for recruitment

Smart sophomore

Sophisticated senior

Sorority / Fraternity party house

Where's mom or dad now that I need them?

The best is yet to be

Time of my life

The undergrad

Top ten list of college favs

Young, broke and still in college

♣ Graduation

It's not the degree but your commitment to using that degree to work toward making your dreams come true

Class of (year)
Degree in-hand and ready to go
Diploma day
Everything is in your reach!
Fast times at (name) High
From diapers to diploma
Glad to be a grad
Goodbye school!
Got degree! Got job?
Grad night
Graduation at last
Graduation day
Graduating with honors
Hard work pays off
Hats off to the class of (year)
Hello world, goodbye school
I did it! I made it!
I got the world on a string
Looks like we made it
My shining hour
Next step (goal)
Oh, the places you'll go!
Put your future in good hands—God's hands
Pomp and circumstance
Reach for the stars
Ready to take on the world
School day memories
The dream is now a reality
The graduate
The road to success
The tassel was worth the gold
These are the best of times
This day we have worked for
This is the first day of the rest of your life
The day I've been waiting for
Way to go!
Welcome to the real world
With honors!
You did it with flying colors
You made it!

♣ High School

A year to remember
Aim high
Back to school
Books are my bag
Brain-builder
Caught thinking
College-bound
College or bust
Explore the genius within
Fantastic freshman
Going on my senior trip
High school memories
High school drama
Homework is fun or not!
Junior years
Lessons in logic
Making the grade
Opportunity knocks
School spirit
Sensational senior
Smart as a whip!
Sophomore years

Spring break
Still learning after all these years
The best of times
The joy of learning
The learning zone
The senior trip

♣ *Prom Night*

A night to remember
All decked out
All dressed up
Dancing the night away
Dream night
Junior prom
Memories of high school
My prom gown
Pretty as a princess
Handsome as a prince
Prom king / queen
Prom night
Senior prom
Swept off my feet
The perfect date

♣ *School Days*

A fine day at school
A good book is your best friend
A kid with class
A year to remember
ABC's and 123's
Adding it all up
All I need to know I learned on the playground –*Linda LaTourelle*
All I really needed to know I learned in kindergarten
As easy as A-B-C
Be the best you can be
Be true to your school
Believe in yourself
Best in my class
Big man / woman on campus
Black board jungle
Books are my bag
Brain-building is my business
Brain overload
Caution! Learning zone!
Class clown
Classmates and friends, too!
Color outside the lines
Diary of a geeky kid
Diary of a straight A student
Do the math
Education is key to everything
Education is not the filling of a pail, but the lighting of a fire –*W. B. Yeats*
Education is key to your future
Elementary school days
Explore the genius within
Fables of a fifth-grader
First day of school
Fourth-grade fairytales
Genius in training
Go figure
Go in the direction of your dreams
Go to the head of the class
Hall pass to fun

Heaps of homework
Hi ho, hi ho, it's off to school I go
High school dances are fun
High school sweethearts
Hitting the books
Home sweet classroom
Homecoming king / queen
Homework makes you smarter
Homework makes you ugly
Honor student
I hate Mondays
I have never let my schooling interfere with my education
–Mark Twain
He that loves reading has the world within his reach
I love brainiacs
I love my classmates
I love school / field trip day
I love standing in lines
I love to go school-clothes shopping
I love to read
I study for weekends
I survived middle / high school
I use to be little, but now I'm going to school
Imagination is more important than knowledge
In a class of his / her own
In a school daze
Kids just wanna have fun
Knowledge itself is power
Late for school / class
Learning curve

Learn all that you can to do all that you want to do
Learning is a lifetime process
Learning is fun
Learning new every day
Learning the basics
Let your light shine
Letter-perfect
Life is an open book, so study
Live and learn
Love for learning
Love my weekly reader
Magic school bus
Making the grade
Me and my brain
Me and my bright ideas
Me and my friends down at the schoolyard
Middle school—too cool!
Miss / Mr. Smarty
Most likely to succeed, _____
Mr. / Miss Academia
My alma mater
My classmates rock
My favorite science project
My favorite teacher and subject
My first day at nursery school
My first day of school...such as, nursery, preschool, elementary, middle, high or profession name
My kid's on the honor roll
My kid rocks learning
My no-good horrible day at school
My old school

My school is better than your school
My school is cool
My weird school daze
National achievement award
New kid on the block
Organization is the key to success
Our little bookworm
Over-achiever
Packing the books
Playing by the books
Preschool blues
Preschool scholar
Pretty / Handsome and smart, too!
Proud parent of an honor student
Reach for the stars
Reading rocks!
Ready for school
Recess is best
Red letter day
Road to success
Rock-n-roll high
Saved by the bell
School according to me
School days, rule days, good old fashioned school days
School is more than just recess
School rules
School's cool and other myths
School spirit
Schoolyard spirit
School zone
School's out for summer
Schoolhouse rock
See you in September
Sensational student
Sharp as a tack
Sixth-grade super star
Smart as a whip
Smartypants goes to school
Sporting school attire
Star of the show
Star student
Still learning after all these years
Stop the bus I wanna get on
Study buddies
Summer school? Oh, no!
Summertime blues
Super kid
Super scholar
Super science
Teacher's pet
Tests overload my brain
The best is yet to be
The best school year ever
The bus stops here
The class clown
The dean's list
The freshman
The future belongs to those who dream
The future belongs to those who work hard
The gangs all here
The good, the bad and the brainy
The great chalkboard mystery
The harder you work, the easier it gets
The learning zone
The littlest Einstein

The magic school bus

The mind is your computer

The National Deans List

The new kid at school

The road to success

The roots of education run deep and the fruit is extraordinary

The smart kids guide to school

The wheels on the bus

The written word

There are no mistakes, only lessons

Thinking outside the box

This is my brain on homework

This too shall pass

Today a reader, tomorrow a leader

Too cool for school

Top student in my class

Top ten things I like about school

Train up a child in the way he should go

Treasure the years you are in school, they will fly by

' Twas the night before preschool

Waiting at the bus stop

We love school

Welcome back students

What you do is determined by you

When the student is ready, the master appears –Buddhist proverb

Whether you think you can or think you can't—you are right

Whole lotta learning going on

You can be the change you wish to see in the world, just try

Way to go!

You must do the thing you think you cannot do -Eleanor Roosevelt

Zany and brainy, too!

♣ Teachers

A child can do anything if he / she is inspired by a great teacher

A class act—my teacher!

A good teacher is a masterpiece

And he hath put in his heart that he may teach –Exodus 35:34

A teacher sees tomorrow in a child's eyes

A wise teacher makes learning fun and exciting for everyone

A teacher may be just one person to the world, but he may give the world to a child through his / her teaching –Linda LaTourelle

Behind every successful student is an exhausted teacher

Every truth has four corners—as a teacher I give you one corner, and it is for you to find the other three –Confucius

First class teacher

Give children your heart and you will teach them to believe in themselves –Linda LaTourelle

Give of your hands to serve and your hearts to love –Mother Teresa

Good children become great adults through the influence of teachers who care

Good teachers make everything write

Great teachers are a class act

The Biggest Book of Words & Prompts for Scrapbooks, Art Journals & Crafts

Great teachers are born with a passion to impart knowledge

Happy teachers have happy students

I cannot teach anybody anything, I can only make them think –Socrates

I love learning

I'm as lucky as can because the world's greatest teacher is teaching me! –Linda LaTourelle

Home, sweet classroom!

If you can read, write and count— thank a teacher! –Linda LaTourelle

It is a wise teacher who gives her children the ability to think

Leading a child to learn is a teacher's hidden treasure

Learning is a journey, not a destination

Children count—ask a teacher

Love is the square root of teaching

Many can teach—few can reach

Math teachers really count

Me and my teacher

Music teachers are really sharp

Music teachers give sound advice

Music teachers play the right note

My teacher has class!

One good teacher outweighs a ton of books –Chinese proverb

Only the educated are free –Epictetus

Precious and few are teachers like you –Linda LaTourelle

Preschool teachers enjoy small blessings

Real learning begins with great teaching

Science teachers have great chemistry!

See (name) teach—see (name) care —see children learn!

Share your knowledge for future generations

She sees tomorrow in every child's eyes!

Teach me, O' Lord—the way of Thy statutes –Psalm 119:33

Teacher's aide—a welcome addition!

Teacher's motto—when all else fails, pray!

Teachers can evoke changes that last a lifetime –Linda LaTourelle

Teachers have homework, too!

Teachers light the way for others to shine –Linda LaTourelle

Teachers lessons last a lifetime

Teachers make the grade!

Teachers make the little things count

Teachers plant seeds of knowledge that will grow forever

Teachers strengthen others when they share their passion to learn

Teachers that love to teach, create kids that will love to learn

Teachers touch the future

Teaching creates all other professions –Linda LaTourelle

Teaching is a lost tradition waiting to be found –Linda LaTourelle

Teaching today touches tomorrow

Tell me and I forget, teach me and I remember, involve me and I learn –Benjamin Franklin

The world need's more teachers like you

There is great joy in seeing the light come on in a child's eyes

There is no nobler profession than to teach

Those who are wise will instruct many –Daniel 11:33

Three good reasons to be a teacher: June, July and August!

Through the love of teaching a heart lives more than once –Linda LaTourelle

To learn is a blessing. To teach is a gift –Linda LaTourelle

To teach a child how to think is the real purpose in school

Treat people as if they were what they ought to be and you help them become what they are capable of becoming –Goethe

What I live by—I will impart

When we learn from God we can teach to man –Linda LaTourelle

When one teaches, two learn

Wisdom has a thousand faces

You can't scare me—I'm a teacher!

SEASONS

SING A SONG
Sing a song of seasons!
Something bright in all!
Flowers in the summer,
Fires in the fall!
–Robert Louis Stephenson

SEASONS
In winter I get up at night
And dress by yellow candlelight.
In summer, quite the other way,
I have to go to bed by day.
–Robert Louis Stevenson

A change of seasons

Autumn hath all the summer's fruitful treasure –Thomas Noshed

Nature gives to every time and season some beauties of its own

One season following another

Seasons in the sun

Seasons change and so did you

There is no season such delight can bring as summer, autumn, winter and spring –William Browne

To everything, there is a season

The four seasons of the year

The seasons change with each passing year

We had joy, we had fun, we had seasons in the sun

No spring nor summer beauty hath such grace, as I have seen in one autumnal face –John Donne

My favorite time of year—everything has beauty

Season of mists and mellow fruitlessness –John Keats

Every season has its treasures

Live in each season as it passes; breathe the air, drink the drink, taste the fruit –Henry David Thoreau

Autumn

AUTUMN

Gleam the apples through the leaves;
Thickly stand the golden sheaves;
Earth is all in splendor dressed;
Queenly fair, she sits at rest,
While the deep delicious day
Dreams its happy life away.

–Margaret Sangster

AUTUMN'S COLORS

Bright leaves we gather one by one,
like gems beneath a tropic sun.
Golden brown with specks of red,
scarlet leaves by sumac shed,
green with amber shades of light,
maple leaves all golden bright,
they'd make a crown so rich and rare,
it would do for any king to wear.

–Watie W. Swanky

A festival of fall colors
Adieu sweet summer
Amazing autumn days
Apple time in the orchard
As autumn leaves turn
Autumn colors
Autumn days are here again
Autumn festival time
Autumn in New York
Autumn leaves are falling
Autumn of my life
Autumn splendor
Autumn's in the air
Autumn's palette
Autumn's glory
Autumn's splendor
Baby's first autumn
Bonfires of autumn!
Bushels of blessings
Chillin' in autumn
Colors of autumn
Cornucopia of blessings
Crisp autumn nights
Fall comes to New England
Fall extravaganza
Fall festival of colors
Fall into autumn
Fall into love
Fall on the farm
Fall's coloring book
First day of autumn
Flavors of fall
Frolic in the leaves
Glorious autumn days
Happy fall, ya'll
Have a good fall, y'all
Here comes autumn
Hi-ho, hi-ho, it's off to rake we go!
I love farmer's markets
I love scarecrows in the fall
I love September—when the leaves come falling down
I love the sound of crunchy leaves as I walk in my garden
Indian summer
Kaleidoscope of colors
Nature's bounty
October is a symphony of color
Playing in the leaves

OCTOBER

O hushed October morning mild,
Thy leaves have ripened to the fall;
To-morrow's wind, if it be wild,
Should waste them all.
–Robert Frost

Autumn is my favorite time of year

Red, yellow, orange and brown —nature's glory does abound

Oh, those autumn colors!

Rakin' in the fun

Rolling in the leaves

Scarecrow on duty

September to remember

Shades of autumn

The apple dumplin' gang

The colors of fall are the most beautiful of all

When the leaves came tumbling down

The majesty of fall

Those golden autumn days

When autumn leaves begin to fall

I saw old autumn in the misty morn stand shadowless like silence... *–Thomas Hood*

Everyone must take time to sit and watch the leaves turn *–Elizabeth Lawrence*

The vineyards are blazing with the blush of fall, this harvest has been the most blessed of all *–Linda LaTourelle*

Delicious autumn! My very soul is wedded to it, and if I were a bird, I would fly about the earth seeking the successive autumns *–George Eliot*

No spring nor summer beauty hath such grace as I have seen in one autumnal face *–John Donne*

I love Autumn's color

In September, when the leaves come falling down...

Windy autumn day

The autumn leaves are falling like rain. You are a thousand miles away. There are always two cups at my table. *–T'ang Dynasty*

Give me juicy autumnal fruit, ripe and red from the orchard
–Walt Whitman

♣ Winter

100% chance of flurries

A blanket of serenity

A blanket so soft and white

A cold winter's night

A cup of cocoa, a warm fire and you

A flurry of friends and lots of fun

A hot chocolate winter day

A rose in winter

A winter's day

A winter's tale

And cold, white winter snow fell softly down *–Louisa May Alcott*

An old man loved is winter with flowers *–Edgar Friedenberg*

Announced by all the trumpets of the sky, arrives the snow *–Emerson*

At the first fall of snow

Baby let's snuggle up together—it's cold outside

Better bundle-up

The Biggest Book of Words & Prompts for Scrapbooks, Art Journals & Crafts

Blizzard conditions
But baby it's cold outside
Cold frosty morning
Coldest winter in years
Cozy by the fire
Cozy winter wishes
Cuddlin' with cocoa
December's child
Delights of December
Digging out again!
Dressed up like Eskimos
Epic snow adventure
Even the coldest winter days can bring the warmest memories
Far away from the cold night air
Give me hot chocolate any day
Gliding along together
Glitter, glamour and frosty friends
God gave us memories so we might have roses in December
Grey December
Hazy shades of winter
Headin' south for the winter
Hot chocolate and you—warm the coldest of days!
I love your Eskimo kisses
I melt with you
I walked to school in three feet of snow when I was your age
I'm dreaming of a warm winter
Ice princess / prince
Icicles as big as the house
If we make it through December
Once upon a winter

In the depths of winter I finally learned there was in me an invincible summer –Albert Camus
In the frosty air
It's a hot chocolate kind of day
It's going to be a long cold winter
Jack Frost nipping at your nose
Jack Frost painting on my windows
Jingle all the way
Just a couple of flakes
Just chilling with my baby
Just me and my sled!
Last blast of winter
Lazy, cozy days of winter
Leaving little paths behind
Let the winter games begin!
Let's go for a sleigh ride together
Let's go sliding!
Listen to the north wind blow
Love like winter
Melting in the sun
Mommy's / Daddy's little popsicles
Mufflers and mittens
My favorite winter hobby
O the long glories of the winter moon! –Alfred Lord Tennyson
O, wind, if winter comes, can spring be far behind? –Percy Bysshe Shelley
Old Man Winter
One kind word can warm three winter months –Japanese proverb
Over the river and through the woods on a wonderful winter day
North Pole or bust!

Peppermint winter
Polar bear, polar bear
Popsicle toes
Promise of a new year
Ridin' the storm out
Scarves and mittens and hats— oh my!
Season of white
Shimmering snow crystals
Short days and long nights
Ski bums
Skiers paradise
Sledding buddies
Sleds for rent
Sleepy winter nights
Sleigh bells ring
Sleigh rides in the moonlight
Slipping and sliding on the slopes
Snuggly and warm
Song for a winter night
Star light, star bright—please let it snow tonight
Sub-zero temperatures
Ten degrees below—getting colder
The coldest winter in fifteen years
The dawn of winter
The fire is so delightful
The first day of winter
The Great White Way
The icicles are melting
The lake effect
The lights of winter
The longest winter
The warmest mittens

The perfect winter day
The Polar Bear Express
The twelve days of winter
The weather outside is delightful
The weather outside is frightful
The winter song
There's a chill in the air
There's a kind of a hush
Tis the season to be freezin'
Two eyes, a carrot and an old top hat
Under the snowdrifts are the seeds of spring
Walking in a winter wonderland
Wanted: Magic hat
Warm and toasty together
Warm woolen mittens
We are little icicles
We're having snow much fun!
Welcome to our igloo
Wet socks and mittens
What fire could ever equal the sunshine of a winter's day? –Henry David Thoreau
When a snowflake, brave and meek, lights on a rosy maiden's cheek –Mary Maples Dodge
White-out conditions
Winter blues
Winter love
Winter lullaby
Winter romance
Winter wonderland

✤ Spring

SPRING
I wandered in the well-known path,
The sky was bright and blue,
The trees were clad in freshest green,
The sunlight streaming through.
O whence this gladness in the air?
And wherefore do ye sing?
The little birds were answering me
"rejoice, for it is spring!
–Mary Morgan

A bouquet of springtime

A new beginning

A pocketful of sunshine

All through the long winter, I dream of my garden

And the rain, rain, rain, came down, down, down…

And then it was spring

April hath put a spirit of youth in everything *–Shakespeare*

A season of flowers and showers

Baby's first spring

Between winter and summer, lies a beautiful spring

Blowing in the wind

Come gentle spring!

Daffodils and daisies

Enchanted spring

First day of spring

First signs of spring

If we had no winter, the spring would not be so pleasant *–Anne Bradstreet*

It's a beautiful day!

SPRING'S SONG
As the first ray of sunlight stole in,
He was awakened by sweet music
It was the morning song of the bees
–Louisa May Alcott

Fresh as a daisy

For the winter is past, the rain is over and gone…Yes, spring is here *–Song of Solomon 2:11–12*

Gather ye rosebuds as ye may

I love spring

I dream of spring

I'm singing in the rain

If you do not sow in spring, you will not reap in the autumn *–Bible proverb*

Imagination is the highest kite that one can fly *–Lauren Bacall*

In like a lion—out like a lamb

In search of spring

In the springtime

It's always spring in a mother's heart

It's finally spring

It's spring—look who's blooming

It's a spring thing!

It's a lovely day in the neighborhood

It's a sunshine day

Little April showers

Look who's blooming!

Mr. / Ms. Blue Sky

My favorite season of all

Only with winter patience can we bring the deep desired, long-awaited spring *–Anne Morrow Lindbergh*

SPRING

Songs of the birds for music-
Flowers bending with grace,
The sky is so blue and pretty;
The sun warm upon my face.
Treasures here for the taking
Spring is bursting forth today,
Days full of many blessings-
Time to go outside and play.
—*Linda LaTourelle*

New beginnings

One spring day

Puddle-jumper

Ready for spring

Songs of spring

Spring, an experience in immortality —*Henry David Thoreau*

Spring ahead, fall back!

Spring and fall, I love them all!

Spring cleaning

Spring had come once more... lingering along through April and May in a succession of sweet, fresh, chilly days, with pink sunsets and miracles of resurrection and growth —*Lucy Maud Montgomery*

Sitting quietly, doing nothing, spring comes and the grass grows by itself —*Zen proverb*

Spring arose on the garden fair— each flower rose from the dreams of its wintry rest —*Percy Bysshe Shelley*

No matter how long the winter, spring is sure to follow —*Old proverb*

Spring into style

Spring is in the air everywhere

Spring is a symphony
Played in my heart
Through winter's
Coldest days
—*Linda LaTourelle*

Spring is the year's pleasant king —*Thomas Noshed*

Spring speaks of love and other beauty

Spring's greatest joy beyond a doubt is when it brings the children out —*Edgar Guest*

Springtime in the Rockies

Springtime promises

Suddenly one spring

Swing into spring

Take time to smell the flowers

The ABC's of spring

The birds of spring

The color of spring

The essence of spring

The fairest of the seasons

The sweetest spring

The flowers appear on the earth; the time of singing has come —*Song of Solomon 2:12*

The hills are alive with the sounds of spring

The promise of spring

This outward spring and garden are a reflection of the inward garden —*Rumi*

Winter is on my head, but eternal spring is in my heart —*Victor Hugo*

Younger than springtime

♣ Summer

RECIPE FOR SUMMER

What is summer made of?
Of opening buds and flowers;
Of sunshine and of shadow,
And gracious little showers,
Of birds that in the tree-tops
Sing sweetly all the day;
Of buttercups and daisies,
And breath of new-mown hay.

Of butterflies that hover
O'er every fragrant rose;
Of bees that gather honey
Where the honeysuckle grows.
Of brooks that murmur softly,
And thro' the meadows glide:
Of shadows shifting gently
Down the mountain-side.

Of rainbows after showers,
Of starlight nights so still;
Of moonbeams shimmering softly
O'er every brook and rill.
Of mornings dawning sweetly
O'er dew-wet grass and flowers,
Oh! Summer time is only
A life of golden hours!
—Mary Dow Brine

100 days of summer

A big summer splash

A bright, sunshiny day

A day at the beach

A little taste of summer

A place in the sun

A ray of sunshine

A summer job for me

A summer to remember

A summer's day

A taste of summer

Baby loves summer

Backyard fun

Basking in the sunshine

Beach ball babes

Beach bums

Bikini bottoms

Camping in your own backyard

Castles in the sand

Celebrate summer

Cool in the pool

Crafts in the park

Crazy summer days

Day camp adventures

Dreaming of summer

Endless summer

Feels like summer's here

Firefly summer

First dip of summer

Flip-flop days

Giggles and goggles

Girls just want to have sun

Going for a swim

Good morning sunshine

Got lemonade?

Got sunscreen?

Gotta wear shades

Grilling and chilling

Happy days are here again

Happy summer days

Havin' a heat wave

Here comes the sun

Hot fun in the summertime

Hot summer nights

I love summer
I love the lifeguard
In summer, the song sings itself –William Carlos Williams
I scream, you scream we all scream for ice cream
I'm walking on sunshine
In the heat of the night
In the summertime
Indian summer
It happened one summer
It's a sprinkler kind of day
It's a sunshine day!
Jump into summer
Just pooling around
Keepin' cool by the pool
Kissed by the sun
Lazy days • Laughter • Lemonade
Lazy, hazy, crazy days of summer
Lemonade for sale!
Little Miss sunshine
Loving the outdoors
Made in the shade
Make fun all summer long!
Makin' waves
Midsummer night's dreams
My sunshine girl
On a summer's day
Once upon a summertime
One bright ray of sunshine
One crazy summer
One hot summer day
One summer night
Our little mermaid
Picnics in the shade
Pool boy / girl
Pool party at my house!
Poolside antics
Popsicles in paradise
Prince / princess of the pool
Ready for summer
Red hot summer
Relaxing and reading
Run in the sun
S is for summer!
School's out!
Shall I compare Thee to a summer's day? –Shakespeare
She's / He's Hot! Hot! Hot!
Sips of summer
Sittin' on the dock of the bay
Sizzlin' fun in the summer sun
Sliding into fun
Sliding into summer
Slippery when wet
Soak city
Soaking in the sun
Soft summer nights
Some like it hot
Splish splash
Star swimmer
Stay-cations are fun
Summer at the seashore
Summer book club
Summer camp adventures
Summer days are here again!
Summer in paradise
Summer in the city

Summer of love
Summer Olympics
Summer rain
Summer reflections
Summer romance
Summer school blues
Summer sunset
Summertime blues
Summertime—the livin' is easy
Sun-burned buns
Sun worshipers
Sun-kissed!
Sunny days are here again
Sunny side up
Sunshine on your shoulders
Surf, sand, and fun!
Swim lessons
Swimming into summer
Swingin' into summer
The ABC's of summer
The boys / girls of summer
The colors of summer
The first day of summer
The greatest summer on earth
The grills of summer
The heat is on
The last day of summer
The littlest swimmer
The long hot summer
The perfect summer
The poolside lounge
The summer solstice
The summer story
The sunshine girls / boys

The sunshine of my life
The sweet fruits of summer
To see the summer sky is poetry – *Emily Dickinson*
The things we did last summer
To sit in the shade on a fine day and look upon verdure is the most perfect refreshment   –*Jane Austen*
Too much fun in the sun
Triple digits
Underwater adventures
Walking on sunshine
Warm, wild and wishing I was swimming!
What are you wading for?
What I did on my summer vacation
You are my sunshine

SHOPPING

All I need is love and two or three shopping cards
Bargains are my business
Friends forever shop together
I came, I shopped, I scored
I decided to start exercising, so I went shopping
I'd rather be shopping
I get allergic cleaning house
I left my heart at the mall
I live to shop
I never met a store I didn't like
I'll take one in every color
I'm out of money, where's my checks?

If at first you don't succeed, try a different store or a different card

Just give me Park Avenue

Madison Avenue here we come

My man knows what turns me on—him cooking in the kitchen and me shopping at the mall

WAH: Women Against Housework meeting at the mall—2:00 daily

Proud member of shopaholics anonymous

Queen of the bargains

Shop 'til you drop

Shopping—my favorite sport

Shopping is great therapy

Shopping makes every day a great day

The sales, the stores, the fun!

To shop or clean—that's a silly question!

What the world needs now is more shopping and less housework

When all else fails—go shopping

SLUMBER PARTY

And to all a good night

At sleep and at play

Caught napping

First one awake

Girls / Boys only!

Good night, moon

I didn't sleep a wink last night

I should be sleeping

Last one to sleep

Late night movies

Midnight snacks

Mister sandman

Mom's / Dad's coming!

No sleep, no dreams

Peace and quiet

Pizzas, parties and pals

Sleeping beauties

Sleepless night

Sleepover—my house!

Sleepy heads

Sleepy-time girls / boys

Slumbering with my friends

Staying up all night

The big sleepover

Who needs sleep?

SMILES & LAUGHTER

A season of love and laughter

A wink and a smile

Belly laugh

Glad all over

Goofy grin

Grins, giggles and laughing wiggles

Happy-go-lucky

He / She was born with the gift of laughter

He / She who laughs last, laughs best

I can still hear the song of your laughter

Just one smile

Keep smiling

Laugh a little—love a lot

Laughing all the way

Laughter in the rain

Laughter is the best medicine
Laughter is the sun that drives winter away
Laughter is a joyful noise
Miles and miles of smiles
Mona Lisa smile
My favorite smiles
Put on a happy face
Share a smile and be a blessing
Smile when your heart is breaking
Smile you're on candid camera
Something in the way she smiles
Sweet sweet smile
The lady / gentleman smiles
You are my laughter in every day
You make me laugh
You make me smile
Your laughter is sunshine to my soul
Your's is the smile I dream about!
Your smile is the light of my life

SNOW

A beary snowy day
A beautiful blanket of peace
A flurry of friends
All covered with snow
All that glitters is snow
A wonderland of white
Angels in the snow
Blizzard conditions
Bright ideas for a snowy day
Dance of the snowflakes
Dashing through the snow
Epic snow adventure
Fast and flurrious
Feelin' frosty
Footprints in the snow
Forecast is flurries and fun
Frosty and his friends
Frosty nights and warm memories
Frosty's snowy day
Got snow?
Have snow, will ski!
Here we go a'shoveling
I love a good blizzard
I love snow globes
I love snowbirds
I'd rather be playing in the snow
I'd rather be skiing
I'm a little snowflake
I'm dressed for snow and ready to go!
In the lane, snow is glistening
It's snowtime!
It's snow cold outside!
It's snow nice to be with you!
It's snow wonder I love you!
I wish it would snow
Just add snow
Just another snowy day
Just me and my snow baby
Let it snow, let it snow, let it snow
Let's make snow angels
Look at him / her snowing off!
Millions of snowflakes
One snowy day

No snowflake ever falls in the wrong place —Zen proverb
Snow adorable
Snowball fight
Snow bird / bunny
Snowbirds in love
Snow buddies
Snow cream cones
Snow daze
Snow happens
Snow kidding
Snow is falling, friends are calling —it's a beautiful day!
Snow play on a winter's day
Snow princess / prince
Snowball fight—join us tonight!
Snowballs for sale
Snowbird lane
Snowbirds welcome
Snowbound and snuggling
Snowed-in and lovin' it!
Snowed-in together
Snowflakes are angel wishes
Snowflakes fall, are you listening?
Snowflakes keep falling on my head
Snow friends forever
Snow girls / boys like to snuggle
Snow white queen / king
Snowy adventures
Snowy splendor
Suzy / Sammy snowflake
Tales of a snowy day
The biggest snowfall ever
The biggest chill
The cutest snow baby of all
The first snowball of the season
The first snowfall of winter
The friendliest snowflake
The greatest snow on earth
The littlest snow angel
The long and snowy road
The moon on the breast of the new-fallen snow gave the lustre of mid-day to objects below...
-Clement Clark Moore
The perfect snow
The perfect blizzard
The smallest snowflake
The snow fairies
The snow is so delightful
The snow king / queen
The snow patrol
The snowiest winter ever
There's snow place like home
Think snow—think happy!
Walking in a winter wonderland

SNOWMEN

A perfect snowman
A snow family
Big-bottom snowmen
Dressed to chill
Frosty the Snowman
Frosty's winter wonderland
I believe in snowmen
I love snow / snowmen
Just add snow
Once upon a snowman

In the meadow we can build a snowman and have lots of fun
Just add snow
Just me and my snowman
No two alike
Our snowman is a very big flake
Season to be freezin'
Snowfolk welcome
Snowman-collector
Snowman soup
Snowmen are a little flakey
Snowmen live here
Snowmen make the coolest friends
Snowmen melt my / your heart
Snowmen smile big
Sub-zero temperatures
Tales of the runaway snowman
The biggest snowman ever
The day the snowman melted
The magic snowman
The snowman
The snowman and the sun
There's no men like snowmen
There's nobody, like a snow-buddy
Wanted—magic hat!
What a snowman wants

SOUTHERN SAYINGS

Ain't seen you in a 'coon's age (haven't seen you in a long time)
Ain't that the berries (that is great)
Bitty bit (a small amount)
Bless your pea pickin' heart (that's special)
Chugged full (full and over-flowing)
Busy as a stump-tailed cow in fly time (very busy)
Directly (in a little while or a couple of weeks)
Don't let your mouth overload your tail (talking too much)
Either fish or cut bait (work or get out of my way)
Fair to midlan (okay, so-so)
Fixing to (about to)
Go hog-wild (have a good time)
Good Lord willing and the creek don't rise (hopefully)
I onst went to (once upon a time)
In a coon's age (a long time)
Mend fences (settle differences)
Piddle (waste time)
Reckon (think or suppose so)
Scarce as hen's teeth (no such thing)
She's as ill as a sore-tailed cat (in a bad mood)
So kiss my grits (whatever, buzz off)
Sweet talking thing (a flirter)
Well, shut my mouth (shocked and speechless)
Y'all (you all—two or more people)

SPIRITUALITY

Amazing grace
Be thou humble
Blessed are the peacemakers
Count your blessings

Future missionary

God allows u-turns

His truth is marching on

I believe in miracles

I hope they call me on a mission

If you can't sleep, don't count sheep—talk to the shepherd

Let your mind dwell on these things

I know now, Lord, why you utter no answer. You are yourself the answer. Before your face questions die away. What other answer would suffice? –C.S. Lewis

Just a closer walk with Thee

Keep His promises in your heart

Let your light shine

Miracles happen

Oh holy night!

Our daily bread

Sometimes the Lord calms the storm; sometimes He lets the storm rage and calms His child

The greatest of these is love

The truth shall set you free

Today I am blessed, tomorrow I am blessed, for eternity I am blessed—because He lived and died for me

We may ignore, but we can nowhere evade the presence of God. The world is crowded with him. He walks everywhere incognito. –C.S. Lewis

When life gets too hard to stand —try kneeling

♣ Angels

Angel flyin' close to my heart

Angel sent from up above, please protect the ones I love

Angels have wings to carry your prayers to God

I believe in angels!

Little angels up above, bless our home with lots of love

Whatever you do, may angels of love always watch over you

Angels gather here

♣ Baptism

Oh, what a wonderful blessed day
God hears every prayer I pray
You are honoring the father and son
By being baptized, my little one!
–Thena Smith

What can I give Him? I will give Him my heart.

Baptism is faith in action

Christened with Christ

Let them come to the water

The living water quenches thirst

Train a child in the way he should go

Washed my sins away

♣ Childrens' Prayers

God make my life a little light,
Within the world to glow;
A tiny flame that burns so bright
Wherever I may go.
–MB Betham-Edwards

The Biggest Book of Words & Prompts for Scrapbooks, Art Journals & Crafts

Thank you God
For all you do,
May my heart
Be ever true!
Amen!

God make my life a little flower,
That giveth joy to all
Content to bloom in sun or shower
Whether big or small.
Amen!

Thou art, O God, the life and light
Of all this wondrous world we see;
Its glow by day, its smile by night,
Are but reflections caught of Thee
Thank you and Amen!

✤ Church Signs

A family altar will alter a family

A half-truth is a whole lie

A parent's life is a child's guidebook

ASAP—always say a prayer

Downn on your knees you will learn to stand

Faith book—the ultimate network

Get rich quick—count your blessings

Have you thanked God today?

How can I keep from singing?

Jesus knows me, this I love

Morning praise makes your day

Our church is prayer-conditioned

Practice random acts of love

Prayer—the wireless connection

The more you invest in marriage, the more valuable it becomes

When God saw you, it was love at first sight

Don't worry? Just pray!

✤ Faith

Birds know the worm will always be there, they do not question—they simply fly –Linda LaTourelle

Faith begins when we choose to let worry end

Faith in God is trusting that His timing perfect for you

Faith is the substance of things not seen—but hoped for

Choose faith—not worry

Faith must be your priority—not your option

Faith shines brightest in the dark, for to have faith, is to have wings, Peter Pan –J.M. Barrie

I don't know what tomorrow holds, but I know who holds tomorrow

Without faith it is impossible to please God

Faith in every footstep is my prayer

✤ Forgiveness

Everyone thinks forgiveness is a lovely idea until he has something to forgive –C.S. Lewis

Forgiven—forever!

Forgiveness is the fragrance that the violet sheds on the heel that crushed it –Mark Twain

The key to forgiveness is me

To be a Christian means to forgive the inexcusable because God has forgiven the inexcusable in you –C.S. Lewis

Forgive and forget, you'll never regret. It's love you will get.

♣ Godparents

Hands to guide with hearts that will love that is Godparents sent from above

Blessed to be a godparent

God created godmother's for an extra touch of love

Godmothers are a special blessing

Godparents—another word for love

Godparents know how to have fun

My angel here on earth

My fairy-godparent

Someone to watch over me

♣ God

A child of God

An everlasting love

Be still and know that He is God

Behold, I make all things new!

Breathe in God's spirit

Delight in the Lord

God can't give us peace and happiness apart from Himself because there is no such thing –C. S. Lewis

God holds your heart in the palm of His hand

God gave us each a song to sing

God has done great things

God is great, God is good

God is in the details

God never asks about our ability, only our availability hands to serve with our heart for God

How great Thou art!

I know who holds tomorrow

I love Thee, Lord Jesus

Jesus loves me

Jesus loves the little children

Kumbaya, my Lord

My Jesus, my Savior

No greater love

Our God is an awesome God

Praise His name

Sweetest name I know

Tell me the stories of Jesus

Thank you Lord

The Lord is my strength

The Lord's been good to me

The presence of the Lord is in this place

There is a sweet spirit...

The touch of the Master's hand

The way of the cross

Walking with Jesus daily

With God, all things are possible

You are God's masterpiece

Yours is the kingdom of God

♣ Prayer

A place of grace—seek His face

Did you take time to pray today?

Don't worry about tomorrow, God is already there

Jesus—
bless what thou hast given,
Feed our souls
with bread from heaven;
Guide and lead us all the way,
In all that we may do and say.
For this new morning with its light,
For rest and shelter of the night,
For health and food,
For love and friends,
For everything
Thy goodness sends,
We thank Thee,
Heavenly father.
–*George L. Conrad*

Hope and prayer is faith in action

Hope puts wings upon your prayers

Leave your worries at the door, you don't need them anymore

Life is fragile, pray faithfully

Life is short, pray hard

Pray and then believe

Praise God from whom all blessings flow

Pray together, stay together

Pray without ceasing

Prayer works

Too busy to pray is too busy

Two hands clasped in prayer can do more than a hundred working

✤ *Scripture*

All things are possible through Christ who strengthens me –*Phil. 4:13*

A merry heart maketh a cheerful countenance –*Proverbs 15:13*

As for me and my house, we will serve the Lord –*Joshua 24:15*

Behold, how good and pleasant it is when brothers dwell in unity! –*Psalm 133:1*

Be not anxious about anything, but in every situation, by prayer and petition, with thanksgiving, present your requests to God. And the peace of God, which transcends all understanding, will guard your hearts and your minds in Christ Jesus . –*Philippians 4:6–7*

Be ye kind one to another, tenderhearted, forgiving one another –*Ephesians 4:32*

Children, obey parents in everything, for this pleases the Lord –*Colossians 3:20*

Create in me a clean heart, o God; and renew a right spirit within me –*Psalm 51:10*

Do not fear, for I am with you; do not be dismayed, for I am your God. I will strengthen you and help you. –*Isaiah 41:10*

But they that wait upon the Lord shall renew their strength –*Is. 40:31*

For by grace are ye saved through faith; and that not of yourselves: it is the gift of God –*Ephesians 2:8*

God has not given me the spirit of fear, but of power and love and a sound mind –*2 Timothy 1:7*

He determines the number of stars and calls them each by name –*Psalm 147:4*

Her children arise up, and call her blessed; her husband also, and he praiseth her –*Proverbs 31:28*

Joy comes in the morning –*Psalm 30:5*

Hear, my son, your father's instruction and reject not your mother's teaching –*Proverbs 1:8*

He will wipe away every tear from their eyes –*Revelation 21:4*

I have a plan for you, declares the Lord, plans to prosper you and not to harm you, plans to give you hope and a future –*Jeremiah 29:11*

I thank my God on every remembrance of you –*Philippians 1:3*

Let all those that put their trust in Thee rejoice –*Psalm 5:1*

Oh, taste and see that the Lord is good; blessed is the one who trusts in Him –*Psalm 34:8*

That everyone may eat and drink, and find satisfaction in all his toil- this is the gift of God –*Ecclesiastes 3:13*

I can do all things through Christ who strengthens me –*Philippians 4:13*

In every thing give thanks –*1 Thessalonians 5:18*

The joy of the Lord is your strength –*Nehemiah 8:10*

The Lord your God is with you wherever you may go –*Joshua 1:9*

Trust in the Lord with all your heart and lean not on your own understanding; in all your ways acknowledge Him, and He will direct your paths –*Proverbs 3:5–6*

Unless the Lord builds the house, those who build it labor in vain –*Psalm 127:1*

We love Him because He first loved us –*1 John 4:9–10*

What does the Lord require of you? To act justly and to love mercy and to walk humbly with your God –*Micah 6:8*

Whatever you did for one of the least of these brothers of mine, you did for me –*Matthew 25:40*

You knit me together in my Mother's womb –*Psalm 139:13*

SPORTS

A sporting proposal

Above the belt please

Action shot

Alive and kicking

American hero

Armchair athlete!

Awarding the winners

Battle of the all-stars

Born to play

Can't be beat

Can't win 'em all

Dream team

Exceed your dreams

Fast and the furious

Future pro

Game of the year

Get your game on

Go for the gold!

Go, team, go

Hall of famers

He's / she's got game

Home team advantage

Instant replay!

It's all in the game

The Biggest Book of Words & Prompts for Scrapbooks, Art Journals & Crafts

It's how you play the game
Junior / senior varsity
Let the games begin
Most valuable player
Number one—we won
On your mark, get set, go
One little all-star
Player of the year
Practice makes perfect
Rookie of the year
Super star status
Taste of victory
The agony of de-feet
The comeback kid
The littlest rookie
The sports page
The sweet smell of victory
The taste of victory is sweet
The undisputed champion
The winning team
They came from behind
Tournament time
Undefeated champs!
Unrivaled talent
We are the champions
We got game
World class athletes
World's best player / team
X-treme sports fanatic
You're an all-star

♣ Archery

All about archery
Brave heart
Blessed is the man whose quiver is full *—Psalm 127:5*
Bowhunt America
Bullseye!
Eat your heart out, robin
I love bowhunting
Lighter than air
My quiver is full
Old archers never die,
Point blank
Quiver no more—I just scored
So close!
Straight shooting
Take a bow
They just bow and quiver

♣ Badminton

Battle for the birdie
Birds of a feather
Got birds?
I love badminton
Love to serve
Meet you at the net
We serve birdies
What a racquet!

♣ Baseball

A grand slam
Attention in the outfield
Baseball is my life
Boys of summer
Buy me some peanuts
Double-play
Field of dreams
Girls / Boys just wanna play ball

Going, going, gone!
He swings and misses
High-fly ball
Home run
I got the dugout blues
It's out of the park
Keep your eye on the ball
Little / big league
Little slugger
Lovin' little league
Major / Minor leaguer
May your bases always be full
Our little all-star
Pitching a hit
Step up to the plate
Take me out to the ballgame…
The life of a baseball mom / dad
The ol' ball game
The pitch is straight and fast
The rookie and the lady
The slugger
Three strikes you're out!
Triple play
Who loves the ump?
World Series, here we come!
You can win, or you can lose, or it can rain —*Casey Stengel*

♣ *Basketball*

A balanced act
All-star!
And he shoots!
Basketball is my life
Baskets of fun
Dishin' and swishin'
Dribble and shoot
Goin' for the hoop
Hanging tough
High hopes in high jump
Hoop dreams
Hoop it up
Jam session
Jammin'
Jumpstart
Kiss the rim
Nothin' but net
Open shot
Pass and score
Ridin' the rim
Shootin' hoops
Slam-dunker
Stop, drop and jump
Swish—it's in
Take it to the hoop
Benchwarmer today—professional all the way!
Wow! That was a slam-dunk!
Zero gravity

♣ *Body-Building*

Awesome abs
Body by choice
Body by trainer
Buff and beautiful
Burn baby burn
Check out the biceps
Cutting up
Eat, sleep, lift

Feel the burn
Got bench?
Gym addict
Hard body—hard work
I love bodybuilding
I love gettin' ripped
Just lift!
Look at them abs
Muscle beach babe
Muscle man / woman
One fit guy / girl
Perfect pecs
Press-on
Ripped and rugged
Squat and burn
Super-body
Tough as steel
Triathlon trainer

♣ Bowling

Born to bowl—forced to work
Bowlers love to score
Bowling with talent to spare
Got pins? Will bowl!
Grip it and rip it
Gutter gals / guys let's party tonight
Hitting the lanes
I live to bowl
I love bowling
Live • Love • Bowl
Sister strikers
Split happens!
Strike out
That's how I roll
These shoes were made for bowling
Walk softly and carry a big ball
Watch me roll
Within striking distance

♣ Boxing

A fighting chance
Champion of the ring
Fight with might
Heavyweight champ
In this corner…
Knockout! TKO!
On the ropes
Ooh! That had to hurt!
Out for the count
Ringside attraction
Takin' it on the chin
The golden gloves
The main attraction
Train don't complain

♣ Bungee-Jumping

Boiiiinnnngggg
Bouncing bouncing
Gravi-drop
Just hanging out
Leap of faith
Stretched to the max

♣ Canoeing • Kayaking

A canoe for you
Always paddle your own canoe
Around the river's bend

Crazy for canoeing
Down a lazy river
Go with the flow
I love canoeing
Kayaking the night away
Paddle-pusher
River of dreams
Smooth floatin'
Still waters run deep
The great outdoors
The long and winding river
The river is wide
Up a creek wishin' for a paddle!
A man of wisdom delights in water –*Confucius*
Everyone must believe in something. I believe I'll go canoeing. –*Henry David Thoreau*
Wherever there is a channel for water, there is a road for the canoe –*Henry David Thoreau*

♣ *Cheerleading*

2, 4, 6, 8—who do you appreciate?
Cheer my way through college?
Cheer them to a win!
Cheerleaders—a jump above
Competition bound
Eat • Sleep • Cheer
Go big red (your school colors)
Go, fight, win—let's go!
Go! Fight! Score!
Hey now, you're an all-star
Hooray for our team
How loud can you cheer
If you're here—we'll cheer
I'm just a cheery girl
Jump • Shout • Win
Loud and proud—rock the crowd
Pom poms and blue jeans
Push 'em back—way back!
Rah rah—siss boom bah
Stand up and cheer
The rah-rah sisters
We can't hear you
We got spirit
Yay, team!

♣ *Croquet*

Addicted to croquet
Croquet anyone?
Croquet chick / dude
Every day is a croquet day
Extreme croquet
Hoop-jumper
I love croquet
Just me and my mallet
Let's play—croquet!
Mallet mama / daddy
Sticky wicket
Wild wicket woman

♣ *Cycling*

American flyers
Biker babe / dude
Born to cycle
Breaking away

The Biggest Book of Words & Prompts for Scrapbooks, Art Journals & Crafts

Eat • Sleep • Cycle
I brake for cyclists
I love cycling
King of the road
Men on bikes
Pedal for the medal
Peddling my life away
Ride like the wind
Speed racer
Trails of a peddler
Train hard—ride harder
Climbing mountains is hard work
See: Transportation / Bicycles

♣ Disc Golf

Baby come back
Bird dog
Bogey band
Fly-by
Fore
Gettin' greasy
Hit the nickel
Nice shot!
Playing the woods
Shoot the moon

♣ Diving

Jewel of the pool
Taking the plunge
Unsinkable
Dive right in
Ready to jump
Hi diving show-off
Under the sea
I dive because I can
The ultimate board game
Rock the board

♣ Fencing

Crossed swords
Don't fence me in
Get the point?
Never give a sword to a man who can't dance *-Confucius*
On the fence
Sword play
Zorro in training

♣ Fishing

A fisherman lives here with the catch of his life—his wife
A river runs through it
At the river's bend
Best catch of the day
Born to fish, forced to work!
Catch of the day
Casting 101
Casting my life away
Daddy's / Mama's gone fishing
Deep sea tales
Early to bed, early to rise, fish all day makes one wise
Field and stream
Fish fry tonight
Fish more, work less
Fish stories told here—some true!
Fishermen are reel happy
Fishing is a tough job to tackle

323 | ultimatebookcompany.com

Fishing is easy, catching is hard
Fly-fishing is the life for me
Get hooked on fishing!
Gone fishin'—back whenever!
Got bait?
He's a keeper—my husband!
Look who caught the big one
Lure of the lake
Never caught a fish I didn't like
Reel men eat, sleep and fish
Rise and shine, it's fishing time!
She's a keeper—my wife!
Swim with the fishes
Take up a reel sport—fishing!
The old man and the sea
The one that got away
The reel story
To fish or not to fish?
Wading and reeling
Wishin' I was fishin'
You catch 'em, you clean 'em

♣ Football

Defense department
Backfield in motion
First and ten
Football fan-atic
Football Friday nights
Football fever
Football super star
Go for the whole nine yards
Guard the yard
Half-time
I get a kick out of playing
Kick off the new season
Let the games begin
My favorite season—football
On any given Sunday
On the bench
Play like a champion
Pride • Power • Victory
Ready to rumble
Rookie of the year
Superbowl, here we come
The longest yard
The tradition continues
Time to tackle another year
Touchdown!
Weekend quarterback
Where pride meets passion
You gotta be a football hero

♣ Golf

An iron a day keeps the doctor away
Anytime is tee-time
At home on the green
Bye-bye, birdie
Driving up to par
Drive it to the green
Fly like an eagle
Fore! Ever-addicted to golf
Give me life, liberty and 18 holes to walk
Golf is my game
Golf suits me to a tee

Golfers need a daily dose of iron
Grandpa / Grandma loves golf
Green is my favorite color
Hooked on golf
How's my driving?
I love birdies and eagles
I love to be my daddy's caddy
I love to go putt, putt, putt
I could swing all day!
I'd rather be golfing
I love tee time!
I'm not over the hill, just on the back nine
Lost in the sand trap again
Masters here I come!
On the green in ___ strokes
Par excellence
Strokes of genius
Tee party for four
The best time is tee-time
Tiger in training
To golf or not to golf—duh!
Was that an eagle or a turkey?
A game in which you claim
The privileges of age, and
Retain the playthings of
Childhood -Samuel Johnson
I've spent most of my life golfing; the rest I've just wasted

♣ *Gymnastics*

Beaming girl
Best foot forward
Falling with style
Fantastic gym-tastic!
Going for the gold
Gravity is not your friend
Gymnasts are better-balanced
Hanging on
I flip for gymnastics
It's all about the landing
Jump, tuck and tumble
Lord of the rings
No fear—no gravity
On a roll
On the beam
Perfect balance
Princess light on her feet
Ribbon dance
Rough and tumble
The king / queen of the rings
Tuck and roll

♣ *Hockey*

My goals
Eat, sleep, breathe hockey
Hat trick
Got stick?
Hide the puck
Hockey with heart
I live for hockey
Icing on the season
In the crease
My "goal" is to play hockey!
Power play
Refuse to lose
The puck drops here!

♣ Horse Racing

Around the turn
By a nose
By the rail
Derby day
Down the backstretch
Down to the wire
Giddy-up
Grand champion
Horse power
Jockeying to win
On track
Race to the finish
Riding high
Right on track
Run for the roses
The best horse doesn't always win the race -Irish proverb
The sport of kings
The winners' circle
Win—place—show

♣ Hunting

A-hunting we will go
Big game hunter
Big old bear
Big shot
Bow hunter champion
Call of the wild
Daddy's / Mama's gone hunting
Deer crossing
Give it your best shot
Going on a bear hunt
Gone hunting!
Gone to the woods
Gunning for trouble
Have gun, will hunt
Hunters will do anything for a buck
I love venison
Oh deer!
Open season
Ready • Aim • Fire!
Right on target
Road kill grill
Sharpshooter
Superior marksmanship
Talking turkey
The big hunt
The buck stops here
The happy hunter
The lone ranger
The mighty hunter
The rifleman
The thrill of the hunt
The woods—my home away from home
Under the hunter's moon
Watching for wildlife
Wild goose chase

♣ Ice Skating

At the rink
Blade runner
Born to skate
Cold feet • Warm heart

Double axel
Gliding light
Going for the gold
Got ice?
Have ice will skate
Ice princess / prince
I love ice skating
Olympic trainer
On one blade
On the edge
Perfect performance
Skater boy / girl
Skating on thin ice
Skating is my life
Skating star
Smooth as ice
Speed skater
The magic skates

♣ Martial Arts

Above the belt
Alive and kicking
Chop, chop, wop
Getting a kick out of karate
Give me your best shot
I am little grasshopper
I got my dojo working
It's a kick
Judy chop
Kick it!
Martial arts—blockbuster
My karate kid
Tae Kwan do it!

♣ Off Road

4x4 hear me roar
Bushwhackers Anonymous
Creek jumper
Down a dusty road
Fun forever four-wheeling
Gittin' down and dirty
Got mud?
I love ATV's
Just give me some dirt
Just me and the mud
Me and my wheels
Monster machine
Mud-slinger
Off-road adventures
Off the beaten path
Stuck in the mud again
Trail-runner

♣ Racing

A night at the races
And they're off!
At the track
Beat the clock
Big boys • Expensive toys
Born to race
Burn rubber!
Caution—yellow flag
Crossing the finish line
Drag-net
Dragster racer
Driving force

Fast, faster, fastest
Full throttle
Go speed racer!
I love the smell of oil
In the driver's seat
In the pit crew
Motor magic
My racer man
Put the pedal to the metal
Race to the finish line
Ready for the pro circuit
Record-breaker
Still playing with cars
Take it to the limit
The checkered flag
The little engine
The thrill of victory
The track—my other home
The victory lap
Winner's circle

♣ Racquetball

Are you game?
Born to play
Get a grip!
Havin' a ball!
King of the court
Lord of the strings
Racquetball MVP
Racquetball rules!
The sweet smell of victory
What a racquet!

♣ River Rafting

A river runs through us
All in a row
Big river keeps on runnin'
Drift a lazy river
I'd rather be rafting
Paddle faster
Paddle the river least taken
Paddling against the current
Racing the rapids
Ride the rapids
River deep, mountain high
Rock and row
Row with it
Soggy bottoms
Up a creek without a paddle
Wet behind the oars
Wet and wild ride
What an adventure!

♣ Rock Climbing

Ain't no mountain high enough
Between a rock and a hard place
Cliffhanger
Climb every mountain
Eat • Sleep • Climb
Friends in high places
Get to the point
Keep calm—climb on
Know the ropes
New kids on the rocks
On higher ground
On the top
Scaling new heights

Sheer pleasure
She'll be coming down the mountain
Upwardly mobile
View from the top

♣ Running

Born to run
From start to finish
Huffing and puffing
I came, I saw, I ran
In the running
Just one more lap
Lightning fast / quick
Look at him / her run
Makin' tracks
Minute man / woman
My first 5k
My first marathon
Perfect timing
Photo finish
Sneaker junkie
Sprint to the finish line
Take it to the limit
The marathon man / woman
The run to victory

♣ Scuba Diving

Air hog
Cave diver
Certifiably wet
Dive chick / guy
Dive deep, live shallow
Dive more, work less
Diver dude / dudette
Eat • Sleep • Dive
Eat my bubbles
Get tanked
I love my wetsuit
I'd rather be scuba diving
Like a shark
Live • Love • Scuba
Live to dive
Meet me at the bottom
Naturally buoyant
Scuba addict
Scuba diver do
Scuba diving is my life
Scuba toys for big boys
Swim with the dolphins
To dive or not to dive?
Under the sea
The sea, once it casts its spell, holds one in its net of wonder forever –*Jacque Cousteau*

♣ Skateboarding

Born to skateboard
Extreme skateboarding
Foot loose
Future skateboarder
Grip it and rip it
Head over heels
I defy gravity
I do all my own stunts
I live for skateboarding

Keep on rollin'!
Kick flip
King of the pack
Less work • More skate
Peace • Love • Skate
Rip up the pipes
Skateboarding is my life
That's how I roll
To skate or not to skate

♣ Sky Diving
Above all else
Fall guy
Falling for you
Free fallin'
High hopes
Just dropping in
Kiss the sky
Know skydiving • Know life
No strings attached
Nothing but blue skies
Sky dancer's delight
Skydiver's sing like a bird
Sky's the limit
Takes my breath away
Things are looking up
Up, up and away
What a view!

♣ Snowboarding
Babes on boards
Board certified
Board games
Board silly
Boarding school
Born to surf
Chairman of the board
Downhill racer
Eat • Sleep • Snowboard
It's a snowboard life
Knowledge is powder
Living on the edge
No snow—no show
Powder princess
Pray for powder
Slope tester
Smoothing the edges
Snowboarders rule
Snowboarding or work? Duh!
Snow surfer
Ticket to slide

♣ Snowmobiling
Away we go!
A ride on the wild side
Dashing through the snow
Frosty the nose-man
Watch it blow!
Popsicle toes
Winter wonderland

♣ Snow Skiing
Ain't no mountain high enough
Alpine adventurers
Bunny hill drop-outs

Dashing through the snow
Downhill racer
Epic run
Got snow?
High mountain drifter
Hittin' the slopes
I'm a mogul freak
Learning curves
No bumps—no lumps
Plowing ahead
Poles apart
Powder hound
Powder peeps
Ski bum
Ski-dazzle
Ski diva and her dude
Ski now—work later
Snow bunny
Steep and deep
The greatest snow on earth
Tip 'em and rip 'em

♣ Soccer

Alive and kicking
Backyard soccer
Best in the field
Goal • Goal • Goal
Goalie dude / dudette
Got soccer?
Head to head
I get a kick out of soccer
Keep your eye on the goal
Kick back—have a great time!
Live • Laugh • Play soccer
Move quick and carry a big stick!
Ready, set, goal!
Soccer is a kick!
Soccer is the universal language
Soccer mom and proud of it
Soccer—rain or shine
Soccer rules!
Use your head

♣ Surfing

Born to surf
Do the wave
Endless surf
Everybody's surfing now
Give me a break
Hang ten
Less work • More surf
Let's go surfin' now
My little surfer girl
One wave at a time
On the right wavelength
Ridin' the big one
Surf fast—rock hard
Surf Hawaii
Surfing the good life
Surfing USA
Surf's up
Surf the earth
Totally tube-ular
Wave on wave
Wipeout

♣ **Swimming**

A big splash
Aqua kid
Belly flopper
Dive right in
Diver dude / diva
In the swim of things
Junior lifeguard
Making the team
Marco Polo
On your mark, get set, go!
Snorkeling in style
Splashing the day away
Splish, splash, we're having a blast!
Swim lessons for mommy / daddy and me
Swim like a fish
The little mermaid
Wet and wild

♣ **Tennis**

A whole lotta love
Clear the net!
Love is me, love is you, love is winning a match or two!
Point-set-match
Tennis anyone?
Tennis bum
Tennis—it's all about love!
Tennis—it's not just a game
Tennis superstar
Tennis—what a racquet!
Tennis! You gotta 'luv' it!
Unrivaled competition

♣ **The Gym**

Arm strong
Body work
Gym dandy
Man / Woman and machine
Men / Women of iron
Need a lift?
Not another dumbbell
Path of least resistance
Pump you up
Get me to the gym on time

♣ **Track & Field**

A need for speed
And they're off!
Around and around…
Back on track
Eat my dust!
Finishers are winners
Get ready, get set, go!
Giant leap
Go the distance
Hammer it home
Have a field day
High hurdles
Javelin lover
Jump for joy
Life in the fast lane
On the right track

One-track mind
Overcoming hurdles
Road runner
Sprint to the finish

♣ Volleyball

Bump! Set! Spike!
It's a net thing
Net attack
Game, set and match!
It's over the net
Set up—slam
Volley girls / boys
What a dig!
What a volley!
Win the rally

♣ Walking

Baby steps
Following in his footsteps
From start to finish
I'm walkin' on sunshine
I'm still standin'
I walk the line
Just a closer walk with Thee
Just one more lap
Makin' tracks
One small step for woman / man
One step at a time
On the move
Run for the money
Step by tiny step
Sweetness in motion
To walk a mile in your shoes
Walk of life
Walkin' the walk

♣ Waterskiing

Float my boat
Going, going, gone
In the drink
Making waves
Rocking the boat
Rope tow
Wake up
Walking on water
Wet, wild and wonderful fun!
Wipe out

♣ Working Out

Ab-solutely fit
Aerobics—fast and furious
Aerobic torture
Body in training
Cardio-tastic
Exercise? What a stretch!
Firm and fit and fine
Fit and fabulous
Gettin' stronger
Gym-dandy
Hamstring you along
Heavily armed
Huff and puff
Man as machine
Muscle-bound
Need a lift?

No pain—not workin'
Skinny Minnie
Sweatin' to the music
What a bod!
Work it out
Zumba to the rumba

♣ *Wrestling*

1,2,3...he's out!
And in this corner...
Down for the count
Face mat
Face to face
Flex appeal
Miracle on the mat
No holds barred
Opposites attack
Ready to rumble
Seeking balance
Taking it to the mat
The winner, and still champion
Wrestle mania

♣ *Yoga*

A perfect Zen
Blessed are the flexible
Flex your body—relax your mind
Practice serenity—practice yoga
Stretched to the max
Slow and quiet
Yoga works if you work it
Your pose grows

SUCCESS

A life spent making mistakes is more honorable and useful than a life spent doing nothing –*George Bernard Shaw*

Dismiss whatever insults your soul –*Walt Whitman*

Do everything through Him who will strengthen you

Do or do not—there is no try
–*Linda LaTourelle*

Do what you can, with what you have, where you are
–*Theodore Roosevelt*

Do your best, that's all you can do

Every day plan your work and then work your plan

Fall seven times, stand up eight!
–*Japanese proverb*

Hard to read a new chapter when you're still stuck on the previous one

In the middle of every difficulty there is a new opportunity

Someone says you can't—but you know you can, so go for it!

Thinking is the door that opens to opportunities that create success

Love yourself first and everything else in life will begin to fall into place

Once you choose hope, anything is possible –*Christopher Reeve*

Once you make a decision, the universe conspires to make it happen –*Ralph Waldo Emerson*

You were born to succeed
–*Thoreau*

Never, never, never, never give up

Passion and persistence are the perfect combination for success

Set your goals and then kick them in the butt and get to work!

Success and rest don't sleep together –Russian proverb

Success comes certainly to those who think they can succeed

Success is going from failure to failure with no loss of enthusiasm –Winston Churchill

Surround yourself with people who lift you higher and you can fly

The biggest secret in life is that there is no secret to life. Just do your best. –Linda LaTourelle

Surround yourself with those who are going in the same direction

Success is not in pleasing others —just God and yourself

How can you climb the ladder of success if you're sitting on your butt?

The Lord will fight for you; if you will only be still –Exodus 14:14

The measure of real success is that which you cannot spend

You will do your greatest work, when you do what you love most

To succeed is not worrying about what anyone else is doing

When talent and passion work together, therein lies opportunity

When you come to a roadblock— make a u-turn or take a detour

You are the only person on earth who can use your abilities –Zig Ziglar

SUNDIAL MOTTO

Time is too slow
For those who wait,
Too swift
For those who fear,
Too long
For those who grieve,
Too short
For those who rejoice;
But for those who love,
Time is eternity.
–Henry Van Dyke

I count none but sunny hours,
be the day weary,
be the day long,
soon it shall ring to even song.

A clock the time
may wrongly tell,
I, never,
if the sun shines well.
–Old English

Let others tell of storms
and showers,
I'll only count your sunny hours.
–Unknown

TEA

A cup of tea and a book for me

Crumpets and tea and Thee

High tea

Let's have a tea party

Not my cup of tea

One lump or two?

Tea for two—it's good for you

Tea is a cup of life

Tea should be taken in solitude
Tea time is quiet time
Tea time tots
Teddy bear tea party
Trading tee time for tea time
You can never get a cup of tea large enough or a book long enough to suit me   –C. S. Lewis

TEENS

#1 teen idol
12 going on 30
A truck of his own
A work in progress
Adventures in babysitting
Are you talking to me?
After midnight—I'm in trouble
Bad hair day
Ballad of a teenage queen
Be kind, I have a teen
Blooming into a woman
Boy crazy / girl
Boys to men
But I need my own car
But mom, everyone is going
Can I borrow the car keys?
Class-action hero
Cool chic
Cooool
Cruising is my life
Curfews are for kids
Dare to be different
Dudes / dudettes

First date
Forever in blue jeans
From a teen to a queen
Gnarly dude
Going steady
Groovy kid
Hang loose
Hanging with the group
Hip to be square
Hot and hip
How I spent my summer vacation
I don't have an attitude
I need gas money
I'm licensed and legal
I'm not texting
Is this cool, or what?
It's a teen thing
Learning to drive
License 2 drive
LOL-laugh out loud
Mah peep-zzz
Material girl
Music is my life
My telephone is my life
No homework zone
No parents allowed
Rock star
So cool, just gotta wear shades
So many boys / girls, so little time
Sports star
Student body president
Sweet and sassy
Teenage crush
Teens just wanna have fun

Texting with 'tude
The birds and the bees
The dos and don'ts of dating
Too young to date
Total geek
Totally cool!
Tweet me please
Video game king
Warning: enter at your own risk!
Warning: loud music zone
What I like about you!
Whatever!
Where's the keys?
Which way to the mall?
Who needs an attitude adjustment?

THEATER

A chorus line
A class act
A star is born
All the world's a stage
An actor's life for me
Another opening, another show
Applause begets applause
Audition time
Baby, take a bow
Behind the scenes
Break a leg
Broadway, here we come!
Casting call
Center stage
Curtain call
Curtains up!
Dressing the part
Encore performance
Enter stage left / right
Follow my lead
Future star
Hooray for Hollywood
It's showtime!
Leading lady / man
Lights, camera, action!
Lullaby of Broadway
Now appearing
On with the show
One shining star
Playing the part
She's / He's the star of the show
Standing room only
The director's chair
The hottest show in town
The show must go on
The star of the show!

TIME

As time goes by
Cherish every moment
For old time's sake
For the good times
Half past late
I've had the time of my life
It was the best of times
Jolly good time
Once upon a time
Past, present and future
Running out of time

Somewhere in time
Tech time
The time of my life
Timeless treasures
Turn back the hands of time

♣ Morning

A new day is dawning
As morning breaks
Daydream believer
Good day sunshine
Here comes the sun
I don't do mornings
In the wee small hours of morning
Lazy days of summer
Mama said there'd be days like this
Oh, what a beautiful morning!
Sunday morning sunshine
Sunrise serenade
The early bird catches the worm
The early show
The glory of daybreak
The sun also rises
This is the day that the Lord has made…
Top o' the mornin' to ya!
Wake up sleepy head
What a day for a daydream

♣ Nighttime

A night on the town
A night to remember
Are you lonesome tonight?
Bedtime is story time
Boys / girls night out
Don't let me be lonely tonight!
Dream sweet dreams
Good night, moon
Goodnight sweetheart
Hard day's night
Honkey tonk tonight
I see the moon
Land of the midnight sun
Lullaby and goodnight
Moonlight serenade
Night night sleep tight
Oh, what a night!
Sleepless in Seattle
Snug as a bug in a rug
Some enchanted evening
Starlight, star bright
Strangers in the night
The cow jumped over the moon
The stars are brightly shining
Time for a nap!
Time for bed, sleepy head
To sleep, perchance to dream
Too pooped to party
We've got tonight
Working on the night shift
Zzzzzz are my favorite letters

♣ Quiet Time

A little place of quiet
A place of my own
Be still and know that I am God
Everyone needs their own spot

Meditation moments
My quiet place
Quiet moments together
Peace like a river
Place of mediation
Refreshing the soul
Rest in the Lord
Restoration for my soul
Search for self
Silence is golden
The sounds of silence
There's a kind of hush
Sitting quietly, doing nothing, spring comes and the grass grows by itself *–Zen proverb*
The happiest of all lives is a busy solitude *–Voltaire*
The good and the wise lead quiet lives *–Euripides*

TOWN

Big dreams in a small town
Boys / Girls are back in town
Hometown girls
Honky tonk town
Little town on the prairie
My little country town
My little town
My kind of town
New kid in town
Night on the town
One-horse town
Painting the town
Small town girl /boy
Downtown's the place to be
The lights of my hometown
Uptown girl / boy

TRANSPORTATION

♣ *Airplanes*

A flying voyage
Born to fly
Check-in and wait
Come fly with me
Fly me to the moon
Frequent flyer smiles
Get me to the plane on time
God is my co-pilot
High above the clouds
I believe I can fly
I'd rather be flying
Into the wild blue yonder
Jr. Pilot in training
Leaving on a jet plane
On a wing and a prayer
Passport to our dreams
Soaring to great heights
Spirit of adventure and fun
We're jet settin' now!
I haven't been everywhere, but it's on my list *–Susan Sontag*
My soul is in the sky *– Shakespeare*
A journey of a thousand miles begins with one airline ticket and a suitcase *–Linda LaTourelle*
Smiles high club
If I had to choose, I would rather have birds than airplanes *–Charles Lindbergh*

Planes, trains and let's boogie!
I've almost been to as many places as my luggage —Bob Hope

♣ Bicycle

Away he goes
Bye-bye trike—I love my bike
Cycling is a family affair
Hang on for the ride
Hittin' the trail
How fast can you go?
Kids on wheels
Look mom, no hands!
No more training wheels
Nothing compares to the simple pleasure of riding a bike
On the bike path again
Poppin' wheelies
Wheelies are such fun

♣ Boats • Cruising

A cabin with a view
Ahoy, matey
Anchors aweigh
Aye Aye, Captain
Beyond the sea
Bon voyage
By the sea, by the sea
Calm waters
Come sail away
Cruising along
Distant shores
Float your boat
Hit the deck
Honeymoon cruise
Island-hopping
Just another day in paradise
Love boat
Love cabin #4
Moonlight on the deck together
Sea cruise
Slow boat to China
Smooth sailing
Stormy weather

♣ Cars • Trucks

A boy and his truck
And the race is on!
Auto-gratification
Buckle-up and put the phone away
Catch me if you can
Caution—legal blonde driver
Classic cruiser
Classy chassis
Classy jalopy and cool chic
Crazy for trucks
Dad, I need gas money
Dirt road trekking
Faster than the speed of sound
Fender-loving career
First race—first place
Gas sucker—fast trucker
Give me a brake!
Goodbye trike, hello bike!
Got mud?
Hit the road
Honk and drive
Honk if you're _____

Hot rod Ford
How's my driving? Call 1-800-mom
Life in the fast lane
Loud car—middle age
Love my car
Make vroom for daddy
Mama's got a brand new ride
Man / Boy and machine
Motor man
My other car is chauffeur operated
My way or the highway
No parking zone
Off road a-traction
Off the show-room floor
Off-road rules
Rocky off-road
'Round and 'round we go!
Steering the course
Tailgate party tonight
Teen driver
The great American race
The ultimate off road vehicle
Torqued and truckin'
Truck power
Zero to sixty—smokin'

♣ Hot Air Balloons

Above the clouds
A flight to remember
Adventure of a lifetime
Amazing sites
Ballooning adventures
Ballooning is a blast
Bird's eye view
Carried away
Drink in the wind
Flying high
Flyin' low—movin' slow
Fly like an eagle
High and mighty
I can see clearly now
I love ballooning
Mile-high club
Ride the wind
Sweetheart flights
Up, up and away
Wind pilot
Wind rider

♣ Motorcycles

A Harley someday
Bad motor scooter
Big boys with big toys
Biker babe / dude
Biking buddies
Born to be wild
Born to ride
Built for speed
Chicks on bikes
Girls just wanna ride
Go speed racer
Good vibrations
Have wheels, will ride
Headin' down the highway
Hog wild
I'm a big kid now!
I'm in hog heaven
Iron horse

Just me and my mope
Keep on ridin'
Kickstart my heart
Leader of the pack
Leather and lace
Live to ride
Love at first bike
Love to ride
Lookin' for adventure
Midnight rider
Motorcycle man / mama
Open road
Outlaw women
Pit crew
Re-tired and ridin'
Ride a hog—forever free
Ride like the wind
Ride to live
Rockin' down the highway
The wild ride
Trikes to bikes
Two wheels—movin' my soul
Un-easy rider
Unknown legend
White lightnin'

♣ Trains

A private railroad car is not an acquired taste. One takes to it immediately. —*Eleanor Roosevelt*

All aboard
At the station
Boogie Woogie Choo Choo Train
Choo-choo caboose
Clickety-clack, makin' tracks
Don't sleep in the subway
Everybody loves a train
Grand Central Station
Hop on board
I love the dining car
Leavin' on the midnight train
Little red caboose
Love train
Makin' tracks
Meet me at the station
No one realizes how beautiful it is to travel until he rides a train
One loose caboose
On the right track
Riding on the Illinois Central
Riding the rails
Ridin' to the city of New Orleans...
Riding trains is my passion—the only way to be sure of catching a train is to miss the one before it
—*G. K. Chesterton*
Romance on the rails
The little engine that could
The littlest engineer
Tickets please!

TRAVEL & PLACES
♣ America

Alabama-bound
Amarillo by morning
America the Beautiful
American classic
At home in the heartland

The Biggest Book of Words & Prompts for Scrapbooks, Art Journals & Crafts

Austin city limits
Back to Boston
Black Hills of South Dakota
Blue Ridge Mountain memories
Boston Tea Party
By the time I get to phoenix
Carolina moon
Chattanooga Choo-Choo
Chi-town
Chicken fried love
City of New Orleans
Climbing the canyon
Coming to America
Country roads
Deep in the heart of Texas
Desert heat
Down home southern cooking
Down in the Ozark
Escape to the Cape
Eureka—I found it!
For the love of country
From the mountains to the prairies
Galveston, oh Galveston
Georgia on their / my mind
Get your kicks on Route 66
God bless America
God blessed Texas
Going to Graceland
Good morning America
Grand Old Opry
Great Lakes, good times
Hills of West Virginia
Home of the brave
I love the Poconos
In old Chicago
In old Mexico
Kansas City
Land of Lakes
Land of the Free
Leavin' Memphis
Little house on the prairie
Meet me in St. Louis
Midnight train to Georgia
Moonlight on Vermont
My kind of town—Chicago
My Old Kentucky Home
North to Alaska
O' beautiful, for spacious skies
Oklahoma!
On the Bayou
On top of Old Smokey
Only in America
On Music Row
Philadelphia story
Pray for America
Riding down the canyon
Rocky Mountain high
Run for the border
Sea to shining sea
Sidewalks of Chicago
Song of the South
South Dakota-bound
Southern comfort
Southern hospitality
Spa-time in Calistoga
Springtime in the Rockies
Sweet home Alabama
Tennessee mountain home

Texas Two-Step
The American dream
The great Niagara
The happiest girl in the whole USA
The Nashville scene
There's no place like home
The wild wild west
The windy city
Traveling around America
Way down south in Dixie
We're not in Kansas anymore
Weekend in New England
Welcome to Music City
Westward Ho
Winter in Chicago
Y'all come back soon
Yankee country
Yellow rose of Texas
Young Americans

♣ Africa

My African queen
A mission to accomplish
Out of Africa
Our African adventure
On a safari with you
Under African skies

♣ Australia

Australia—my favorite place
Down under
I left my heart in Adelaide
I love kangaroos
I love the outback
Sydney, I love you

♣ California

A day at the winery
Aged to perfection in Napa
All aboard the wine train
All the gold in California
California sunshine
Catalina is calling me
City of Angels
Coronado nights
Do you know the way to San Jose?
Hello, Hollywood!
I left my heart in San Francisco
LA story
Love in the Valley of the Moon
Napa—wine lover's paradise
Old San Diego
On the vine in Napa valley
San Francisco nights
Sittin' on the dock of the bay
Sunset on the Golden Gate
Sunset Strip
Tahoe or bust
The city by the bay
Treasure of the Sierra Madre
Ventura Highway
Wear some flowers in your hair
Wine country romance
Wine tasting in Napa
Yosemite—God's wonderland

♣ Canada

Alberta skyline
Beautiful British Columbia
Heart of Newfoundland
Hello Montreal
Home to the northland
I love Prince Edward Isle
Joys of Quebec
Land of maple
Manitoba morning
Meet me at Niagara Falls
My own Canadian home
North of the border
O Canada!
On Vancouver Island
Ontario—I love you!
Take me back to Nova Scotia
Team Canada
The fields of Saskatchewan
Twilight in the Yukon

♣ England

A foggy day in London
Across the River Thames
Autumn in London Town
Big Ben boogie
Changing of the guards
In London Town
Kensington gardens
Merry ol' England
My London
Night flight to London
On London Bridge
Piccadilly Circus
The River Thames
The Tower of Big Ben
Westminster Abbey

♣ Florida

Daytona nights
Key largo
Key west
Moon over Miami
On old Tampa Bay
Spring break in Panama City
Talladega speedin'
Tallahassee lassie
The garden state

♣ Holy Land

O' little town of Bethlehem
O Jerusalem!
Pilgrimage to the Holy Land
Rivers of Babylon
Shalom Israel
The crusaders
The Promised Land

♣ Hotels

Another motel memory
A room of our own
Beach house memories
Bed and breakfast—you make em' both
Check-in' the view
Cottage on the shore
Dew-drop inn

Do not disturb
Grand hotel
Heartbreak hotel
Home away from home
Home sweet hotel
Honeymoon haven
Honeymoon suite
I love room service
Inn for the holiday
Motel memories
Mountain retreat
Mr. / Ms. Elevator Man
Our romantic bungalow
Room with a view
Sittin' at the Ritz
Suite retreat
Swiss chalet
The inn crowd
The suite life

♣ *Ireland*

An Irish lullaby
My wild Irish rose
Summer in Dublin
The wearing of the green
When Irish eyes are smiling

♣ *Las Vegas*

Broke • Busted • Kaput
Deal me in
Eat • Drink • Win
Glitz and glamour
I hit the jackpot
Lady Luck
Leaving Las Vegas
Listen to the bells
Lost wages
Playing the game
Spin to win
The city that never sleeps
Viva Las Vegas

♣ *New York*

42nd Street
Live on Broadway
Apple of my heart
Autumn in New York
Big yellow taxi
Boy from New York City
Broadway baby
Brooklyn on my mind
Christmas in New York
Coney Island memories
Empire State of mind
First night in New York City
Fog on the Hudson
Give my regards to Broadway
Gotham City
I Love New York
Lullaby of Broadway
New York central
New York City nights
New York state of mind
New York, New York
Off Broadway
One night in New York
Only in New York
Rockefeller Center

The Biggest Book of Words & Prompts for Scrapbooks, Art Journals & Crafts

Statue of Liberty
Tales of Manhattan
The Big Apple

♣ Paris

A country girl in Paris
A walk through Paris streets
Adieu, Paris
An American in Paris
April in Paris
Bonjour, Paris
Evening in Paris
I love Paris
Last tango in Paris
Lights of Paris
Paris after midnight
Paris in the spring
Paris nights, New York mornings
Paris was made for lovers
Parisian love affair
Passport to Paris
Strolling the Champs-Elysees
The last time I saw Paris
The streets of Paris
The windows of Paris
Under Paris skies

♣ Scotland

A highland fling
Bonnie Scotland
Mist-covered mountains
Scottish fantasy
The pipes are calling

♣ Travel

Ahh! Relaxation
All bets are off
All roads lead to home
All roads lead to Rome
Are we there yet?
Around the river's bend
At the water's edge
Back roads and byways
Backyard vacations
Bon voyage
Break away from the ordinary
Come away with me
Cruisin' down a country road
Didn't we just go down this road?
Down in old Mexico
Down Mexico way
Dream vacation
Enjoying the sweet life
Escape to the cape
Exploring life together
Far and away
Foot-loose and fancy-free
From here to eternity
From the mountains to the prairies
Far from the ordinary
Globetrotting professionals
God's country
Gone to the mountains
Great adventure
Having a grand time
Here comes the sun
Hidden hideaways

Hit the road
Homeward bound
How we gonna get there?
In old Chicago
In search of…
Incredible journey
Indulge yourself
Leave the driving to us
Let the good times roll
Location, location, location
Lonesome highways
Looks like we made it
Lost again?
Lost our luggage?
Magnificent countryside
Maps and legends
Meals on wheels
Not all who wander are lost
Off the beaten path
Oh, the places we'll go!
Oh, the places we've gone!
On the road again
Our romantic getaway
Passport to adventure
Places to go and sites to see
Planes, trains and automobiles
Play more—work less
Professional tourist
Romantic vacation
Scenic detours
Seashells by the seashore
Seize the moment
Some enchanted journey
Southern hospitality
Southern traditions
South of the border
Summer vacation
Taking the scenic route
Tale of two cities
The great Niagara
The incredible journey
The land down under
The long and winding road
The open road is a'beckoning
The road less traveled
The stories we can tell
The trip of a lifetime
The world is a beautiful place!
Town and country travels
Travel more, work less
Traveling shoes
Traveling the world
Uncharted territory
Walking tour
Wave chaser
Way down south in Dixie
We love to see the world
We'll sing in the sunshine
Weekend getaway
Westward ho!
What a view!
What a wonderful world!
What I did on my summer vacation…
Where the road leads us
World traveler
Yankee country
Yellow rose of Texas

♣ Travel Inspiration

A man travels the world in search of what he needs and returns home to find it —George Moore

All that is gold does not glitter, not all those who wander are lost —Tolkien

He who does not travel does not know the value of men —Moorish proverb

I have found out that there ain't no surer way to find out whether you like people or hate them than to travel with them —Mark Twain

I haven't been everywhere, but it's on my list —Susan Sontag

Happiness is a way of travel

I may not be where I intended to go, but I am exactly where I am meant to be —Linda LaTourelle

I travel not to go anywhere, but to go. I travel for travel's sake. —Robert Louis Stevenson

It is not down in any map; true places never are —Herman Melville

Life's a voyage that's homeward bound —Herman Melville

The journey of a thousand miles must begin with a single step —Lao Tzu

The traveler sees what he sees, the tourist sees what he has come to see —G. K. Chesterton

There are no foreign lands. It is the traveler only who is foreign. —Robert Louis Stevenson

Two roads diverged in a wood and I took the one less traveled by —Robert Frost

When you are everywhere, you are nowhere. When you are somewhere, you are everywhere. —Rumi

♣ Tropical

Almost paradise
Aloha adventure
Another day in paradise
Bahama mama
Blue Hawaii
Blue lagoon
Caribbean cruising
Changes in latitudes
Come on I wanna lei you
Down by the bay
Here today—gone to Maui
Honeymoon in paradise
Island hopping
Island paradise
Jamaican me crazy
Paradise found
So this is paradise
South Pacific
Sweet aloha
Sweet paradise
Tropical honeymoon
Tropical persuasion
Tropical punch
Two tickets to paradise
Under the sea

TREES

The trees are nature's music
Her living harps are they,
On which the fingers of the wind
Majestic marches play
–*Unknown*

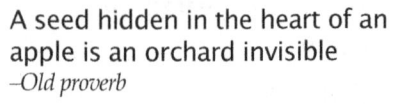

A seed hidden in the heart of an apple is an orchard invisible
–*Old proverb*

Happy is the man whose delight is in the law of the Lord, and on his law he meditates day and night. He is like a tree planted by streams of water, that yields its fruit in its season, and its leaf does not wither. – *Psalm 1:1–3*

May my life be like a great hospitable tree, and may weary wanderers find in me a rest
–*John Henry Lowett*

Even if I knew that tomorrow the world would go to pieces, would still plant my apple tree – *Martin Luther*

The creation of a thousand forests is in one acorn –*Emerson*

Keep a green tree in your heart and perhaps a singing bird will come –*Chinese proverb*

Trees give peace to the souls of men –*Nora Waln*

He that planteth a tree is a servant of God, he provideth a kindness for many generations, and faces that he hath not seen shall bless Him –*Henry Van Dyke*

The wonder is that we can see these trees and not wonder more –*Emerson*

TROUBLE & MESSES

A little dirt never hurt
Always into something
Bless this mess
Caught in the act!
Crime doesn't pay
Crimes and misdemeanors
Diggin' the dirt
Don't sweat the small stuff
Down and dirty
Fun in the mud
Happiness is dirt
Here comes trouble!
High grime and messy demeanor
In the dog house
Little mud puppy
Love me, love my messes
Mommy's little mess maker
Mud Pies 101
Muddy buddies
Partners in grime
Playing dirty
Puddle jumper
The good, the bad and the ugly
The maid's day off
Topsy-turvy
What dirt, mommy / daddy?
Who dude-it?
Who's sorry now?
Wild thing, you make a big mess

TWINS & TRIPLETS

A double blessing
And then there were two / three
Army of two
Baby, baby—can you hear our heart-beats?
Double exposure
Double / triple the fun
Doubly delightful
Father of twins—twice the man
Got twins? Got triplets?
Just the two / three of us
It takes two / three
It's so much better with two
Me and my womb-mate
Mommy's miracles
My two / three loves
My three sons / daughters
One little, two little, three ...
Our family grew by four / six feet
Peek-a-boo, two for you
Perfect trio
Power of two / three
Seeing double / triple
Terrific triplets
Then came two
There's womb for two
The three musketeers
They came two by two
Three of a kind
Three's company
Triple treasure
Twice as much love
Twice as nice
Twice / thrice blessed
Twinkle, twinkle tiny twins
Twins / triplets are so much fun
Twins / triplets in training
Two of a kind
Two peas in a pod
Two to tango
Uno, dos, tres
We three siblings
What a pair / trio

VOLUNTEERS

A lifetime of service
Do good and care not to whom
Do what you can, where you are, with what you have
Every Day heroes
Giving is the best way to receive
Helping others helps yourself
I shall pass through this world but once—let me do all I can to make it a better place
Love brings universal healing for the world
Love is action in motion
Love isn't love until you give it away
Make this world a better place by volunteering
Making a difference
No act of kindness is ever wasted

No greater love for a brother / sister than to give

Pay it forward, it will return ten fold

Random acts of kindness

Selfless devotion

The greatest gift we can ever give someone is our time

Together we accomplish much

Treat others like you would want to be treated

Volunteers are angels in disguise

You can't do everything but you can do something

WEATHER

A flood of blessings

Blame it on El Nino

Future meteorologist

Hail, hail, it's coming down

The weather outside is frightful

Lost without an umbrella

Rough weather ahead

There's a chill in the air tonight

Weathering heights

Winter thaw

♣ *Clouds*

A walk in the clouds

Cloudy day

Every cloud has a silver lining

Head in the clouds

Like floating on a cloud

Pushing the clouds away

Uncloudy days

♣ *Heat*

Hot fun in the sun

Hot, humid and hungry

It's a sizzling day

Summer sizzler

Turn up the heat

Walking on sunshine

We're having a heatwave

♣ *Rain*

THE RAIN SONG
Across the harp strings of the pane
I hear the belling rain
Plucking music from the glass;
Singing in the grass;
Chiming the flowers
With its showers
And the rain song
Singing to the blooms
With its booms
The oldest song in the world
—Edwin Curran

A rainy day is the perfect time for a walk in the woods *—Rachel Carson*

After the rain

And me without my umbrella

And the heavens opened up

April showers— pretty May flowers

Baby the rain must fall

Can you hear the rain?

Come rain or shine

Crying in the rain

Don't rain on my parade

Foggy misty mornings

Have a ducky day!

The Biggest Book of Words & Prompts for Scrapbooks, Art Journals & Crafts

Have you ever seen the rain?
Here comes the rain
I can see clearly now
I wish it would rain
In the misty morning
Is it raining at your house, like it's raining at mine?
It's a wonderful rainy day
It's raining again
It's raining cats and dogs
Kentucky rain
Let it pour!
Like a child in the rain
Nobody here but us ducks
Puddle jumpin'
Rain, rain go away, come again another day
Raindrops keep falling on my head
Raining cats and dogs
Rainy days are play days
Rainy night in Georgia
Rhythm of the rain upon my roof
Shower the people
Singing in the rain
Smoky mountain rain
Soaked to the bone
Splish splash
Summer rain
The rain song
Under the umbrella
Walking in the spring rain

✤ Rainbows
All the colors of the rainbow
Chasing rainbows
Everybody needs a rainbow
Have a rainbow day
I love the colors of the rainbow!
Make today a rainbow day
May your days be filled with rainbows
My end of the rainbow
Rainbow's end
Somewhere over the rainbow
Sunshine, lollipops and rainbows
The rainbow connection
The whole spectrum
Where the rainbow ends

✤ Snow
- See **SEASONS—WINTER** section

✤ Storms
I love a good storm
Lightnin' strikes
Morning thunder
Pushing the clouds away
Storm clouds on the horizon
Storms across the water
The perfect storm
Thunder and lightning—can be rather frightening
Weathering the storm
Without a cloud and a storm
Zig zag, what a loud crash
After winter comes the summer
After night comes the dawn
And after every storm, there comes clear, open skies

353 | ultimatebookcompany.com

–Samuel Rutherford

♣ *Wind*

A blustery day
Gone with the wind
Blowin' in the wind
Look at her blow!
High winds and hurricanes
One windy day
There she blows
The very no good horrible windy day
The windiest day ever
When the wind blew
Where the wild winds blow
Whippin' winds
Whoosh went the wind!

WISDOM

Be yourself—not an imitation of someone else
Believe in the impossible
Don't sweat the junk
Don't waste time on nonsense
Don't worry, keep laughing
Express yourself
Hands that serve are holier than hands that pray
If it doesn't feel right, don't do it
If you want it, ask for it
It's okay to color outside the line
Laugh until your cheeks hurt
Learning is a journey, not a destination
Lighten up on yourself

Make up your own rules
Nothing is a mistake, just an opportunity to learn
Organization is the key to success
Out of clutter, find simplicity. From discord, find harmony *–Einstein*
Share with your friends
Somewhere something incredible is waiting to be known *–Carl Sagan*
The best way to find yourself is to lose yourself by serving others
The gem cannot be polished without friction, nor man without trials *–Confucius*
The greatest strength is kindness
The height of your accomplishments will equal the depth of your convictions *–William Scolavino*
To thine own self be true *–Shakespeare*
To be yourself in a world that is constantly trying to make you something else is the greatest accomplishment *–Emerson*
Whatever you are, be a good one

WOMEN

And God created woman
Behind every successful woman is herself
Blooming into a woman
Damsel in distress
Earth's noblest thing—a woman
Exclusively feminine
Girl meets boy
I am a woman in love
Ladies first

The Biggest Book of Words & Prompts for Scrapbooks, Art Journals & Crafts

Lady Godiva
Lady in waiting
Little women
Lovely lady
Mad about the girl
Mama loves mambo
Mama—that's my lady!
Mirror, mirror on the wall, I've become my mother after all!
Modern woman
My gal
My lady in red
My wife, my life
My woman, my woman, my wife
On the 6th day, God created woman...
Pretty woman
Red roses for a blue lady
Romeo and his lady
Sexy lady
She loves you
She's a lady
The woman of my dreams
This girl's in love with you
To know her is to love her
Too sexy for her shoes
Wanted: good woman
What women want...
When a woman loves a man
Who's that lady?
Woman of the year
Women don't work as long and hard as men, they do it right the first time
Women rule all the men

Women—we're just better
World's best girlfriend
World's best wife

WORK & JOBS

A lifetime of service
A woman's work is never done
Another Saturday night...
Blue collar man / woman
Bringing home the bacon
Dream job / team
Dressed for the job
High cost of low livin'
If you want a job done right, ask a woman / man
I got the payday blues
I just work here
It takes someone special to drive a school bus
It's a jungle out there
It's five o'clock somewhere
It's my job
Jack of all trades
Labor today—labor tomorrow
Laid off and gettin' lazy
Love your job—love life
Movin' on up
Moving up the ladder of success
Mr. / Mrs. Businessman / Woman
Night shift / crew
Open for business
Poundin' the pavement

355 | ultimatebookcompany.com

Professionally unemployed
Professional student
Quittin' time
She's / He's just a working girl / guy
Take this job and shove it
Takin' care of business
The apprentice
Whistle while you work!
Workin' at the car wash blues
Workin' class hero
Workin' on the railroad
Working for a livin' / weekend

♣ *Accountants*
Accountant number one
Balanced to the penny
By the numbers
Count on the accountant
I love figures
In the money
Losing my balance
Money business
Number crunching time
See red or black
Taxed beyond measure

♣ *Authors*
Have thesaurus, will write
Editor in training
I write the words
Journaling life's stories
The pen that writes your life story must be held in your own hand *–Irene C. Kassorla*

Type time is my time
Write from the heart
Write the book
Written on my heart

♣ *Auto Mechanics*
Bust my knuckles repair shop
Cars, cars and more cars!
Garage guru
Got tools?
Groovin' in the grease
Junkyard wars
Love the uniform
Motor manager
My body man / woman
My garage, my rules
Nuts and bolts
Out of gas
So many engines, so little time
The car / truck guys
Tool pusher
Tools of the trade
Tuned up and turned on
Well-fueled mechanic lives here with his hot-rod honey
What happens in the garage stays in the garage
Wrench warfare

♣ *Chief Executive*
A head above
Executive decision
Follow the leader

Head honcho
I'm the consultant
Make a plan, work the plan
Minding your / our business
Mr. / Ms. Bossman
Suited for this
The big cheese
Top notch exec

♣ Computer • Technical

Ctrl-alt-delete
Keyboard commander
Technically speaking
Working bit by bit
One byte at time
Information highway
Geeks write the code
Crashed again!
Needs more memory
Geeks save
Googly girls / guys
Socially challenged / connected
May the code be with you
Nerd is the word for the day
Hardwired and hardware
Tweet success
Search and ye shall find
Wi-fi wizard

♣ Construction

Build it one piece at a time
Built to last

Contractors measure up
Duct tape—my best friend
Electrifying results
Hard hat days
He / She fixed me up
If I were a carpenter
Know the drill
Men / Women at work
Mister painter
Mr. / Ms. Fixer-upper
My cool tool dude / chick
Plumb smart
Trust me—I can fix anything
Up on the roof
We built this city
Wired to the max
Workin' for a livin'
Working man / woman blues
You color my world

♣ Cooks & Chefs

Baked with love
icancook.bizz
iFat.com
Kiss the cook
Kitchen helper
Cookie man can
Big iron skillet
Pot watcher

♣ Dentists

The tooth brush man / woman
Floss man / woman works here
I get paid one bite at a time

Mr. / Ms. Braceman
I make smiles
Tooth teller
Totally toothful
Yackety yak, don't bite back

♣ Doctors

Doctor's orders
Dr. Fix you right up
Healer at work
Mr. / Ms. Mend's a lot
Boo-boo fixer
Dr. Feel-good
Calling Dr. Love

♣ Farmers

Bringin' in the sheaths

Chasing the sheep

Chores and more

From sun-up to sun-down a farmers work is never done

Herdin' them cows

Home, home on the farm

Been to two rodeos and a calf-ropin'

Make hay while the sun shines

Mendin' fences

Mr. / Ms. Blue Jeans

Plantin' and pickin'

What happens in the barn-stays, in the barn

Yes, I was born in a barn

♣ Firefighters
All in a day's work
Baby, light my fire

Big red fire truck
Burning love
Cool it down!
Fire workers are hot stuff
Flames of desire
Four alarm kid
Fun at the firehouse
Great balls of fire
I volunteer for you
Some like it hot
The big engine that did
Today's heroes

♣ Gardeners

We dig dirt
Plants are us
Come to my garden party
Hoe down tonight
Garden girls / guys
Gardner's keep it green
Compost happens
I'd rather be gardening
I like to play in dirt
Seeders and reapers
The Plant Lady / Man
There is a season
Peace • Love • Dig
I love green
Totally organic
Well-seasoned
We sow love to reap

♣ Hairstylist
A cut above the rest
A job to dye for

358 | ultimatebookcompany.com

The Biggest Book of Words & Prompts for Scrapbooks, Art Journals & Crafts

Beauty expert
Beauty is my business
Color him / her beautiful
Combing through life
Hairstylist are a shear delight
I'm a beautician—not a magician
Mr. Bodacious and his beauty
Shampooin' my days away
Snippin' and clippin'
Stylists permanently wrap & roll
The barber and the beautician
This comb is not a magic wand
Wrapper at heart—perms that is!

❖ Housekeeping

A woman's work is never done
Born to mop
Domestic Goddess
Mr. Honey do-man
Organized grime fighters
Sponge maid, dirty apron
We do messes
We get down and dirty
We kill dust bunnies
Windows are us

❖ Lawyers

Behind every good lawyer is a paralegal doing the work
Circumstantial excellence
I fought the bar and won
Jailhouse rocker
Just the facts mam
Law and order

Legal eagle
Mr. / Ms. Razzle Dazzle
Mr. / Ms. Litigator
Passing the bar
Trust me, I'm a lawyer

❖ Medical

Nurses care
LPN—loving, patient, nurturing
Masters degree in caring
Nurses are IV Leaguers
Nurses call the shots
Nurses give intensive care
Nursing is a work of heart
Fear the nurse
Nurses are 98.6
Got medicine?
Proud to be a nurse
Pediatric nurses give baby love
Physical therapists work it out
ENT—excellent nursing trainer
RN—ready now
World's best CNA
Nursing—the doc stops here

❖ Military

A force to be reckoned with
A sailor went to sea, sea, sea
A wing and a prayer
American pride
America's heroes
An officer and a gentleman
Anchors away
Army times

At sea and on shore
Bound by honor
Brave little soldier
Bring our troops home
Coast guard, we are for you!
D-day memories
Defender of freedom
Fighting Seabee
For the love of country
G. I. _____ (name)
Great American hero
Guardians of freedom
Heroes of the sea
History makers
Home safely
Honor, courage & commitment
Hooray for heroes
I am my brother's keeper
In honor of those who serve
In the company of soldiers
Jump-master makes the grade
Keep America proud
Keep him / her safe
Kiss the boys goodbye
Letters from home
Magnificent marines
Make peace, not war
Man / woman behind the uniform
Military brat
Military moments
My daddy's a ruff-tuff marine
My hero
Navy brat

Once a marine, always a marine
Peace and liberty for all
Please God, bring us peace
Real life heroes
Risking their safety for ours
Seals—intense training!
Seek and destroy
Serving his country
Soldier boy
Soldiers for freedom
Stars and stripes forever
Take to the skies
The few, the proud, the Marines
The life of a military wife
The real American Idols
The road to victory
To serve God and my country
Veterans are valuable
We salute you—our military!
We're in the army now!

♣ Office Workers

Cubicle, sweet cubicle
Desk jockey
Do not disturb—I'm on break
Don't ask me—I just work here
Excellence is doing ordinary things extraordinarily well
Good morning—let the stress begin
I love deadlines!
I thought I wanted a career—but I was wrong, I just needed a paycheck
Instant human—comes to life after morning coffee

Just the fax please
My job is secure—no one wants it!
Let's get personal and I'll assit
Pushing the envelope
Real secretaries take notes the shortcut way
Sweet reception
The workin' girl
To serve God and my country
World's greatest secretary

♣ Pilots
Comin' down the runway
Fly the friendly skies
Flyin' high
Jet-settin'
Leavin' on a jet plane
Mile high management
On cloud nine
Pilots soar

♣ Police Officer
Angels in blue
Law and order
Serving the community
The rookies
The mod squad
Badge of courage
Real men / women wear blue
The dedicated few
Star man / woman
Pedal to the medal
Men / Women in blue
Mr. / Ms. Lawman
An arresting smile

Committed to community
Walking the beat
Will work for donuts
May the force be with you
Blessed are the peacemakers

♣ Postal Workers
Bagged. bundled and delivered
We deliver the goods
I deliver!
Eat • Sleep • Mail
It's a mail world
Got stamps?
Weather warrior
Mr. Postman bring me a letter
They / We deliver
Postal workers got it in the bag

♣ Religious Workers
Amazing grace
Celebration of our faith
Friends in high places
Great is thy faithfulness
He's a soul man
How great thou art
I come to the garden to pray
I love you Lord
Mr. Preacher man
Old habits are hard to break
Onward Christian soldiers
Promised land guide
Son of a preacher man
The altar boy
Servants of the Lord
Serving the savior

Soul saver
Souled out to Jesus
Sweet hour of prayer
We will glorify

♣ *Salesperson*
Sold out for sales
Just a travelin' man
Salesman blues
Mr. Wheeler-dealer
Salesman of the year
Selling ice cubes to the eskimoes
Top dog in sales
I love sales!

♣ *Teachers*
- See **SCHOOL** section

YARD SALES
A new deal at dawn
Bargain-hunting babes
Born to yard sale!
Buy of a lifetime
Dressed for hunting
Dumpster diving diva / dude
Fantastic finds
Flea Market Fanatic
Garage sale guru
Hoarder in training
Hunting for treasure—one yard sale at a time
I love dumpster diving
I love rummage sales
I love yard-sales
Junkyard addicts
Junk warriors
Look what I found!
Keep Calm—Hit the sales
One man's junk is another man's treasure
Our crap could be yours for the right price
Pack rat to the max
Shabby chic couture
Sold to the highest bidder
So many yard sales—so little money
Stuff you may need this way
The bigger the sale, the better the bargains
Turning trash to treasure—that's my pleasure
Up at dawn to do a deal
What a deal!
Yard sale diva / dude
Yard sale queen / king

ZOO • CIRCUS • FAIRS
♣ *The Zoo*
A day at the zoo
A real swinger
A wild and crazy place
All creatures great and small
Born to be wild
Clown college

Don't monkey around!
Feed the animals
Got peanuts?
Giraffic park
Hug a giraffe
I love the rainforest cafe
I love the zookeeper
It's a jungle out there
It's a zoo around here
Just monkey'n around
Living the zoo life
Monkey business
On a safari
Our little monkey
Our private zoo
Out of Africa
Something wild
Swinging from the trees
The big adventure
The mighty jungle
This place is zooriffic
Tiger cubs on the prowl
Trip to the zoo
Walk like the animals
Wild things I love…
Where the wild things are
Wildlife safari in _____
Yes, they are alive!
You're my "mane" man!
Zebras rock
Zoo bi do bi do—we love you!
Zoo pitti do dah
Zoo-pendous fun!

✣ The Circus

All aboard the circus train
All roads lead to the circus
Carousel fanatics
Candy apples and sugar kisses
Circus girl
Clownin' around at the circus
Corn dogs and cotton candy
Echoes from the big top
Everybody loves a clown
Get your red hots here
I love elephants
Just clownin' around
Lions and tigers and bears, oh my!
March of the clowns
My fair lady
My mane man
Peanuts for sale
Send in the clowns
Tears of a clown
The big top
The circus came to town!
The dancing horses
The elephant walk
The flying trapeze
The greatest show on earth
The ringmaster
The water boy
Three-ring circus
Tiger in training
Walkin' the tightrope
Walk like an elephant
When the circus comes to town

♣ The Fair

A fair to remember
At the fair
At the world's fair
Best of show
Big fun at the fair
Blue ribbon goes to...
Carnival of dreams
Catchin' the country spirit at our county fair
Celebrate country living
Come out and play
Demolition Derby
Fair enough
Fair-endipity
Free admission
Goin' to the fair
Going to the tractor pull
Home spun fun
I love country fairs
It's all happening at the fair
It's fair time
Let's rodeo
Meet me at the fair
Old-fashioned country fair
Palisades Park
Pig races
Prize pickle princess
Queen of the fair
Riding the carnival
Riding the rodeo
Roaming at the renaissance fair
Sew it, grow it, show it
State fair competition

The best in show
The best time of the year
The county fair
Two goat ropin's and a county fair

♣ Your Favorites

The Biggest Book of Words & Prompts for Scrapbooks, Art Journals & Crafts

Notes & Quotes

People to Interview

Create a list of people to interview
And then coordinate a time talk with them

INDEX

A

accomplish, *34, 49, 77-78, 90, 92, 219, 344, 352*
accountants, *356*
adoption, *10, 72, 92-93, 97, 278*
africa, *344, 363*
aging, *94*
albums, *4, 9, 38, 96*
alphabet, *17, 100, 114, 164, 279*
america, *120, 203, 230-231, 235, 238, 319, 342-344, 359-360*
amusement, *75, 99*
angels, *56, 115, 123, 216, 268, 311, 314, 344, 352, 361*
animals, *78, 100, 128, 147, 200-201, 277-278, 282-283, 363*
anniversary, *50, 83, 98, 101-102*
apology, *104*
apples, *104-105, 210, 301, 363*
archery, *319*
art, *4, 10, 12, 33, 38-39, 49, 78, 105-107, 118, 122, 156, 164-165, 167, 169, 172, 192, 194-195, 205, 212, 216-217, 250, 254, 266, 275-277, 286, 315-316, 361*
artists, *105, 166*
attitude, *24, 74, 107, 126, 235, 241, 287, 336-337*
aunt, *180-181*
australia, *344*
authors, *32, 356*
autumn, *74, 160, 252, 264, 287-288, 300-302, 305, 345-346*

B

baby, *11, 26, 34, 38, 57, 59, 70-72, 76, 92-94, 97, 107-120, 123-125, 129-131, 135-137, 139, 144, 46-147, 149, 160, 172, 175-177, 182-183, 190-191, 193, 205, 207, 210, 218, 222, 226-227, 242, 253-254, 256, 260, 264-265, 267, 272-273, 275, 277, 279, 281-282, 284-286, 289-290, 292, 301-303, 305, 307, 311-312, 320, 323, 333, 337, 346, 351-352, 358-359*
baby poems, *114*
badminton, *319*

baking, *206, 292*
ballet, *117-118*
balloons, *126, 129, 341*
band, *75, 118, 160, 180, 261, 270, 273, 323*
baptism, *314*
barbeque, *207*
baseball, *319-320*
basketball, *144, 320*
bath, *109-110, 112, 123, 144, 209*
bears, *112, 118-119, 147, 150, 218, 224, 281-282, 363*
beautiful, *19, 21, 23, 32, 35, 39, 44-45, 51, 54, 64, 68, 88, 102, 105, 108-109, 115, 117, 119-121, 123, 127-128, 135-136, 139, 148-149, 159, 175, 183, 189, 191-192, 199, 210, 212, 214-215, 218, 220, 222, 224, 230, 233, 237, 244, 246-247, 249, 256, 263-264, 266, 268, 271, 282, 284, 302, 305, 311-312, 320, 338, 342-343, 345, 348, 359*
beauty, *59, 100, 113, 117, 119-121, 133, 136, 140, 160, 175, 203-205, 207, 212, 214, 216, 220, 231, 243, 251, 263, 276, 290, 300, 302, 306, 359*
bedroom, *74, 76, 84, 288*
bedtime, *51, 73, 75, 79, 112, 155, 247, 272, 338*
bees, *59, 104, 141, 149, 215, 233, 261, 277, 305, 307, 337*
belated, *128-129*
best friends, *118, 181, 194, 196, 213, 279, 282*
bicycle, *73, 340*
bingo, *95, 213, 223*
birds, *59, 121-122, 195, 209, 214-216, 305-307, 315, 319, 337, 339*
birth, *11, 36, 57, 70-73, 79, 84, 123-124, 160, 193, 195, 204, 252, 284*
birthday, *39, 50, 57, 73, 76, 98, 100, 111, 125-135, 217, 227, 231*
blanket, *71, 110, 114, 124, 150, 168-169, 189, 194, 202, 251-252, 302, 311*
blessing, *5, 26, 31, 33, 37, 44, 54-55, 57-59, 65-66, 69, 87, 92, 98, 116-117, 124, 127, 145-146, 149, 180, 182, 190, 192, 194, 200, 219, 236, 245, 249, 300, 311, 316, 351*
blue, *25-26, 106, 122, 129, 136, 144-145, 153, 160-161, 173, 175, 183, 193, 202-203, 205-206, 231, 233, 262, 272, 277, 285, 290, 305-306, 322, 330, 336, 339, 343, 349, 355, 358, 361, 364*
boats, *135, 340*
body, *46-47, 95, 135, 141, 187, 205, 253, 276, 286, 320-321, 332-334, 336, 356*
book, *141-143*
bowling, *76, 321*

boxing, *321*
boy, *95, 102, 108, 119, 131, 139, 142-150, 157, 159-160, 165, 173-174, 184, 187, 202-203, 227, 230, 244, 247, 252, 257-260, 269-270, 277-279, 281-284, 286, 291-292, 308, 327, 336, 339-341, 346, 355, 360-361, 363*
boyfriends, *148*
boys, *77, 143-147, 150, 172, 176, 184, 187, 208, 218, 223, 227, 231, 241, 290, 292, 309-310, 312, 319, 327, 329, 333, 336, 338-339, 341, 360*
bride, *11, 57, 189, 259-263*
brother, *98-99, 112, 181-182, 195, 197-198, 245, 352, 360*
brown, *26, 120, 135, 161, 215, 217, 301-302*
brownies, *142*
bugs, *108, 144, 149-150, 157, 216*
bungee, *321*
butterfly, *149, 215-216*

C

california, *344*
camping, *74, 147, 150, 307*
canada, *345*
candy, *99, 155-156, 158, 161, 207-208, 231, 236-237, 246, 252, 71-272, 285, 363*
canoeing, *321-322*
cars, *85, 200, 238, 270, 328, 340, 356*
castles, *151, 290-291, 307*
cat, *97, 151-152, 174, 188, 231, 277, 279, 313*
cats, *151-152, 175, 278, 353*
celestial, *152-153*
cheerleading, *322*
chefs, *357*
chess, *214*
chickens, *167, 201-202*
chief executive, *357*
child, *10, 12, 33-34, 39, 44, 63, 69, 71-80, 85-86, 92-93, 97-98, 100, 106-109, 112, 114-117, 123, 131, 136-137, 154-159, 171, 173-174, 180, 185, 188-195, 216, 227, 260, 267-268, 275, 283-286, 289, 298-300, 303, 314-316, 353*
childhood, *17, 36-37, 72-80, 96, 126, 155, 159, 181-182, 192-194, 196, 198-199, 206, 213, 325*
children, *11, 32, 40, 59-60, 69-70, 85-87, 93, 98, 108, 116, 124, 141, 154-155, 158-159, 180, 185-186, 189-195, 226, 228, 246, 268, 276, 278, 298-299, 306, 316-317*

christmas, *10, 39, 50, 54, 73-74, 76, 78, 80, 83, 85, 97-98, 110, 162, 226-228, 234, 346*
church signs, *315*
cinco de mayo, *229*
circus, *75, 345, 362-363*
clouds, *122, 146, 179, 216, 277, 339, 341, 352-353*
coffee, *5, 39, 207, 209-210, 241, 250, 255, 267, 287-288, 361*
cold, *189, 228, 242, 280, 302-303,311, 326*
college, *37, 73, 80, 84, 220, 293-294, 322, 363*
color, *19-21, 29, 34-35, 50, 59, 71, 74, 100, 103, 105-107, 120, 122, 152, 159-162, 167, 184, 191, 199, 209, 252, 277, 282, 295, 301-302, 306, 309, 325, 354, 357, 359*
computer, *2, 8, 12, 16, 18, 39, 47, 49-50, 65, 69, 145, 162-163, 298, 357*
construction, *239, 285, 287, 357*
cooking, *83, 150, 206-207, 240-241, 310, 343*
cooks, *357*
couples, *163*
cousin, *182*
cowboys, *164-165*
cowgirls, *164-165, 176*
cows, *200-201, 278, 358*
crafting, *105, 165-166, 208*
crawling, *110-111*
creative sparks, *32*
croquet, *322*
cross stitch, *166*
cruise, *263, 291, 340*
cry, *78, 84-85, 108, 125, 146, 172, 241-242, 267, 274, 285*
crying, *25, 172, 224, 352*
cub scout, *143-144*
cuddle, *26, 108*
cupid, *75, 236*
cycling, *322-323, 340*

D

daddy, *97, 106, 108, 112, 123, 127, 136-138, 140, 145-147, 153, 155-158, 168, 172, 182, 184-185, 193, 207, 217, 230, 240, 242, 260, 263, 270, 279-280, 284-286, 303, 322-323, 325-326, 332, 341, 350, 360*
daisies, *142, 305, 307*
dance, *17, 19, 29, 76, 90, 103, 117-118, 127, 134, 172-173, 189, 201-202, 204, 217, 223, 244, 251, 253-256, 258, 261, 263, 290, 311, 323, 325*

dancing, *47, 78, 82, 113, 117, 149, 172-173, 223, 247, 264-265, 290, 295, 363*
dating, *11, 55, 73, 256-257, 337*
daughter, *107, 132, 136, 157, 159, 163, 182-184, 189-190, 192, 202, 217, 230, 233*
days, *173-175*
dentists, *358*
diet, *209-210*
digital journaling, *12*
disc golf, *323*
diving, *323, 329-330, 362*
doctors, *358*
dogs & puppies, *174*
dolls, *279*
doodling, *4, 19, 31, 33, 90, 166*
dreams, *4, 10, 13, 44, 48, 87, 90, 92-94, 100, 104, 109, 111-112, 116, 118, 124-125, 131, 134, 144, 152, 156, 166, 175, 179, 181, 207-208, 211, 215-217, 220, 223, 237, 243, 259, 264, 270, 289, 293, 295, 301, 306, 308, 310, 318-320, 322, 338-339, 355*
dress up, *175*
driving, *96, 177, 241, 324-325, 328, 341, 348*
drooling, *114*
ducks, *177-178, 353*

E

earth, *96, 105, 152-153, 203-204, 206, 212, 216, 219, 228-229, 243, 266, 268, 275-276, 301-302, 306, 309, 312, 316, 331, 335, 354, 363*
easter, *74, 176, 229-230*
education, *11, 59, 76, 84, 178, 295-296, 298*
elementary, *80, 295-296*
encouragement, *59, 178*
engagement, *11, 80, 257-258*
england, *55, 301, 344-345*
evening, *35, 83, 86, 164, 206, 257-258, 278, 338, 347*
eyes, *5, 33, 45, 51, 54, 102-103, 109, 116, 120-121, 123-124, 128, 135-136, 145-146, 154, 159-161, 167, 185, 205, 235, 251-252, 256-259, 262, 264-266, 268, 272, 285, 298-300, 304, 318, 346*

F

face, *9, 27-28, 31, 38-39, 47, 49, 51, 93-94, 107, 109, 111, 114, 116-117, 120-121, 123-125, 136, 139, 145, 154-155, 163, 173, 188, 191, 197, 203-204, 214,* *223-224, 245, 257, 260, 263, 272, 275, 284-285, 300, 302, 306, 311, 314, 316, 334*
fairs, *165, 362, 364*
fairytales, *93, 108, 141-142, 164, 179, 188, 259, 279, 295*
faith, *11, 27, 91-93, 149, 155, 227, 235, 243, 246, 272, 289, 314-315, 317, 321, 361*
family, *9-12, 20, 31-33, 36-38, 44, 50, 64-72, 74-77, 80, 83-87, 92-93, 97-98, 103, 108, 116, 118, 123, 126, 147, 151, 155-156, 166, 168-170, 174, 179-180, 183, 185, 88-190, 194-195, 199, 213, 224, 226-228, 230, 232-233, 235-238, 240, 264, 269, 278, 285, 288-289, 312, 315, 340, 351*
family trees, *170, 183*
farm, *75, 100, 155, 200-203, 277, 301, 358*
farmers, *358*
farming, *200, 202*
fashionista, *175, 203*
father, *73, 76, 78-79, 91, 112, 114, 136, 145, 147, 157, 183-186, 190, 192-194, 221, 226, 230, 252, 260, 262, 271-272, 314, 317-318, 351*
father's day, *76, 230*
favorites, *4, 17, 32, 73*
feet, *91, 109, 113, 115, 117, 138, 152, 157, 172, 181, 196, 221, 237, 242-243, 275, 284, 295, 303, 319, 325-326, 351*
fencing, *323*
firefighters, *358*
firsts, *72, 98, 110*
fishing, *146-147, 323-324*
florida, *345*
flowers, *19, 57, 81, 95, 105, 137, 155, 182, 198, 202, 204-205, 214, 216, 221-222, 225, 237, 276-277, 290, 300, 302, 305-307, 344, 352*
food, *17, 70, 72, 82, 110, 176, 182, 206, 221, 235, 274, 317*
football, *235, 324*
forgive, *104, 268, 315-316*
forgiveness, *104, 192, 315*
fourth of july, *230*
freckles, *210*
freedom, *149, 205, 211, 231, 287, 360*
friend, *13, 16, 33, 40, 44, 55, 63, 65, 77, 79, 96, 118-119, 133-134, 142, 144, 152, 157, 160, 168, 174, 180-183, 186, 189-191, 196-199, 202, 211-213, 222, 233, 243, 245, 256, 258-259, 262-263, 265, 287, 289, 295, 325, 357*

iii

friendship, *101, 133-134, 170, 193, 195, 198, 211-213, 285*
fruits, *207, 210, 216, 289, 309*
fun, *3-4, 19, 31-32, 47-48, 50, 57, 68, 97, 103, 106, 109-110, 112-113, 115, 117, 119, 125, 127-132, 135, 138-139, 142, 145, 150, 152, 155-157, 165, 167-168, 170-171, 174-175, 181, 187, 196, 198-199, 213, 217, 223, 229, 237, 243, 248, 278-281, 283, 291-292, 294-296, 298, 300, 302, 304, 307-311, 313, 316, 320, 327, 333, 336, 339-340, 350-352, 358, 363-364*
funny, *22, 95-96, 120, 130-132, 136, 158, 67, 194, 201, 236, 257, 272*

G

games, *73, 79, 132, 157, 213-214, 231, 279-281, 303, 319, 324, 330*
gardeners, *102, 212, 221, 358*
gardens, *214-216, 345*
genealogy, *10, 31, 36, 87*
gift, *33-35, 39-40, 44-45, 48-50, 53-60, 66, 68, 76, 87, 91, 93, 97, 102, 107, 113-114, 116-117, 123-128, 134, 138, 144, 182, 186, 192, 195-196, 199, 211, 218, 225, 228, 230, 246, 249, 252, 265-267, 269, 284-285, 289, 300, 310, 317-318, 352*
girl scouts, *142*
girlfriends, *213*
girls, *77, 120, 143, 146, 165, 169-170, 172, 182, 186, 191, 203, 207-208, 212, 217-218, 227, 255, 259, 292, 307, 309-310, 312, 319, 333, 336, 338-339, 341, 357-358*
giving, *18, 27, 45, 48, 66, 68, 114, 212, 218-219, 224, 235-236, 243, 246, 351*
glasses, *96, 161, 194, 219*
goals, *11, 34, 37, 57, 66, 69, 77, 84, 219-220, 243, 325, 335*
God, *56, 61, 63, 65, 90, 92-93, 100, 105, 107-108, 113, 115-117, 124, 135, 137-138, 141-143, 145, 152, 154, 156, 158, 166, 179, 181, 186, 189-190, 192, 195-197, 203, 205-206, 211-214, 216, 218, 221, 224, 226, 230-237, 243-246, 249-251, 254, 261, 266, 268-269, 273-274, 276, 284-285, 289, 294, 300, 303, 314-318, 335, 338-339, 343-344, 347, 350, 354-355, 360-361*
godparents, *316*

gold, *1, 46, 104, 124, 129, 139, 147, 154, 156-157, 160, 185-186, 209, 224, 230, 235, 259, 261, 265, 277, 294, 318, 325, 327, 344, 349*
golf, *76, 288, 323-325*
graduation, *12, 37, 57, 66, 220, 293-294*
grandchildren, *185-187*
grandma, *37, 97, 155, 167-169, 171, 186-187, 213, 228, 278, 293, 325*
grandpa, *97, 155-156, 158, 186-187, 228, 293, 325*
grandparents, *10, 12, 39, 69, 72-73, 83-85, 114, 186-187*
gratitude, *3, 10, 22, 32, 34-35, 195, 220-222, 224*
green, *100, 123, 152, 160, 177, 206, 234-235, 276, 281, 301, 305, 324-325, 346, 350, 358*
grilling, *207, 307*
groom, *11, 57, 189, 259-260, 262-263*
growing, *11, 34, 74-80, 84, 86, 111, 128, 131, 137, 145, 156-157, 159, 180-181, 183, 185*
gym, *282, 321, 325, 332-333*
gymnastics, *325*

H

hair; *71, 95-96, 139, 167, 176, 186, 222, 241, 336, 344*
haircuts, *222*
hairstylist, *359*
halloween, *74, 76, 231*
hands, *31, 59, 93, 99, 116-117, 124, 136-137, 157, 164-166, 168, 171, 181, 185, 188, 193, 196, 214, 216, 220, 236, 242, 244, 256-257, 262, 272, 288, 294, 298, 316-317, 338, 340, 354*
handwritten, *2, 39-40, 47, 54, 69*
hanukkah, *232*
happiness, *35, 91, 102, 104, 106-108, 116, 121-122, 126, 131, 149, 151, 156, 160, 164-165, 169, 174, 186, 188, 193, 206, 209, 213, 215, 218, 223-224, 231-232, 237, 251, 255, 263, 271, 286, 316, 349-350*
happy, *20, 22, 29, 31, 34, 57, 65, 80, 90, 93, 95, 101-103, 106, 109, 115, 119, 121, 125-134, 136, 138, 145-146, 149-150, 152, 156, 159, 162-163, 167, 169-170, 172-175, 179-182, 184-186, 189, 191, 193-194, 196, 198, 200, 202, 204, 207-208, 210, 212-216, 221-225, 227, 229-237, 240, 242-243, 246-247, 250, 255, 261-263, 269, 277, 280-283, 287-289, 299, 301, 307, 310-312, 323, 326, 350*

iv

harvest, *74, 202, 218, 224, 302*
hats, *161, 164, 176, 220, 234, 294, 304*
heart, *2-3, 6, 8, 11-12, 15-16, 19, 27, 31, 33, 39, 44-54, 56, 58-60, 65, 68-69, 87, 91, 93-94, 97-98, 102-103, 105-108, 113, 115-117, 119-126, 135-138, 144-146, 148, 151-152, 158, 160-162, 164-166, 169-171, 175, 179-187, 189, 191-192, 194-199, 201, 204, 208-209, 211-213, 215, 218-223, 225-227, 230, 232-233, 236-237, 241, 246-247, 250-252, 254-258, 261-267, 269-270, 274-275, 279, 288, 298, 300, 305-306, 309, 311, 313-319, 325-326, 342-346, 350-351, 356, 359*
heritage, *12, 36, 39, 97, 155, 180, 188, 225, 238*
high school, *73, 78, 80, 96, 294-296*
hiking, *74, 142, 150*
historical, *31, 37*
hockey, *74, 325*
holidays, *10, 72, 74, 76, 83, 85, 97, 225-228*
holy land, *345*
home, *5, 11, 31, 51, 55, 59, 66, 70-77, 82-83, 85-86, 92-94, 97-98, 106, 114, 117, 123, 125, 141, 146, 149-152, 154-155, 163-165, 171, 174, 180, 184-195, 199-201, 206, 211, 217, 224-228, 230-232, 236-240, 248, 251, 254, 256, 271-273, 278-279, 282, 287-289, 296, 299, 312, 314, 318, 320, 324, 326, 328, 332, 343-347, 349, 355, 358, 360*
horse, *201, 280, 326, 339, 342*
hot, *9, 21, 26, 96, 138, 161, 163, 165, 174, 177, 200, 203, 207, 209, 222, 237, 264, 280, 302-303, 307-309,*
house, *5, 122, 141, 152, 154, 157, 167, 187-188, 198, 200, 203, 212, 226, 228, 237-240, 248, 269, 273, 278-279, 282, 293, 303, 308-310, 317-318, 343, 345, 350, 353*
housekeeping, *359*
housework, *169-170, 240-241, 310*
hugs, *109, 118-119, 145, 163, 225, 236, 252*
humor, *241-242*
hunting, *149, 227, 229, 281, 326, 362*
husband, *33, 49, 54-55, 71, 120, 136, 163, 171, 187-188, 190, 199-200, 208, 239-240, 254, 262, 270, 287-288, 317, 324*

I

ice skating, *74, 326-327*
illness, *240-241*
injuries, *241*

inspiration, *21, 38, 40, 47-48, 69, 72, 107, 242, 349*
inspire, *17, 31-33, 37, 44, 68, 105, 193*
introduction, *65*
ireland, *234, 346*

J

journal, *3-4, 8-13, 18, 31-34, 37-38, 49, 54, 65-66, 69-72, 97, 202*
journals, *2, 4-5, 8-10, 12-13, 31, 54, 66, 68, 97*
journey, *2, 4, 9, 44, 46, 57, 59, 64, 69, 93-94, 125, 138, 153, 155, 162, 168, 211-212, 243-244, 250-251, 259, 269, 299, 339, 348-349, 354*
joy, *3, 17, 27, 33, 44, 48-49, 56, 60, 85, 87, 101, 107, 112, 116-117, 120, 122, 124, 128-130, 133-134, 144-147, 159, 171-172, 180, 182-183, 185-187, 195-196, 199, 211-212, 214, 216, 221-224, 226-227, 232, 236, 244, 246, 250-252, 256, 258-259, 262-263, 266, 268, 271, 276, 280, 284, 295, 300, 306, 315, 318, 332*
joyful, *3, 19-20, 23-24, 64, 223, 274, 311*
jumping, *145, 272, 280, 321*
jumpstarts, *4, 16-17*

K

kayaking, *135, 321-322*
kids, *50, 76, 96, 99, 106, 119, 155-159, 167, 170, 173, 184, 187, 201, 222, 268, 280-281, 296, 298-299, 328, 336, 340*
kind, *28, 46, 49, 71, 75, 78, 80, 84, 100, 108-109, 141, 146, 155-156, 158, 166, 182, 188-189, 193, 195-196, 198, 200, 211, 213, 221, 229, 232, 242, 245-247, 264-265, 268, 274, 303-304, 308, 317, 336, 339, 343, 351*
kindness, *22, 28, 193, 216, 221, 245-246, 350, 352, 354*
kings, *247, 326*
kisses, *28, 50, 97, 111, 115-116, 118, 126, 128, 134, 145, 149, 155, 163, 202, 207, 209-210, 218, 225, 234-236, 250, 252, 263, 277, 303, 363*
kitchen, *166, 187, 192, 206-207, 226, 228, 240, 247, 288, 310*
kites, *157, 281*
kittens, *151-152, 157*
knitting, *166-167*
kwanzaa, *232*

L

lake, *248, 290, 304, 324*
languages, *248*
las vegas, *346*
laundry, *192, 240-241, 289*
lawyers, *359*
leaves, *74, 95, 144, 169, 193, 215, 301-302*
letters, *10, 19, 32, 34, 39-47, 49-52, 54, 164, 184, 256, 265, 291, 338, 360*
love, *3-4, 6-7, 10-12, 17-18, 20, 24-25, 28-29, 32-34, 38-40, 43-60, 63-64, 66-67, 69, 80-81, 85, 87, 91-94, 96-98, 100-104, 106-127, 129-130, 132-138, 140-152, 154-160, 162-172, 174, 176-203, 205-219, 221-240, 243-270, 272-280, 282-286, 288-293, 296, 298-306, 308-312, 314-319, 321-323, 325-330, 332, 334-335, 340-348, 350-353, 355-364*
love letter, *33, 43-48, 50-52*
lullaby, *34, 113, 115-116, 267, 279, 289, 304, 337-338, 346*

M

maid, *191, 240, 263, 271, 350, 359*
make-believe, *99, 268*
mama, *97, 108, 110, 113-114, 119, 123, 125, 127, 136-137, 145, 147, 150, 157, 161, 166, 168-170, 176, 190-192, 203, 207, 218, 232-233, 251, 255, 260, 274, 284, 286, 290, 322-323, 326, 338, 341-342, 349, 355*
manners, *268*
marriage, *11, 81, 83, 86, 101-103, 188-189, 199, 251, 261, 264, 315*
martial arts, *327*
masterpiece, *19, 21, 38, 45, 68, 105-106, 166, 211, 223, 298, 316*
mechanics, *356*
medical, *359*
memorial, *42, 76, 97, 268*
memories, *1-2, 4, 7, 12, 15-19, 28, 36-37, 40, 44-45, 54, 57, 59-61, 63-65, 67-69, 72-76, 78, 80, 82-85, 88, 96-98, 100, 103, 117, 144, 154, 159, 168, 170-171, 173, 181, 185, 194, 196-197, 199, 205, 207, 212-213, 224-227, 235, 239, 268-269, 272-273, 287, 289, 293-295, 303, 311, 343, 345-346, 360*
men, *94-96, 145, 152-153, 155, 160, 167, 181, 184, 186-188, 200, 207, 211, 228, 240, 251, 255, 262, 269-270, 287, 313, 323-324, 332, 336, 349-350, 355, 357, 361*
merry christmas, *227-228*
messes, *350, 359*
middle school, *73, 296*
midnight, *227, 234, 278, 310, 336, 338, 342-343, 347*
milestones, *10, 36, 97-98, 129, 157, 249*
military, *10, 84, 200, 359-360*
miracle, *28, 72, 93, 108-109, 116, 124-125, 144, 205, 215, 284-285, 334*
miscellaneous, *271*
mom, *73, 77, 98, 100, 104-106, 109, 116, 139-140, 147, 155-158, 167-168, 170, 184-187, 189-194, 196, 201, 207, 210, 228, 230-236, 241-242, 252, 271-272, 278-280, 284, 288, 293, 310, 320, 331, 336, 340-341*
mom & dad-isms, *271*
moments, *2, 4-5, 12, 16, 18, 31, 44, 49, 59-60, 69-70, 72, 78-79, 85, 87, 90, 98, 103, 107, 118, 144-145, 149, 191, 214, 244, 249, 269, 288, 290, 338-339, 360*
mommy, *97, 105-106, 108, 112, 115, 123-124, 129, 137, 140, 146, 155-158, 190-193, 242, 279-280, 284-286, 292, 303, 332, 350-351*
money, *54, 86, 141, 220, 239, 250, 262, 272, 288, 309, 333, 336, 340, 356, 362*
moon, *112-113, 138, 145, 150, 153, 160, 164, 185, 202, 224, 228, 257, 264, 277, 289, 303, 310, 312, 323, 326, 338-339, 343-345*
moonbeam, *264*
morning, *76, 83, 85, 90, 95, 114, 119-120, 126-127, 153-154, 173-174, 189, 204, 206, 210, 212, 215, 217, 220-221, 223, 226, 234-235, 241, 250, 253-255, 259, 265, 267, 278, 290, 302-303, 305, 307, 315, 317-318, 338, 342-343, 345, 353, 360-361*
mother, *39, 73, 76, 78-79, 90, 98, 106-107, 109, 112, 114, 117, 136, 144-145, 153-154, 157, 181-183, 186, 189-194, 197, 200, 217-218, 229, 232-234, 240, 246, 252, 259-260, 262, 266-267, 271-272, 276-277, 280, 285, 298, 305, 318, 355*
mother's day, *76, 232-233*
motorcycles, *341*
mountains, *146, 237, 272-273, 323, 343, 347*
moving, *19, 28, 79, 95, 143, 238, 245, 273, 355*

music, *9-10, 19, 32, 46, 55, 57, 73, 81-82, 85-86, 96, 103, 117-118, 148, 204, 211, 249, 252, 256, 264-266, 273-275, 299, 305-306, 334, 336-337, 343-344, 350, 352*

N

nap, *108, 236, 338*
nature, *10-11, 126, 142, 150, 167, 211, 217, 229, 275-277, 300-302*
neighbor, *39, 238*
new year's day, *234*
new york, *301, 346-347*
newlyweds, *82-83, 261*
nighttime, *338*
nursery rhymes, *277, 280*

O

occasions, *18, 34, 49, 148, 255*
ocean, *92, 135, 153, 222, 225, 277, 290-292*
off road, *327, 341*
office workers, *360*
orange, *153, 161, 302*
order, *65, 69, 195, 237, 271, 359, 361*
overcoming, *31, 333*

P

pacifier, *71, 111*
painting, *105-106, 167, 229, 234, 303, 339*
papa, *97, 113, 119, 185, 203, 286*
paradise, *107, 121-122, 128, 135, 141, 201, 216, 277, 304, 308, 340, 344, 349*
parents, *33, 36, 69, 73, 75, 83-86, 147, 157, 193-195, 199, 278, 317, 336*
paris, *347*
parks, *75, 99*
parties, *11, 75-76, 81, 126-127, 278, 310*
passion, *3, 24-25, 38, 43, 45, 48-49, 92, 103, 122, 148, 155, 161, 167, 178, 203, 214, 250, 252-253, 266, 275, 278, 282, 290, 299, 324, 335, 342*
pearls, *33, 53, 59-61, 175, 260, 262, 290*
pets, *80, 83, 98, 100, 147, 152, 158, 278-279*
photo, *33-34, 70, 162, 167, 170, 329*
photography, *59, 167*
picture, *2, 18, 36, 46, 51, 64, 76-77, 79, 84, 87, 97, 105, 120, 167-168, 182*

pigs, *200-202*
pilots, *361*
pink, *20, 23, 115, 161-162, 165, 177, 202-203, 205, 229, 285, 306*
planet, *72, 153, 194, 229*
play, *31, 79, 113, 117, 131, 137-138, 145-146, 152, 156, 158-159, 165, 197, 213-214, 233, 238, 245, 248, 268, 271-272, 274, 276, 278-282, 299, 306, 310, 312, 318-320, 322-325, 328, 331, 348, 350, 353, 358*
playground, *146-147, 157, 280, 295*
playing, *74, 78, 100, 103, 119, 138, 145, 147, 244, 259, 275, 279-280, 291, 297, 301, 311, 323-324, 328, 337, 346, 350*
pms, *209, 283*
poems, *81-82, 114, 277*
police officer, *361*
potty, *283*
praise, *93, 101, 220-221, 236, 283, 315-317*
prayer, *44, 46, 57, 92-94, 103, 115-116, 209, 221, 239, 244, 246, 254, 275, 314-317, 339, 359, 362*
prayers, *10, 57, 112, 114, 125, 129, 182, 191, 224, 285, 314, 317*
pregnancy, *10, 70-72, 194, 284*
pregnant, *70-71, 284-285*
preservation, *37*
prom, *295*
proverbs, *183, 186, 190, 198-200, 218, 317-318*
pumpkin, *210, 285-286*
purple, *54, 89, 161, 204, 233, 273*

Q

queens, *247*
questions, *4, 16, 37, 64-69, 72, 84, 87, 179, 210, 314*
quiet, *7, 9, 23-24, 46, 64, 86, 108, 114, 154, 166, 169, 193, 214-215, 222, 242-243, 270, 310, 334, 336, 338-339*
quilting, *168-169*

R

racing, *326-328*
racquetball, *328*
rain, *51, 59, 149, 155, 158, 161, 203, 212, 216, 234, 244, 256, 275, 302, 305, 309-310, 320, 331, 352-353*
rainbows, *247, 307, 353*

vii

reading, 8, 10, 47, 49-50, 66, 141-142, 186, 286-287, 296-297, 308
red, 104-105, 114, 118, 122, 129, 139, 153, 155-156, 158, 160-161, 176-177, 201, 203-204, 216, 230-231, 237, 277, 281-282, 290, 292, 297, 301-302, 308, 322, 342, 355-356, 358
religious, 361
remember, 5, 15, 18-19, 32-34, 36-37, 39-40, 46-48, 50, 55, 64, 77-78, 80-81, 83, 87, 94-99, 102-103, 112, 116, 121, 125, 135, 146, 156, 170, 180, 184, 189, 192, 196, 199, 222, 224-226, 228, 231, 234, 242-245, 247, 253, 256, 260, 263, 268-269, 278, 294-295, 299, 302, 307, 338, 341, 364
repairs, 287
retirement, 248, 287-288
river rafting, 328
rock, 100-101, 107-108, 113, 118, 122, 124, 132, 135, 144, 158, 163-164, 196, 198, 204, 218, 247, 253, 267, 272, 274-275, 277, 281, 284, 288, 296-297, 322-323, 328, 331, 336, 363
rock climbing, 328
romance, 11, 25, 45, 57, 102, 253-254, 257, 259, 262, 266, 304, 309, 342, 344
romantic, 25, 44-48, 54, 57, 81-82, 101, 253-254, 258, 263, 346, 348
room sayings, 288
roses, 5, 65, 127, 129, 160-161, 191, 217-218, 236, 258, 260, 277, 289-290, 303, 326, 355
rubberstamping, 169
run, 12, 113, 138-139, 145-146, 183, 202, 241, 248, 291, 298, 308, 320, 322, 326, 329, 331, 333, 343
running, 143, 176, 187, 244, 271, 291, 329, 337

S

sad, 25, 31, 80, 106, 114, 163, 181
sailing, 135, 251, 340
salesperson, 362
sand, 33, 44, 49, 223, 265, 276, 290-292, 307, 309, 325
santa, 75, 292-293
school, 10, 37, 46, 48, 57, 73, 75-80, 86, 96, 98, 106, 114, 178, 257, 272, 277, 293-298, 300, 303, 308-309, 322, 330, 355, 362
school days, 37, 57, 98, 295, 297
scotland, 347
scrapbooking, 12, 31, 38, 170

scripture, 35, 57, 82, 317
scuba diving, 8329
seasons, 9-10, 17, 37, 98, 159, 196, 252, 266, 270, 300, 306, 353
senior, 94, 293-295, 319
sentimentally, 51
sewing, 170-171
shoes, 90, 113, 117-118, 138, 152, 160, 173, 176-177, 185, 203-204, 248, 291, 321, 333, 348, 355
shopping, 176, 204, 226, 241, 296, 309-310
showers, 71, 81, 123, 127, 236, 259-260, 305, 307, 335, 352
siblings, 10, 36, 69, 72-74, 77, 79, 83-85, 181, 195, 351
significant other, 16, 35, 70, 72
silly, 23, 50, 119, 132, 148, 198, 218, 224, 241, 257, 310, 330
silver, 51, 95, 104, 122, 160, 186, 204, 222, 259-261, 352
sing, 17, 70, 91, 96, 108, 116, 159, 179, 216, 237, 249, 267, 274-275, 292, 300, 305, 307, 316, 330, 348
sister, 98-99, 112, 139, 181, 195-199, 321, 352
skateboarding, 329-330
skies, 122, 124, 153, 160-161, 204, 216, 292, 330, 343-344, 347, 354, 360-361
sky diving, 330
sleep, 100, 104, 109, 111-113, 115, 141, 149, 173, 175, 185, 189-190, 209-210, 213, 247-248, 256, 267, 280-281, 293, 310, 314, 320, 322-325, 328-330, 335, 338, 342, 361
slumber party, 310
smiles & laughter, 310
snow, 103, 155, 162, 228, 234, 247, 302-304, 311-313, 330-331, 353
snow skiing, 330
snowboarding, 330
snowmen, 312-313
snowmobiling, 330
soccer, 331
soldier, 146, 200, 360
song, 17, 34, 50, 55-57, 81, 91, 103, 108, 122, 170, 179, 192, 203, 221, 228, 249, 256, 261-264, 273-275, 300, 304-306, 308, 310, 316, 335, 343, 352-353
soulmate, 28
southern sayings, 313

viii

special, 4, 7, 16, 18, 20, 31-34, 36, 40, 45-46, 49-50, 54-57, 66, 70-75, 77-78, 80-82, 84-87, 100, 118, 123, 125, 127, 129, 131-132, 134, 144, 148, 158, 161, 171, 174, 180-181, 184, 186, 188-189, 196, 198-199, 207, 211, 213, 233, 238, 262, 267, 269, 271, 281, 313, 316, 355
spirituality, 3, 86
sports, 10, 73, 77-78, 98, 147, 185, 318-319, 336
spouse, 35, 40, 44, 59, 69, 80-81, 84-87, 238-239, 247, 283
spring, 73-74, 144, 160, 196, 205, 214, 216, 223, 230, 237, 252, 267, 295, 300, 302-306, 339, 345, 347, 353
st. patrick's day, 234
standing, 56, 113, 117, 139, 217, 296, 337
stars, 106, 122, 145, 150-151, 153-154, 175, 179, 199, 206, 228, 231, 252, 256, 264, 294, 297, 317-318, 338, 360
storms, 198, 244, 353
storytelling, 1, 59
success, 34, 57, 90-92, 179, 220, 243-244, 294, 297-298, 334-335, 354-355, 357
summer, 73-75, 78, 97-98, 103, 142, 144, 147, 159, 173, 207, 216, 239, 248, 252, 292, 297, 300-303, 305, 307-309, 319, 336, 338, 346, 348, 352-353
sun, 96, 112, 123, 129, 144-145, 149, 151, 154-155, 164, 204-206, 210, 214, 216, 248, 252, 264-265, 276, 291, 300-301, 303, 306-309, 311, 313, 315, 335, 338, 352, 358
sunrise, 214, 249, 252, 338
sunset, 59, 154, 161, 249, 309, 344
sunshine, 94, 108-109, 113, 125, 127, 139, 146-147, 149, 151, 154-155, 158-159, 167, 173, 183, 186, 205-206, 212, 215-219, 223-224, 241, 247, 249, 267, 290-292, 304-305, 307-309, 311, 333, 338, 344, 348, 352-353
surf, 47, 290-292, 309, 330-331
surfing, 331
sweet, 11, 16-17, 26, 40, 47, 54, 69, 91, 94, 104-105, 108-116, 120, 122, 125-126, 129-136, 138-141, 146-151, 158, 168-169, 174-175, 179, 182, 185, 187-190, 198, 202-208, 212, 215, 218, 221, 223-225, 231-233, 236-237, 240, 248, 250, 252-254, 257, 259, 264-267, 275, 277, 281, 284-285, 288-290, 293, 296, 299, 301, 305-306, 309, 311, 313, 316, 319, 328, 336, 338, 343, 346-347, 349, 360-362

sweetest tale, 63
swimming, 74, 309, 332

T

tapestry, 66, 97
tea, 9, 16, 65, 99, 142, 197, 242, 267, 335-336, 343
teachers, 37, 74, 178, 194, 274, 298-300, 362
technical, 357
teddy bears, 118-119, 147, 281-282
teen, 34, 74-80, 86, 98, 132-133, 177, 193, 256, 336, 341
teens, 336
teeth, 139-140, 160, 200, 226, 313
teething, 114, 140
tennis, 76, 332
thank you, 39, 102, 167, 221, 233, 236, 245, 247, 268, 315-316
thankful, 22, 35, 76, 92, 171, 220, 223-225, 235-236
thanksgiving, 74, 76, 83, 212, 220-221, 235-236, 317
theater, 337
thoughts, 2-5, 7-9, 13, 16-19, 32, 34, 36-37, 40, 44-46, 48-49, 51, 54, 65, 68, 85, 87, 106-107, 122, 148, 193-194, 196, 198, 204, 223, 233, 243, 249, 256
tidbits, 33
time, 4, 7-9, 11, 16-18, 33-34, 38-40, 44-46, 50-51, 53-55, 57, 59-61, 63-65, 70-71, 73-74, 77, 80-82,84-86, 91, 93, 96, 98, 101-102, 104, 106-112, 114, 118, 123-134, 137-142, 144, 146, 148-149,155-157, 159, 165-168, 170-174, 176, 178, 183, 186, 192-194, 198-199, 202-203, 207-211,215-216, 220, 225-226, 228-229, 231, 233-237, 239-243, 245, 255, 259, 262-264, 268-269, 272-273, 277-278, 281, 284-293, 300-302,306-307, 310, 313, 316, 319, 324-325, 331-333, 335-339, 343, 347, 352, 354-358, 362
tips, 4, 9, 15, 31-33, 36, 48, 57, 117, 138
tools, 4-5, 7-9, 38, 44-45, 239, 356
tooth, 75, 110, 114, 139-140, 208, 358
town, 75, 84, 127, 158, 227-228, 234, 237-238, 248, 256, 273, 278, 292, 337-339, 343, 345, 348, 363
toys, 71, 73, 96, 110, 112, 118, 144-145, 147, 157-158, 280, 282, 329, 341
track, 99, 326-328, 332-333, 342
trains, 282, 340, 342, 348

transportation, *323, 339*
travel, *10, 35, 79, 98, 240, 342, 347-349*
trees, *105, 170, 183, 246, 272, 276, 305, 350, 363*
triplets, *351*
tropical, *128, 349*
trouble, *78, 147, 158, 187, 190, 326, 336, 350*
truck, *161, 164, 336, 340-341, 356, 358*
trucks, *144, 165, 340*
turkey, *200, 235-236, 325-326*
twins, *351*

U

uncle, *199*
us, *3, 5, 11, 36, 40, 44, 51, 54-56, 59-60, 65, 97-98, 102-108, 124-125, 128, 135, 143, 149, 157, 163, 167-168, 174, 177, 190, 192-193, 195-196, 208, 211-213, 215, 217-218, 221, 226-227, 232-233, 235-236, 243-244, 251-252, 254-255, 258, 261, 265-266, 269, 273, 275-276, 279, 284-285, 289, 293, 303, 312, 316-318, 328, 348, 351, 353, 359-360*

V

valentine, *50, 236-237*
valentine's day, *236*
veggies, *210*
volleyball, *333*
volunteer, *358*
volunteers, *351-352*

W

walking, *20, 39, 56, 91, 110, 113, 138-139, 154, 175, 185, 204, 245, 304, 308-309, 312, 316, 333, 348, 352-353, 361*
weather, *71, 81, 96, 197, 304, 340, 352, 361*
weaving, *171*
wedding, *10-12, 34, 50, 55, 57, 66, 80-83, 98, 256, 258-263*
week, *114, 173*
white, *48, 74, 96, 100, 122, 139-140, 159-160, 162, 205, 228, 231, 238, 262, 292, 302, 304, 311-312, 342*
wife, *120, 136, 162-163, 188, 199-200, 203, 208, 239-241, 254, 262, 270, 287-288, 323-324, 355, 360*

wild, *29, 95, 100, 110, 139, 142, 144, 148, 151-153, 158-159, 164, 174, 188, 194, 200-201, 204-205, 217, 235, 254, 257, 267, 270, 276-277, 292, 302, 309, 313, 322, 326, 328, 330, 332-333, 339, 341-342, 344, 346, 351, 354, 362-363*
wind, *59, 146, 214-215, 219, 228, 238, 281-282, 290, 302-303, 305, 323, 341-342, 350, 354*
winter, *74, 95, 98, 103, 144, 162, 216, 226, 252, 264, 288-289, 300, 302-306, 311-312, 330, 344, 352-353*
wisdom, *33, 44, 90, 95, 117, 198, 222, 225, 274, 300, 322, 354*
wishes, *36, 101, 114, 118, 123, 125-134, 145, 155, 207, 216, 220, 226, 252, 263, 277, 303, 312*
wonderful, *11, 16, 29, 35, 37-39, 44-45, 55-56, 59, 61, 64, 66, 68, 72, 82, 87-88, 97, 103, 106, 108-110, 115, 119, 125, 127, 129, 131, 154, 158-159, 180-181, 190, 192, 197, 200, 209, 212-213, 226, 228, 233, 241-244, 250, 256-257, 261, 263, 266-267, 269, 276, 288, 290, 303, 333, 348, 353*
word games, *214*
word palette, *20-21, 30, 65*
work & jobs, *355*
workers, *358, 360-361*
working out, *333*
wrapped, *89, 104, 114-115, 117, 124-125, 137, 168, 226, 228, 247, 252, 254*
wrestling, *334*
writer's block, *9, 19, 30-31, 38, 46*
writer's tools, *4-5, 7*
writing, *2-5, 9-10, 12, 15-20, 29-31, 33-34, 37-40, 44, 46-50, 53-54, 64, 66, 68-69, 84, 87, 171-172*
writing tips, *15*

Y

yard sales, *362*
yellow, *162, 177-178, 229, 300, 302, 327, 344, 346, 348*
yoga, *334*
yummy, *106, 110-111, 130-131, 156, 206, 210, 229*

Z

zoo, *78, 128, 362-363*

x

About Us

The Ultimate Book Company Inc. website will be offering freebies, a quote-a-day and as we build our site, we'll be adding digital downloads, unique gifts, photographs, and even more books to add to your crafting stash. Everything we offer will focus on words because that's what we're all about.

We hope you will visit often and share the link with family and friends. As we grow, we hope to offer videos, a monthly newsletter and more. Books can be ordered through us or at a variety of stores, both large and small. Our goal is to spread "the word" (pun intended) and share our love for words.

The Ultimate Book Company also has a blog and we invite you to subscribe for updates. We hope to create a community for old friends and new. Our desire is to offer an environment that will inspire and educate our readers. Your input will be a valuable part of achieving that goal. We look forward to getting to know you as we bring inspiration and ideas to our site, blog, social media and newsletters that will help you tell your story and preserve your memories. We hope you'll find useful ideas for creating cards, journals, scrapbooks and more, leaving a legacy of love to those near and dear to you.

Thanks for buying my book; it has been a blessing for me to share it with you. Please share it with your friends and local scrapbook store,too. I look forward to getting to know you.

Joy and love—

Linda

The Ultimate Book Company Inc.
PO Box 615 • Mayfield KY 42066
Tel (270) 251-0022
ultimatebookcompany.com

Bonus Stuff

Please visit our website to download free blank forms to help you organize your favorite quotes, poems and thoughts, for instant access when you are at a crop or craft event. There is also a downloadable blank form to jot down questions you might like to ask when interviewing someone for your family history and also a form to list the names of potential interviewees.

Time is our precious gift and making time for getting to know our family is a wonderful opportunity to learn more about your history and keep your relationships special—because love is all that ultimately matters. May you have fun!

We will be adding additional forms to our website, so please keep us bookmarked for easy access. ultimatebookcompany.com

I hope that you find this book very valuable when you need that perfect word for any project or occasion. Happy creating! May you be blessed!
Thank you!

The Biggest Book of Words & Prompts for Scrapbooks, Art Journals & Crafts

NAME

ADDRESS

CITY / STATE	ZIP CODE

AREA CODE • PHONE NUMBER
( ) _____ − _____

EMAIL

QTY	TITLE	COST
	ULTIMATE WORD- Vol 2 x 19.95 each	
	Please add $3.25 shipping **per book** (Discount on orders of 3 or more books) — SHIPPING	
	Kentucky residents must add 6% sales tax on total — KY TAX 6%	
	TOTAL ORDER	

Thank you for your order!

ORDER ON OUR WEBSITE OR BY SENDING THIS FORM WITH PAYMENT TO:
Ultimate Book Company • PO Box 615 • Mayfield KY 42066
Office / 270 251-0022 • *sales@ultimatebookcompany.com*
www.ultimatebookcompany.com

Made in the USA
Las Vegas, NV
02 January 2024